Projects for the Birder's Garden

Projects for the Birder's Garden

OVER **100** EASY THINGS THAT YOU CAN

MAKE TO TURN YOUR YARD AND

GARDEN INTO A BIRD-FRIENDLY HAVEN

Edited by
Fern Marshall Bradley
and the Editors of
YANKEE MAGAZINE.

YANKEE BOOKS.

A portion of chapter 7 is reused from *The Original Birdhouse Book*, by Don McNeil © 2003 Bird Watcher's Digest Press with permission from Bird Watcher's Digest Press (PO Box 110, Marietta, OH 45750; www.birdwatchersdigest.com).

Library of Congress Cataloging-in-Publication Data

    Projects for the birder's garden : over 100 easy things that you can make to turn your yard and garden into a bird-friendly haven / edited by Fern Marshall Bradley and the editors of Yankee Magazine.

        p.   cm.

    Includes index.

    ISBN 0–89909–392–2 hardcover

    ISBN 0–89909–393–0 paperback

    1. Bird feeders—Design and construction.   2. Birdhouses—Design and construction.   3. Birdbaths—Design and construction.   4. Gardening to attract birds.   I. Bradley, Fern Marshall.   II. Yankee Magazine.

    QL676.5.P76   2004

    639.9'78—dc22   2004008367

Distributed to the trade by Holtzbrinck Publishers

2 4 6 8 10 9 7 5 3 1   hardcover
2 4 6 8 10 9 7 5 3 1   paperback

Yankee Publishing Staff

President: Jamie Trowbridge
Book Editor: Fern Marshall Bradley
Contributing Writers: Susan Burton, Sally Cunningham, Rose Kennedy, Sally Roth, Anita Small, Delilah Smittle
Book Designer: Jill Shaffer
Illustrator: Michael Gellatly
Copy Editor: Barbara Jatkola
Manuscript Review: David M. Bird, Ph.D.
Indexer: Lina B. Burton
Proofreader: Nancy Rutman

RODALE

Rodale Inc. Editorial Staff

Editor: Christine Bucks
Editorial Production Manager: Marilyn Hauptly
Editorial Assistant: Emily Williams
Cover Designer: Anthony Serge

FOR MORE OF OUR PRODUCTS
WWW.RODALESTORE.COM
(800) 848-4735

Contents

Acknowledgments vi

Building It for the Birds vii

CHAPTER 1   Fast-and-Easy Projects for First-Timers 1

CHAPTER 2   Supplying Seeds 29

CHAPTER 3   Bird Treats 65

CHAPTER 4   Feeding Stations 105

CHAPTER 5   Creating Backyard Bird Habitats 133

CHAPTER 6   Water for Birds 173

CHAPTER 7   All about Birdhouses 203

CHAPTER 8   Hummingbird and Butterfly Projects 243

Projects at a Glance 287

Who Eats What? 290

Resources for Backyard Birders
and Gardeners 292

Recommended Reading 296

Index 298

USDA Plant Hardiness Zone Map 312

ACKNOWLEDGMENTS

The editors wish to thank David M. Bird, Ph.D., professor of wildlife biology at McGill University, for his thorough review of the manuscript and his corrections and insightful comments on current practices in feeding and attracting birds. The writers and editors also wish to thank the many people who offered information and ideas for this book: Harry L. Abel, owner of Shinkigen, for instructions and sketches for a bamboo dripper and information about Japanese garden style; Ken Burton for his review of and input on chapter 7 and for supplying excellent scrap art; Ann Hoffert of Pipestem Creek in Carrington, North Dakota, for suggestions about edible garlands for birds; Chris Keating for advice on fasteners for use in making feeders; Chaz Macdonald for technical advice on computers and birds; Mike Masterson of Masterson's Garden Center in East Aurora, New York, for his expert advice about pumps and fountains; Carolyn Schaeffner of Buffalo, for her idea for an improvised birdbath using a fireplace grate; Mike Shadrack of the London and East Aurora water garden scene, for explanations of the fine points of in-ground ponds; Bill Thompson, editor of *Bird Watcher's Digest,* for helpful comments and corrections to text concerning birdhouses; and members of the Niagara Frontier Koi and Pond Society—including Greg Young, Marlene Hyden, and Gordon Ballard—for information on water gardens.

Building It for the Birds

Watching birds from the comfort of your living room or patio is like living in a private nature preserve. You'll enjoy the proverbial bird's-eye view of beautiful feathered visitors eating, drinking, bathing, preening, courting, and possibly even feeding their young. Whether or not you ever become a birding expert who can identify every bird you see, you're sure to love the feeling of connection with nature that you'll get when you take steps to attract birds to your yard.

There's no great secret to attracting beautiful birds such as cardinals, chickadees, and goldfinches. Just buy a feeder, fill it with seeds, and hang it outside, and chances are birds will find it. Although feeding birds by hanging a store-bought feeder is easy, there's a deeper satisfaction in watching birds gobble seeds and other treats from a feeder that you've made yourself. And you'll feel the warmth of parental pride when a mother bird tends to her babies in the protective hideaway of that homemade wooden birdhouse you built in your garage or workshop.

That's what *Projects for the Birder's Garden* is all about: affordable, doable projects that will make your yard a bird magnet. There's so much to try: making a simple feeder, whipping up a bird treat, adding a burbling water feature, crafting a hummingbird nectar feeder, creating a garden of natural materials for birds' nests, or building your very first wooden birdhouse. You'll find more than 100 great projects in this book, including more than 20 different feeder designs, 17 recipes and projects for bird and butterfly treats, 5 feeding station designs, 10 birdbaths and water features, 14 birdhouse and nesting projects, 9 designs for baffles and other protective features to foil predators and pests, and more than 20 garden designs and projects featuring plants that will lure songbirds, hummingbirds, and butterflies to your yard.

Projects for the Birder's Garden begins at the beginning, with a dozen simple projects that are perfect for newcomers to the pleasures of backyard bird watching. The easy projects in chapter 1 include a simple tray feeder, a woodpecker feeder fashioned from a cedar roof shingle, and a beautiful minigarden with a birdbath centerpiece. Many of these projects are simple enough to assemble in half an hour or less, using materials that you probably already have around the house.

From there, you can branch out to the types of projects that interest you most. If you love to make bird treats, check out the recipes for Suet Muffins and Dough Ball Treats and the directions for creating a Doughnut Sandwich feeder in chapter 3. If you're ready to create a larger-scale feeding station, consult the recommendations and projects in chapter 4, including the Woodland-Look Feeding Station and the Cat's Delight Window Feeding Station. Want to build a birdhouse? Chapter 7 has complete instructions for building a classic bluebird house, a traditional birdhouse, a wren house made from PVC (polyvinyl chloride) pipe, and even a window-mounted birdhouse with a see-through back that allows you to watch as mama bird tends her eggs and babies. If gardening projects are first on your list, you'll find great ideas in nearly every chapter, ranging from a front yard makeover for the birds to a hummingbird window box garden and a container garden for butterflies.

Since feeders and birdhouses can sometimes attract unwanted predators and pests, *Projects for the Birder's Garden* also explains how to create baffles and barriers to keep squirrels, raccoons, and other problematic visitors away from the birdseed. If, however, you enjoy watching the antics of squirrels, you can build them a feeder of their own, following the step-by-step instructions for the Stump That Squirrel (Not!) Feeder and the Through-the-Roof Nut Feeder in chapter 4.

If you're not sure where to start and you want a fast take on the complete range of project choices, turn to "Projects at a Glance" on page 287, where you'll find a list of all the projects in this book. You can find leads to projects that will attract specific types of birds by consulting the detailed index that begins on page 298.

The projects in this book run the gamut from very simple to somewhat complex. But every reader can be successful with even the most challenging project, thanks to the detailed materials lists, clear illustrations, and straightforward step-by-step instructions.

The contributors to *Projects for the Birder's Garden* are veteran gardeners and bird watchers who write from experience. They know that these projects will bring birds flocking to your yard because they've used them in their own gardens. And along with the instructions for making unique feeders and planting beautiful bird-attracting gardens, these bird-loving writers also provide plenty of interesting tidbits about bird behavior. Watch for these highlights in repeating features throughout the book, including "Nests and Eggs," "Regional Viewpoint," and "For the Record."

Watching birds is so satisfying because the learning never ends. As you plant the gardens and set up the feeders, birdhouses, and other projects you'll find in *Projects for the Birder's Garden*, you'll discover that your curiosity about birds and their habits will increase. You may want to invest in a good field guide and a pair of binoculars, because the more you learn, the more you'll enjoy these fascinating feathered friends. This is just the start of a lifetime of companionship with some of nature's loveliest creatures—so choose a project and let the fun begin!

CHAPTER I

Fast-and-Easy Projects for First-Timers

Your yard can be a natural magnet for all kinds of birds, whether you live in the most dramatic or the most ordinary surroundings. Satisfy their basic needs for food and protection from enemies, and your yard will soon be alive with feathered visitors. Add special touches with treats, water, safe places to nest, and a few other necessities, and birds won't be visiting your yard only now and then; they'll be spending much of their time there and checking it out as a place to raise their families.

ENJOYING THE FRUITS OF YOUR LABOR

Bird-tempting features are fun and easy to add to a home landscape, and it's very satisfying to watch birds enjoy a feeder, nest box, or garden you've added just for them. In fact, you'll soon discover that making projects for birds will also make you a better bird watcher. When you've set out a homemade feeder or designed a special birdbath garden, you'll naturally be inclined to check it frequently to spot new customers arriving and to watch how those birds react to your "present."

Simple Projects for Starters

Included in this chapter are a dozen do-it-yourself projects that will draw in perky goldfinches, sleek mourning doves, native sparrows, and a flock of other interesting birds, as well as the usual crowd of robins, chickadees, and jays. Even if your toolbox is limited to the hammer and screwdriver in a kitchen drawer—or if you have little free time for making things—you can still enjoy crafting simple bird-friendly projects. From a woodpecker feeder to a feather board to supply materials for nest-building birds, most of these projects can be completed in an hour or two, and some take just a few minutes. They will quickly increase the bird appeal of your yard—in some cases, birds will arrive to enjoy the fruits of your efforts within just a few hours of your finishing the project.

New Surprises Every Day

Backyard bird watching is full of surprises. Until we start looking, most of us have no clue how everyday bird life works. But once we begin watching birds, we discover the thrill of learning something new about even the most common winged visitors to our yards. You may have shared your breakfast time with chickadees on the other side of the window all winter, but your friendship will deepen when you discover that they're as fond of peanut butter as a 4-year-old—and as prone to squabbling over which one gets the biggest share.

The more you watch, the more you'll learn. You'll find out how the habits of backyard birds vary and how you can take advantage of different bird behaviors by tailoring your projects to fit the needs of your favorites. By adding a couple of very simple feeders to your yard, for instance, you can increase its appeal to specific birds, such as the shy song sparrow, which would rather nibble seeds near the low branches of shrubbery than dine at a high feeder out in the open.

Benefits for All

Birds certainly benefit from these projects, but we get the better end of the deal: year-round entertainment, a lifelong hobby that fits every age and every budget, a helping hand with insect pest control, and that satisfying feeling of nurturing the living creatures that share our space. Watching birds is the fun part: seeing how they search for food and what kinds they like best, laughing at the free-for-all and the wet-hen aftereffects of a bath, and feeling an almost parental pride when you discover a nest filled with perfect eggs or tiny peeping babies.

If you have children or grandchildren, these projects are ideal candidates for a joint venture. Be sure to enlist the children's help in watching for the first takers.

Once you've tried a few of the simple projects in this chapter, you'll be eager to move on to the wider variety of projects in chapter 2 and beyond.

Backyard Buddies

Birds are programmed to flee at sudden movements or startling sounds, and most of them quickly retreat to a safe hiding spot when an intruder arrives. Dedicated birders know that the key to spotting birds is to stay still and remain quiet until the birds venture out again.

Backyard birds, however, are a special breed. They're the species that have adapted to living right alongside humans,

---

FEEDERS Song Sparrow Favorite

Song sparrows are among the most common backyard birds, but you may not notice them in your yard until you put out a feeder especially designed for them. Although these native sparrows live in close proximity to people, they have a real knack for keeping out of sight.

Song sparrows prefer to eat on or near the ground. Take advantage of this habit with this truly simple feeder. House sparrows will show up to feed also. You'll be able to tell the two kinds of sparrows apart because song sparrows have noticeable brown streaks on their breast.

Step 1. Scout around your yard for a rock that's at least 12 inches long × 18 inches wide and between 4 and 8 inches high, with a slightly concave top. If you can't find such a rock in your yard—or if your lifting capabilities aren't up to lugging it around—visit a garden center and buy a lightweight faux rock with at least part of its surface slightly dished.

Step 2. Choose a site for the rock in the shelter of a landscape plant such as a shrub, a clump of ornamental grass, or a shrub rose.

Step 3. Tuck the rock partway under the foliage, so that the sparrows will feel safe and unexposed when enjoying their seeds. Be sure to leave part of the rock in open view so that you can catch a glimpse of your charming visitors.

Step 4. Pour about 1/2 cup of white millet seeds into the depression on top of the rock. Little brown song sparrows will quickly investigate and enjoy this new feeder that's tailored exactly to their needs.

such as the cardinal that nests in your climbing rose or the wren in the birdhouse by the vegetable garden. Some species of backyard birds will keep a cautious distance from people, but they're not nearly as shy as birds of the forests or fields that take flight when humans come near.

Because backyard birds are well-adapted to human activity, it's easy to entice them to dine and bathe within full view, and many will raise their families right in our yards. These species know that people are big, loud, and active, and they'll stick around even when there's a game of catch or a patio party going on. That's the best part of backyard birds: They fit right into the rhythm of our everyday lives.

Knowing Where to Look

Chances are your yard already plays host to more birds than you realize. The cheerful robin that sings in your maple or hops about on your lawn every morning has lots of shier friends, including the streaky-bellied song sparrow, which may frequent your forsythia bush or hedge. Fabulous hummingbirds have probably visited, zooming so fast from one flower to another that you may have missed them altogether. Other backyard birds actually live in other places, including nearby fields, woods, or roadsides, but they leave their usual residences frequently to visit your yard and garden in search of food, water, or other needs. Every corner of the continent has a slew of birds that will readily visit backyards. Consult "Winged Wonders in Your Backyard" on page 6 to see who may visit you.

All-Season Backyard Birds

Just like the flowers in your garden, many backyard birds come and go with the seasons. Lucky gardeners in the cold North welcome their slate-colored juncos home when spring is in full bloom. Meanwhile, those of us who hosted the juncos over the winter are saying good-bye, knowing that spring is really here when the little gray snowbirds depart. Other backyard birds are with us year-round. Here are some to look for, no matter what season it is.

Northern cardinals. In the winter, cardinals often frequent feeders in flocks. In the spring and summer, they feed singly or in pairs. The male cardinal's feathers brighten to an almost glowing red as spring approaches.

American goldfinches. It's easy to spot goldfinches in the spring and summer, when the males are a sunny yellow and black. Fall through winter, the males' plumage turns to olive drab and the birds are easy to miss.

House sparrows. Although they are an imported species, house sparrows are common in cities and towns across the country and usually arrive at feeders in flocks. This species is not a true sparrow, and the plumage of the female is similar to that of the female house finch, another common feeder bird.

House finches. Originally a western bird, the house finch is now widespread over North America. Once these finches discover a feeder, they may arrive in flocks numbering dozens of birds.

Jays. Several species of these boldly colored birds are boisterous at feeders in the fall and winter; which species you'll see depends on where you live. Notice how silent jays become in the spring, when they're adept at keeping the locations of their backyard nests a secret.

Mourning doves. Small flocks of doves may appear in your yard in the fall and winter. In the spring, it's fascinating to observe the fierce behavior of rival males as the birds pair off for mating. Watch for "billing and cooing" courtship behavior, where male and female birds appear to kiss and make cooing calls to each other.

Starlings. When they're not at the feeder looking for suet and other soft foods, starlings stalk the yard in the spring, summer, and fall to seek out grubs.

BUILD ON WHAT YOU HAVE

Feed them, and they will come. It's that simple when it comes to attracting backyard birds. Food is the number one enticement. When birds are hungry—which is most of the time—they'll even put themselves in risky situations to eat, whether that means a cat slinking nearby or a car bearing down on them.

Putting out a feeder is the obvious first step to entice birds, but don't stop there. One generously stocked feeder in the middle of a barren yard is like a single cookie on a plate: The birds will grab the goodie and run. Before birds will relax and spend a lot of time in your yard, or select it as a place to raise their families, they need to feel safe from danger. And to create that feeling of safety, nothing beats plants. The leafy protection of shrubs, flowers, and shade trees is vital to birds. Start with simple projects that provide food and protective cover, and you're well on the way to creating a bird

lover's garden. To encourage birds to hang around after they've finished eating, you'll want to supply them with other creature comforts, such as water and nesting materials.

Natural Features for Birds

Birds and backyard gardens are a natural fit, because the landscape features that make birds feel at home are the same ones that appeal to people. A bed of bright flowers, a shady spot under a tree, colorful fall berries, evergreen plants in winter, and a privacy hedge are all pleasing both to humans and to backyard birds.

continued on page 8

A robin may follow behind as you dig your vegetable garden, snatching up worms from the loose soil as fast as you uncover them. Chickadees are famed for their fearlessness and will alight at a feeder—or on your head—while you're still pouring out the seeds.

Winged Wonders in Your Backyard

The list of backyard birds easily runs into the dozens of species, no matter where you live. Here are some of the most widespread and abundant backyard birds. In most regions, you can expect these birds to be regulars at your feeder or in your yard.

BIRD NAME	DESCRIPTION	BEHAVIOR NOTES
Northern cardinal	Male, solid bright red; female, grayish brown with reddish accents and orange beak; not usually found in western United States, but its range is expanding	If you see a male feeding a female at the feeder (part of the courtship routine), the pair may have a nest in your yard; look among dense vines, roses, or conifers
Chickadees	Dapper, active, small gray birds, most species with black accents and pale bellies	Nest in cavities or birdhouses; particularly fond of dog hair and hairbrush combings for lining nests
Mourning dove	Soft taupe gray; long tail; watch for iridescent pinkish purple patch on male's neck to develop as breeding season nears	Endearing habit of nesting very near human activity; may select a hanging basket as nest site
House finch	Male, light brown with reddish head and back; female, lightly streaked pale brown; sparrow size	Often confused with purple finch, a much less common visitor; male purple finch has a deeper raspberry or purple color; female is more darkly streaked and has a distinctive light eye stripe
American goldfinch	Male, yellow and black; female, olive green	Listen for the happy-sounding call given in flight, with a distinct upward inflection at the end; it sounds like "potato chip"
Grackles	Big, bold birds; solid black with iridescent sheen on head; long tail	Often confused with stubby-tailed starlings, but much more elegant in shape; frequently nest in blue spruces, cedar hedges, and other dense backyard conifers
Hummingbirds	Unmistakable tiny, hyperactive birds with shining, iridescent feathers and long, thin bills	Visits may be fleeting as birds patrol the neighborhood, going from one favorite nectar source to the next

BIRD NAME	DESCRIPTION	BEHAVIOR NOTES
Jays	Biggest of the usual backyard birds; blue feathers with white-and-black trim; loud calls	Other birds scatter when a jay arrives, a good reason to include more than one feeder at your station; nuts are a favorite, so try a game of hide-and-seek by setting peanuts in the shell in odd but visible places
Juncos	Gray on top, white below, a color scheme that echoes dark clouds and snow-covered ground, giving them the nickname *snowbirds*	Their arrival is a reminder that winter is on its way; they often scratch below feeders to forage for dropped seeds; look for them beneath the standing stems of garden flowers in winter
White-breasted nuthatch	The "upside-down bird," which travels headfirst down tree trunks; dapper suit of dark above, white below	Watch for companionable flocks of chickadees with a nuthatch or two patrolling your trees in winter
American robin	Familiar backyard bird with classic orange breast and brown-gray back	Won't be tempted by a seed feeder, but loves a daily bath, with plenty of splashing
House sparrow	Small, warm brown bird; male has gray to black bib	Full-grown cicadas, grasshoppers, and Japanese beetles are great treats to this small bird; it doggedly pursues and subdues the large insects before consuming them
Song sparrow	Common backyard resident but usually heard more often than seen; dark brown with streaky white belly	Learn the sweet song of this bird and search for it, low to the ground, in undisturbed areas of your yard
Starlings	Chunky, short-tailed birds with blackish feathers decorated with small whitish chevrons or "stars" in fall or early winter	A lawn lover's best friends, these often-reviled, imported birds feast on the sub-terranean larvae (grubs) of pest insects, including Japanese beetles, May beetles, and European crane flies, all of which eat grass roots and give lawns a patchy appearance
Titmice	Fearless, chipper, small birds with jaunty head crest; gray with paler underparts; sometimes with black head markings	Big fans of dog hair to line their nests in tree cavities or birdhouses
Downy woodpecker	Typical woodpecker shape; smaller than other woodpecker species, with patterned black-and-white plumage; male has red dot on its head	Often works away quietly at suet feeder for long stretches of time; ardently eats poison ivy and Virginia creeper berries (seedlings of these plants may crop up in your yard from seeds in this bird's droppings)

continued from page 5

Birds no doubt already visit your yard, even if you haven't done a single thing to attract them. That's because many of the same backyard ideas that please people also satisfy birds' needs.

Shade trees. That maple or other shade tree you planted as a skinny sapling or were lucky enough to inherit full-grown looks mighty inviting to birds. It gives them a sheltered place to perch and maybe a good place to build a nest. Even a young tree supplies a lot of food in the form of insects living among its leaves and branches or in the grooves of its bark.

Foundation plantings. The shrubs that soften the outline of your foundation and hide unattractive features of your house are appealing to birds, too, thanks to their dense branches—a good spot to hide or travel from place to place for the species that naturally live at lower levels.

Vegetable gardens. Birds think that garden pests are yummy. They love a meal of stinkbugs, cutworms, Mexican bean beetle grubs, and other insects. They also like the nice loose soil in a vegetable garden, where it's easy for them to find worms or grubs.

Mulch. The earthworms, beetles, and other creatures that live in or beneath mulch are free food for robins, thrushes, and other birds.

Lawns. Your lawn is a great place for robins, flickers, and starlings to hunt for worms, ants, and grubs.

Flowerbeds. Blossoms attract butterflies and myriad smaller insects, all of which make a tasty meal for a bird. A colorful spread of blooms is also bound to attract hummingbirds, which sip nectar at geraniums, petunias, scarlet sage, and other common flowers. When flowers go to seed, they catch the eye of goldfinches and other small seed-eating birds, which eagerly devour the seeds right on the plant.

Driveways. Got a gravel driveway or a rock garden? Doves, finches, and other birds pick up tiny bits of grit to aid their digestion.

See how easy it is to make birds feel welcome? Just by having a yard with plants, you're doing things right from the birds' perspective. Food and a safe place to dine are the top attractions to backyard birds, and plants fill the bill.

WHAT BIRDS WANT

For the fastest payoff in increased bird visits, start your backyard improvement program with well-stocked feeders and a few plantings that will provide cover. Most bird behavior is governed by trying to reduce the threat from hawks, which typically perch or fly high above. Shrubs and other plants that keep a bird hidden are highly desirable, and plant groupings that allow for travel without much exposure are most welcome.

You can see how food goes hand in hand with cover when you consider two different locations for a feeder. Put that feeder in the middle of a neatly mowed lawn with not a tree or shrub in sight, and you won't see any customers for a long time. The few birds that do visit will be nervous and won't linger.

Now imagine the same alluring feeder positioned under a large shade tree or near shrubs or a hedge. The feeder is an easy hop, skip, and jump from safety, so birds will visit often and dine at leisure, allowing you to enjoy their extended visits instead of a fast eat-and-run.

Having cover nearby is also important when birds visit a water feature, another desirable addition to a backyard bird habitat. And, of course, birds need a safe and private location for nesting and raising young.

Coping with Cats

Backyard birds have learned that cats (and sometimes dogs) can be dangerous, but the presence of pets won't deter them totally; they'll just be extra careful. If your bird-catching pet often stalks birds' favorite food sources, however, the birds may trade in the dangers of your yard for a neighbor's less risky space. It's not fair, though, to invite birds into your yard if you have threatening pets or neighborhood cats that like to visit. Try these tips to keep your yard safe for birds.

Keep your cats indoors. Cats are a prime reason for the decline of songbirds. If you have a cat, keep it indoors. Many folks let their cats roam only at night, but that's still bad news for many birds that roost in low shrubs, particularly youngsters. It's especially important to keep cats indoors during nesting season (late spring through late summer). Not only can they clean out an entire nest in minutes, but they also can nab young birds that have left the nest but aren't yet strong fliers.

Eliminate stalker hideouts. Keep birdbaths and feeders out in the open, away from shrubs or bushy plants where cats can hide. But do place these attractions near a tree so that birds can fly to a safe haven.

Stock tube feeders with "no waste" seeds. Some styles of feeders allow a lot of seeds to fall to the ground, where birds will congregate to pick them up, becoming sitting ducks for prowling cats. Birds extract seeds one at a time from tube feeders, so fewer seeds escape. "No waste" seeds are those without hulls, such as sunflower chips and hull-less millet. Birds can eat them right away, reducing the chances that the seeds will fall to the ground while birds work on shelling them.

Raise feeders well above ground level. Consider feeders that attach to your deck railings, or mount them on 5-foot posts so that cats can't make a deadly bound.

Educate your neighbors. If you know that a neighbor's cat is allowed to roam outdoors, courteously share information with its owner about the dangers that cats pose to songbirds. One place to find such information is the Cats Indoors page of the American Bird Conservancy at www.abcbirds.org/cats.

Make a lot of noise. Train wandering cats to stay away by shaking a metal soda can that contains a handful of gravel or dried beans. The noise alone may make them scoot, or you can accompany the shaker noise with a loud "Shoo!" Clapping your hands may be enough to scare them off, too.

Reach for the squirt gun. If all else fails, or if a cat learns that you're all bark and no bite, give the cat a short burst from a hose or a high-power squirt gun. Unless it's very cold outside, water is harmless but highly unpleasant to cats.

Call out the dogs. A dog is the perfect cat deterrent. Walk yours frequently and at irregular times, and stray cats will skedaddle.

Food

It takes a lot to fill a belly when you eat one bug or seed at a time. Spend a few minutes watching a bird, and you'll see that its life is spent in an almost nonstop quest for food. When a bird isn't singing, nesting, or sleeping, it is snacking—grabbing a few seeds or berries here, an ant there, a cutworm over there—from daybreak to dusk.

Dining Styles Differ

Foraging styles are so different from one bird species to another that you may not realize how universal this pursuit of the daily grub (or grubs!) actually is. The robin casually hopping about on your grass is every bit as intent on finding food as the chickadee that flits from twig to twig in your shade tree, the woodpecker that hammers at a log, or the hawk that soars overhead. They're all looking for the next tasty thing to go down the hatch.

Foraging is a lot of work for birds, and providing food is a great place for a bird watcher to start. A well-stocked feeder is the key, because feeders keep birds in easy view, and you can fine-tune the foods you offer to attract specific birds. But to encourage those birds to linger in your yard, and to attract birds such as tanagers and flycatchers (which don't usually visit feeders), you'll want to make sure your garden appeals to birds, too.

Feeder Foods

Three basic foods—small millet seeds, sunflower seeds, and suet—plus insects and worms will satisfy every bird that is likely to visit a backyard in North America. So why is there such a confusing selection of seeds and food products available? Because, just like us, birds have their favorites. By offering specialty foods and homemade treats, plus particular plants in your garden, you can keep the birds coming back for more and ensure that your backyard is the busiest on the block. Jays, for instance, will readily eat sunflower seeds. But if you put out peanuts at your feeder, they'll quickly forsake your neighbor's sunflower spread in favor of your peanut supply.

Feeders

Feeders for basic as well as specialty bird foods come in a bewildering array of shapes, styles, and prices, but the simple suggestions on the following pages will get you up and running quickly. (You'll find in-depth information about the various types of feeders in chapter 2.)

Why a Feeder?

The name of the game is temptation. And yes, thou shalt tempt thy neighbor's birds to thy own backyard—all's fair in love and bird feeding. Because every yard on your block supplies some kind of natural bird food, you'll want to add special treats that birds can find only at your place. The simplest way to do that is to put up a feeder, where you can offer the most tempting foods for the birds you seek to entice. You also may want to exclude certain birds, such as starlings, and feeders of various designs will allow you to do so. Naturally, you'll want to add plants that birds find tempting, such as berry bushes, but keep in mind that birds will quickly consume a bountiful crop of berries, whereas feeder foods can be refreshed whenever they run out.

Bring gentle mourning doves to your garden with an offering of cracked corn in a clay plant saucer. Cracked corn is a favorite of doves, and it's one of the cheapest foods available, especially if you buy it at a farm supply store.

Doves tend to feed in the open, and they solve the problem of possible predator attack by feeding in groups, with one dove acting as lookout while the others peck. Put your dish of corn atop a short pedestal on the lawn, backed by a flowerbed if you like, and make sure there's an open escape route. Doves will gather around the dish and reach up to feed on the corn, or they may step up on the rim or even right into the dish. Many other kinds of ground-feeding birds will join the picnic, too.

Step 1. Settle a flat-topped rock that's at least 4 inches long × 4 inches wide and 1 to 3 inches tall in an open area of your yard to serve as a base for the feeder. Or use two bricks laid side by side. The base will help deter rodents and also makes the feeder more visually appealing.

Step 2. Choose a clay plant saucer that is slightly smaller than the rock or bricks. (If the saucer extends over the base, it may tip when birds land on the edge.) Set the saucer on the base.

Step 3. Pour a few handfuls of cracked corn into the saucer. The corn will be highly visible in this feeder and will quickly tempt customers. For a fun additional touch, place the feeder near columbine plants: Their curved-spur flowers look just like a group of doves feeding at the dish with heads in, tails out.

A shallow open tray or platform feeder, such as the one on page 12, is one of the easiest types of feeders to make. A tray feeder can serve many birds at once—and it's the best type of feeder for viewing birds, too. Dozens of birds can dine at the same time, and the overflow crowd can look for dropped seeds underneath the feeder.

Choose a site for your feeder where you can watch the birds in comfort. Place it outside a window that is an inviting vantage point for viewers. Or if you spend a lot of time outdoors, position it near your porch, patio, or garden bench.

Suet feeders and peanut butter feeders, such as the one on page 14, will attract different and equally fascinating birds.

You can use scrap wood to make this feeder or ask your supply store to cut the wood to size; most stores will do it for free or for a nominal fee. Vary the size of this feeder to suit yourself and your site. A tray measuring about 10 by 24 inches is satisfyingly large but requires only one mounting post. If you decide to make a larger feeder, support it with a post at each end so that it doesn't look ungainly. Such a feeder will visually overwhelm a very small yard, however, so if your yard is modest in size, choose feeder dimensions to match.

HELPFUL HINTS

To save on the cost of materials, you can use scrap lumber for the base and sides of this feeder. Two sections of 2 × 6s would work fine as the base. Nail two metal cleats into the undersides of the scraps to hold them together.

MATERIALS

8-penny nails

2 sections of pine 1 × 4 cut to the length of the short dimension of the plywood

Rectangular piece of ¾-inch exterior plywood

2 sections of pine 1 × 4 cut to the length of the long dimension of the plywood plus 1½ inches

Flat-topped 4- to 6-inch-diameter wooden post, 4 to 5 feet tall

Two 12-penny nails

Step 1. Use 8-penny nails, about 4 inches apart, to attach one of the short sections of pine to the plywood base. Nail through the strip into the edge of the plywood, so that one edge of the strip is flush with the bottom edge of the base.

Step 2. Attach the other short section in the same way.

Step 3. Position one long section of pine flush with the bottom edge of the base and covering the ends of both short sides. Nail it in place along the bottom with 8-penny nails, about 6 inches apart.

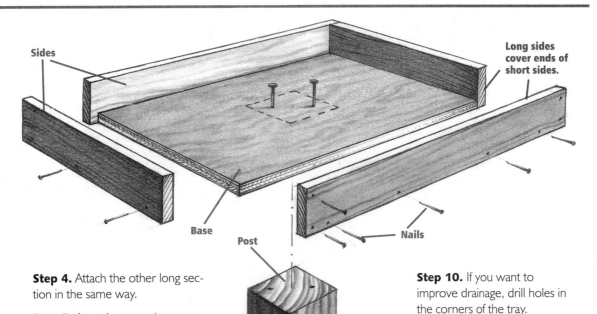

Sides

Long sides cover ends of short sides.

Base

Post

Nails

Step 4. Attach the other long section in the same way.

Step 5. At each corner, hammer two 8-penny nails through the long strip into the edge of the short strip.

Step 6. Dig a hole about 1 foot deep for the post. A tool called a posthole digger works well for this unless your soil is very rocky.

Step 7. Insert the post and refill the hole, stamping the ground very firmly when you're done. Make sure the post stays straight as you fill the hole; enlist a helper to hold it in position if you can.

Step 8. Mound the soil to slope away from the post so that water doesn't collect around it, which could cause the wood to decay quickly.

Step 9. Nail the feeder securely to the top of the post with the 12-penny nails.

Step 10. If you want to improve drainage, drill holes in the corners of the tray.

Step 11. Fill the feeder with seeds and await the arrival of your first guests.

Dealing with Drainage

Drainage is a tricky issue with a tray feeder. Many store-bought versions, and some homemade ones, use screening for the floor of the feeder to provide fast drainage. Solid-bottom tray feeders have been in use for many years, however, and those who tend them know that drainage rarely causes big problems. Rainwater and snowmelt seep out through the wood or through cracks where the sides are attached, and birds readily eat wet seeds (but not spoiled ones, which can make them sick).

Maintain the feeder by using a wide plastic or metal kitchen spatula or linoleum scraper to remove shells and other debris as needed. You are likely to find that this is seldom necessary because the wind blows out much of the chaff and birds often kick out the rest while scratching for a choice bit. After a rain, use the same tool to lift and spread out the seeds so that they don't get moldy.

Woodpecker Wonder

Every bird likes a feeder that mimics its natural habit, and for a woodpecker, that means gleaning goodies from a tree while clinging to the tree with its feet and bracing itself with its stiff tail feathers. Spread some peanut butter on a vertical surface where woodpeckers can reach it, and they'll nibble off every bit. Watch for chickadees, titmice, and nuthatches at this feeder, too. All are big fans of peanut butter, especially the chunky variety, with its bonus of bigger nutty pieces. The rough surface of a cedar roofing shingle is perfect for providing a smear of peanut butter pleasure. You can use the recipe for peanut butter feeding mix at right or you can slather on peanut butter straight from the jar. Note that peanut butter is high in oil and will quickly stain a wooden porch post or deck railing if you apply it directly.

Step 1. Buy a single cedar shingle, or shake, at a home supply store. The classic siding for Atlantic seacoast houses, these rectangular strips of wood are thin but sturdy.

Step 2. To help prevent peanut oil from seeping through the shingle, cut a piece of heavy-duty aluminum foil to a size slightly larger than the shingle. Wrap the back of the shingle with the foil and tightly crimp the edges all around.

Step 3. Nail the shingle to a vertical support, such as an arbor post or feeder mounting post, as high as you can reach without a ladder. Woodpeckers feed on tree trunks, which is what you're trying to imitate.

Step 4. Spread a thin area of peanut butter or peanut butter mix near the top of the shingle so that woodpeckers have room to grip the wood without getting their feet or tail feathers messy.

Peanut Butter Stretch

Birds can go through a jar of peanut butter lickety-split. This recipe will save you some money because it combines other tasty (but low-priced) ingredients with the peanut butter. As long as the mix tastes like peanut butter (sample it yourself), a variety of birds will eagerly gobble it up. Kids love to help with this recpe, especially the hand mixing.

INGREDIENTS

16-ounce jar of peanut butter, any kind

1½ to 2 cups yellow cornmeal, coarse grind

1 cup plain bread crumbs or crushed unsweetened breakfast cereal

Peanut oil, as needed

Optional: ½ cup total of one or all of the following: chopped unsalted nuts (any kind), chopped raisins, chopped apple

The basic method for making this mix is simple. Combine the peanut butter, 1½ cups cornmeal, and bread crumbs in a large bowl. Using a squeezing motion, mix the ingredients by hand until the dry ingredients are well incorporated with the peanut butter (wear thin plastic gloves for easy cleanup).

You'll want to temper this recipe according the type of feeder you plan to use. A crumbly texture is perfect for a tray or other horizontal feeder, but you'll need a stickier spread for a vertical feeder. If you want a crumbly mixture, add the remaining cornmeal ¼ cup at a time until you achieve the desired texture.

For a stickier result, add less cornmeal and drizzle in peanut oil 1 tablespoon at a time, mixing well after each addition. Test the stickiness of the mixture by spreading it on the inside of the bowl with a knife or the back of a spoon. If it clings well, it is ready for a vertical feeder.

Once you have the right texture, add any or all of the optional ingredients, if desired. To save yourself the time and effort of chopping raisins or apples, substitute thawed frozen blueberries or raspberries.

Match Feeder to Customer

The type of feeder you use will determine who gets to partake of this peanut butter treat. If you use an open tray, aggressive jays and mockingbirds and crowds of starlings will get the lion's share. Slathered on a vertical surface, the mixture will be accessible only to more agile birds with well-adapted clinging feet, such as woodpeckers, chickadees, titmice, and nuthatches.

To make sure smaller birds get their share, put some peanut butter treat in a store-bought birdseed feeder that bars entry to large, heavy birds, such as a hopper-style feeder equipped with a weight-triggered guard, or a plastic, globe-style feeder. Keep a batch on hand for a bout of late-spring cold or snow, when robins, catbirds, and wrens also may enjoy some of this soft, nutritious food. (If you're lucky enough to live near bluebird habitat, you may see some bluebirds at the feeder, too.)

Natural Foods

Birds would get along just fine without a single feeder in the world. Their natural diet is readily satisfied as they hop about the yard or patrol through the trees. The fact that birds forage for their own food is helpful to us gardeners because insects and weed seeds are high on their preferred food list.

Your yard already supplies lots of different natural foods. In fact, some of the best "feeders" are your plants! They supply seeds, berries, fruit, nectar, and an everlasting supply of nutritious, delicious insects. They also expand your bird watching beyond the feeder. It's fascinating to see how birds forage and what they forage for when they're not jockeying for a perch at your feeder.

Insects Are Important

One of the best arguments for not using insecticides is the fact that birds depend on insects for a large part of their daily diet. You may have noticed that feeders draw many more visitors in the winter but that the numbers dwindle quickly once spring sets in. That's because birds are busy eating bugs in the spring and summer.

Every plant in your yard is apt to host insects. You probably never notice them, but birds sure do. They'll scour your plants to pick off beetles, caterpillars, ants, aphids, and thousands of other insects, plus spiders (which are technically arachnids). A yard with plenty of plants and no insecticides already has a big head start on attracting birds.

Insects are a year-round food for birds, another good reason to plant abundantly. In the winter, birds will hunt for insects beneath tree bark, under leaf litter, and in cocoons or other hiding places. Every species of bird has its instinctual foraging places and style. It's fun to watch the variety in the action when several kinds of birds hunt for insects in your yard.

Underground Offerings

Robins, flickers, starlings, and a few other backyard birds regularly patrol lawn and garden areas searching for tasty un-

---

✔ *For the Record*

You Can't Please 'Em All

Not all birds take to living in our yards and gardens. Some have habits that are so specialized we can't satisfy them. Chunky, stubby-tailed meadowlarks, for instance, would rather walk or run than take to the air, so they need the wide-open spaces of large grasslands or farm fields, with thick, deep grass to provide cover as they move about. The legendary sweet song of the wood thrush is heard from the dim shadows of leafy woods, not from the housetops. And ducks, of course, look for water to paddle around in. When conditions are tough, though, unusual birds may show up in your yard. Watch for rare visitors—from small, sparrowlike dickcissels to giant-size pheasants and wild turkeys—especially in winter after a snowstorm or ice storm, when they're desperate for food. Tired, hungry birds, including bobolinks, wood warblers, and tanagers, may also unexpectedly alight during the spring or fall migration. In sustained summer drought, the birdbath or water feature is likely to draw in some seldom-seen customers, such as cuckoos, flycatchers, and thrashers. Keep your bird identification guide handy, because just about anybody may drop by: Great blue herons, scissor-tailed flycatchers, and even a young bald eagle have all been recorded at feeders.

derground morsels. Earthworms and plump grubs (the developing larvae of various beetles) are the prime targets, which is another good reason to avoid upsetting the natural balance with quick-fix chemical controls. A loose mulch of lawn mower–chopped fall leaves around plants creates ideal conditions for worms.

Supplies for All Seasons

Consider seasonality when you take stock of your existing plants. Spring-blooming trees such as crabapples attract large numbers of insects—good news for spring-migrating birds. Fall and winter berries—the decorative displays on plants such as dogwoods and hawthorns —are popular during the fall migration and later, when the weather turns cold. On a sultry summer day, the small, juicy fruits of strawberries, raspberries, and blueberries are just as popular with birds as they are with us.

Best Bird Plants

Once you see how nicely varied a menu your present plantings offer, you're apt to be surprised at how good a bird garden you already have. Look around your yard to see if you have any of these bird favorites currently growing. If not, add them to your wish list for future plantings. You'll find more suggestions for using plants like these in chapters 3 and 5.

Berries. Many shrubs, groundcovers, and other plants produce berries that are favored by birds for food but are considered mainly decorative (or inedible) by gardeners. Birds devour some berries as soon as they ripen; they leave others alone until late winter, perhaps when other food sources become scarce. Holly and dogwood berries are particular favorites of thrushes, including robins and bluebirds, plus catbirds, mockingbirds, tanagers, and other songbirds.

Small fruits. Birds will test your willingness to share when you grow delectable, desirable small fruits such as raspberries, strawberries, blueberries, grapes, and cherries. Backyard birds also adore the fruit of mulberry trees, which, although it's tasty, usually goes unpicked and gains our notice only when it drops to stain the pavement below. A single mulberry tree can host a virtual aviary of some of the most spectacular birds. Orioles, tanagers, bluebirds, great crested flycatchers, vireos, and other colorful beauties alight to gorge on the fruit as soon as it ripens.

Self-sowing annual flowers. Old-fashioned garden favorites, including bachelor's buttons, marigolds, cosmos, zinnias, common flax, scarlet flax, and cockscomb, produce abundant seeds so that new generations keep sprouting in the garden year after year. Birds like that bounty of seeds. They'll pluck them off as soon as they ripen and continue the work right through the winter, scratching below the stems to uncover any seeds that may have dropped.

Honeysuckle, trumpet vine, wisteria, and grapes. These old-fashioned, long-lived favorites for covering a porch or sturdy arbor retain their value to birds for 50 years, and possibly as long as 100 years. Honeysuckle and trumpet vine attract hummingbirds to their flowers. Wisteria and grapes bring in gazillions of

continued on page 20

Self-Renewing Beginner Bird Garden

This easy-care planting

is so full of color that nobody but you and the birds will know that its real purpose is to provide a feast for your wild friends. Even better, the agreeable old-fashioned annual flowers are easy to grow and quick to bloom from seed. Plus, they produce so many seeds that, even with birds sharing the bounty, plenty will be left to sprout next year. You plant this garden once and enjoy it for years thereafter.

Except for the coneflowers and marigolds, you can select the color scheme to suit your taste. For best results, choose a site that receives full sun.

PLANT LIST

3 bareroot or potted purple
   coneflower plants

1 packet bachelor's buttons
   seeds or 6 started plants

1 packet 'Sensation Mix' cosmos
   seeds or 6 started plants

1 packet 'Lemon Gem' or
   'Tangerine Gem' marigold
   seeds or 6 started plants

1 packet dwarf zinnia seeds or
   6 started plants

1 packet tall zinnia seeds or
   6 started plants

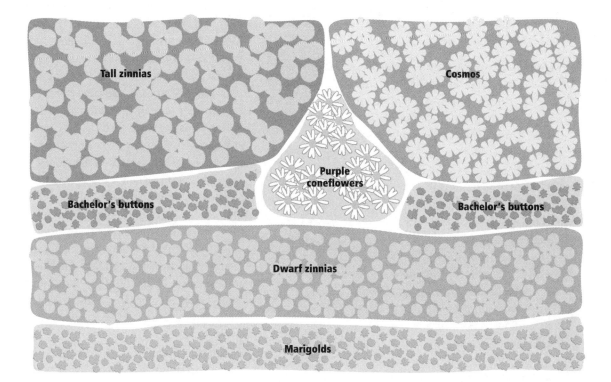

Tall zinnias

Cosmos

Purple coneflowers

Bachelor's buttons

Bachelor's buttons

Dwarf zinnias

Marigolds

Step 1. Prepare a 3 × 5-foot area in your yard for planting by removing all existing vegetation and loosening the soil.

Step 2. Plant the purple coneflower plants as shown in the garden plan above.

Step 3. Sprinkle seeds from the seed packets or transplant the started plants as shown in the garden plan above.

Step 4. Water well with a gentle spray until the soil is thoroughly moist.

Step 5. If you've used plants, mulch the bed with grass clippings immediately after watering. If you've sprinkled seeds, wait until after the seeds have sprouted to mulch. Gradually add to the thickness of the mulch as the seedlings grow until the mulch is about 2 inches deep.

Step 6. During the summer, keep a close eye on the flowers as they begin to mature. You're likely to spot foraging goldfinches in particular, but also buntings, sparrows, and other seedeaters.

Step 7. Let the plants stand after frost. Birds will continue to glean seeds from the seedheads and scratch for them in the ground.

Step 8. In late winter, pull out the annuals and cut back the coneflower plants to ground level.

Step 9. In the spring, watch for sprouting flower seedlings in your bird garden. If any invasive weeds pop up, pull them out. Once the flower seedlings get growing, they're likely to shade out weed competition for the rest of the season, especially if you renew the mulch.

Seven Speedy Flowers to Grow from Seed

Annual flowers live only a single growing season, so they have to produce plenty of seeds to make sure there's a next generation. Their abundant seeds quickly draw seed-eating birds, from big, bold ones such as cardinals and jays to quieter, smaller types such as sparrows and juncos. If you're new to growing plants from seed, pick any of the flowers from this list to start with. They're all hardy and reliable, sprouting in just a few days after planting and zooming to blooming size in as little as 8 weeks. Just-sprouted seedlings are big enough to spot easily, too, so you can tell when your crop is up and growing.

- Bachelor's buttons (*Centaurea cyanus*)
- Spider flower (*Cleome hassleriana*)
- Cosmos (*Cosmos bipinnatus* and *C. sulphureus*)
- Sunflowers (*Helianthus annuus* cvs.)
- Flax (*Linum* spp.)
- Marigolds (*Tagetes* cvs.)
- Zinnias (*Zinnia* spp. and cvs.)

continued from page 17

insects when they're in bloom, and that's good news to the birds that follow to pick them off. The gnarled tangle of vines is also an inviting homesite for catbirds and other backyard nesters, and it creates a safe roosting place at night.

Acorns and nuts. If there's an oak tree in your yard, you have a homegrown bird banquet. Strong-billed jays and woodpeckers will hammer the nuts open, and many small birds will scavenge for the smaller bits they drop. The same is true for walnuts, pecans, and other nuts.

Weeds. Less-than-perfect weeders, take a bow! You may be creating more headaches for next year, but you're also helping out the birds with every weed you overlook—as long as it sets seed. Backyard birds will feast on nearly all types of weeds, from tiny chickweed to giant ragweed and shrublike pokeweed. Smartweeds are particular favorites, and the pink-flowered species are pretty enough to consider as an intentional garden flower. Birds eat weed seeds as they ripen and also scratch about to pick up those in mulch or soil. The much-maligned dandelion is a top choice for many backyard birds, including some special migrants that fly through right about the time those notorious puffs are ready to let loose. Tolerate a few dandelions going to seed in your yard, and you may get a look at a gleaming indigo bunting or dashing white-crowned sparrow as your reward.

Cover

Except for open-space lovers such as robins and starlings, most backyard birds prefer the protection of a tree, shrub, or patch of plants while they forage or rest. When these types of plantings are staggered throughout your yard, birds can move from one place to another without much fear of hawks, because they don't have to cross large areas of open space.

Chances are your yard already has a good start on the kinds of cover birds seek and the kinds of food that attract them—even if you don't have a single feeder. Think of the shrubs, trees, and beds in your yard as stepping-stones that birds use to crisscross the area. Can they get around your yard by following the stepping-stones, or are there wide gaps where they'll have to make life-and-death dashes across open space? When plantings of cover plants are continuous or have only small gaps, they're called *corridors* and are highly attractive to birds as a way to travel safely around your yard. A good travel corridor can be as simple as a hedge along your property, augmented by several shrubs or flowerbeds. You'll find more details on creating corridor plantings in chapter 5.

Water

Water is high on the list of bird needs. But like a feeder, a birdbath or water garden is a feature that makes it easier for us to view birds in our yards, not (in most cases) a necessity for bird survival. Except during times of extended drought or when birds are fatigued on migration, water won't necessarily attract more birds to your yard. Even so, adding a water feature, whether it's a birdbath or a faux rippling brook, is certainly lots of fun. Water projects such as the simple birdbath improvements in this chapter and the more extensive water feature projects in chapter 6 will give you plenty of pleasure watching birds sip and splash.

You may wonder how birds find water on their own in nature. The supplies are all around them.

Dew and Rain

Dew and rain supply a lot of the water that birds need. Keep watching your birds, and you'll see that they're adept at sipping moisture from a cupped leaf or a blade of grass. Chickadees, hummingbirds, and other tiny birds can even bathe on a leaf. They'll rub their bodies and wings in the wetness, and then ruffle their feathers just as they do after a dip in the birdbath.

Wet Foods

Lots of tidbits that go down a bird's gullet are moist. Juicy caterpillars, fat-bellied spiders, and ripe fruits and berries all contain moisture that reduces the need for a drink of pure H_2O.

Bodies of Water

The regular visitors or nesters we think of as "ours" actually have larger territories that may include half the block or much more. That means they can easily get to water anywhere within a reasonable distance. A puddle on the street, a nearby stream or lake, a pet's outdoor water bowl, or, perish the thought, the neighbor's burbling garden pool all serve just fine as a pit stop for a drink or a bath for the birds.

Private, Please

Here's a method for making part of your yard instantly more inviting to birds, especially those seeking nest sites: Stay out of it! An undisturbed area is ideal for birds looking to raise a family. Many choose nest sites in branches high overhead or in thorny bushes that keep out intruders, but the birds that nest at lower heights or on the ground will avoid choosing a site that is frequently interrupted by a gardener weeding, clipping, sniffing the flowers, or simply strolling. Find a corner of shrubs, flowers, or herbs that you can leave to its own devices for weeks at a time, and your birds will thank you for the privacy. Just because you can't walk through it doesn't mean you can't watch it. Sit quietly on a nearby bench or chair with a view of the area, and you can admire the thrashers, towhees, thrushes, sparrows, and other shier species that may be calling it home.

Prettified Pedestal Birdbath

A shallow water basin elevated on a pedestal base has been a popular garden feature for more than a hundred years. Concrete birdbaths with a flared base are inexpensive and widely available, and they're excellent drinking and bathing facilities for birds. The rough surface provides a secure no-slip footing, and the basin is shallow, so the water won't be too deep for birds to bathe in.

A plain concrete birdbath may be too nondescript for your taste. If so, try one of these ideas to prettify an ordinary bath.

■ Curve a piece of wire fencing or chicken wire behind the birdbath and plant fast-growing scarlet runner beans (hummingbird nectar!) along the base of the fence for a grotto effect. Allow at least 8 feet between the birdbath and fence to ward off cat ambushes.

■ Ring the base with a 10- to 12-inch-wide collar of sweet alyssum or creeping thyme. These low-growing plants don't pack much visual punch from a distance, but you'll appreciate them every time you refill the birdbath. The alyssum smells as sweet as honey, and the thyme, when bruised, will delight you with a fresh, spicy fragrance.

■ Paint the base and outside of the basin, stopping an inch from the rim. Do not paint the inside of the bowl. Ask a salesperson at your hardware or paint store for advice on appropriate paint and primer. You can choose a single color or go for festive vertical stripes or a faux meandering vine on a solid-color background.

■ Set a small potted water plant, such as a miniature papyrus, in the basin. If wind is a problem in your yard, anchor the pot with a few stones on top.

■ Place a birdbath near each end of a flower border.

■ Wrap natural raffia around the base, just below the basin. Knot the raffia and let the ends dangle. Sow seeds for hummingbird-attracting cypress vines, and their tendrils will catch the raffia and climb up the base.

■ Back the bath with an arched iron trellis planted with a grapevine. Keep the trellis well away from the birdbath so that cats can't use it as an ambush area.

■ Use black iron shepherd's crooks at staggered heights to hold hanging baskets nearby.

■ Fill the basin with potting soil. Nestle a clay plant saucer in the center to hold water, then plant the space between the saucer and the basin rim with hens-and-chicks and other succulents.

Nesting Needs

Everybody knows that birds make nests, but birds are as individual in their nesting habits as the buyers of custom homes. Instead of granite countertops, Mrs. Robin demands a mud foundation; rather than a soaring great room, Mrs. Chickadee seeks a cozy bungalow. Consulting a bird behavior guide to learn about the most prized construction materials and the favorite locations of certain birds will help you become the best landlord on the block, with a steady stream of interesting tenants.

What we often take for granted is really a small miracle. The typical bird's nest is formed from dozens to hundreds of twigs, plant stems, and blades of grass—building materials that require trip after trip to the local home supply store of your backyard. Watch to see where a bird is carrying a twig, and you may get a good view of the construction process, too. It's quite a feat for an animal that's working mainly with its beak! You'll marvel when you see the bird select just the right twigs or glean stray dog hairs from your patio for a soft lining.

Vine-Draped Birdbath

For a lush, junglelike effect around a birdbath, plant seeds of a climbing nasturtium in the soil around the base. The vines, which tend to recline rather than climb, may need your help (in the form of Velcro plant tape) to stay semierect against the base. To support the vines, measure off a section of ½-inch-wide green Velcro plant tape long enough to wrap around the base about halfway up and add 2 inches. Position the stems of the plants loosely and naturally, then gently wrap the tape, which is barely noticeable even at close range, around the base and the stems. Overlap the end of the tape and press to seal it to itself. Add a second strip of tape as the plants grow if needed.

Velcro plant tape

"Plant" a Residence for Birds

To the chagrin of some home owners (and the delight of many others), the nests of songbirds have become fixtures in outdoor hanging baskets and wreaths. House finches and robins are the two most common nesters. At first, the trusting birds are charming, but as your lush green fern begins looking like a bedraggled mess, or as unsightly white streaks appear on the cheerful silk flowers of your wreath, you may find yourself considering eviction.

Under the Migratory Bird Treaty Act of 1918, it's a crime to interfere with a songbird or its nest. Although you can seek permission from the local office of your state's fish and wildlife service to stop a songbird from nesting in an inconvenient spot, it's simpler—and more fun—to enjoy your feathered guests. Why not plant a basket in a special way to leave room for a nest or hang a wreath specifically for birds to nest in, and hope your backyard birds take to those decoys instead of your own personal favorites.

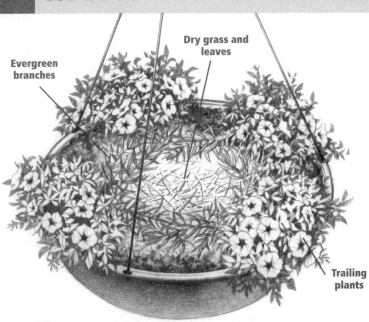

Evergreen branches

Dry grass and leaves

Trailing plants

A HANGING BASKET FOR BIRDS

Step 1. Fill a large hanging basket with soil-based potting mix, mounding the mix higher at the edges and hollowing out the center slightly to create a shallow bowl-like effect.

Step 2. Plant the perimeter with sturdy, vigorous trailing plants, such as 'Wave' petunias, Martha Washington geraniums (*Pelargonium* × *domesticum*), or fan flowers (*Scaevola aemula*). Avoid delicate edging lobelia, sweet alyssum, and other thin- or brittle-stemmed plants that would be damaged by frequent bird traffic.

Step 3. Line the inside edge of the circle of plants with short branches of needled evergreens, such as firs or spruces. This will help protect your flowering plants from damage.

Step 4. In the center of the pot, lay clippings of dry ornamental grass blades or dry fall leaves.

Step 5. Wait until the basket is adopted before you hang other, standard planted baskets. If birds don't move in, add a bright geranium or other plants in the unplanted middle. Just as washing your car seems to bring on rain, beautifying your basket may bring you a tenant within days!

A BIRD-BRAINED WREATH

Step 1. Choose a grapevine wreath that is relatively plump, not one that hangs flush to the wall, so that the inside bottom curve of the wreath is deep enough to support a nest.

Step 2. Decorate the wreath, limiting your decorations to the top and sides; leave the bottom center bare of trimmings. Loosely woven jute ribbons or raffia bows are a great choice, because they'll double as desirable nesting materials. Birds will tug at the fibers to collect them for nest building.

Step 3. Hang the wreath on a seldom-used door or on the wall next to a window—someplace where you'll be able to observe any developments without disrupting the mother bird while she's sitting on the eggs.

Step 4. Place a rubber mat beneath the wreath to catch droppings. A car floor mat works great. Use your garden hose to wash off droppings occasionally.

Many species of backyard birds add feathers to the framework or lining of their nests. White feathers seem to be extremely prized. A municipal duck pond is usually a terrific source of feathers, free for the collecting (and perfectly legal, since there's no law against collecting molted feathers). Or if you live near a poultry breeder, ask the owner for permission to collect some dropped feathers. Gather those that are soft and curled, and the palest ones you can find. Tan or gray feathers also will have takers.

The simplest way to supply feathers to nest-building birds is to scatter them on the lawn, but they'll blow away at the slightest breeze. To slow down flyaway feathers, try this sneaky trick for securing them to a wooden fence or garden furniture, so you get a better view of the feather-collecting phenomenon.

Step 1. Gather feathers and put them in a resealable plastic bag. Bring the feathers home with you.

Step 2. In your kitchen, make a sticky paste of flour and water by dribbling water into a few tablespoons of flour in a cup. Aim for a very thick, highly sticky mixture.

Step 3. Take the cup of paste and the bag of feathers outside to your wooden fence or garden furniture.

Step 4. Dab the back of a feather lightly in the paste. Press the feather against a flat surface on the fence or furniture and hold it in place for a few seconds. Repeat, spacing the feathers several inches apart.

Step 5. Retreat to a hidden vantage point and see which bird spots the feathers first.

Make a "Featherboard"

You can also use flour paste to attach feathers to a piece of cardboard or plywood. Lay the board on the lawn, feather side up. Even though it's an unnatural-looking object, birds will be so bewitched by the white feathers that they will soon overcome their hesitancy and approach to steal the treasures.

TAKING INVENTORY

Now that you've learned about the four big attractions for birds—food, cover, water, and nest sites—inventory your yard to see how many bird-attracting possibilities it already holds. The few minutes it takes for this "quiz" will give you a great starting point for deciding which types of bird-attracting projects your yard needs most. Just for fun, you can figure out the bird attraction score of your current, unimproved yard, then year by year compare your scores to see how your yard is increasing in bird appeal.

With this book, a notepad, and a pencil in hand, take a walk around your yard and make a point tally based on the table below. If your yard is small (city size), a total score of 50 or more means you already have a good start on a bird-worthy backyard. For a medium-size lot (less than ¼ acre), aim for a score of 100 or more. For a property of ¼ to ½ acre, a score of 150 or more means your place is already holding out a welcome mat. If you dwell on more than half an acre, roughly divide your property into quarter acres and evaluate the potential of each parcel.

Your Backyard Scorecard

Many common landscape features help provide birds' needs for food, cover, water, and nest sites. The listing below ranks features and lists their potential benefits.

LANDSCAPE FEATURE	BENEFITS FOR BIRDS	POINT VALUE
Young shade tree (deciduous)	Possible nest sites, some insects	10 points
Mature shade tree (deciduous)	Nest sites, moderate shelter from elements, protective cover, insects, seeds or nuts	25 points
Young conifer (less than 10 feet) with widely spaced branches	Some shelter from elements, protective cover, some insects	10 points
Young or dwarf conifer (less than 10 feet) with dense branches	Nest sites, nighttime roosting place, excellent shelter from elements, protective cover, insects, possible seeds from cones	20 points
Large conifer (such as fir, spruce, hemlock)	Nest sites, nighttime roosting place, shelter from elements, protective cover, insects, seeds from cones	30 points

continued on next page

LANDSCAPE FEATURE	BENEFITS FOR BIRDS	POINT VALUE
Single flowering deciduous shrub (such as forsythia, lilac)	Nest sites, nighttime roosting place when in leaf, shelter from elements when in leaf, protective cover, insects, possible nectar	10 points
Single thorny flowering shrub (such as rosebush, barberry)	Nest sites, nighttime roosting place when in leaf, shelter from elements when in leaf, protective cover, insects, possible berries or other fruits	10 points
Single evergreen shrub	Nighttime roosting place, shelter from elements, protective cover, some insects	10 points
Hedge of flowering deciduous shrubs	Nest sites, nighttime roosting place when in leaf, shelter from elements when in leaf, excellent protective cover, insects, possible nectar, travel corridor	30 points
Group or hedge of thorny flowering shrubs	Nest sites, nighttime roosting place when in leaf, shelter from elements when in leaf, protective cover in all seasons, insects, possible berries or other fruits, travel corridor	30 points
Group or hedge of evergreen shrubs	Nest sites, nighttime roosting place, excellent shelter from elements, protective cover, insects, possible seeds from cones, travel corridor	30 points
Established woody vine (such as grape or wisteria)	Nighttime roosting place, protective cover, insects, possible nectar, nesting materials from strips of bark	15 points
Flowerbed or flower border of mixed heights	Some protective cover, insects, possible seeds, possible nectar	10 points
Flowerbed or flower border with shrubs or small trees	Possible nest sites, protective cover, insects, possible seeds or fruits, possible nectar	15 points
Flowerbed or flower border left to stand over winter	Protective cover, insects, seeds, travel corridor	20 points
Container garden	Possible insects, possible nectar	5 points
Vegetable garden	Protective cover, insects, travel corridor	10 points
Undisturbed weedy area	Possible nest sites, protective cover, insects, seeds, possible nectar, travel corridor	20 points

CHAPTER 2

Supplying Seeds

Seeds work like magic to bring colorful birds into close view. Toss some striped sunflower seeds in a ground-level tray feeder, and the striking red male cardinal will appear. Fill a tube feeder with nyjer seeds, and swarms of brilliant yellow-and-black goldfinches will come to feed. Pour black oil sunflower seeds into a hopper feeder and watch rose-breasted grosbeaks alight. Plant a few dwarf zinnias in the window box, and rusty-capped chipping sparrows will peck for fallen seeds on the ground close at hand. In this chapter, you'll learn how to use seeds as your magic wand to fill your garden and yard with your favorite everyday visitors and also how to entice some not-so-ordinary birds to stop by.

FEEDERS FIRST

Now that you've sampled a few simple do-it-yourself projects to attract birds, what's the next step? You may be inspired to transform your yard into a true sanctuary for birds, complete with as many types of inviting habitats as possible. Creating bird habitats takes time, though, and while you're developing backyard habitats (see chapter 5 to learn how), become a regular supplier of birdseed for your feathered friends.

When you stock a few feeders in your yard, you do a world of good for the birds, for yourself, and for the environment. Many birds use feeders like truckers use truck stops: as convenient spots to find a meal without having to waste a lot of time. But just as truckers prefer home cooking, many seed-eating birds would rather feast from trees, flowers, and other natural spots when seeds are abundant there. As far as we know, your feeders won't change the natural habits and instincts of birds, but they will give birds a reliable spot to find fuel for a life in perpetual motion.

Providing a Power Source

From dawn to dusk, birds are on the move. They need power to fly, grow, change their feathery coats, and stay warm at night. Males need energy to mark and defend their territories and to court a mate—often at a feeder with a seed delicately placed in a female's bill. Females need strength to build nests and incubate eggs. Seeds at feeders are like energy bars for parents to eat on the run while they ferry protein-rich insects from your garden to their babies in the nest.

Feeders are also training camps for young birds where they learn how and what to eat. Feeders invite migrating birds to rest and refuel. When snow and ice bury natural food supplies, feeders brimming with seeds can be a bird's best chance for survival.

By offering seeds with feeders and garden plantings, you help restore a piece of the wild lost to suburban sprawl and intensive agriculture. The bonds that feeders help build between people and birds often inspire in us a renewed respect for our natural resources.

GUESS WHO'S COMING TO DINNER?

Carolina chickadees, purple finches, scrub jays, dark-eyed juncos, white-breasted nuthatches, song sparrows, and pine siskins are just a few of the birds you can lure to your yard with seeds. More than a dozen different types of common backyard birds like to eat seeds, with many species within each type. Observing the variety of shapes, colors, and behaviors of feeder birds is a treat that's well worth the effort of maintaining a few feeders.

A Question of Place

Of course, which seed-eating birds visit your yard will depend on where your yard is located. If you live near Massachusetts woodlands, an American tree sparrow may stop by. Green-tailed towhees can be expected in desert areas, and multicolored painted buntings may frequent feeders in the South. Black-headed grosbeaks are likely to show up in mountainous regions, and you might see dickcissels in grassy prairie areas. Wherever you live, continental birds such as dark-eyed juncos and black-capped chickadees are practically a sure thing.

Seasonal Visitors

The time of year also determines which birds to expect. Cold-weather storms may force horned larks in from corn-fields. Indigo buntings may stop over for a few days in the spring to refuel for the rest of their journey to their breeding grounds. In late summer, a young, fluffy-feathered white-breasted nuthatch is a special treat.

Although the average yard can expect visits from roughly 15 to 20 different bird species on a regular basis, not all of them

Seed-Loving Birds

The most common backyard seed-lovers can be classified into 12 broad groups of birds. Each of these categories contains lots of individual species (some found only in certain regions). Plus, other birds that usually favor insects or berries will grab seeds when times are tough. All in all, a bountiful variety of birds are waiting to taste the seeds in your yard.

SEED-LOVING GROUP	SOME FAMILIAR SPECIES
Blackbirds, cowbirds, and starlings	Red-winged blackbird, yellow-headed blackbird, brown-headed cowbird, common grackle, starling
Buntings	Indigo bunting, lazuli bunting, painted bunting
Chickadees and titmice	Black-capped chickadee, Carolina chickadee, mountain chickadee, plain titmouse, tufted titmouse
Doves	Mourning dove, rock dove (pigeon)
Finches	Northern cardinal, dickcissel, Cassin's finch, house finch, purple finch, American goldfinch, pine siskin
Game birds	Northern bobwhite, ruffed grouse, ring-necked pheasant, Gambel's quail, wild turkey
Grosbeaks	Black-headed grosbeak, blue grosbeak, evening grosbeak, rose-breasted grosbeak
Jays and crows	Blue jay, scrub jay, American crow
Nuthatches	Pygmy nuthatch, red-breasted nuthatch, white-breasted nuthatch
Sparrows	Dark-eyed junco, chipping sparrow, fox sparrow, house sparrow, lark sparrow, song sparrow, white-throated sparrow
Towhees	Green-tailed towhee, rufous-sided towhee
Woodpeckers	Northern flicker, downy woodpecker, hairy woodpecker, red-bellied woodpecker

will be seed lovers. Many birds, such as robins, house wrens, and scarlet tanagers, like to fill their bellies with insects first. Cedar waxwings and northern orioles are just two species from the big berry-loving bird group. Woodpeckers love suet-based treats and shelled peanuts best. Ruby-throated and rufous hummingbirds, of course, fill up mostly on flower nectar. You'll learn more about making bird treats, treat feeders, and nectar feeders to attract these birds to your yard in chapters 3 and 8. And if you'd like a broad view of bird food preferences, including seeds, nuts, suet, insects, fruit, and more, check out "Who Eats What?" on page 290.

Even those birds that usually shun seeds may one day show up at your feeders, especially in the winter if their preferred food is scarce. Or perhaps a young fledging will do a taste test to see what the excitement at your feeders is about. Place a good bird identification guidebook for your region at your favorite bird-spotting window so you can pick out the regulars and the unusual visitors. That's part of the fun of feeding birds.

SETTLING ON SEEDS

In chapter 1, we took a quick look at the wide range of foods that appeal to birds, but in this chapter, we focus on seeds. When you're looking to lure more birds to your yard, seeds are your best bet for bait. Nothing works faster than these tiny powerhouses of fat and protein to bring birds to your yard.

The best lures are the seeds preferred by the birds you most want to see. Read on for a guide to the seeds birds most like to eat.

Common Feeder Fare

Birds can be picky about the seeds they eat, and one seed does not suit all.

Sunflower and nyjer are two of the most common seeds for stocking feeders, along with millet, safflower, cracked corn, and milo.

Sunflower

It's hard to find a bird that doesn't like the taste of a sunflower seed. The wings-down favorite of nearly all feeder birds (except doves), sunflower seeds will draw the biggest variety of birds to your yard. Birds love these seeds because it's easy for them to crack open the thin shells to get to the fat-laden seeds. If you put out only one type of seeds, make it sunflower.

There are three kinds of sunflower seeds: black oil, striped, and hulled. Each type has its advantages.

Black oil. The most popular type, black oil sunflower seeds are small, oval, black seeds. They contain more fat than the larger striped sunflower seeds, so birds get a bigger bang for their buck.

Striped. Cracking the larger, tougher shell of gray- or white-striped sunflower seeds takes a bigger beak. Cardinals, jays, and grosbeaks may actually seek out striped sunflower seeds because there's less competition for them.

Hulled. As they crack open seeds, birds shed a lot of shells—beneath the feeder. Hulled sunflower seeds (also known as sunflower hearts or chips) leave no waste or mess behind. No shells to break apart also means that other birds—such as woodpeckers, mockingbirds, and even robins—may be tempted to visit your

continued on page 35

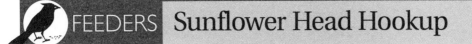
Say "I love you" to goldfinches, chickadees, and other sun worshippers by hanging the head of a ripened sunflower on a porch post, fence, or tree branch, or any other likely location in your yard. These easy-to-make instant feeders are sure to please a crowd.

You can buy sunflower heads from feed or craft supply stores and farmers' markets, or collect them, with permission, from knocked-down stalks in farm fields after the harvest. Or you can plant them to shine in your own garden (see "Sized-to-Fit Sunflower Plantation" on page 60). Wear gloves for protection against the spiny heads and clip them off at the top of the stalks with garden clippers.

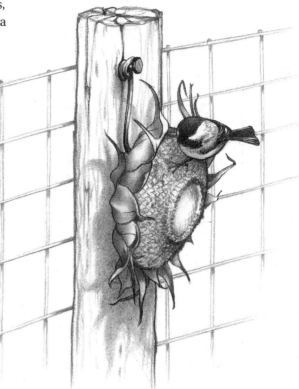

Step 1. Use wire cutters to cut through a metal clothes hanger at one angle bend.

Step 2. Make a second cut just below the hanger hook but on the opposite side of the hanger from the first cut. This will leave you with the hanger hook and an attached wire "tail" about 6 inches long. Discard the cutoff section.

Step 3. Wearing gloves, impale the sunflower head onto the hanger hook, thrusting the hook into the back of the head.

Step 4. Bend the wire tail into a rough hook shape to hang from a tree branch or other support, or wrap the end of the wire around a nail in a garden fence post, and let worship services begin.

A Steady Stream of Sunflowers

A black-capped chickadee needs to eat 150 sunflower seeds (or the equivalent) in an average day. When a hard frost hits, it must consume 250 sunflower seeds per day. Based on roughly 10 hours of winter daylight, this means a chickadee—forever obedient to its feeding style—needs to take one seed from a feeder, fly to a branch, put the seed under its foot, break the shell with its beak, swallow the seed, and return for another seed every 2½ minutes, all day long.

A Sporty Nyjer Tube Feeder

Serve up some nyjer

in this feeder made from a plastic tube that tennis balls come in. The tiny slots cut in the tube are the perfect size for dispensing the tiny black seeds. This feeder proves that you can think outside the soda bottle to make a tube feeder.

MATERIALS

1 clear plastic tennis ball tube with lid; balls and labels removed

Sharp knife, such as a box cutter, paring knife, or craft knife

12 to 14 inches of heavyweight picture-hanging wire

Duct tape or clear packing tape

Drill

5/16-inch twist drill bit

Handful of pebbles

Paper towels

5/16-inch-diameter dowel, 7 inches long

Step 1. Remove the lid from the tennis ball tube and set the lid aside.

Step 2. Use the point of a sharp knife to poke a hole 1 inch below the top on each side of the tube.

Step 3. Cover the holes with duct tape to keep out the rain. Thread one end of the wire through both holes and twist the ends together tightly to form a loop for hanging.

Step 4. Hold the tube steady and, using the drill with the 5/16-inch twist drill bit, slowly drill a hole through the bottom for drainage.

Step 5. Measure 1 to 1 1/2 inches up from the bottom of the tube and slowly drill a hole through the side. Drill a hole at the same height on the opposite side of the tube.

Dowel

Paper towels

Pebbles

Step 6. Drop a small handful of pebbles into the tube, then place paper towels on top of the pebbles. Press the towels down firmly, filling the tube to just below the holes. (The pebbles will give the feeder some weight and stability. The paper towels will keep the seeds from falling to the bottom of the feeder and out of reach.)

Step 7. Insert the dowel through the holes. This makes two perches about 2 inches long on each side of the feeder.

Step 8. With the knife, carefully cut slits 1/4 inch × 1/8 inch wide about 1 1/2 inches above each perch.

Step 9. Pour in some nyjer seeds, place the lid on top, and hang the feeder.

HELPFUL HINTS

If you'd like to use a tennis ball tube as a sunflower seed feeder rather than a nyjer feeder, follow these directions, but in step 8, use your drill and 5/16-inch bit to drill seed holes above the perches instead of cutting slits.

---

continued from page 32

feeder. However, some undesirables, such as starlings, also may try to feast on those easy-to-eat nuggets.

Nyjer

These thin, tiny, black seeds, sometimes called niger or thistle seeds, come from a golden-petaled daisy imported from Ethiopia, India, and Nepal—not from our native thistle plants. Nyjer seeds are heated to prevent germination, so you're not likely to get a patch of weeds growing below your nyjer feeder.

The high fat content of nyjer seeds is nutritional dynamite for the many finches that devour them. You may even find doves and the elusive woodland ovenbird scavenging the ground beneath a nyjer feeder for leftovers.

Millet

No bigger than a pinhead, millet seeds are those little round white, red, or golden seeds found in most seed mixes; you can serve millet by itself, too. White proso millet, as it's officially known, is the most popular mix seed and the type birds like best. Its white color will draw attention to a new feeder because birds readily see the color white.

These high-protein seeds are slightly sweet, which may explain their popularity with so many birds, even the lovely orange-and-blue varied thrush. Millet is a good choice for ground-feeding birds and other small seedeaters such as doves, buntings, juncos, pheasants, quail, sparrows, cardinals, and towhees.

Safflower

Safflower, another white seed, often appears in mixes with millet. It is conical, has a thin shell, and is about the same size as a black oil sunflower seed. It's sometimes offered by itself and has the reputation of being a favorite among cardinals, perhaps because of its high oil content. Grosbeaks, chickadees, finches, and jays also will partake of safflower seeds.

Safflower's biggest claim to fame may be its bitter taste, thought to deter unpopular grackles, starlings, and house sparrows and the dreaded eastern gray squirrel.

Cracked Corn

Cracked corn is pulverized dried corn kernels. Like millet, it's a popular ingredient in birdseed mixes or as a single offering. (It's best not to buy whole corn ker-

 FEEDERS **Flowerpot Seed Bell**

A seed bell is tailor-made for small birds that can cling and eat, and it's an easy project. The only materials you need are an egg, some seeds, and a small terra-cotta flowerpot. You can expect black-capped chickadees, tufted titmice, or white-breasted nuthatches to dig in their toes and start pecking at this feeder made of nothing but seeds.

Around the holidays, make several bells, freeze them, and then hang them in a row on separate branches to help decorate an evergreen tree outside with goodies.

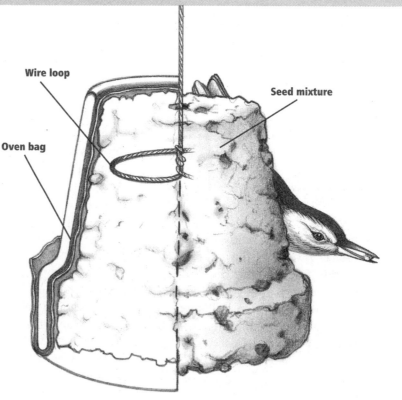

Wire loop

Oven bag

Seed mixture

nels, because they are too hard for most birds to digest.)

Cracked corn attracts almost any feeder bird, particularly ground feeders, including those that can eat whole kernels. Because either the cracked or whole kernel variety ranks high with unpopular birds such as starlings and pigeons—as well as with squirrels—you can offer corn in a spot away from your other feeders as a diversion for these pesky intruders. Leftover cracked corn is a good winter food. In the spring, rake leftovers onto flowerbeds for a natural fertilizer.

Seed Blends

A bag of mixed seeds offers ready-made variety, which is important in attracting a diverse bunch of birds. The trick is providing a quality blend that birds will pick clean. Mixes with lots of sunflower seeds, some millet, a dash of nyjer, and a little cracked corn have something for everyone.

MATERIALS

8 inches of heavyweight picture-hanging wire

1 cup seed mix (see page 38 for a recipe)

1 egg white, lightly beaten

3-inch terra-cotta flowerpot with drainage hole

1 large oven bag, cut into quarter sections

Step 1. Wrap one end of the wire around your index and middle fingers to form a loop about 2 inches in diameter. Twist the end against the straight length of wire to hold the loop in place. Angle the loop at 90 degrees to the rest of the wire and set aside.

Step 2. Mix the seed mix and egg white in a bowl until the seeds are well coated.

Step 3. Line the flowerpot with a quarter section of an oven bag, folding the extra plastic over the sides.

Step 4. Fill the pot one-quarter full with the seed and egg mixture.

Step 5. Poke the end of the wire into the mixture and through the hole in the bottom of the pot. Pull the looped end of the wire through the mixture until it is close to the bottom of the pot.

Step 6. Pour the remaining mixture into the pot.

Step 7. Set the pot on a rack in your oven with the wire hanging down. Place a cookie sheet on the rack below the pot to catch any drippings from the hole. Bake at 200°F for 1 1/2 hours.

Step 8. Remove the pot with oven mitts and let it cool.

Step 9. Use the exposed part of the oven bag to gently pull the seed mixture out of the pot. Peel away the oven bag.

Step 10. Bend the wire into a small hook, and your seed bell is ready to hang.

Simple Seed Mix with a Winter Kick

As an alternative to commercial seed mixes that may contain unappealing seeds such as wheat or barley, try a basic, low-cost recipe recommended by the bird-feeding experts at the Cornell Lab of Ornithology in Ithaca, New York. The combination of black oil sunflower seeds and millet with inexpensive cracked corn makes it appealing to a large variety of seed-eaters, especially ground feeders such as white-throated sparrows and dark-eyed juncos.

When winter rolls around, kick up the energy-producing punch by adding more high-fat, high-calorie seeds and an energy-boosting treat of peanut hearts to the mix. These will help the birds survive the cold days and nights. Plus, the heavy mixture of sunflower seeds with some safflower seed will appeal to large seedeaters such as cardinals and blue jays.

To make either of these mixes, pour the seeds into a large metal trash can, stir with a broomstick (or your hands) to combine, and cover the can with a tight-fitting lid.

BASIC MIX

25 pounds black oil sunflower seed

10 pounds white proso millet

10 pounds cracked corn

SPECIAL WINTER MIX

15 pounds black oil sunflower seed

5 pounds gray-striped sunflower seed

5 pounds hulled sunflower seed

10 pounds millet

5 pounds peanut hearts

3 pounds safflower seed

2 pounds cracked corn

Specialty seed mixes are hot items at many seed supply stores. Finch mixes, cardinal blends, and the like typically combine the foods most preferred by these species so that you can fine-tune your offerings. The popular waste-free mixes offer small, no-hull seeds such as hulled sunflower seeds, peanut pieces, and millet. You can use these to avoid having a mess on the ground around your feeders. They are especially good for feeders located on a balcony, patio, or windowsill. Even birds that usually shun seed feeders, such as catbirds, bluebirds, and thrashers, may sample no-mess mixes.

Milo

Some say there's a bad seed in every bunch, and milo has that rap when it comes to feeding birds. Milo, or sorghum, is a round reddish seed that's a common ingredient in cheap grocery store blends. It's the last, desperate choice for most eastern and midwestern birds, except doves and game birds such as pheasants. Red milo, however, is a favorite seed of many western birds, particularly in the Southwest.

Out of the Ordinary

Want more choices for filling your feeders? You won't see the following types of seeds on the everyday menu, but they make a great blue plate special for your bird diner.

Flax seed. This flat, oval, shiny brown seed is so loaded with energy-packed oil that it practically gushes. The biggest flax seed fans are small birds such as sparrows and finches.

Rapeseed. A tiny round seed from a European mustard plant, rapeseed is also known as canola—of canola oil fame. As you might expect, rapeseed is loaded with energy-boosting oil and is especially good for cold-weather feeding. Small seedeaters, including juncos, finches, towhees, sparrows, doves, and buntings, enjoy sampling rapeseed.

Canary seed. Shiny and brown, canary seed is most often found in mixes, including pet bird mixes, but it may be available by itself from some bird supply stores or feed mills. It is a special treat for finches—canary relatives—and other small birds such as sparrows and indigo buntings.

Grit

Not actually a kind of seed, grit is nonetheless an important supplement to any bird's diet. Grit can be any small,

Budgeting for Birdseed

The price of birdseed varies by region, so it's difficult to make specific cost comparisons of various types. But to help you decide what to buy and how much your can afford, check these general guidelines for the relative expense and value of various kinds of birdseed.

TYPE OF SEED	COST AND VALUE
Black oil sunflower	A high value seed even at its medium-range cost because it feeds so many kinds of birds
Striped sunflower	Expect to pay a little more for this compared to black oil on a per pound basis.
Hulled sunflower	Although priced higher than black oil sunflower, hulled seeds are actually a better value, because you're not paying for bulky hulls (which birds can't eat).
Nyjer	One of the priciest seeds, but there's lots of seeds to the pound and a wealth of beautiful birds to be lured.
Millet	More expensive than sunflower on a per pound basis, but seeds are tiny, so it's actually a great buy.
Safflower	A mid-priced seed that offers some birds a change of pace.
Cracked corn	The least expensive choice among popular birdseeds.
Seed mixes	Generally a good value, but some special blends can be pricey. Mixing your own blend to suit the birds you want to attract (or already have in your yard) will keep the birds happy and save you money.
Flax seed	Since it's expensive, you may want to save this seed for times of high-energy need, such as during nesting season or bad weather.
Rapeseed	Try offering it as one ingredient in a mix to help dilute its high price tag.
Canary seed	Its appeal seems to be regional, so serve a small amount as a test before investing big-time in this expensive seed.

hard substance that birds can swallow and hold in their gizzards. Grit works for birds as our teeth do for us. In the gizzard, the grit acts to grind up seeds and other foods for better digestion. Flocks of birds will gather around road gravel or sand spread by road maintenance trucks for grit. You can use coarse builder's sand (not children's play sand), small pieces of charcoal, or crushed shells to supply grit for birds.

Crushing and heating the shells from your breakfast eggs is an easy way to serve a daily dose of grit to birds. Smash the shells between pieces of waxed paper and then bake the shells (but not the paper) for 20 minutes at 250°F to kill salmonella bacteria. Eggshells also provide calcium, which female birds need to produce eggs and strong-boned chicks. Toss grit and crushed eggshells on the open ground, or serve them in a separate dish at a feeder.

BUYING AND STORING GOOD SEED

Bags of birdseed can be found just about everywhere nowadays. Garden centers, hardware stores, feed mills, discount stores, bird supply stores, grocery stores, and corner convenience stores all stock at least a few bags of birdseed. If lugging bulging sacks of seed is not for you, you can even order seed (usually 5-pound bags) by mail or phone or on the Internet for delivery straight to your door—at an extra price for the convenience.

In the seed business, the smaller the bag, the higher the price per pound will be. If you have a convenient place to store it, buy quality seed in bulk and save big bucks in the long run. If, however, you store your seed in the hall closet of your third-story apartment or your back just isn't up to carrying 25- or 50-pound bags anymore, the convenience of smaller bags or mail delivery may be worth the price. (For information on mail-order seed suppliers, see "Resources for Backyard Birders and Gardeners" on page 292.)

Finding Quality and Value

With so many options for buying birdseed and so many types to choose from, it pays to recognize quality and value. High-quality seed is fresh and free of debris, insects, and webbing (a sign of insect infestation). Buying seed that the birds will eat to the last kernel gives your seed-buying bucks real value. Inspect bags carefully before you buy, keeping the following guidelines in mind.

■ Seed bagged in plastic or heavy paper stays fresh longer than seed sold from open bins.

■ Seeds, particularly sunflower seeds, should be plump and well-formed. (Ask for permission to inspect a sample if you can't see through the packaging to the seeds inside.)

■ If you see a lot of empty hulls, small sticks, or webs in a bag of seed, walk away.

■ Avoid buying seed packaged in burlap bags, because insects like to lay eggs in burlap.

■ Reject any bags that have patched holes, which could mean mice or other rodents have hit.

Grapevine Wreath Feeder

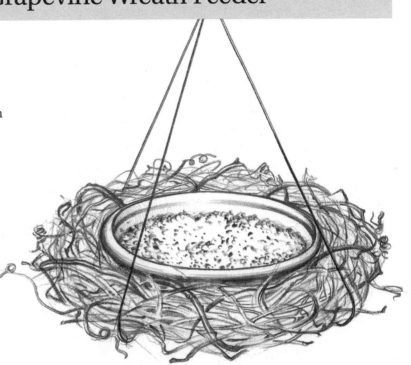

A grapevine wreath

is so simple yet elegant that it has become a classic American home decoration. You can use the cuttings and trimmings from your garden grapevine or buy an inexpensive grapevine wreath to fashion a natural, classy-looking outdoor feeder full of seeds.

MATERIALS

Grapevine trimmings, about 2 feet long, or premade grapevine wreath, 18 inches in diameter

22-gauge florist's wire

12-inch plastic plant saucer

Drill

5/16-inch twist drill bit

Strong wire

4 long S hangers (often used to hang flowerpots)

Step 1. If you're using grapevine trimmings from the garden, soak the trimmings in a large tub or sink of warm water for at least 30 minutes. If you're using a premade wreath, skip ahead to step 4.

Step 2. Make a ring about 12 inches in diameter with one vine and tie the ends with florist's wire.

(You can use a small bucket or other round object as a form to wrap the grapevine around.)

Step 3. Weave additional trimmings around the ring until you achieve the thickness you want, tucking or tying the ends to secure them (12 times around is about average).

Step 4. Turn the saucer upside down and use the drill with the 5/16-inch twist drill bit to make several holes for drainage.

Step 5. Lay the saucer right side up in the opening of the wreath. If

it feels too loose, use three pieces of strong wire to form a cage across the opening of the wreath to support the saucer.

Step 6. Hook three of the S hangers into the wreath at three equidistant points. Hook the remaining hanger to a branch or nail in a good observation spot. Then gather the three S hanger ends together and attach them to the suspended hanger.

Step 7. Fill the saucer with seeds and watch the birds enjoy your handiwork.

When a Bargain Isn't

So-called bargain mixes, commonly sold next to the potato bin at the grocery store, are rarely bargains. They contain lots of cheap grain seeds, such as wheat, oat, barley, and milo, that most feeder birds avoid like a red-tailed hawk. A quality seed mix will consist largely of the seeds that birds prefer to eat: Little is wasted, and there's value to the dollar.

Choose mixes that list sunflower, millet, safflower, nyjer, peanuts, peanut hearts, or other treat seeds near the top of the list of ingredients. Bags with filler or junk seeds near the top of the list are seldom worth the price. (Remember, though, that if you live west of the Mississippi, milo in a seed mix shouldn't raise a red flag. Unlike their eastern brethren, many western birds love milo.)

When the seed bins are bare and that 5-pound bag of seed at the convenience store starts to look good, don't despair. You probably have plenty of items on hand that you can use to fill your feeders. (For ideas, see "Kitchen Cupboard Treats" on page 84).

Storing Seed Safely

You've hauled that 50-pound bag of striped sunflower seed home from the store. Now where to keep it? Leaving the seed in the bag is not the best idea, because it leaves the seed vulnerable to insect infestation or being consumed by pest animals. Instead, store your seed in a metal can with a tight-fitting lid and keep it in a cool, dry place. An unheated garage or shaded garden shed are two suitable locations. Trash cans are great for holding large quantities of seed. For smaller amounts, try pretzel or popcorn tins with snug lids.

Moth Woes

Moths and other insects often lay their eggs in piles of birdseed. The eggs can lie dormant for months until they are warmed by summer heat. If you find what look like cobwebs in your seed, it's evidence that the larvae of flour moths or weevils have been eating the seed. When you find cobwebs, the only recourse is to discard the seed. Worse, the moths are very hard to get rid of once they are established in your home or garage.

Other Headaches

Warm summer days or direct sunlight can turn the oil in seeds rancid, ruining them for birds. If moisture sets in, mold may follow. In addition, mice, squirrels, raccoons, and other rascals will gorge

A Moth-Repelling Folk Remedy

Throwing away moth-infested birdseed is throwing money down the drain. To save money in the long run, spend a little on a small bag of bay leaves. You can also use California laurel (*Umbellularia californica*) leaves, which are less expensive but more pungent than regular bay leaves. For years, people have used bay leaves to keep bugs out of flour, and they work to protect birdseed from moths, too.

As you fill a metal storage container with birdseed, drop in one or two bay leaves at about 5-inch intervals in the seed. When the can is full, set three or four bay leaves on top. Cover the container snugly. You can reuse the leaves until they become brittle. Then just add them to your compost pile.

themselves on your stockpile of seed if given half a chance.

FEEDERS GALORE

Birds will take seeds from almost any kind of container—from a pie tin to an ornate gazebo with separate bins for four different kinds of seeds. There is an infinite variety of feeders, but if you look closely, they're all just variations of a few basic models: tray or platform feeders, hopper feeders, and tube feeders.

Let's look at the features of these basic seed feeders, which birds like to use them, and which seeds work best in them. Chapter 3 will fill you in on feeders for other bird foods, such as suet, fruit, and nectar, and chapter 4 will teach you how to coordinate feeders to create great feeding stations (groupings of feeders in locations that offer birds the conditions they need to feed safely).

Tray or Platform Feeders

The door is always open when you serve seeds in an open-sided tray feeder, also called a platform feeder. True to its name, a tray feeder looks like a serving tray with a flat surface and low rim. The open sides let birds come and go easily and put all the seeds in plain sight, just begging to be grabbed. Trays and platforms with large feeding areas give a variety of big and small birds enough room to feast together. This type of feeder will draw a crowd in a hurry. For directions for making a basic tray feeder, see "A Buffet Tray" on page 12. If you'd like to try your hand at a platform feeder with more style and charm, try the "Gazebo-Style Platform Feeder" on page 45.

Feeding High and Low

Just as birds have preferred foods, they have preferred feeders, which fit in with their natural feeding niches. Basically, that means on the ground or among the branches of trees and shrubs.

Ground-Feeding Birds

In nature, ground feeders scavenge the ground for fallen seeds or pick off insects from leaf litter. They like to eat as close to the earth as possible. Dark-eyed juncos, mourning doves, chipping sparrows, eastern towhees, and game birds such as Gambel's quail are typical ground feeders.

Tree-Loving Birds

Tree lovers, for want of a better name, pick insects and seeds off the leaves, branches, and trunks of trees or shrubs. Their idea of a good place to eat is someplace out of the dirt and up in the air. Tufted titmice, downy woodpeckers, rose-breasted grosbeaks, and goldfinches are a few of the many birds that like to eat in a location with a view.

The good news is that birds are not overly fussy about eating in their favorite spots. You'll see ground-feeding chipping sparrows on hanging tube feeders and tree-loving chickadees at low tray feeders. The lure of a favorite food usually takes precedence over the venue.

Protection Problems

The wide-open space of a tray feeder also creates its biggest problems. The seeds are sitting ducks for ruin by bad weather or pilfering by other wildlife, especially squirrels, raccoons, and vermin. A screened bottom or drainage holes are important for a tray feeder to let water drain and allow air to circulate so the seeds won't turn moldy. Adding a roof, such as the one on the "Picture-Perfect-Tray Feeder" on page 48, of course, provides better protection.

Wire guards can protect tray feeders from squirrels and, for better or worse, big birds. To deter nighttime raids, try serving only enough seeds for the daytime crowd. Expect to fill this feeder daily.

Low Platform Feeders

Low-level platform feeders just a few inches or a couple of feet above the ground are the first choice for doves, sparrows, juncos, and other ground-feeding birds. Other seedeaters, such as cardinals, jays, chickadees, nuthatches, titmice, grosbeaks, buntings, crossbills, and finches, will use low trays but favor post-mounted platforms that ground feeders avoid.

Place a low tray feeder on your lawn near a cluster of shrubs and trees, which simulate the forest's edge, an environment where small wildlife feels safe. If the feeder has a roof, turn the feeder so that the low side of the slanted roof faces the prevailing wind to help bird visitors conserve body heat while feeding in the winter.

Stock the feeder with with straight millet (favored by ground feeders) or black oil sunflower seeds to attract cardinals, chickadees, crossbills, finches, tufted titmice, and other birds. Add mixed birdseed, and you'll also see Carolina wrens, mourning doves, juncos, and thrashers. Sprinkle in some peanuts, and you'll be rewarded with visits from woodpeckers and nuthatches. (Expect the occasional chipmunk and squirrel, too.) These feeders are not good for serving light seeds such as nyjer.

Windowsill Feeders

Small platform-type feeders that fit on a windowsill are highly appealing because they bring birds so close to your view. In your grandmother's day, people didn't use a feeder; they simply opened the window and sprinkled bread crumbs or seeds directly on the sill.

There's no better way to enjoy the company of your feathered friends than inviting them to hop onto your windowsill for a snack of seeds or suet. After a few visits, the birds will become accustomed to your presence and may even grow bold enough to tap on the window with their beaks to remind you that it's time to fill the feeder.

Modern commercial windowsill feeders are made of clear plastic and mounted with suction cups. This is a great option for windows without ledges or for gardeners who have tiny city yards that afford no room for a feeder. Beware that sometimes the feeders will slip unless there is a sill to support the bottom. Try waste-free mixes or hulled sunflower seeds in this type of feeder for less mess beneath the window.

You can make your own deluxe version of one of these plastic windowsill feeders by following the instructions for the "Clear-View Windowsill Feeder" on page 50.

Make sure you have easy access to refill your windowsill feeder, because goldfinches, chickadees, and sparrows will be feeding close-up often.

This rustic feeder

makes an elegant addition to a bird garden. Even better, you can make several of these feeders for less than the cost of just one of the trendy commercial models that you see at garden centers and advertised in high-end mail-order catalogs. This feeder is ideal for all types of seeds, including large pieces of cracked corn and peanuts.

MATERIALS

Large plastic funnel, about 8 inches in diameter (available in the automotive department of discount stores)

Scrap of 1 × 10, or 10 × 10-inch piece of ½-inch-thick exterior plywood

4-foot-long rounded fence post or turned, untreated deck-stair spindle or newel post

Wood glue

3-inch #12 wood screw

½-inch-diameter straight tree branch with bark, 2½ feet long

Four 1-inch #10 screws

Small bark-covered twigs

¾-inch metal brads

Four ¾-inch #10 screws

Aquarium silicone sealant

Small, unpainted wooden finial or drawer knob with screw

TOOLS

Band saw

Cordless drill

⅛-inch drill bit

¹⁄₁₆-inch drill bit

Screwdriver

Hammer

Pruning shears

Pruning saw (optional)

MAKING THE PLATFORM

Step 1. Set the large end of the funnel on the scrap board and draw a circular cutting line 1½ inches out from the rim of the funnel.

Step 2. Cut the board to size with a band saw. (If you don't have a band saw, you can buy a scrap of wood at a home center and ask them to cut it for you.)

Step 3. Using a ⅛-inch bit, drill a pilot hole into one end of the fence post and another hole through the center of the wooden platform piece.

continued on next page

Gazebo-Style Platform Feeder *continued*

Step 4. Switch to the $1/16$-inch bit and drill four pilot holes through the platform around the perimeter at evenly spaced intervals. (The gazebo pillars will be centered above these holes.) Set the pilot holes about 2 inches in from the edge of the platform to allow room to attach a perching ledge.

HELPFUL HINTS

An easy way to ensure that the pilot holes for the gazebo pillars are evenly spaced is to draw two straight lines that intersect at right angles across the center of the platform, as if you were slicing a pie into four servings. Use the center hole you drilled into the base as your guide. Lay a ruler across the platform and mark a line. Then use a carpenter's square or other right-angled edge to line up the intersecting line at exactly 90 degrees. Measure in $7/8$ inch from the edge along each line and mark a dot for the pilot hole.

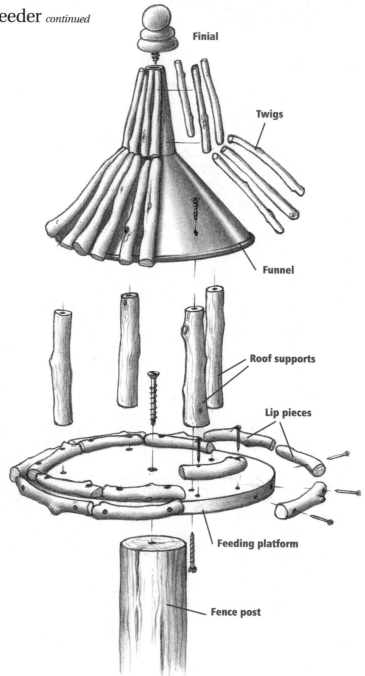

Finial

Twigs

Funnel

Roof supports

Lip pieces

Feeding platform

Fence post

Step 5. Dab wood glue onto the end of the post or spindle and screw the post to the platform using the 3-inch #12 wood screw.

Step 6. Take the platform assembly to the site you have chosen for the feeder and drive the post or spindle about 6 inches into the ground by hammering on the center of the platform. If your yard tends to have hard or heavy soil, water the site well a couple of days in advance to make this job easier. If you're using a thick post, you may want to try one of the methods shown in chapter 7 for installing a mounting post.

ATTACHING THE PILLARS

Step 7. With the platform firmly situated, you can now begin building the gazebo from the base up. Use sturdy pruning shears or a pruning saw to cut the tree branch into four pieces, each about 8 inches long.

Step 8. Use the 1/16-inch bit to drill pilot holes into both ends of all four branch pieces.

Step 9. Dab wood glue on one end of one of the branches. Fasten that end to the platform by screwing a 1-inch #10 screw from underneath the platform, through the pilot hole and into the branch. (It helps to have a friend hold the branch steady while you line up and drive the screw.)

Step 10. Repeat step 9 with the other three branches.

ATTACHING THE LIP

Step 11. Using the pruning shears, cut short lengths of twigs to attach around the rim and edge of the platform to form a lip that will prevent seeds from spilling out of the feeder.

Step 12. Using the 1/16-inch bit, drill two pilot holes in each twig.

Step 13. Align a twig with the rim of the platform and hammer brads through the pilot holes to fasten the twig in place. Repeat until the entire rim is disguised by twigs.

Step 14. Align a twig at the outside edge of the top surface of the platform and secure it with brads. Repeat with more twigs until you've covered the entire outer edge.

ADDING THE ROOF

Step 15. Rest the funnel upside down on the pillars and drive a 3/4-inch #10 screw through the funnel into each pillar to secure the roof.

Step 16. Cut twigs to the length of the funnel and glue them, one at a time, to the outside of the funnel, using the aquarium silicone sealant. Cover the roof with one layer, and if there are gaps, fill them in with smaller twigs as needed for full coverage.

Step 17. When the funnel is "shingled," screw the finial into the small funnel opening at the top of the roof. Use sealant to create a waterproof seal between the finial and the funnel opening.

Quick-and-Easy Tiki Roof

If you don't want to fuss with gluing individual twigs to make the twig roof, substitute a flexible grass mat (either a small floor mat or a couple of grass cloth place mats) instead. To do this, fashion a pattern by taping a sheet of newspaper to the funnel and cutting it to fit. Then remove the pattern from the funnel, lay it on the grass mat, and draw around it with a marker. Cut the mat along the pattern lines and glue it to the funnel with aquarium silicone sealant.

You may need to replace the mat yearly due to wear from the weather or from birds stealing pieces of grass as nesting material.

Picture-Perfect Tray Feeder

A used picture frame

is the base on which this tray feeder is built. Any size frame will do. A frame that measures about 11 by 17 inches will make a feeder that holds a week's worth of seeds but is still small enough for one person to move when it's time to mow the grass.

This feeder rests on three legs instead of four to accommodate uneven ground. The slanted roof protects birds from driving wind and rain and hides them from the eyes of soaring raptors.

MATERIALS

Wooden picture frame, any size

Aluminum window screening

$3/8$-inch-long staples

3 turned, untreated deck-stair spindles

$5/8$-inch-thick exterior plywood, cut about 4 inches longer and wider than the picture frame

Three $1 1/2$-inch #10 screws

TOOLS

Heavy-duty scissors or shears

Staple gun

Saw

Drill

$3/16$-inch drill bit

Screwdriver

Carpenter's square (optional)

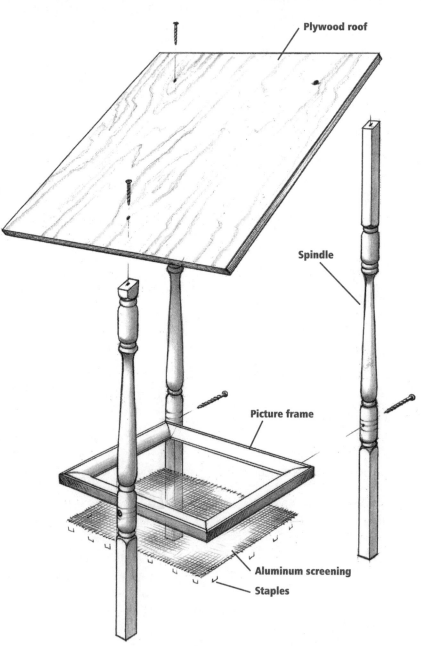

Plywood roof

Spindle

Picture frame

Aluminum screening

Staples

MAKING THE TRAY

Step 1. Remove the backing and glass from the picture frame and discard them. Lay the frame right side down on your worktable.

Step 2. Cut a piece of screening large enough to cover the opening of the frame plus enough extra so that you can staple it to the back of the frame. Or go to a glass supply store and ask them to cut the screening for you.

Step 3. Staple the screening to the back of the frame, stretching it tightly as you go.

ATTACHING THE LEGS

Step 4. Use a saw to shorten one of the spindles by 6 inches.

Step 5. Center this short spindle along one of the long sides of the frame, so that the "leg" portion that projects below the frame is 9 inches long. Mark and drill one pilot hole into the frame and another into the spindle.

Step 6. Screw the leg to the frame using one screw.

Step 7. Draw a diagonal line at about a 30-degree angle across the top of each of the remaining two spindles. Cut the tops of the spindles at this angle so that when the roof is attached, it will slant toward the back of the feeder.

Step 8. Following the same technique as in steps 5 and 6, attach one spindle to each corner of the long side of the frame opposite the short spindle. Orient the spindles so that the slanted ends point up when the tray is set upright.

Step 9. Turn the tray right side up so that it rests on its legs.

ATTACHING THE ROOF

Step 10. Cut the plywood to the same dimensions as the picture frame plus 2 inches all around, plus the width of the spindles.

Step 11. Rest the plywood roof on the slanted spindles, and push the plywood forward until it touches the inside edge of the short spindle. Mark the angle of the slant against the side of the short spindle, and set the roof piece aside.

Step 12. Cut the spindle along your mark. (You may need to remove the spindle to cut it, then reattach it.)

Step 13. Set the roof in place and adjust its position until the over-hang is approximately equal on all sides. Drill pilot holes through the roof into the spindle tops.

Step 14. Drive one 1-inch screw through each pilot hole to secure the roof. To ensure that the frame is level, hold a carpenter's square against the frame and spindle as you attach the roof.

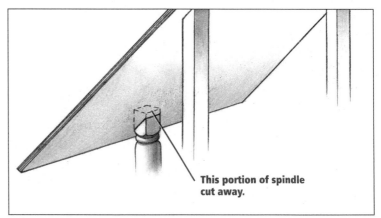

This portion of spindle cut away.

FEEDERS Clear-View Windowsill Feeder

This simple-to-make, see-through windowsill feeder has a lot going for it. It's roomy enough to accommodate several small birds or even a hungry woodpecker, and it's much cheaper to make than buying a commercial clear plastic windowsill feeder.

You'll want to save your richest seeds, such as nyjer, black oil sunflower, and peanut hearts, for this feeder and add a suet cake to one or both ends to entice a wide variety of birds. Cardinals, Carolina wrens, catbirds, black-capped chickadees, chipping sparrows, downy woodpeckers, mockingbirds, mourning doves, red-bellied woodpeckers, red-breasted nuthatches, robins, song sparrows, tufted titmice, and white-throated sparrows will all be tempted by these treats.

MATERIALS

Clear plastic shoe box with lid

Two 2½-inch-diameter safety suction cups with S hooks

Scrap of 2 × 4, less than 1 foot long

12-inch-long piece of 1-inch trim board (such as quarter round)

Wire cage suet feeder

Aquarium silicone sealant

Spool of craft wire, such as 20-gauge steel or brass wire

Two #6 stainless steel washers

Two #4 stainless steel flat-head screws

TOOLS

Drill

⅝-inch twist drill bit

5/64-inch twist drill bit

7/64-inch twist drill bit

Saw

Diagonal wire cutters or heavy-duty scissors

Screwdriver

PREPARING THE COMPONENTS

Step 1. Lay the shoe box on its side. With one hand, hold a suction cup against the back (bottom) of the box near an outside upper corner. With the other hand, mark a dot on the inside of the box where the center of the suction cup touches the box.

Step 2. Repeat step 1, placing a second dot in the other upper corner.

Step 3. Rest the box open end up on the 2 × 4. Using the ⅝-inch drill bit and very light pressure (to keep from cracking the plastic), drill a hole through each of the dots.

Step 4. Using the saw, cut a piece of trim board to fit inside the lip of one long side of the box. Because the box has rounded corners, the trim won't fit precisely, but that's okay. The gaps will allow water to drain out of the feeder.

Step 5. Turn the box on its side and place the trim board on the inside lip of what will be the floor of the feeder. Make a mark 1 inch in from each end of the box, centering these marks below the thickest part of the trim board. Make a corresponding mark on each end of the trim board.

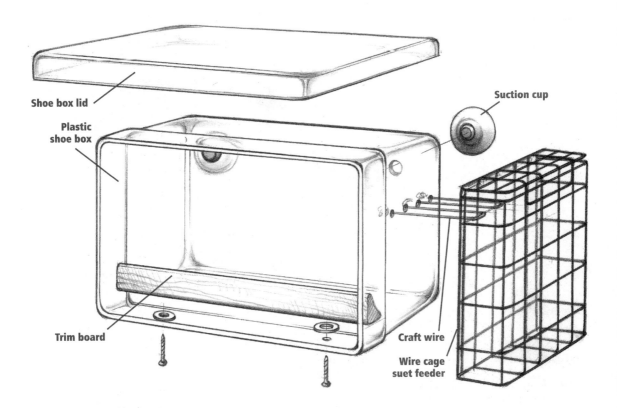

Shoe box lid

Plastic shoe box

Suction cup

Trim board

Craft wire

Wire cage suet feeder

Step 6. Set the box on its side on the 2 × 4. Using the 5/8-inch bit, drill a hole from the inside of the box through each mark.

Step 7. Switch to the 5/64-inch drill bit and drill a pilot hole into each end of the trim board.

Step 8. Hold the wire cage against the outside of one of the short box ends (keep the cage flush with the back of the feeder). Mark the spots for four holes through which you can feed wire to attach the cage to the box.

Step 9. Place the box marked-end down on the 2 × 4. Using the 5/64-inch bit, drill a hole through each mark. (If you want a suet cage on each end of the feeder, simply repeat steps 8 and 9 on the opposite end of the box.)

ASSEMBLING THE FEEDER

Step 10. Remove the S hooks from the suction cups and push the button on the back of each cup through one of the 5/8-inch holes that you drilled in step 3, so that the buttons end up inside the box. If the buttons don't fit perfectly in

the holes, dab some of the aquarium silicone sealant around them to secure them in place.

Step 11. Hold the suet cage in place against the end of the box, and thread a piece of craft wire from inside the box through one of the holes and into the cage. Thread the other end of the wire through another hole. Twist the ends of the wire together inside the cage. (They will end up safely tucked behind a suet cake after you've installed the feeder.)

continued on next page

Clear-View Windowsill
Feeder *continued*

Step 12. Repeat step 11 with another piece of wire, threading it through the other two holes in the end of the box.

Step 13. To attach the trim board, place a washer on the inside of the box above one hole in the floor and push a screw up through the hole and washer. Position the trim board so that the screw aligns with one pilot hole and drive the screw partway into the trim. Align the other end, then drive both screws into the board for a fit that is snug but not tight enough to crack the plastic. The washers will reinforce the plastic beneath the perch and allow water to drain from the floor of the feeder.

Step 14. Create a weather-resistant awning by gluing the shoe box lid to the top of the feeder with the silicone sealant. (When applying the sealant, work in a well-ventilated place and follow the package directions.) Align the lid so that it is flush with the back of the feeder. Allow the sealant to cure overnight before hanging the feeder.

Step 15. Dampen the suction cups and press them to the outside of a window next to your easy chair or breakfast table, or even outside a child's bedroom window. For firm support, be sure to attach the feeder low enough on the window so that the bottom of the feeder rests securely on the windowsill.

Step 16. Fill the feeder with high-quality seeds and suet, then sit back and enjoy the show.

Super-Size It

If you're expecting a crowd, you can super-size this project by substituting a clear plastic storage box (or other bin of your choosing). Just be sure to add more suction cups to hold it steady against the window, and adjust the length of the wooden perch to fit the front edge of the bin.

Hopper Feeders

A hopper feeder is like a self-loading, semiautomatic tray feeder. Seeds are stored in a holding bin, and when a bird pulls a seed from the little slot at the base of the bin, another one drops onto the feeding tray. Most hopper feeders, also called house feeders, have a roof covering the storage bin and tray. Hoppers hold a good pile of seeds, anywhere from a quart to many gallons, and the roof keeps them fresh and dry in all but the nastiest weather. Glass or plastic bins make it easy to see when you need to refill.

Think of a hopper as the melting pot of the backyard bird world. Big or small, birds love to eat at a hopper. Look for tree-loving cardinals, grosbeaks, chickadees, nuthatches, titmice, woodpeckers, buntings, jays, and finches. Ground-feeding sparrows and doves will join the crowd, too, if the feeding area is big enough. With all this bird action, no wonder a hopper is a popular first feeder.

Drawbacks of Hopper Feeders

Because of the storage space required for the seeds, feeding areas on hoppers are often small, holding just a few birds at a time. (A few commercial models have large feeding trays.) Expect lots of wasted seeds at hoppers, because it's easy for birds to knock off undesirable seeds from seed mixes and to sit and munch favored sunflower seeds. In addition, the seeds and the wood or plastic used to make many hoppers are easy targets for squirrels. A good option is an all-metal box hopper with a spring-loaded bar or counterweighted perch that shuts off access to the seeds when a squirrel lands on it to feed.

What to Serve

Any large or small single seeds, like black-oil or striped sunflower or safflower, do well in a hopper. (One way to deter starlings at a hopper is to offer only black-oil sunflower.) Tiny nyjer, however, should not be served, because it's easily knocked off. Mixes go well in a hopper, too, but less-preferred seeds may be pushed aside.

Eating Like a Bird

When someone says you "eat like a bird," should you (a) kiss her or (b) kick her? Either reaction, depending on your perspective, may be appropriate.

Kiss her. Birds, especially small birds, have a high metabolic rate. They burn calories superfast because they're constantly on the move. The burn for small birds is about 20 percent higher than for people. Ever see a fat bird?

Kick her (figuratively speaking). A red-hot calorie burn means that birds must eat enormous amounts of food to maintain their daily activity—quantities far above their body weights. Wild birds consume between 10 and 30 percent of their body weights daily. Ouch!

Colorful Coffee Can Feeder

Even if you're accustomed to stopping at a drive-thru latte vendor for your morning java, you'll want to change your routine long enough to use up the contents of a 1-pound can of good old-fashioned coffee, so that you can use the empty can to make this perky hopper-style feeder.

For a festive-looking feeder, choose colorful, patterned picnic dishes or retro melamine ware from a flea market.

MATERIALS

Church key can opener

Clean 1-pound coffee can with plastic lid

Nontoxic enamel spray paint

2 sturdy, colorful plastic plates or aluminum pie tins

Aquarium silicone sealant

Wooden drawer knob with screw

Metal screw-in hook

Drill

Twist drill bits of appropriate size to match the drawer knob screw and the metal hook

S hanger

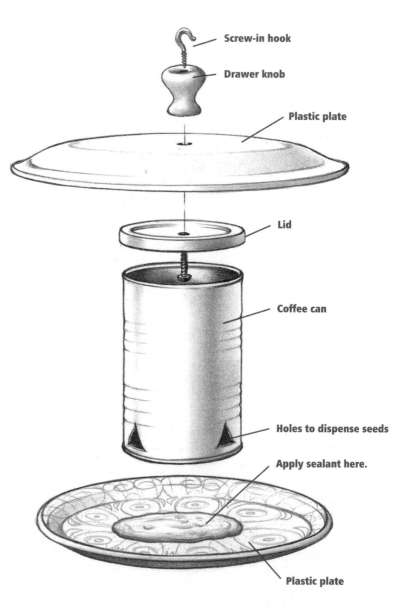

Screw-in hook

Drawer knob

Plastic plate

Lid

Coffee can

Holes to dispense seeds

Apply sealant here.

Plastic plate

Step 1. Use the can opener to punch three or four evenly spaced holes in the side of the coffee can, as close to the base as possible.

Step 2. Following the manufacturer's instructions, spray-paint the outside of the can a color that coordinates with the plates you've chosen.

Step 3. When the paint has dried, use the aquarium silicone sealant to attach the base of the can to the top of a plate. (When using the sealant, follow the package directions and work in a well-ventilated place.) If you're using a pie tin instead of a shallow plate, poke a few holes through the edge of the tin for drainage.

Step 4. Invert the plastic lid from the coffee can and attach it to the top of the second dish with the sealant. (When you put the lid back on the can, the curved bottom of the dish will shed rain like an umbrella.) Let the sealant dry for 24 hours.

Step 5. Drill a hole through the plastic lid and its attached dish, making it big enough to accept the drawer knob screw.

Step 6. Thread the screw up through the hole. Thread the knob onto the end of the screw and tighten it, sandwiching the dish and plastic lid snugly in place.

Step 7. Drill a smaller pilot hole through the top of the wooden knob just deep enough to allow you to screw the metal hook in place.

Step 8. After all the pieces are together, use the wooden knob to pull the lid off and fill the can with seeds of your choice. The holes in the can will be big enough for everything from millet to sunflower seeds and peanuts to trickle out of the can and into the dish below.

Step 9. Slip one end of the S hanger through the screw-in hook and hang the other end from a tree branch or shepherd's crook.

Tube Feeders

The tube feeder is a small bird's dream machine: a long cylinder of plastic, metal, or mesh loaded with seeds; short perches that keep big birds off; and feeding holes (portals) just big enough for one bird to eat in peace. Tubes keep seeds well protected and dry, and they're easy to fill and clean. The grab-and-run feeding style of most customers usually means fewer spilled and wasted seeds.

Drawbacks of Tube Feeders

Tubes feeders appeal only to certain types of birds, so there is less variety in the birds that use them. Also, fewer birds are able to eat at one time because there are only a handful of portals. Unless you refill the feeder often, the portals at the top become useless as the seed level drops.

Lightweight tube feeders can spill seeds easily as they wave in the wind, so look for one that has a metal cap and bottom for stability. Metal reinforcements around the portals are a good idea, too, because they thwart gnawing squirrels.

Who Likes Tubes?

Tubes are a favorite type of feeder for small tree-loving birds, including nuthatches, chickadees, titmice, finches, woodpeckers, pine siskins, and redpolls. Small ground feeders such as sparrows will occasionally use a tube feeder, too. If you attach a tray to the bottom of a tube feeder, jays and other larger birds also will feed.

Tube feeders are great for the single seeds, such as black-oil or hulled sunflower seeds, that their small customers favor. A tube is the only type of feeder suitable for nyjer. Save the seed mixes for trays or hoppers, because tube users will toss out undesirable seeds such as millet to get to the others.

Specialized Tubes

Here are a few specialized tube feeders you may want to include in your backyard.

Globe feeder. Take a tube feeder, transform it into a hollow ball, and throw away the perches: The result is good for birds that can cling. This round, clear plastic feeder usually has its feeding portals on the bottom half to further hamper big bird use. Chickadees, woodpeckers, nuthatches, titmice, and finches will be frequent visitors to a globe feeder filled with black oil or hulled sunflower seeds.

Wire mesh tube feeder. Large seeds and peanuts are perfect for a wire mesh feeder. The all-mesh design caters to tree-loving birds that can cling, such as chickadees, woodpeckers, and nuthatches. Larger birds such as cardinals, starlings, and grackles will use this type of feeder if you add a perch. Without the protection of plastic, this feeder is very vulnerable to weather and squirrels, but a baffle above it will help deflect problems.

Nyjer feeder. If the tube feeder wasn't invented for nyjer seeds, it should have been; they're the perfect couple. A nyjer feeder is a tube that has narrow slots instead of the conventional feeding portals. Many birds, such as pine siskins and chickadees, enjoy the taste of nyjer, but goldfinches and house finches tend to monopolize nyjer feeders. If you'd like more goldfinches and fewer house finches, choose a feeder with slots that are below the perches, because house

continued on page 58

A coconut is not your run-of-the-mill seed feeder. However, many birds enjoy the sweet, nutty taste of coconut meat as a treat. This feeder appeals to small birds that can cling to a shell without perches. It takes a slow and patient hand to make a feeder out of a hard coconut shell without crushing or cracking it, but your careful work will be rewarded. The birds will first peck their way through the hole in the coconut and then clean out the inside, leaving an empty shell that you can fill with seeds. Nuthatches and chickadees will be nibbling at this little feeder for a long time.

Note: Never feed shredded or flaked packaged coconut to birds, because it is dry and will swell in their stomachs after they consume it.

MATERIALS

1 coconut

Claw hammer

1 medium-size #6 common nail

1 thin, small #4 common nail

1-inch-long screw eye

Pliers (optional)

Flat-head screwdriver or knife (optional)

12 inches of twine or heavyweight picture-hanging wire

Step 1. Locate the three round depressions, called eyes, at one end of the coconut. Using the hammer and #6 nail, punch a hole in each eye and let the coconut milk drain out into a cup or bowl.

Step 2. At the other end of the coconut, hammer just the point of the #4 nail into the coconut. Twist the screw eye into the indentation. Use the pliers if it is hard to turn.

Step 3. With the hammer and #4 nail, carefully make a series of holes very close together in the side of the coconut. The holes should form a circle about 1 1/2 inches in diameter. (The shell is less likely to crack if you make a series of small holes.)

Step 4. Carefully remove the shell inside the circle of holes with the hammer claw (or use a flat-head screwdriver or knife blade) to expose the white coconut meat underneath.

Step 5. Thread the twine through the screw eye and hang this unusual feeder on a branch, shrub, or pole.

continued from page 56

finches have trouble feeding upside down. For a simple homemade nyjer tube feeder, see page 34. Small mesh bags, sometimes called thistle socks or nyjer socks, are also used to serve nyjer. The birds cling to the cloth and pull seeds out through the mesh. These bags are easy to fill but offer no protection from the weather.

CHOOSING A FEEDER

Whatever type of feeder you decide to buy or build, knowing which features separate the worthwhile from a waste of money will help you sift through the enormous variety of styles and materials available.

Don't Fall for Looks

The beauty of a feeder is often in the eye of the beholder. Feeders come in all shapes and sizes, made of cedar, oak, or pine; PVC (polyvinyl chloride) tubing or metal; thin or thick plastic; terra-cotta or ceramic. In many backyards, feeders made of recycled tuna cans, soda bottles, milk cartons, plastic trays, or scraps of lumber host birds with simplicity and creative flair.

Plain or fancy, store-bought or hand-made, a feeder's worth is measured by how many birds come to visit. The birds don't care how it looks as long as it's filled with tasty seeds. But before you shell out your money, cut up a plastic jug, or saw some wood, consider these features that every feeder should have.

Easy to fill, easy to clean. You need simple, easy access to the guts of a feeder so that you can quickly restock the food supply and reach all the nooks and cran-

nies with a cleaning brush. Feeder tops and roofs should open with little effort.

Keeps seeds dry. To prevent pooling of rainwater and the ensuing mold or disease, a feeder needs good drainage or decent cover. A tray or platform feeder, the most vulnerable type, should have a heavy screen bottom or a roof. The roof on a hopper feeder should extend at least 1 inch beyond the feeding tray. If seeds at the feeding holes of a tube feeder are getting wet, try placing it under a baffle or protective tree canopy. Use waterproof materials for a homemade feeder, and remember to poke holes in the bottom or use screening.

Shows off the seeds. Birds are attracted to feeders by the sight of food or other birds eating. Easy-to-see seed levels also let you tell when more seeds are needed.

Room to eat safely. Birds like a little wing room when eating and will keep a certain distance (varies by species) away from one another at a feeder. A good-size feeding area will host more birds. Make sure there are no sharp points or edges on the feeder, and avoid decorative touches that might hinder birds from getting to the seeds.

No toxins or hazards. Do not reuse containers with possible residues that could be poisonous to birds, such as detergent, bleach, or medicine. To protect life and feet, cover anything sharp with masking tape or duct tape. This includes the ends of wires and the jagged or sharp edges of cut plastic or metal.

Signs of Quality

Feeders can last for years or a weekend. You may choose to go the budget route when making a feeder yourself, but it's worthwhile to invest in a quality feeder when you're buying a commercially made product. You should expect to pay more for a well-made feeder. You also should expect it to last for years and years. Look for these quality features when buying a feeder.

- Feeding holes reinforced with metal
- Seed bins protected by glass, metal, or heavy-duty plastic
- Solid wood rather than plywood or flimsy plastic
- Metal perches instead of wood or plastic (it's a myth that birds' feet will freeze to a metal perch in winter)
- Nails or screws at joints, not staples
- Strong attachment for hanging

SEEDS AU NATUREL

While you're thinking about feeders, don't forget the other powerful source of seeds that your yard can supply: flowering plants and grasses and grains.

Grasses and Grains

If you've ever tried to start a lawn, you know how much birds love to eat grass seed. Bird favorites include ryegrass, weedy crabgrass, millet, milo, grains such as wheat, and ornamental or native perennial grasses such as switch grass.

You can let grasses grow tall in patches along the edges of your property or leave the sprouts beneath a feeder to see what develops. Sparrows, juncos, buntings, quail, and other ground-feeding birds will scavenge for seeds wherever they lie.

It's also easy to incorporate grasses into a full-sun area of your garden by loosening the soil and sowing groups of seeds thickly about 6 inches deep.

Grasses grow fast, so by mid- to late summer, birds will start pulling down seedheads, and they will continue on into the fall and winter. If you don't like the idea of raising annual grasses, consider planting a row of native perennial grasses as part of a perennial garden or along a boundary line of your yard. You can let the birds feast directly on the plants, or harvest the grasses and include them in decorative feeders like "An Incredible, Edible Garden" on the next page.

Flowering Plants

Which can hold the greater number of seeds: A single zinnia flower or a 2-quart hopper feeder filled with sunflower seeds? Believe it or not, the zinnia flower can. Although a single zinnia won't feed an army of birds for long, a garden full of flowers, ornamental grasses, and even weeds produces enough seeds to last through the fall and winter, a bird's toughest seasons. Feeders brimming with seeds are huge attractions to lure birds into your backyard, but they can't match the powerful pull of gardens holding a gazillion tasty, juicy seeds. When natural seeds are ready for plucking, a garden is the first stop on a bird's daily rounds for food.

A garden in full, glorious bloom also attracts birds looking to pick off yummy spiders, aphids, caterpillars, and other insects creeping along stems, leaves, and petals. Feeder-shy insect lovers such as thrushes, warblers, and catbirds will join the regular feeder crowd of sparrows, chickadees, cardinals, juncos, towhees, and finches in your garden for a much sought-after bug feast.

continued on page 61

An Incredible, Edible Garland

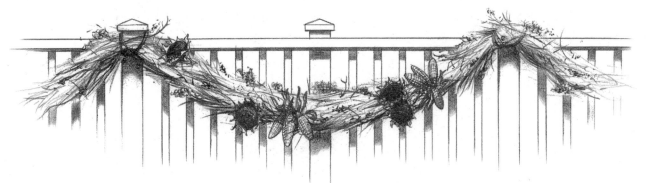

Decorate your fence,

trellis, porch, or deck for fall with an all-natural garland loaded with seeds your bird visitors will feast on for months. Any kind of grass or grain with seeds will work, so the hardest part of making this swag is deciding what to use for the base. You can harvest plants from your garden or search for raw materials from quality craft supply stores or Internet suppliers.

MATERIALS

Any grasses or grains with seeds still in the heads

Florist's wire

Thin rope, such as a clothesline, cut to the desired length

Wire cutters

Sunflower heads, 4 to 8 inches in diameter

Miniature Indian corn

Seasonal Specialties

Fall Garland Ingredients

Ann Hoffert, owner of Pipestem Creek near Carrington, North Dakota, creates and sells handmade edible feeders from the crops in her fields. For a great fall garland, she suggests using white popping sorghum and the popular 'Purple Majesty' ornamental millet. White popping sorghum has graceful, fluffy, cream-colored seedheads. 'Purple Majesty' millet holds its bountiful seed supply in thick, cattail-size, deep purple seedheads. The contrasting textures and colors of these grasses will give this garland real eye appeal. Add some small sunflower heads and ears of miniature Indian corn to provide an early Thanksgiving for the birds.

Other grasses that work well in a garland for birds include little bluestem (*Schizachyrium scoparium*), big bluestem (*Andropogon gerardii*), Indian grass (*Sorghastrum nutans*), wheat, and barley.

Step 1. Gather a handful of grasses or grains, keeping the seedheads in a bouquet. Clip off the stems evenly at about 12 to 14 inches.

Step 2. Use florist's wire to wrap the stems together, forming a dense bunch. Securely attach the bunch to the end of the rope with another piece of wire so that the seedheads align with the end of the rope.

Step 3. Make several more bunches in the same way.

Step 4. Lay the seedheads of the second bunch over the stems of the first so that both heads fit snugly together. Wrap the stems of this bunch with wire and then attach it to the rope with more wire.

Step 5. Continue attaching bunches along the entire length of the rope.

Step 6. Randomly insert sunflower heads and ears of miniature Indian corn among the bunches of grasses along the garland, securing them with wire.

Step 7. Hang the garland on a fence or deck railing, or wrap it around a feeder post, using long nails as spikes to drape the garland around. You can also simply loop the garland around itself at the ends of the railing or post, or on a deck railing, you can use twine to support the garland. Look for cardinals, finches, juncos, doves, and others to start feasting.

continued from page 59

Birds will continue to bustle about your garden through their busy fall and winter seasons if big seed-producing plants are included in your beds. Just as your garden starts to look scruffy and its beauty is but a memory, sparrows, buntings, cardinals, titmice, chickadees, grosbeaks, towhees, juncos, and finches will bring it back to life, scouring seedheads and dancing beneath the stems for the hidden bounty of nutrition-packed seeds.

We'll cover how to enhance your garden as a bird food supply in chapter 5, but for now let's look at how you can supply some of the more common kinds of seeds, such as sunflower seeds, as well as some unusual seeds, right from your garden.

Some Special Choices

You seldom see safflower seeds, rapeseeds, or flax seeds outside of high-priced mixes. These special seeds actually come from easy-to-grow garden plants that display lovely blue, yellow, or orange flowers before the seeds are ready for the birds. Beautify a spot in the garden with these plants and save the money you would have spent on seeds. Cardinals, goldfinches, chickadees, fox sparrows, and other small birds will happily pick their own treat seeds in your garden for months.

Mustard (*Brassica napus*). Also known as rapeseed or canola, mustard bears small, airy, sunshine yellow flowers. Scatter the seeds freely in informal flowerbeds; this annual grows vigorously in almost any soil with little care. The flowers ripen into long pods full of tiny,

continued on page 64

Sized-to-Fit Sunflower Plantation

A single $2 packet

of seeds is all you need to create a tall sunflower hedge for summer-long privacy. When the patio season is over, you can cut the ripened seedheads for winter bird food. Growing tall sunflowers is great for lazy gardeners, because the plants stay upright better if you plant the seeds in unprepared soil rather than a loosened bed. At maturity, a tall sunflower in loose soil is apt to keel over as its head grows heavy with the ripening seeds. The plant maintains a better grip in uncultivated soil.

For this sunflower plantation, sow single seeds 6 inches apart in triple, staggered rows. About 100 plants (or a triple row 15 feet long) can yield 25 to 100 pounds of sunflower seed. Growing the plants close together also provides more support by breaking the force of any windy gusts that zip through your yard. Here's how to get things growing.

Step 1. Pick a spot in full sun. Sunflowers live up to their name, thriving in heat, and they can take dry soil, too, once they're up and growing. Use stakes and string to mark rows for precise planting (three rows is best).

Step 2. At the end of the first row, dig a hole about 2 inches deep with a trowel. Crumble a bit of the removed soil into the hole and drop in a single sunflower seed. Crumble the rest of the removed soil over it.

Step 3. Continue planting down the rows, spacing the seeds about 6 inches apart in all directions.

Step 7. Stand back! Sunflowers grow fast.

Step 8. When petals wither and heads begin to nod, the seeds are beginning to ripen. Keep a close eye on the seedheads so you can beat the birds to the harvest. Or drape bird netting over the heads as ripening time approaches.

Step 9. Use loppers or a sharp, sturdy knife (careful!) to slice through the stalks. Dry the heads on screens in a cool, dry place.

Step 10. When the seeds and seedheads are completely dry, store them in a tightly covered metal trash can with crumpled newspaper at the bottom to absorb any lingering moisture.

Getting Mammoth Results

Sunflowers come in all colors, heights, and styles, from fluffy knee-high 'Teddy Bear' and delicate branching 'Italian White'—both at home in any ornamental garden—to stalwart 'Russian Mammoth', whose single golden head grows as high as 15 feet against the summer sky. For the biggest return in seeds for space, stick to tall, single-stemmed varieties like this one. Because these types grow up, not out, you can cram a lot of plants into a small space.

If you plant 'Russian Mammoth' in your plantation, you'll discover that each seedhead will supply from ¼ to 1 pound of seeds! You can remove ripe seeds by rubbing the face with your thumbs, but why bother—it's more fun to offer the seedhead whole and watch songbirds extract their own tidbits. (See "Sunflower Head Hook-up" on page 33.)

Growing your own sunflower plantation, whether it's small or large, will supply plenty of free seeds, but it will also reward you with a longer look at the birds visiting this tempting "feeder." No more snatch-and-run dining: You'll get to see chickadees, titmice, jays, finches, and other seedeaters cleverly working the plump seeds free from this birdseed banquet.

Step 4. When you finish planting, remove the stakes and string and water with a gentle spray.

Step 5. Keep the soil moist until the seedlings are established. Water daily, if necessary. The seeds typically sprout within 5 days.

Step 6. Mulch around seedlings to eliminate weeding. Grass clippings make an ideal mulch.

continued from page 61

round, oil-rich seeds that delight many small birds, especially goldfinches, purple finches, sparrows, and towhees.

Safflower (*Carthamus tinctorius*). With shaggy blossoms in vivid golden orange, this annual grows easily from seeds sown directly in sunny soil. The flowers yield plump white seeds often enjoyed by cardinals.

Annual flax (*Linum usitatissimum*). Wire-thin stems with small needlelike leaves hold clusters of silky, sky blue flowers. The flowers put on a show by unfolding in the morning and closing in the afternoon. Plant this annual in a sunny spot by thickly scattering the seeds and pressing them into prepared soil. As the flowers fade, finches, sparrows, and buntings will enjoy eating the oil-rich, shiny brown seeds.

Bringing In the Seeds

If you stay a step or two ahead of the birds, you can grab some of the flowers and weeds growing in your garden and harvest their seeds for later use at the feeder.

Look for seedheads with plump green seeds that are just starting to turn yellow. The seeds aren't completely ripe, which beats the birds to the punch. Clip off the seedheads and spread them in a shallow cardboard box, such as the cut-down type used for canned foods. Put the box in a dry place out of sight of birds and rodents. If you want to use the seedheads in wreaths or other decorations, keep them on long stems.

Check the seedheads daily for ripeness. The seeds will change to a golden or brown color when they are fully ripe and dry. Transfer the ripe seedheads to a paper bag, close tightly, and shake briskly to release the seeds.

Pour the seeds into a container with a tight-fitting lid and label the container. You won't be able to fill your big storage containers, but you should be able to garner a few jars and tins of tasty seeds. Mix some of your stash with regular store-bought feeder fare when snow covers natural supplies or hectic spring activities mean that birds need a boost. Some easy flowers and weeds to try are cosmos, purple coneflowers, zinnias, pigweed, and lamb's-quarters.

CHAPTER 3

Bird Treats

Backyard birds respond just like the family dog (or the family!) when you offer them tasty foods that are a cut above the ordinary. Try offering birds some of the special treats included in this chapter, and you'll see just how much your winged visitors enjoy a choice of foods. Birds that never before appeared at your feeders may stop by—including bluebirds looking for peanut butter concoctions or bold brown thrashers picking over homemade suet cakes (see the recipe on page 83). When you plant fruit-bearing shrubs and trees, you'll attract other species, too, such as waxwings and orioles.

TREATS FOR EVERY TASTE

In chapter 2, you learned that birds favor some foods over others. Each species that visits your backyard seeks a different selection of natural foods in the wild. Swallows eat mainly insects, for example; field sparrows eat mainly seeds. The suet that downy woodpeckers find so tempting is no attraction at all for cardinals, but pumpkin seeds in the feeder tray will bring cardinals flocking.

When you make bird treats yourself, you can tailor your offerings to those birds you most want to attract. You'll discover the treats that appeal to a wide range of birds, as well as those out-of-the-ordinary foods that attract a limited but highly desirable audience, such as bluebirds or purple martins. You'll find out, too, what you can feed your birds when your seed supply is unexpectedly low—a trick that can be a literal lifesaver in bad weather, when natural foods are scarce.

Fun for Kids, Too

Making bird treats is a great pastime to try with your children or grandchildren, because the projects are simple and undemanding—and the results happen fast. Put out a suet treat, for instance, and birds will probably arrive within minutes. Whipping up bird treats is easy for kids because precise measurements aren't nearly as important here as they are when preparing foods for people, and no special skills are needed. (You will want to supervise children when a project involves using the stove.) Even if your young cooks' recipe doesn't turn out quite as expected, the birds are still likely to eat it. After all, birds don't care how lumpy or odd-looking a finished project is!

Old and New Favorites

Supplying your regulars with special foods they really enjoy is a simple project. Thanks to observations by many bird watchers, and also to scientific research, the favorite foods of many feeder birds are well-known. And with the advent of Web sites about bird feeding, it's become easy to share and compare notes about treats that really please birds. (For specific listings, see "Who Eats What?" on page 290.)

Tempting the Rare Birds

Rare birds, in this case, means birds that you usually don't see at feeders stocked with seeds and suet. Many of these birds aren't rare at all; it's just that we rarely see them. For instance, tanagers spend most of their time in the treetops. So do flycatchers, even though they may perch on a branch overhead to conduct their aerial chases after flying insects. Brown creepers often visit backyards, but chances are you won't notice these unobtrusive birds hitching about tree trunks in search of insect snacks.

Patience, Please

Tempting rare birds to visit a feeder takes more patience and a different menu than the typical handout of a bagged seed mix. First of all, these birds tend to be insect or fruit eaters, not seedeaters. But it's not enough to put out a plate filled to the brim with cherries or blueberries. Unlike the seed-eating birds that flock to feeders, these birds are accustomed to foraging for themselves in brush or treetops. Their natural foods are abundant, so there's no need for them to seek out the offerings at some nonnatural structure in your yard.

Nonfeeder birds also tend to lead more private lives than birds that are used to eating near us. Unlike chickadees and other regulars, these species haven't learned to associate humans with a handout.

Also, nearly all of these rare birds are migratory. Following long-established instinctual patterns, most of these migrants depart from their nesting grounds in the fall, when their natural food sources are growing scarce. In the winter, the foods they depend on won't be available. But by the time the migrants return in midspring, the world will be alive again with insects and burgeoning fruit.

The extra effort to attract rare birds is worthwhile, though, because once the birds learn that your offerings are a reliable food source, they are likely to make the shift from rare feeder birds to regulars.

Three Birds That Made the Switch

Beautiful rose-breasted grosbeaks and flashy indigo buntings used to be rare sightings at feeders, but these days both birds often seek out feeding stations as they travel on their spring migration.

The northern oriole, a gorgeous orange-and-black creature, also has been changing its ways. Nowadays, many backyard bird lovers have discovered that a sweet treat of grape jelly will tempt these brilliant songbirds to a feeder—and the orioles are learning to look for it. It's real cause for celebration when you host an oriole or other rare bird at a feeder in your yard, whether it's for the entire summer or only a few days.

Matching Beaks and Treats

Soft foods are the key to attracting unusual birds that don't rely on seeds and nuts. Treats based on suet, fruit, or bakery items are your best bets. Crumble the treats into smaller pieces. Birds are more likely to eat small bits of suet or doughnut crumbs, for instance, than large chunks. Also, when you're introducing a new food or attempting to lure a new species, offer the food first in an open-tray feeder so that it's easily visible and accessible.

One helpful strategy is to learn how the shape of a bird's beak (also called a bill) relates to its feeding habits. Once you understand that relationship, you'll be better able to decide what types of treats to offer your favorite species of birds.

Chisel Beak

All types of woodpeckers, from the cute little downy and the raucous flicker to the striking black pileated, have large, stout beaks that are shaped like a chisel. Woodpeckers use their chisel beaks to peck at wood, with the goal of ferreting out insects under the bark or within the decaying heart of a tree. The power of that beak also can crack nuts and acorns to free up the tender nutmeat inside, or loosen dried corn kernels from a cob.

Treats for chisel beaks. Most of us aren't about to fill the feeder tray with those yummy grubs, no matter how many *Survivor* episodes we've watched, but we can put out plenty of treats that will appeal to woodpeckers. Different kinds of nuts, dried field corn (on the cob), peanut butter treats, and suet (which mimics the soft morsel of a grub) are all high on the favorites list of these hammer-beaked birds.

Large Conical Beak

The bright red feathers of a cardinal are so eye-catching that you may have never taken a close look at the bird's beak: It's short and wide, roughly conical in shape. That beak is built for cracking big, hard-shelled seeds. Rose-breasted, evening, and black-headed grosbeaks also have this type of beak. These birds all naturally seek out some of the biggest or toughest seeds around. In the wild, they nibble out the goodies hidden in the hard husks of tree seeds such as ash and catalpa.

Treats for large conical beaks. Sunflower seeds are the feeder staple for grosbeaks and cardinals. For a treat, try other big seeds, such as pumpkin seeds, watermelon seeds, dried corn kernels, dried peas, and the incredibly hard-shelled safflower seeds.

Large All-Purpose Beak

The sturdy, medium-long mouthpiece of a crow, magpie, or jay is made for eating practically anything. Their beaks can crack, whack, rip, stab, or nibble—whatever technique and eating utensil a meal requires. The natural habit of birds with a large all-purpose beak is to put some food aside for that proverbial rainy day. These birds load their beaks with as many seeds as they can cram in, then use those same sturdy tools to push seeds into soil or mulch. That habit of storing food may be why birds with this kind of beak tend to prefer hard, dry foods at the feeder. Sticky, soft, or juicy foods such as peanut butter, bread, fruit, or suet aren't as appealing to large-beaked birds, and they may avoid this kind of treat.

Treats for large all-purpose beaks. Shelled nuts are the favorite.

Small Conical Beak

Take a close look at any sparrow, and you'll see that its beak is a miniature version of the large, strong bill of the cardinal. This type of beak is tailored to small seeds. Birds that have a small conical beak include native sparrows, such as white-throated and song sparrows; finches, such as the house finch and American goldfinch; juncos; buntings; and the imported house sparrow.

Birds with small conical beaks are big consumers of weed seeds and grass seeds. These birds often feed on the ground, where such seeds drop, but they may also cling to the plants to get at the seeds.

Treats for small conical beaks. Serve out-of-the-ordinary small seeds such as flax seed, nyjer seed, mustard seed (also called canola or rapeseed), and canary seed, as well as snipped seedheads of marigolds, zinnias, and cosmos from your garden.

Short Thin Beak

Chickadees, wood warblers, bushtits, and a few other birds sport diminutive bills that look as if they're made for eating tiny morsels of food. In this case, looks can be deceiving. All of these small-beaked birds snap up an abundance of insects, but some of them also eat berries, and chickadees are well-known connoisseurs of sunflower seeds and nuts. Offer these birds a mix of treats, including soft foods, suet, and peanut butter.

Treats for short thin beaks. Soft foods in bite-size morsels are best. Chopped suet, suet blocks, and suet mixes without seeds will suit all species. Chopped dried fruit and chopped nuts are also fine.

Long Thin Beak

A long thin beak is a sign that a bird is an insect or fruit eater. Flycatchers and orioles eat insects almost exclusively, and you probably won't be able to lure them to a treat feeder. The exception is that orioles will visit nectar feeders. Thrashers, tanagers, thrushes, mockingbirds, and catbirds also have beaks on the thin side, but they are adapting to eating at backyard feeders (as are some orioles). Their beaks aren't built for cracking seeds or eating hard foods, so provide them with soft treats.

Treats for long thin beaks. Suet and suet treats, as long as they're served in a feeder that allows these perching, non-acrobatic birds easy access, are a sure bet. Try bread, doughnuts, and other soft treats, too.

Build on the Basic Four

The foods that birds devour first at feeding stations fall into four general categories: seeds, nuts, fats, and fruit. You can invent your own feeder treats by serving any items in your cupboard that fall in any of these categories. If you're offering a new food, put out a scant handful at a time, until you can gauge how readily it's accepted. If the new item disappears in a flash, you know it qualifies for treat status. If it's still sitting in the feeder days later, scoop it out and cross it off your list.

Long thin

Large all-purpose

Chisel

Small conical

Short thin

Large conical

All species within a bird family share the same type of beak. The beaks may vary a bit in size or heft, but the basic shape is similar, and so are the uses to which that eating apparatus is put.

Seeds

Check your grocery store's shelves, and you'll find flax seeds, dried peas, pumpkin seeds, and other unprocessed seeds. Breakfast cereals, bread, and other products based on grains are other possibilities in the seed category, although birds won't accept them as readily as seeds and grains in the raw.

Nuts

Buy nuts in pieces and in bulk to save on the cost of these cherished but expensive bird treats. Supermarkets and health food stores usually have a selection of nuts in bulk, which may include peanuts, walnuts, pecans, filberts, and almonds, all highly appealing to birds. Those sold as pieces are perfect for the feeder, since small chickadees can manage them as well as large jays, and they're usually less expensive per pound than perfect whole nuts. You may want to put whole nuts in a feeder that allows only limited access— one or a few birds at a time—to slow down the consumption. Nut feeders are cylinders constructed of wire mesh with openings large enough to allow birds to tug out a single nut at a time. You can find them in bird supply stores or

 **BIRD TREATS** | ## Seed Mosaic for a Snowy Day

Fresh snow? Kids home from school? This outdoor project will keep you all busy making edible art for the birds. When you're finished, head inside, serve up some steaming hot chocolate, and watch the cardinals, chickadees, sparrows, juncos, and many other art lovers come to appreciate your masterpiece.

If you're working with children younger than 4 years old, make a simpler shape such as a circle, and pour the seeds into the stamped-down shape in alternating stripes.

MATERIALS
Snow-covered area, 4 × 6 feet or larger
Sturdy stick
Scoop
Sunflower seed
Cracked corn
Millet or mixed birdseed
Flax seed
Nyjer seed
Chopped nuts

Step 1. Choose an open area of snow that will be visible from a bird-viewing window of the house. Use the stick to draw a very large five-pointed star in the snow. If you waver while drawing one of the lines, just pat over it and redraw.

Step 2. Stamp down the snow with your feet in each triangular "arm" of the star and in the center section. When you're done, the level of the snow inside the star should be lower than that in the surrounding area.

Step 3. Fill a scoop with sunflower seeds and pour the seeds in the center section of the star.

through mail-order or online suppliers.

Since we covered many of the details about seeds and nuts in chapter 2, most of the projects in this chapter focus on suet-based and fruit treats, but the imaginative treat described below combines seeds and nuts to attract a variety of feathered friends.

Fats

Suet is immensely popular with birds in all seasons. Suet works like magic to draw in birds that might pass on your seed-filled feeders, including woodpeckers, nuthatches, chickadees, and blue-birds. Other solid fats, including peanut butter, lard, and hardened meat drippings, have the same appeal.

Fruit

Many fruit-eating birds don't usually visit feeders. Instead, consider adding a fruit tree, bush, or vine to your yard to attract vireos, tanagers, and other lovely birds that rarely investigate feeding stations. At a feeder, birds that do eat fruit seem to be particular about how the fruit is presented. Dried fruit, chopped into bite-size pieces, works well when added to treat recipes.

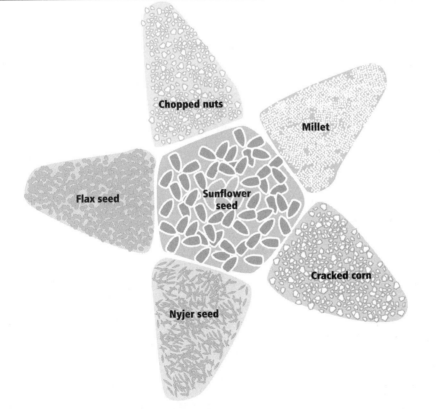

Step 4. Fill a scoop with cracked corn and pour it in one of the arms of the star.

Step 5. Repeat with the other seeds and the nuts, one type per arm.

Step 6. Put away the scoop and foods and head inside to admire your artwork (from an upstairs window, if possible, to get a better perspective on the shape). Settle down to watch the star fill up with appreciative visitors.

SUET TREATS

Technically, suet is the layer of fat around the kidneys of an animal, but in bird-feeding parlance, suet has a much broader definition. Suet may be the fat trimmings from a steak as well as a block of pure, rendered, actual suet. All of the projects in this chapter will work equally well whether you use pure suet or fat trimmings from meat.

Seasonal Suet

Many backyard bird lovers limit using suet to the winter months, when an extra helping of fat is vital to help birds survive cold winter nights. But keeping your suet feeder stocked year-round has benefits that make it well worth the small amount of maintenance required.

Spring Suet Feeding

Spring is migration time, and that means millions of birds are winging their way across every corner of the country as they head north. Those birds are working hard, and they're hungry. If you keep a suet feeder stocked, you may spot unusual visitors such as yellow-rumped warblers, brown creepers, hepatic tanagers, and other bird travelers.

Another benefit of spring suet feeding is that it helps birds cope with unpredictable seasonal weather. Should a cold snap hit overnight, your suet feeder may be popular with guests such as tree swallows and bluebirds, which normally feed on insects during the spring.

Summer Suet Feeding

Oh, those fuzzy-headed baby birds! There's no word but adorable to describe a lineup of chickadee fledglings settled near your feeder, waiting for Mom or Dad to bring them a bite.

Parent birds often augment their youngsters' insect diet with soft foods from feeding stations, and suet is highly popular. Bird watchers report seeing parents use a beakful of suet as a bribe to encourage shaky youngsters to attempt a short flight or to move farther out on a branch.

In hot weather, suet can get soft and messy, which can cause greasy heads and feather loss in birds that try to feed on it. Commercially made blocks are less apt to melt in summer heat, but it's always a good idea to move your suet setup to a shady spot once the temperature starts to climb. If it is very hot and your suet is melting, take it down until cooler temperatures prevail.

Black mildewlike mold also can develop on summer suet, and the outside surface of the chunk may get hard and look extremely unappetizing. Refill the feeder with fresh fat if you like, but birds don't seem to mind how the suet looks as long as there is fresh white stuff beneath the surface. They'll tear or peck away at it until they uncover a palatable area to feed on.

Fall Suet Feeding

In the fall, birds migrate in the opposite direction from their spring journey. There's a reversal foodwise, too. Instead of a scarcity of natural foods, there's often a rich supply as Indian summer hangs over the land. Insects still buzz, flowers still bloom, and fruit and berries still abound. Even better for birds, weed seeds are ripening along roadsides and streams and in some gardens, supplying plenty of meals for migrating seedeaters. With all that good stuff out there for the taking, you might think that fall migrants would turn up their noses at a block of suet. Not so! Occasional birds may still show up to eat your suet offerings.

Fall also is the season when birds are claiming winter feeding territories. As young birds fan out looking for likely spots, they're bound to zero in on your suet feeder. Visits by woodpeckers and other suet eaters dramatically increase— a great signal to get your bird-feeding supplies in shape for the coming season.

Winter Suet Feeding

Suet feeders can't usually accommodate more than one or two customers at a time, so add a few more suet feeders to make sure all your friends are well-fed during the winter. The pure fat of suet is super high in calories, just what birds need to create body heat and stay warm in cold weather.

Even in mild-winter areas, a suet feeder is a popular hangout for woodpeckers and other birds. Although they don't require as many calories to maintain body warmth, they still enjoy the treat.

Should the temperature really sink, especially in areas that are usually somewhat milder, expect the suet feeder to be bustling all day. Make it easier on the birds by finely chopping another chunk of fat to put in a tray feeder or to scatter on the ground. All winter feeder birds will gladly eat suet, especially in brutal cold. Juncos, sparrows, finches, and other birds that have a hard time clinging to a wire cage suet feeder or a sandwich-style feeder will flock to easy-to-reach suet offerings.

Suet Blocks

A suet feeder is the easiest type of feeder to maintain. A block of suet lasts for a long time, creates no debris, and is a real bargain compared to birdseed.

A commercially produced block of suet is hard to beat. For a dollar or two, you'll have a supply that lasts for a month or more. Each packaged block slides neatly into a wire cage sold as a suet feeder. Another bird-feeding bargain,

 *Regional Viewpoint*

Serving Suet When It's Super Cold

If you live in North Dakota, Maine, or International Falls, Minnesota—which holds the dubious self-appointed title "Icebox of the Nation"—you know that frigid cold is a fact of life in the winter. At feeders in the northern tier of the country and in high mountain regions, homemade suet treats can freeze so solid that birds have trouble pecking out a bite to eat. Or they may expend so much energy working at the food that they wipe out any caloric gain the nourishing treat provides.

Solve this dilemma by serving bite-size mouthfuls instead of solid slabs. Chop or crumble your suet and peanut butter offerings into pieces. Pour the pieces into the feeder or sprinkle them on the ground. If you make more than you can use at one time, distribute the extra pieces on a cookie sheet, making sure they're not touching, and stick the cookie sheet in the freezer. When the pieces are frozen, transfer them to resealable plastic bags and store them in the freezer. When it's time to restock the feeder, use your hands to break apart any pieces that have become stuck together in the bags.

a basic wire cage suet feeder costs just a few dollars.

There is no easy way to avoid touching the suet when you fill the feeder, and your fingers will become quite greasy. Wash your hands as soon as you finish filling the feeder to avoid getting your clothes and other surfaces greasy.

Fat Trimmings

Second in ease to buying commercially prepared blocks of suet is to ask the clerk or butcher at the meat counter of your supermarket for fat trimmings. A few years ago, stores often gave away such scraps for free. Nowadays they usually charge a small price per pound, but even so, trimmings cost less than suet blocks.

Meat often arrives already cut at some markets, but most places still do some trimming to remove excess fat. If the clerk says they have no fat scraps, ask whether there is a good day and time to get some trimmings.

Starlings and Suet

Suet is one of the favorite foods of starlings, and that can be a problem. Not only will starlings devour your suet in a hurry, but they'll also decorate the surroundings (and the feeder) with their white droppings, and their presence will prevent chickadees and other birds from getting a bite. If starlings are a problem in your yard, try special types of suet feeders that deter starlings, or use some decoy tactics.

Sandwich-style feeder. The sandwich-type feeder holds suet between two boards. Starlings aren't agile enough to cling to the vertical sides, but chickadees and woodpeckers are. Starlings will, however, attempt to reach the fat if they can find a foothold on top of the boards. If you don't mind a few determined starlings and still want to enjoy plenty of visits from woodpeckers, chickadees, titmice, wrens, and other desirable suet eaters, try a sandwich-style feeder.

Horizontal feeder. This type of feeder holds suet horizontally, beneath an overhanging roof, with a wire grid placed underneath the suet block. Starlings can't get at the suet, but unfortunately the feeder also is not very popular with other suet-eating birds. First of all, they can't see that alluring white treat, so they don't know that it's there. What's worse, they seem to struggle to find a place to cling. If you want no starling traffic at all at your feeder, this type of feeder may be right for you, even though it will result in fewer visits from other suet eaters as well.

Cage-type feeder. Another option is to serve suet in a feeder that has an outer cage that bars large birds. This type of feeder will exclude bigger woodpeckers as well as starlings, but titmice, nuthatches, chickadees, bushtits, and other small birds will have a safe supply of suet.

Decoy feeder. If you set up a decoy feeder to appeal mainly to starlings, they will leave your suet feeders alone. Fill a tray with old bread products, apple cores, meaty soup bones, softened dog food, and other such "goodies," and the starlings will flock to that feast, allowing the more desirable birds to visit your suet feeder in peace. Alternatively, keep an extra wire cage suet feeder stocked and ready to go in the freezer. Should the black horde of starlings descend on the usual feeders, hang your spare elsewhere for the other suet eaters to enjoy at their leisure.

When you bring

home a quantity of fat trimmings, you'll need to cut them to size and repackage them, because if you put the entire plastic-wrapped package in the freezer, it will freeze into a solid, unmanageable lump. Here's how to work with trimmings with a minimum of mess.

MATERIALS

Disposable plastic tablecloth

Old board (to use as a cutting surface)

Large, sharp, sturdy knife

Disposable rubber gloves

Suet feeders or plastic mesh bags

Fat trimmings

Cookie sheet (optional)

Resealable plastic bags (optional)

Step 1. Set up a spot outdoors to work with the trimmings, such as your patio table. Cover the table with the tablecloth.

Step 2. Take the old board, knife, rubber gloves, suet feeders, and fat trimmings out to your workstation. If you have a large amount of trimmings, also bring along a cookie sheet.

Step 3. Sometimes fat trimmings will slide neatly into a suet feeder as is. If, however, you received large chunks from the grocer, you'll have to cut them down to size. Use the knife to slice through the fat. There's no need to remove any bits of meat or other tissue attached to the fat; birds will eat what's edible, and the rest will dry out for easy removal later.

Step 4. Fill your suet feeders, stuffing the trimmings in tightly. You can use commercial feeders or plastic mesh bags that onions and sometimes potatoes come in. If you use a bag that has a lace at the top, loosen the lace, drop in some pieces of fat, and tie the bag closed. Or just tie the top end of the bag around the tree branch.

Step 5. If you have fat left over after filling your feeders, freeze it for later use. Spread the pieces on the cookie sheet, making sure they're not touching, and pop the sheet into the freezer. The pieces should freeze solid overnight. Slip the frozen pieces into resealable plastic bags and store them in the freezer.

Step 6. For easy cleanup, take off the rubber gloves and put them on the tablecloth along with the wrappings from the fat trimmings. Bundle up the tablecloth and throw it immediately in the garbage. Wash the knife well in warm soapy water.

Making a suet feeder

from a recently fallen tree branch or a hunk of trunk from the woodpile is easy. A log feeder lasts for years and brings that natural look to your yard with little effort or expense. This bird favorite is a great project to share with your children or grandchildren. Each log feeder is unique because you have many choices: type of wood, length and thickness of the log, and whether to add perches.

MATERIALS

7- to 18-inch-long log or branch, 3 to 10 inches in diameter, from a softwood tree such as pine, white birch, or ash

Drill

1½-inch spade bit

¼-inch twist drill bit (optional)

Wood glue (optional)

¼-inch-diameter dowel, cut into 3- to 4-inch lengths (optional)

1 large eyebolt or lag screw

10 to 15 inches of sturdy wire or rope

Suet or peanut butter mix (see recipes on page 80)

Tea light tin (optional)

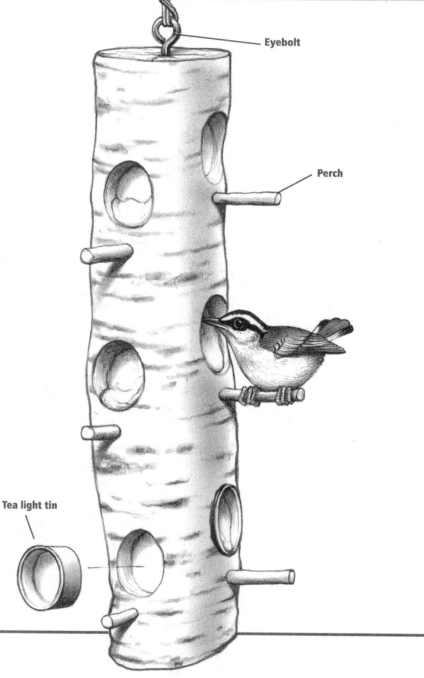

Eyebolt

Perch

Tea light tin

Step 1. In your yard or along a wooded path, look for a fairly straight, rot-free softwood log. Logs that are 3 to 10 inches in diameter will be sturdy enough to support feeding birds.

Step 2. If the log is longer than 18 inches, cut it to length. (A longer feeder will sway too much in the wind.)

Step 3. For logs that are 7 to 12 inches long, use the drill and 1 1/2-inch spade bit to drill three holes, each about 1 inch deep, in one side of the log. Make one hole near the top, one in the middle, and one near the bottom of the log. They don't have to be in a straight line. For longer logs, you may want to drill four holes.

Step 4. Give the log a quarter turn and drill three more holes in similar fashion.

Step 5. Repeat step 4 two more times.

Step 6. If you want to add perches, use the drill and 1/4-inch twist drill bit to make a hole about 1 inch deep and 1/4 to 1 inch below each of the large holes.

Step 7. Glue the dowel pieces in the holes, leaving 2 to 3 inches of dowel exposed.

Step 8. Drill a pilot hole in the center of one end of the log and screw in the eyebolt. Loop the wire through the eye for hanging.

Step 9. Fill the holes with your favorite suet mix or peanut butter recipe, and you're good to go.

Perch Pros and Cons

If you leave your feeder perch-free, you'll make it the exclusive domain of woodpeckers and nuthatches. The toes on these birds, unlike those on most birds, are specially aligned—two toes pointed forward and two toes pointed back—so they can cling to tree bark as they hunt for insects (or suet). These birds don't need perches. You may even spot an elusive brown creeper, lured to the log by the peanut butter. Going perchless also helps keep starlings away.

Adding a few perches, however, will draw chickadees and other birds that relish power-packed suet but have trouble clinging to bark for long. Fashion perches less than 3 inches long to reduce the probability that starlings and other large birds will land on them and steal the goodies.

HELPFUL HINTS

To avoid getting chilled while refilling your suet feeder in cold weather, insert a round aluminum tin from a small tea light candle into each hole in the feeder. Keep extra tins on hand indoors. Fill the replacement tins with suet or peanut butter mix in the warmth of your kitchen, then step outside to the feeder to pop out the old tins and insert the new ones.

Suet Substitutes

Almost all types of animal fat are highly desirable bird treats. You'll need to serve them in solid form, though, so birds can eat, not drink, them. You can also mix melted fat with other ingredients to create a variety of appealing treats for birds.

Lard. A block of lard makes a perfectly acceptable substitute for real suet or fat trimmings. Look for lard in the dairy case at your supermarket, or you may find it near the hot dogs and bacon.

Fatty bones. A fatty ham bone left over from Easter dinner also will be welcome, if you can spare it. Set it in an open-tray feeder or even on the ground. (Remove the bone at night so nocturnally prowling cats or raccoons don't snitch it.)

Rendering Suet

Heating suet so that it turns to liquid fat is called rendering. Melting suet can create a strong odor. To prevent this odor from permeating your kitchen or house, cover the pot containing the suet with a tight-fitting lid and turn on the fan in your stove hood (if you have one) to draw away the smell.

Commercial suet blocks and true suet are fairly free of solid substances that won't melt, but chunks of meat trimmings do contain some of these bits. Birds welcome these delectable pieces, so smash them with a fork if they're large, then use them along with the liquid suet in any of the projects in this chapter that call for liquid fat.

Bone marrow. This unusual bird treat provides hours of entertainment, too, as you watch the ingenious ways birds attempt to reach the marrow inside the hard outer bone. Use wire or string to hang the bone from a support, or set it in a tray feeder. Ham bones and beef soup bones are the best choices.

Bacon grease or pan drippings. Use these as binders for other foods, because they don't solidify past the semisolid stage. Mix in some cornmeal, cracker crumbs, chopped nuts, or other foods to make an excellent wintertime treat for all feeder birds.

Dairy fats, such as cheese and butter, are usually not appealing to birds, although anecdotal records exist of a catbird that liked sour cream!

Some bird watchers believe that treats containing suet or suet substitutes mixed with seeds or chopped nuts can be detrimental to birds. They say that birds may get grease on their head feathers when they stick their beaks deep into the suet to retrieve a seed, and they are concerned that the fat will interfere with the natural insulation of the birds' feathers. Most feeder watchers have not observed this; they note that birds pick at seeds exposed on the surface and don't dip their heads into sticky or greasy offerings. The only time birds may have trouble with suet on their feathers is during hot weather when the suet melts. If you're concerned about this problem, try the suet muffins on page 81. The recipe has no tantalizing seed additions and uses creamy peanut butter rather than chunky, so there are no peanuts to tempt birds to dig into the suet and risk getting messy.

Simple Pinecone Treats

Pinecones make a generous holder for peanut butter, suet, and other bird treats. If you don't have a ready supply of pinecones, you can substitute corncobs.

All are simply irresistible. Expect chickadees, nuthatches, titmice, and woodpeckers to be among the satisfied customers. Woodpeckers and nuthatches often cling to the top of a cone or to the hanging wire and eat head down.

MATERIALS

Pinecones

Thin wire or twine

Cookie sheet or waxed paper

Peanut butter

Cornmeal

Tablespoon

Butter knife

Shepherd's crooks or nails (optional)

Step 1. Working carefully to avoid breaking off the pinecones' scales, wrap the wire around each pinecone, slipping it under the second or third tier of scales from the stem end. Knot the wire to secure it, allowing an extra 6 to 12 inches for hanging.

Step 2. Set the cones on a cookie sheet or waxed paper for easy cleanup.

Step 3. Mix equal amounts of peanut butter and cornmeal until blended. Use the tablespoon to spread some of the mixture on each pinecone. Allow one or two small sections of the cone (a row or two of scales, roughly 2 inches across) to remain free of the spread, so birds can alight without getting sticky feet. Use the knife to push the mixture into the crevices between scales.

Step 4. Hang each pinecone treat from a shepherd's crook, a nail hammered into a post of any kind, or a low branch of a tree.

Suet–Peanut Butter Filling for Pinecones

Once you've mastered the technique for making pinecone treats, you'll enjoy trying different recipes for the filling. Here's a basic mixture that combines two favorites, suet and peanut butter.

INGREDIENTS

1 cup suet

1 cup creamy or chunky peanut butter

Melt the suet in a saucepan over low heat. Stir in the peanut butter until it is melted and well blended with the suet. Remove the pan from the heat and let the mixture cool until it is slightly thickened. Working on a cookie sheet to catch drips, spoon the mixture onto pinecones prepared with wire for hanging as described on page 79. Set the cones stem end down in the loaf pan, so that they are supported vertically. (This helps to prevent the melted mixture from dripping off the cones.) Put the loaf pan in the freezer and freeze the cones until the filling is hard. This may take as little as 2 hours or as long as overnight.

Filling Variations

Changing the ingredients of your pinecone filling gives your customers variety. By adding fruit to the mix, you won't deter the usual clientele, and you may attract some more unusual fruit-eating birds, including mockingbirds, bluebirds, thrashers, and wrens.

Nutty peanut butter pinecones. Melt 2 cups creamy or chunky peanut butter in a saucepan, stirring frequently. Add 1 cup coarsely chopped unsalted nuts (any kind) to the melted peanut butter and stir well to combine.

Seedy pinecones. Melt 1 cup suet or lard in a saucepan over low heat. Stir in 2 cups hulled sunflower seeds until well blended.

Fruity pinecones. Melt 1 cup suet or lard in a saucepan over low heat. Remove the pan from the heat. While the mixture cools, chop a few grapes and half an apple into pieces about ¼ inch wide and ¾ inch long. When the mixture has slightly thickened, stir in ½ cup each of the chopped apple and grapes.

Hanging wire

Set pinecones stem end down in pan.

Suet Muffins

A muffin tin is perfect for molding much-desired suet treats. Use a tin with shallow cups, not the extra-large size. Use only pure suet or lard, not fat trimmings, to make these treats.

INGREDIENTS

1 cup suet

1 cup creamy peanut butter

3 cups cornmeal, regular grind (not coarse)

½ cup whole wheat flour

Melt the suet in a saucepan over low heat. Add the peanut butter and stir until melted and well blended with the suet. Remove from the heat and allow to cool for about 15 minutes. Meanwhile, measure the cornmeal and flour into a large bowl (a glass bowl is easiest to clean) and mix them together with a large spoon. When the suet mixture begins to thicken slightly, scrape it into the bowl. Stir until well blended (about 100 strokes). Fill the cups of your muffin tins about 1 inch deep with the mixture. Put the tins in the freezer. When the muffins are frozen solid, remove them from the tins and slip a few into a suet holder or mesh onion bag. Freeze the rest in a resealable plastic bag.

Note: Check thrift shops and garage sales for battered muffin tins at a bargain price. Then hang up the entire tray as a muffin tin suet feeder! Fill the cups to the rim instead of halfway. After the muffins are well chilled, remove them from the freezer and poke a Popsicle stick or 4-inch-long twig into each muffin to serve as a perch for birds. Hang the tin by attaching a piece of wire.

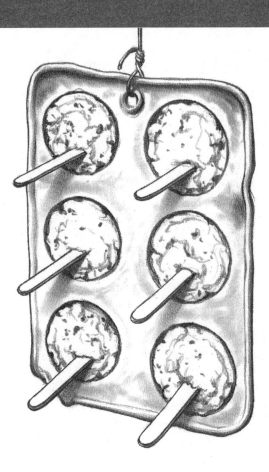

A Simple Suet Smear

If you're short on time, grab a kitchen spatula and the bowl of suet muffin mixture and head out into your yard. Use the spatula to smear the mixture onto wooden posts or tree trunks around your yard. Birds will land on the posts or trunks and peck at the mixture. Keep in mind, though, that the oils in this mixture will stain bark and wood.

Suet Pie

Recycle those aluminum pie tins by filling them with this simple suet-based treat. It's best served in winter, because that's when birds most need an extra source of fat. Also, when the weather is cold, the pie won't melt and slide out of the tin. Hang this suet pie out of direct sunlight, such as on a tree branch, where you can watch the birds enjoy their treat. Birds will cling to the rim of the tin while they eat.

When you hang a suet pie, the weight of the filling can cause the wire to tear through the aluminum. So before you start filling a suet pie tin, poke a hole through the crimped side of the tin and thread through a *loop* of florist's wire, not a single strand. If the side of the tin begins to tear, it should tear only as far as the reinforced rim of the tin.

INGREDIENTS

1 cup suet
1 cup creamy or chunky peanut butter
1 cup lard
1 cup coarsely chopped unsalted nuts, any kind

Melt the suet, peanut butter, and lard in a saucepan over low heat, stirring frequently. When the mixture is melted and well blended, remove the pan from the heat and let the mixture cool until slightly thickened. Pour the mixture into a pie tin, stopping at least 1/2 inch below the rim. If you have extra mixture, pour it into any small, shallow containers you have on hand to make smaller treats. Put the pie (and other treats) in the freezer and freeze until almost solid. Sprinkle the chopped nuts on the pie and use the back of a tablespoon to press them into the surface. Return the pie to the freezer and freeze until frozen solid.

Dough Ball Treats

Not a baked good but a frozen ball of dough enriched with small treats, this easy recipe will please nuthatches, brown creepers, woodpeckers, thrashers, Carolina wrens, bluebirds, catbirds, mockingbirds, and jays. Other birds may sample it, too.

Serve these treats on a nail. Hammer a large 12-penny nail about 1 inch deep into a wooden post that supports another feeder. Carefully push a dough ball onto the nail, all the way to the post, supporting it by wrapping your fingers around the ball so that it doesn't break apart. Woodpeckers, nuthatches, and brown creepers will cling to the post while dining, and other birds will perch on the exposed end of the nail.

INGREDIENTS

2 cups unseasoned bread crumbs
1/4 cup cornmeal, coarsely ground
1/2 cup whole wheat flour
1 cup coarsely chopped unsalted nuts, any kind
1 cup hulled sunflower seeds
3 apples, peeled and finely chopped (not cored)

1 cup raisins

½ pound suet, finely chopped

8-ounce jar of creamy or chunky peanut butter

½ cup bacon drippings or corn oil, if needed

Combine the bread crumbs, cornmeal, and flour in a large bowl and stir to blend well. Add the nuts, sunflower seeds, apples, raisins, and suet. Stir well to combine. Add the peanut butter and mix by hand or with a mixer until well distributed. Test the consistency of the mixture by squeezing a handful. If it crumbles apart, add the bacon drippings 1 tablespoon at a time until the dough holds its shape. Form the dough into balls about 3 inches in diameter and put them on a cookie sheet. Freeze until hard, which may take as little as 3 hours or as long as overnight. When the balls are frozen solid, place each one in a resealable plastic sandwich bag.

Homemade Suet Cakes

This hardened mixture works well as a homemade substitute for store-bought suet cakes. Before you mix the cake batter, measure your feeder so that you know how big to cut the cakes.

INGREDIENTS

2 cups suet

½ cup creamy peanut butter

Melt the suet in a saucepan over low heat. Add the peanut butter and cook, stirring frequently, until it is melted and well blended with the suet. Pour the mixture into a 9 × 13-inch heatproof baking dish and put the dish in the freezer. When the mixture is frozen solid, remove the dish from the freezer and cut the mixture into pieces. Slide individual cakes into resealable plastic sandwich bags (one cake per bag) and store in the freezer until needed.

Suet Cake Variations

Cooking up a batch of suet cakes is a gratifying task because birds take to them immediately. Squabbles often break out at the feeder over these prized cakes, as woodpeckers threaten nuthatches or blue jays shriek at Carolina wrens. Fine-tuning the recipes lets different bird species choose their favorites, reducing the number of quarrels.

Woodpecker delight suet cakes. Adding corn to suet cakes makes them extra special to corn-loving woodpeckers, especially the red-bellied and red-headed species. After melting and mixing the suet and peanut butter, remove the mixture from the heat and let it cool until slightly thickened. Stir in 2 cups yellow corn meal and 2 cups cracked corn.

Quick-oat bird cakes. This variation is highly popular with the usual suet-eating birds, and it's also a draw for thrashers, catbirds, and Carolina wrens. Use 2 cups lard instead of suet; lard is less dense than suet and thus easier for thin-billed birds to nibble. After melting and mixing the peanut butter and lard, add 2 cups quick-cooking oats, 2 cups cornmeal, and 1 cup whole wheat flour, stirring until well blended.

Insect suet cakes. Tempt the taste buds of bluebirds, thrashers, thrushes, woodpeckers, brown creepers, and wrens with these insect-enriched cakes. Add about 1 cup turtle, reptile, or fish food that contains only insects (available at pet supply stores) to 2 cups melted suet. Stir until blended.

Vegetarian "Suet" Treat

For those who prefer not to handle suet or lard, vegetable-based shortening is an acceptable alternative that is also palatable to birds. Plus, it's a good trick to know for those winter days when the suet supply is nil but the birds are hungry for a quick fix of calorie-rich fat.

INGREDIENTS

1 cup creamy or chunky peanut butter

1 cup solid vegetable shortening, such as Crisco

3 cups cornmeal

1 cup cracked corn

Melt the peanut butter and shortening together in a saucepan over low heat. Stir in the cornmeal and cracked corn. Spread the mixture in a 9 × 13-inch baking dish and freeze until thickened but not frozen solid, about 30 minutes, depending on your freezer setting. Use a butter knife, plastic spatula, or tablespoon to spread the mixture in a suet log feeder (see page 76). Or cut the mixture into pieces and use it to fill a wire cage suet feeder. Store any leftover mixture in a resealable plastic bag in the freezer until needed.

KITCHEN CUPBOARD TREATS

Leftovers from your pantry and refrigerator are another rich source of materials for creating bird treats. The best aspect of whipping up bird treats from the kitchen is that you don't need to be a gourmet cook—feeder birds will chow down on just about anything you put in front of them.

Consider Size and Shape

Think about what birds normally eat and how they eat it as you devise imaginative goodies for them. Small seedeaters will investigate tiny bits of food such as cracker crumbs or crushed cereal, because it resembles their typical menu. For instance, juncos will usually ignore a large slice of bread, but if you sprinkle bread crumbs on the ground, they'll pick up every one.

Many birds have learned to recognize bread and other baked goods as suitable food. Jays, robins, blackbirds, magpies, and mockingbirds (as well as starlings and house sparrows) will greedily grab for whole slices or chunks of bread, bagels, and other bakery goods.

One easy way to serve doughnuts and other bakery goods is to use an old wire- or plastic-bristle hairbrush as the feeder. Thread a piece of twine through the hole in the handle of the brush (or use duct tape to fasten twine to the handle). Center the doughnut or other treat over the bristles and gently push, so that the bristles poke securely into the treat. Hang the feeder in a discreet area where your family can enjoy watching birds use your clever feeder but passersby won't wonder about your grooming habits.

Serve Customers Selectively

Think about where and how you will serve kitchen treats before you mix them up. Big, interesting pieces of unusual foodstuffs will quickly grab the attention of scavenger birds: starlings and house sparrows, and possibly pigeons and crows. If you live near the habitats of ravens and gulls, they also may spot your big, intriguing treats and come to inspect what's for breakfast. If you prefer not to attract these birds, put your treats in a

continued on page 86

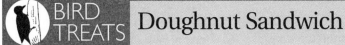

Thanks to their elevated fat content, doughnuts (even stale ones) are a big hit with chickadees, titmice, and other small birds. However, it can be tricky to serve doughnuts to small birds, because the doughnuts tend to fall apart into chunks that are quickly carried off by jays and other larger birds.

In this feeder, the doughnut is the sandwich filling, and the plastic lids that serve as the "bread" preserve the doughnut intact for small birds to nibble. Choose lids that are about the same size as the doughnut, such as those from cottage cheese containers.

Lid

Doughnut

Twine

Lid

Knot

MATERIALS

2 plastic lids, clear or opaque, about 4 inches in diameter

Large nail

12 to 18 inches of twine

Day-old doughnut (a plain cake doughnut is ideal)

Step 1. Poke a hole in the center of each plastic lid with the nail. The outside of the lid (the top surface of the container) is the outside of the feeder.

Step 2. Knot one end of the twine. Thread the other end through the hole in one of the lids,

with the knot on the outside of the lid.

Step 3. Place the lid knot side down on a flat surface.

Step 4. Thread the twine through the doughnut and lay it on the inside of the lid.

Step 5. Thread the twine through the hole in the second lid, making sure that the outside of the lid faces up.

Step 6. Pull the twine taut so that the doughnut is firmly held between the lids. Knot the twine at the point where it exits the second lid.

Step 7. Tie the doughnut sandwich to a low branch, deck or porch railing, or shepherd's crook.

continued from page 84

roofed feeder, where they will be less visible to scavenger birds on the wing.

Start small with kitchen treats, until you see how much the birds in your backyard like a particular offering. Once you hit on something that suits their taste, it's easy to make more.

Breakfast Eggs

It may seem odd, but birds love to eat eggs. Bluebirds, finches, brown thrashers, and wrens seem to be especially partial to a treat of cooked eggs (chicken eggs, that is). Next time you cook hard-boiled eggs for your family, throw in a couple of extras to keep on hand for your birds.

To serve hard-boiled eggs to birds, peel the eggs and coarsely chop the white and yolk. Crumble the eggshells into fine pieces and add them to the chopped eggs. Gently scrape the mixture into an empty open feeder, then watch to see which birds enjoy eggs for breakfast.

Baking for the Birds

Perhaps the ultimate step in making bird treats is to create baked delicacies especially for birds. On a rainy afternoon or quiet evening when you have some free time, give it a try. Make up your own recipe, or try "Corn Bread Deluxe" at right. You'll be so pleased with the response that you may decide to designate one day a month "Baking for the Birds Day."

Baking for the birds is a great way to use up small quantities of ingredients that are cluttering up your cupboards

FEEDERS   Bagel Feeder

Leave a bagel out on the kitchen counter, and it soon hardens into a solid mass that's almost impossible to break apart. Instead of recycling the bagel as crumbs or chunks for birds to eat, use the whole bagel as a feeder to hold other treats.

Step 1. Spread lard or peanut butter on the bagel to within about ½ inch of the inner hole (so that birds can perch on the inside of the bagel). Leave part of the outside edge of the bagel uncoated, too, to give birds more clinging space.

Step 2. Sprinkle sunflower seeds or chopped nuts (any kind) on a plate.

Step 3. Press the coated bagel into the seeds or nuts.

Step 4. Thread a piece of string through the hole and hang the feeder from a tree branch or shepherd's crook. Or place it on a large nail hammered into a post.

and to put ingredients that have gone stale to good use. Don't use rancid nuts or oils in these baked treats, though.

FRUIT AND BERRIES

The best way to offer fruit or berries to birds is right on the tree—or bush, vine, or groundcover. Many kinds of birds that particularly relish fruit and berries rarely visit a feeder. These birds find all they can eat among the branches of wild and cultivated plants in their habitats. The cedar waxwing, for example, rarely or never shows up at feeders. A sleek taupe-colored bird with an elegant crest, the waxwing sports a dashing black mask and jaunty red, waxy wing dots. But it's hard to appreciate the fine points of its style when the bird is high up in the trees, a common perching place. If you grow an American holly or fruiting cherry tree, however, you'll be able to enjoy a close-up view of waxwings as they descend in a group to feed on the berries or fruit.

Plants for Fruit

Fruit trees are easy to grow, and some may even bear fruit the first year you plant them. Fruit trees also are pretty trees, with a drift of fragrant soft pink or white flowers in the spring, glossy foliage, and a naturally attractive form. They grow fast, so they're an excellent choice for a hedge or as a focal point tucked into a large flower border.

You can choose a standard tall or a patio-size dwarf cultivar, whichever best matches the size of your yard. Fruit trees are often sold bareroot in early spring, with a dormant young tree protruding from a plastic bag filled with roots and a

BIRD TREAT RECIPES

Corn Bread Deluxe

This highly nutritious treat is jam-packed with nuts, seeds, and fruit. The mixing is fun and the baking easy, because the recipe is based on inexpensive packaged corn bread mix. Expect to see juncos, native sparrows, jays, mockingbirds, and possibly thrashers, wrens, and robins enjoying this treat.

INGREDIENTS

2 packages Jiffy brand corn bread mix
Eggs (one more than called for in the package instructions)
Apple juice
½ cup cracked corn
½ cup fresh or frozen blueberries
½ cup hulled sunflower seed
⅛ cup raisins or currants
¼ cup flax seeds
¼ cup millet

Preheat the oven to the temperature specified in the package instructions. Grease a 9 × 13-inch baking pan. Prepare the corn bread mix according to the package directions, but add one egg and substitute apple juice for the milk. Add the corn, blueberries, sunflower seeds, and raisins and stir until blended. Spread the batter in the greased pan. Sprinkle the surface with the flax seeds and millet. Bake until the corn bread pulls away from the sides of the pan and is golden brown on top. Let the bread cool completely, then cut it into 1-inch cubes. Don't worry if the corn bread crumbles; the birds will eagerly eat every tiny morsel. Gently place the cubes and any crumbled pieces in a resealable plastic bag and freeze. Remove two or more cubes at a time and serve them in a tray feeder.

peaty soil mix. Plant bareroot trees, shrubs, and vines in early spring as soon as the soil is dry enough to dig, because they will decline if they leaf out before planting. Plant potted nursery stock anytime; keep the soil in the pot regularly watered until you're ready to plant.

At the bush level, blueberries are the number one choice for bird fruit. Robins, bluebirds, catbirds, thrashers, mockingbirds, wrens, some flycatchers, orioles, and all other fruit-eating birds can't resist a beckoning blueberry. Raspberries, blackberries, currants, and other small, juicy fruits are favorites, too.

Try the projects on the pages that follow to provide fruity treats for your backyard birds. To learn more about growing fruit and berries as part of a habitat planting for birds, turn to chapter 5.

Most-Favored Fruit and Berries

It seems as if it should be easy to gauge the attractiveness of a fruit or berry plant for birds, but birds evidently know something we don't. They are quick to descend on certain types, leave others alone until last resort in the winter, and ignore still others completely.

The plants listed here are among those that birds like best. Interestingly, many of them will sprout of their own accord in your backyard, planted courtesy of birds that swallow the fruit and deposit the seeds in their droppings. (You'll also find plenty of seedlings of pokeweed, poison ivy, and other weedy plants sprouting in garden beds thanks to birds. That just shows how popular their fruit and berries are.)

Birds will glean the crop right from the plant, so be sure to choose a planting lo-

cation that's part of your feeding station, where you can have a close-up view of the visitors. It's also fun to collect some of the fruit or berries yourself and serve them in an open feeder to see who comes to dinner. Start with some of the plants listed below; then experiment with others from your fruit bin.

Trees
- Hackberry (*Celtis occidentalis*)
- Flowering dogwood (*Cornus florida*)
- Hawthorn (*Crataegus* spp.)
- American holly (*Ilex opaca*)
- Mulberry (*Morus* spp.)
- Sweet cherry (*Prunus avium*)
- Sour (pie) cherry (*Prunus cerasus*)
- Chokecherry and other wild cherries (*Prunus* spp.)
- 'Bradford' callery pear (*Pyrus calleryana*)
- Mountain ash (*Sorbus* spp.)

Shrubs
- Winterberry (*Ilex verticillata*)
- Privet (*Ligustrum vulgare*)
- Oregon grape holly (*Mahonia* spp.)
- Pyracantha (*Pyracantha* spp.)
- Currant (*Ribes* spp.)
- Elderberry (*Sambucus* spp.)
- Blueberry and huckleberry (*Vaccinium* spp.)

Vines
- Virginia creeper (*Parthenocissus quinquefolia*)
- Grape (*Vitis* spp.)

Groundcovers
- Bearberry (*Arctostaphylos uva-ursi*)
- Strawberry (*Fragaria* spp.)
- Liriope (*Liriope* spp.)

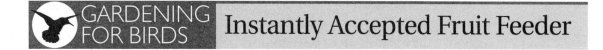

Want to try a project guaranteed to bring almost every bird within a mile to your backyard? Plant a cherry or mulberry tree. Many backyard birds, including titmice, orioles, cedar waxwings, and great crested flycatchers, can be spotted feeding among the leafy branches of a cherry or mulberry when the fruit is ripe.

Note: Mulberry trees are often hard to find at nurseries, because the trees are considered akin to weeds in many areas. If you can't find a mulberry tree locally, look to mail-order sources instead. (See "Resources for Backyard Birders and Gardeners" on page 292.)

Step 1. Select a site in full sun appropriate to the eventual size of the tree. If you're planting a bareroot tree, set the roots to soak in a bucket of water for at least 1 hour before planting.

Step 2. Dig a hole deep enough and wide enough to accommodate the rootball or bare roots. Check to be sure that the tree will sit at the same level as it was growing in the container or at the nursery.

Step 3. Fill the hole with water and let it drain. This will saturate the surrounding soil so that it won't wick moisture away from the newly planted tree.

Step 4. Remove the pot or the plastic wrapper. Gently set the plant in the hole. If you're planting a bareroot tree, spread out any large roots that may be tangled or wrapped around one another.

Step 5. Refill the hole, sloping the soil slightly away from the trunk. Form a mounded berm of soil about 2 inches high around the root area to create a moat that will hold water so that it doesn't run off.

Step 6. Tamp the soil inside the moat moderately hard with your feet. Fill the moat with water.

Step 7. Spread a 2-inch-deep layer of mulch over the planting area, but leave a ring about 6 inches in diameter around the base of the trunk clear of mulch.

Step 8. For the first 2 years of growth, water the tree weekly from spring through fall (or year-round in frost-free areas), except during periods of significant rainfall.

Fuss-Free Maintenance

Fruit trees, bushes, and vines will bear a crop no matter how much or how little care you give them. They are, after all, descended from wild plants that produce fruit regularly with no help from humans. Sure, the crop may not be picture-perfect, but birds don't care about blemishes: They'll happily devour cherries, grapes, and other fruit despite wormholes (an extra bite of protein!) or other bad spots.

When you're growing fruit for birds, there's no need to worry about pruning and the other mysteries of fruit cultivation. Just snip off wayward branches that interfere with passersby (or escape the arbor, in the case of grapes and other fruiting vines). It is also a good idea to thin the interior of the plants once a year so that sunlight can reach and ripen the fruit that is growing near the center or base of the vines.

Fruit in Containers

Even gardeners with no in-ground garden space can provide fruit treats for birds, because growing cherries, apricots, or other fruit is super simple when you plant a dwarf tree in a container.

Plant trees in large containers such as half barrels. Use a high-quality potting mix and add some compost to the mix, if you have it available. Keep the plants well-watered and plan to feed them monthly with fish emulsion or compost tea. Top-dress the plants with compost if you can. See the instructions on page 93 for protecting container fruit trees during the winter in cold climates.

continued on page 94

Blemished Fruit Won't Bother Birds

When you're selecting a fruit tree cultivar to produce fruit for yourself and your family, disease resistance is often a prime concern. Not so when you're planting fruit trees or bushes for birds. Although a disease-resistant tree is still a fine choice because of its usually greater vigor and better crops, birds will eat imperfect fruit just as eagerly as they will fruit without a blemish. It is important to choose a cultivar that is suitable for the climate of your particular area and the conditions of your yard. Select your trees and bushes from stock available at local nurseries and garden centers, because these plants should be well adapted to your climate. Read the labels when there is a choice of cultivars, and if you intend to harvest part of the crop for yourself, select the most disease-resistant one.

Also keep in mind that for plants that bear dry rather than soft fruit (including crabapples, hollies, and pyracanthas), an unimproved plant is a better choice than a cultivar. Crabapples are notorious for having lost their attractiveness to birds as breeders have fiddled with them to make trees with better flowers, more disease resistance, and apparently less tasty fruit. You'll find unimproved forms of plants at native-plant nurseries (see "Resources for Backyard Birders and Gardeners" on page 292) and sometimes at garden centers. If a plant has a cultivar name attached to its botanical name, it's not the tried-and-true original and may or may not attract birds.

A wooden half barrel

will happily support a dwarf fruit tree. Select a site for the container that gets full sun. You'll want to pick a spot that won't be busy with human activity at the time that the fruit ripens. (If you're planting an apple tree, a patio that goes unused in late fall and winter can be a good location, because birds will keep visiting the tree to eat as long as a few apples continue to cling to the branches.)

MATERIALS

Bareroot or potted dwarf fruit tree
Bucket
Wooden half barrel, approximately 25-gallon capacity
Soil-based potting mix

Step 1. If you're planting a bareroot fruit tree, set the tree's roots in a bucket of water to soak for at least 1 hour before you plant it. Prune off dead or broken roots.

Step 2. Set the barrel in place at your chosen site. Use a level to make sure the barrel is sitting straight.

Step 3. Add 5 inches of potting mix to the barrel.

Step 4. Set the fruit tree in the barrel. If the plant is bareroot, create a small raised cone of potting mix in the center of the barrel to support the roots, then flare the roots out over the cone.

Step 5. Fill in around the roots or rootball with potting mix. Your goal is to have the tree sitting at the same level in the soil as it grew at the nursery.

Step 6. Water thoroughly.

If your only open

garden space is a paved patio or you want a fast-growing arbor plant, choose a grapevine. Like fruit trees, grapevines bear amazingly large crops with little care. Choose a variety that thrives in your climate; check farmers' markets and local nurseries and garden centers to find vines that are well adapted to your area. Any container that is at least 15 inches deep will work. You can buy a decorative container or reuse a large, black plastic nursery pot or even a 5-gallon plastic bucket.

MATERIALS

Bareroot or potted grapevine

Bucket

Extra-large plastic container with drainage holes

Freestanding trellis, with attached legs that can be pushed into the ground

Soil-based potting mix

Twist ties or other holders

Step 1. If you're planting a bareroot grapevine, remove the wrappings from around the roots and set the roots in a bucket of water to soak for 1 hour before planting.

Step 2. Place the plastic container in a corner of your patio, in full sun, in a location that will allow you to install the trellis beside the container.

Step 3. Add about 4 inches of potting mix to the container.

Step 4. Set the rootball in the container. If you have a bareroot plant, spread the roots out if they are tangled.

Step 5. Fill in around the roots with potting mix, up to the level at which the vine was previously growing.

Step 6. Tamp the mix down firmly and water well.

Step 7. Install the trellis beside the container by pushing the legs into the ground to their full extent.

Step 8. As the vine grows, fasten it loosely to the trellis with twist ties until the tendrils gain a secure hold.

Step 9. Prune errant branches as needed to confine the vine to the trellis.

Step 10. When the fruit ripens (in the first or second year after planting), watch for birds visiting the vine, especially very early in the morning. Yellow jackets and wasps will visit as well. Clean up dropped grapes to reduce the insect nuisance, and keep in mind that birds will devour the insects as well as the grapes.

Regional Viewpoint

A Winter Blanket for Fruit Roots

Gardeners in cold-winter areas, such as the Northeast or upper Midwest, need to protect the roots of fruit trees in containers before extreme cold weather sets in by surrounding the container with a leafy blanket.

In late fall, after the ground freezes and the fruit tree has dropped its leaves, encircle the container with a cylinder of chicken wire or wire fencing set about 1 foot away from the sides of the container. Fasten the ends together by bending the wires or with twist ties.

Fill the wire enclosure with fallen leaves, piling them up to about 6 inches above the soil level of the container. Spread additional leaves over the soil in the container.

The leafy blanket will insulate the roots against frigid temperatures. In early spring, remove the leaves (you can put them in your compost pile) and the enclosure.

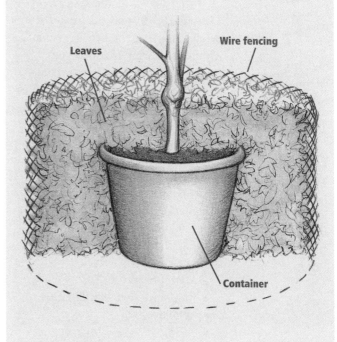

continued from page 90

Growing Berries for Birds

A hanging basket filled with strawberries, like the one shown on page 96, is sure to attract birds. Berry bushes, however, do best planted in the ground rather than in containers, because they need room to ramble.

A berry hedge will have the best bird appeal and be easiest to maintain. Berry plantings for humans require pruning so that fruiting is maximized. But for birds, the less you interfere with the plants, the more appealing the birds will find them. Prune once a year if you like, or let the bushes grow au naturel. (For directions for planting a hedge, see "Bargain Bareroot Bird Hedge" on page 140.)

Berry Bushes for a Bird Hedge

Various cultivars of all the berries listed below will thrive in Zones 3 through 9. Most need a period of winter chill, so if you live in an area without cold winters, check your garden center for cultivars that are adapted to your climate. Or choose tender fruit trees, such as pineapple guava (also called feijoa), strawberry guava, or loquat. Because the growth habits of berry bushes vary from one kind to another, it's best to plant all the same kind for a hedge.

- Blackberry
- Blueberry and huckleberry
- Elderberry (red, black, purple, or blue)
- Marionberry
- Raspberry (red, black, purple, or golden)
- Tayberry

Sharing the Crop

Seems like the fruits that birds like best are the same ones that we covet most. Just about the time your mouth starts watering for those blueberries that are beginning to ripen, the birds are likely to make it a race to the harvest.

Gardeners have a grab bag of tricks to scare birds from the fruit, beginning with the old-fashioned fun of making a scarecrow. Unfortunately, scarecrows work better as garden objets d'art than as defense against fruit-eating birds.

Scare tactics such as scarecrows, rubber snakes, or fluttering strips of reflective material are effective only for as long as it takes the birds to figure out that they're not in any real danger—which is generally not long at all.

Instead of relying on scare tactics that probably won't work well in the long run, you can buy peace of mind for about $10 in the form of reusable bird netting. The lightweight plastic mesh is sold in large sheets that are sized for draping over an entire bed, bush, or tree.

Fruit from the Feeder

Naturally, many folks want to offer fruit for the birds at their feeding stations. Fruit tastes so good to us that we expect birds to flock to it as a welcome change from dry, hard seeds. Unfortunately, this is not always the case. Most of the species we think of as feeder birds—sparrows, chickadees, jays, and other everyday visitors—would rather dine on seeds than fruit.

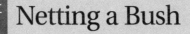
Netting a Bush

Covering a blueberry

or raspberry bush with protective plastic mesh is much easier if you enlist a helper, so arrange for a family member or friend to assist with this project. Once the cover is in place, leave it on until the fruit is perfectly ripe. Then you can remove the net, harvest as much fruit as you like, and leave the rest for the birds to feast on.

Step 1. Stand to one side of the bush you want to cover and ask your helper to stand on the opposite side.

Step 2. Flare the netting up and over the bush—much like shaking out a bedsheet. Retain your hold on the edge of the netting.

Step 3. Have the helper catch the edge of the netting on the other side.

Step 4. Gather the netting around the bottom stems of the bush.

Step 5. To prevent birds from sneaking up under the netting, weight it down at the edges with rocks, or gather it with a tie around the base of the tree or shrub. Birds may peck at any fruit they can reach through the mesh, but they won't be able to pluck fruit within the branches or beneath the leaves.

Who Likes Fruit?

On the brighter side, some regular feeder birds, including house finches, Carolina wrens, and mockingbirds, will readily indulge in servings of fruit. Fruit is a desirable part of their natural diet, and these birds are already accustomed to the feeder setting. Sometimes you can even coax other fruit-eating birds, such as brown thrashers, catbirds, and orioles, to overcome their reluctance with a tempting offering of fruit at a feeder. Robins will eat fruit at ground level and may feed at an elevated tray once they're accustomed to visiting your feeding station or after a winter snowstorm, when they're desperately hungry. But before you begin adding fruit to your feeder, consider that starlings also like fruit.

It will probably take a while to coax fruit-eating birds to your feeding station, because they're not used to looking for their favorite foods there. Make sure the offerings are easily visible in an open-tray feeder that is not obscured by overhanging branches. Once the birds discover your fruit platter, you can bet they'll soon be back.

An Apple a Day

One of the simplest and most appealing fruit treats is an apple cut in half. Birds will peck out every bit of flesh (and squirrels will like it, too). If you prefer not to have half-eaten apples lying around on your lawn, you can keep your feeding station looking tidy by securing the apple to a nail poking up from a horizontal board. Or you can impale the apple cut side up on a branch stub or a simple homemade fruit feeder like the one shown on page 98.

Faux Grape Tree

Another way to coax shy fruit-eating birds to accept your fruit offerings is to

continued on page 99

Hanging Strawberry Basket

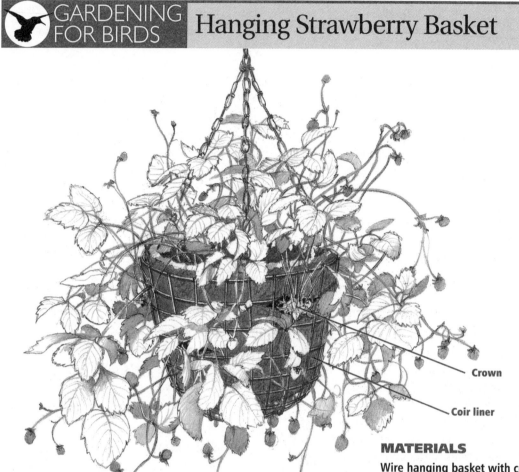

Crown

Coir liner

MATERIALS

Wire hanging basket with coir liner, at least 18 inches in diameter

Sharp, sturdy kitchen knife

Soil-based potting mix

Compost

Plastic bucket or tub

Water-retentive granules

12 to 15 everbearing strawberry plants

Sturdy metal hook

Water-soluble fertilizer, such as fish emulsion or compost tea

Strawberries are ideal for a hanging basket, where the runners can trail over the sides. Depending on which birds live in your neighborhood and when your strawberries ripen, you may see mockingbirds, thrashers, Carolina wrens, robins, or other fruit-loving birds plucking and swallowing the berries from your basket.

The best location for this basket is an area that is protected from afternoon sun but gets plenty of sun early in the day. Make sure the basket is sheltered from the full force of the wind. A basket of 12 to 15 plants will yield 5 to 8 quarts of berries in the first year—enough for you to snitch a few handfuls when the birds aren't looking!

SETTING UP FOR PLANTING

Step 1. Settle the coir liner into the wire basket.

Step 2. Using the knife, make several slits in the liner in a circle all around the basket about 4 inches up from the bottom. These will be planting slots, so that you can plant strawberries along the sides of the basket as well as at the top.

Step 3. Make a second circle of slits about 4 inches above the first.

Step 4. Mix together 3 parts potting mix and 1 part compost in the bucket. Add water-retentive granules in the proportion recommended on the package. Moisten the mixture with water.

Step 5. Add the mixture to the liner, filling the liner to a level about 2 inches above the first (lower) row of slits.

PLANTING THE SIDES

Step 6. Insert the roots of one strawberry plant into one of the slits, so that the roots are inside the basket and the crown and foliage protrude from the side. Tamp the soil moderately around the roots. (Don't pack it down with all your strength; plant roots need air.)

Step 7. Repeat, working around the pot to insert a plant in each slit.

Step 8. Add more of the soil mixture to a level about 2 inches above the next row of slits.

Step 9. Repeat steps 6 and 7.

PLANTING THE TOP

Step 10. If necessary, add more soil mix until it is nearly level with the top of the coir liner. Plant the top of the basket, working outward from the center, and spacing the plants 3 to 4 inches apart.

Step 11. Fill in with additional soil mixture and tamp down, until the soil surface is about 2 inches below the rim of the liner.

Step 12. Hang the basket from the hook in a location with nearby shrubs or trees so that fruit-eating birds can feel sheltered as they approach.

Step 13. Using a gentle spray from a watering wand, water the container well, until water drips rapidly out of the bottom.

Step 14. Maintain the container by using the water-soluble fertilizer to nourish the plants. Follow the package directions for frequency of application and dilution instructions. Generally, a once-a-week application will keep the plants growing lushly and setting plenty of fruit.

HELPFUL HINTS

To make it easier for perching birds to get at the berries cascading out of your strawberry basket, you can add bamboo perches. If you decide to add perches, be sure to hang the basket well out of the way of passersby, because the protruding sticks could cause injury, if someone accidentally walked too close to the basket.

You'll need four thin bamboo stakes and a pair of loppers. After planting the sides of the basket, use the loppers to cut the stakes into sections about 8 inches long. Push the sections into the sides of the basket at random intervals, allowing 5 to 6 inches of each to protrude.

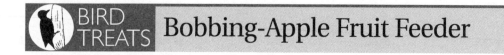

Bobbing-Apple Fruit Feeder

Suspend an apple or pear from a coat hanger, and you have a fruit feeder that's easy to refill. Peel away a strip of the apple or pear skin to expose the flesh, so that birds with weaker bills do not have to work to break the skin but can begin nibbling right away.

MATERIALS

Needle-nose pliers
Heavy wire coat hanger
Wire cutters
Paring knife
Apple or pear
3 corks, such as from wine bottles

Step 1. Use the pliers to untwist and separate the joint of the coat hanger.

Step 2. With the wire cutters, cut off the curved end and twisted neck of one side of the coat hanger. Cut off the somewhat kinked end on the other side of the hanger.

Step 3. Using the knife, slice off a thin strip of peel around the apple, then cut the apple in half.

Step 4. Holding the fruit cut side out, push it onto one end of the wire. Allow 3 to 4 inches of the wire to protrude from the cut side of the fruit.

Step 5. Push a cork onto the exposed piece of wire all the way to the cut side of the fruit, to prevent the fruit from sliding off.

Step 6. Push a second cork onto the tip of the exposed wire. (This is for safety, to prevent passersby from getting poked by the sharp wire tip.) The section of wire between the corks will serve as a perch, if needed.

Step 7. Push a cork onto the other end of the wire, sliding it up against the skin side of the fruit to hold it in place.

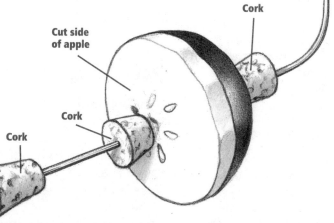

Cut side of apple

Cork

Cork

Cork

Step 8. Hang the feeder from a low tree branch, deck railing, or shepherd's crook where the birds and you can see it. To do this, bend the long free end of the wire around the support, then use the pliers to twist the wire around itself.

Step 9. Bend the "perch" part of the wire, if needed, until it is nearly horizontal, so that birds can get a good grip.

continued from page 95

fashion a faux fruit tree—a real shrub or small tree hung with grapes, a favorite of all fruit-eating backyard birds. This project is best done in the winter, when shrubs are bare of leaves, so that you can better see the mockingbirds, catbirds, wrens, thrashers, and even bluebirds that seek out your faux feeder. Just snip a bunch of grapes into small clusters and hang the clusters over the branches and twigs of a shrub or small tree that you can see from your favorite bird-watching window.

MEALWORMS AND EARTHWORMS

Creepy crawlies are definite treats to birds, although they may not be something you yearn to add to the menu. Keep in mind that even though it takes a little extra effort to serve insects and worms in a feeder, they just might bring you an up-close look at some fabulous as well as some familiar birds.

Mealworms

Mealworms are the larvae of the darkling beetle. Although to our eyes these whitish grubs look much less than appetizing, they must taste delicious, because they make great fishing bait and birds love them, too. You'll find them for sale at very reasonable prices at bait shops; a half-pint goes a long way at the feeder. You can also raise your own mealworms. (To learn how, see "Add Mealworms to Your Station" on page 111.)

Once birds discover mealworms at a feeder, they'll keep coming back, and so will others of their kind. Bluebirds are the

BIRD TREAT RECIPES

Meaty Medley

Many insect-eating birds also enjoy meat. Serve this treat to entice jays, Carolina wrens, mockingbirds, catbirds, woodpeckers, and bluebirds.

INGREDIENTS

2 cups chopped suet

½ cup raw hamburger

½ cup coarsely crushed whole wheat or cracked wheat crackers

½ cup hulled sunflower seeds

Using your hands, combine all the ingredients thoroughly. Pack the mixture into a suet log feeder (see page 76), or serve a small amount at a time in an open tray. Form leftovers into small balls and freeze. Always wash your hands thoroughly after handling this mixture.

best-known fans of mealworms, and who wouldn't love to attract these gorgeous birds! Purple martins also will swoop from the sky to dine on an accessible offering of mealworms.

When insects become dormant in the winter, many of the birds that depend on them, including warblers and flycatchers, migrate south to find still-active bugs. Now and again, unusually mild winter weather lures insect-eating birds, including northern flickers, Carolina wrens and pine or yellow-rumped warblers, to stay in the north for the winter. If you spot any of these visitors in your yard in the winter, offer them mealworms as

continued on page 101

Orioles don't overwinter in the United States, but the most widespread species, the northern oriole, returns just in time for the breeding season—around April 1 in the South and April 15 to May 1 in the North. You can kick off the spring birding season with this oriole feeder positioned on your deck. Other songbirds also will find some of the treats attractive.

MATERIALS

4-foot-long 1 × 12

Drill

¼-inch twist drill bit

2 cup hooks

Double-bowl metal cat food dish with straight sides at least 1½ inches deep

Four 8-penny finish nails

Hammer

2 bricks

Oriole or hummingbird nectar feeder (must have a perch for orioles)

Nectar solution (see page 268 for a recipe)

Wire cage suet feeder

Suet cake

Grape jelly

Mealworms

Juice oranges

Step 1. Along one long edge of the 1 × 12, measure in 6 inches from the ends and mark spots for pilot holes. Drill a pilot hole at each mark, then screw the cup hooks into the holes.

Step 2. Lay the board flat and center the cat dish on it. Mark a line at each end of the dish.

Step 3. Remove the dish and hammer an 8-penny nail at each mark, leaving ¾ inch of each nail protruding. (These nails will help keep the dish from sliding.)

Step 4. About 8 inches from each of these nails, hammer in another nail, leaving ¾ inch protruding.

Step 5. To assemble the station, rest the board diagonally across a corner of the deck railing, about

1 foot from the corner point, with the nails facing up. Allow an overhang of at least 10 inches on each side.

Step 6. Place the bricks on the board, one over each spot where the board rests on the deck railing.

Step 7. Fill the nectar feeder with nectar solution and hang it from one of the cup hooks.

Step 8. Hang the suet feeder with a suet cake from the other cup hook.

Step 9. Wedge the cat dish in place between the two center nails. Fill one side of the dish with

Grape jelly

Mealworms

Brick

continued from page 99

½ cup grape jelly and the other side with mealworms.

Step 10. Spear orange halves pulp side up on the other two nails.

HELPFUL HINTS

Most of the treats offered at this feeder are quickly perishable. Here's how often to renew your offerings.

Orange halves. Replace when all the pulp is gone, or within 3 days of putting them out (sooner if the juice dries out or if mold develops).

Mealworms. Discard mealworms if they develop an ammonia smell. More likely, though, the birds will keep you racing to replenish the supply.

Grape jelly. Replace every 2 days in hot weather or after a rain. When the weather is cool, the jelly may stay fresh for up to 1 week. When you change the jelly, hose off any residue on the feeder and dry the container.

Nectar solution. Empty the nectar feeder and add fresh solution every other day in hot weather (70°F or above). When it's cool outside, add fresh solution every 4 days or when the feeder is empty, whichever comes first.

well to satisfy their need for insect protein. Small, overwintering songbirds such as chickadees and nuthatches will appreciate mealworms, too.

Look for a commercial feeder specially made to serve this delicacy. It prevents the wiggly worms from escaping. (For suppliers, see "Resources for Backyard Birders and Gardeners" on page 292.)

Earthworms

Birds that are fond of earthworms are perfectly capable of finding them on their own in the lawn, flowerbeds, and other places around your yard. You can make it easier for them by keeping a compost pile, a favorite source of food for foraging birds. Robins will soon learn to keep close watch near the bottom of the pile for earthworms.

Robins also will make use of a homemade earthworm farm, such as the one described on page 102, as will wood thrushes. These birds usually shy away from feeder setups, so offering worms in a location that's easy for you to see will yield an opportunity to watch the birds' habits up close.

Earthworms grow quickly, and they multiply fast. Their numbers will double in about 3 months. That means if you start with a farm of 200 worms in April, you are likely to be caring for 400 in June and 800 in August. Obviously, your little worm city can soon get overcrowded, even with robins helping to get rid of the extras. The simple solution is to liberate some of the worms into an area of your garden where the soil is loose and moist, so that they can quickly burrow underground to safety. Be sure to watch for birds, which are likely to gather fast to snatch up any stragglers.

A Worm Farm for the Birds

A worm farm is especially welcome to birds during dry times, when worms retreat deeper into the soil to seek moisture. This worm farm is basically a glorified compost pile in a container that birds can easily access. Red wiggler worms are available at bait shops and pet supply stores or by mail order. Pick a container in a discreet, outdoorsy color such as dark green that will blend in with the surrounding vegetation.

MATERIALS

Opaque plastic storage container, about 2 feet long × 1½ feet wide × 1 foot deep

Drill

¼-inch drill bit

Fiberglass, plastic, or nylon window screening, about 28 inches × 22 inches

Wheelbarrow

Spading fork or shovel

Peat moss

Composted nonsmelly manure (such as composted steer or chicken manure sold at garden centers)

About 200 red wiggler worms

Nonmeat and nondairy kitchen scraps, including vegetable parings, apple cores, and eggshells

Step 1. Turn the container upside down and drill several ¼-inch drainage holes in the bottom.

Step 2. Turn the container right side up and press the screening into the bottom. The screening will extend about 2 inches up the sides.

Step 3. Set the container in a level, shady spot. A site with dappled shade is okay, but full shade is best.

Step 4. In a wheelbarrow or on the ground near the container, use the spading fork to mix 1 part peat moss with ½ to 1 part composted manure.

Step 5. Fill the container with the mixture to within about 3 inches of the rim.

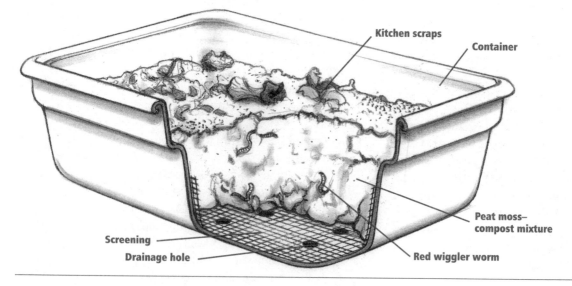

Kitchen scraps

Container

Peat moss–compost mixture

Screening

Drainage hole

Red wiggler worm

Step 6. Add water until the mixture is thoroughly moist but not sopping wet. Do not tamp it down.

Step 7. Wait for 1 to 2 weeks. During this time, the soil mixture will heat up as the composting bacteria do their work. That excess heat would kill the worms, which prefer cool, moist conditions.

Step 8. After the first week, check the temperature of the mixture by sticking your hand deep into it. If it feels even slightly warm to the touch, wait a few more days and test it again.

Step 9. When the soil mixture is consistently cool, buy worms and dump them onto the surface of the mixture. The worms will settle in quickly and work their way down into the soil.

Step 10. Lay a handful of kitchen scraps on the surface of the mixture for the worms' first feeding.

Worm Farm Chores

A worm farm needs routine care to keep the population thriving. Here's your chore list.

■ Once a day, lay a shallow layer of kitchen scraps on the surface of the mixture. Avoid any greasy or oily foods, such as salad greens coated with dressing. One-half pound of worms will devour about ½ pound of organic materials every 2 days.

■ Once a week, scatter a handful of finely ground cornmeal over the surface of the mixture.

■ As needed, water lightly with a watering can or a gentle spray from the hose to maintain a moist consistency. Dry soil will kill the worms, because their skin must be moist to take in oxygen. Overly wet soil also can be fatal, because the worms can drown.

■ If you expect a downpour, cover the container with a sheet of plywood to prevent the worms from drowning. Remember to remove the plywood after the rain stops.

■ As the worms increase in number and size, add grass clippings, leaves, weeds, and strips of newspaper to the top of the soil mixture. All these organic materials will be transformed into rich compost with the aid of the worms' appetites. Depending on the number and size of worms in the container, you'll need to replenish their food supply from about once a week to once a month. Refresh the material whenever the supply begins to look scanty.

■ Once a week, use a short-handled garden pitchfork or other tool to turn the soil mixture so that you can keep it well supplied with air—and admire how fast your worm wealth is increasing!

Make Your Own Blend

Experiment with combinations of bird foods from the four basic groups to make your own feeder treats. Be sure to watch the feeder to see which birds find your custom blend first and whether they come back for more. An open-tray feeder works best when you're introducing new foods, because the items are immediately visible to passing birds, especially those that are less inclined to visit feeders, and accessible to all types of birds. Once the birds are accustomed to the food, you can offer additional handouts in the feeder of your choice, as long as it is of the right design for the birds you want to attract.

BLEND	BIRDS ATTRACTED	TYPE OF FEEDER
4 parts seeds 2 parts nuts	Jays, woodpeckers, cardinals, grosbeaks, chickadees, titmice, nuthatches	Open tray, roofed tray, hanging globe (for small birds), hopper, nut
2 parts seeds 2 parts nuts 1 part fats	Jays, woodpeckers, cardinals, grosbeaks, titmice, nuthatches, chickadees	Open tray, roofed tray, hanging globe (for small birds)
2 parts nuts 2 parts fats	Jays, woodpeckers, titmice, nuthatches, chickadees, brown creepers, mockingbirds, thrashers, bluebirds	Open tray, roofed tray, hanging globe (for small birds)
1 part fats 1 part fruits	Mockingbirds, thrashers, tanagers, waxwings, bluebirds, catbirds, thrushes, robins, wrens, orioles	Open tray, roofed tray

CHAPTER 4

Feeding Stations

Variety is truly the spice of life when you create a feeding station for birds. Imagine a dozen mourning doves cooing as they comb the ground for crumbs, while above them cheeky blue jays, timid woodpeckers, and gorgeous goldfinches throng a pole-mounted feeding station. When you combine seed, fruit, and suet options in one station, you can attract birds year-round. Set up a station on whatever scale you like, and even bring birds to dine right at your window. In this chapter, you'll learn how to take your single-feeder success and expand the party, as well as how to maintain feeding stations throughout the year.

SETTING UP A FEEDING STATION

Creating a feeding station is like designing a garden—the possibilities are endless. You choose the feeders that will draw the birds you most want to attract, then figure out the optimum arrangement for them in your yard. Plants play a role in feeding stations, too, because the fruit and nectar they provide also will draw in birds.

Unlike a garden, though, a feeding station can require four-season maintenance, as birds are present and hungry all year round. Keep that in mind as you decide how large and varied a feeding station you want to manage.

Making Decisions

Like any designer, you'll be influenced by your personal preferences as you create a feeding station: Would you like to concentrate solely on birds that eat the most common foods, such as the cardinals and chickadees that favor black oil sunflower seed? Or are you willing to specialize—for example, offering mealworms to draw bluebirds in spring when they're feeding their young? Would you like to attract fruit eaters such as waxwings and tanagers to a berry bush, or would you prefer to save that fruit for your family?

There's no set formula for a feeding station, and the projects in this chapter are meant to fire your creative juices as you figure out how best to combine and situate feeders in your yard. One generality holds true, though. It may sound counterintuitive, but the most effective way to attract the largest variety of birds to your yard is to put out separate feeders for each type of food you plan to offer, rather than mixing everything together.

Much like a fussy toddler, a bird that doesn't eat a certain type of seed in a mix won't carefully push it to the side for someone else to enjoy. Instead, it will toss the offending food on the ground—where it will become a magnet for squirrels and other rodents. Seeds that wind up on the ground are also likely to be contaminated by dampness and bird droppings. So, as you develop feeding stations, focus on offering specific types of seeds in specific types of feeders, such as nyjer in a nyjer tube feeder, and add feeders as you go.

Where to Start

Chances are, you've already got at least one feeder in your yard. For example, if you've made the song sparrow feeder shown on page 3, try hanging a suet feeder and a tube or hopper feeder filled with black oil sunflower seed from a pole nearby. Voilà! You now have a station and should see chickadees, cardinals, and jays, while your sparrows continue to visit the low rock feeder.

Regardless of whether you decide to focus on a few square feet or a quarter acre, consider the answers to the following questions before you embark on setting up a feeding station.

■ What's the best place, or places, in my yard for a feeding station?

■ How can I make it convenient to maintain the feeding station?

■ How much time am I willing to devote to it?

■ What kind of feeding station will suit my landscape style?

- How will my local climate affect the feeding station?
- What's my budget?

Choose the Right Site

It's important to find a spot for your feeding station where you'll have a good view of the fun. But for the birds, the most important aspects of a feeding station site are shelter, protection from predators, and freedom from pests.

Ideally, you should choose a spot where there's a tree or some other type of shelter within several feet of all feeders in the station. Even if your feeders are on a deck, you can provide a perching spot by putting out a potted evergreen such as a Norfolk Island pine. To supply a windbreak and a safe escape route if a predator swoops down, consider planting a shade or flowering tree near your deck, such as a dogwood, hawthorn, mountain ash, or crabapple.

In some instances, your station will include several feeders and take up 10 square yards or more, due to different species' likes and dislikes. And you may want to allow enough space so that you can occasionally shift the position of the feeders by a foot or so to help prevent the accumulation of uneaten seeds.

If your space is limited, don't despair. You may not be able to attract as wide a range of birds, but you can still enjoy variety, even with a small feeding station such as the one shown on page 108.

Make It Convenient

Creating a feeding station is a labor of love, but maintaining the station over time will be much easier if you locate the

The Ultimate Feeding Station

A feeding station designed for the widest possible appeal to the spectrum of backyard birds would include the following:

- Hopper feeder for sunflower seed
- Tube feeder for nyjer
- Hopper or platform feeder for millet
- Wire mesh cage feeder for peanuts
- Starling- and grackle-resistant suet feeder
- Hopper tray with hulled sunflower seed for less hardy winter birds (seasonal)
- Nectar feeder for orioles and hummingbirds (seasonal)
- Mealworm tin (sometimes seasonal)
- Fruit feeder
- Special treat feeder
- Birdbath

station near an outdoor hose (for cleaning feeders and refreshing water) and reasonably close to your food storage area. If you can, place the station near an existing footpath, or make one yourself, so that you can readily restock, even after heavy rain has turned the area into a mud hole. Having a stepladder handy is important if you need to restock a high hanging feeder.

Even so, these conveniences are just "nice to haves," not "have to haves." You can always adjust your feeding station plans to accommodate any materials or site advantages you can't provide. If you don't have a nearby shed to store seed, for example, you might want to try nyjer feeders, since they take lighter seed and less of it, and you could easily keep a jar of nyjer seed on your work desk indoors.

Little Red Wagon Portable Station

If maintaining a large feeding station takes more effort or time than you can manage, create a portable station in a child's wagon. Although it's small, this station includes three different types of feeders plus a petite birdbath.

You can roll this feeding station over to the hose when it's time to clean the feeders, or over to your shed or garage when you need to recharge the seed supply. This also comes in handy if you want to change the location of your station with the seasons for optimum viewing (near your patio in the spring; outside your kitchen window during the winter). And if a hawk or other predator poses a threat, you can wheel the whole operation out of sight for a week until the bad guy moves on to another neighborhood.

MATERIALS

Child's metal wagon with handle
20-penny nail
Hammer
Rust-inhibiting metal primer
Hay or dry pine needles
2 rectangular glass dishes, one at least 2 inches shorter than the other and capable of being nested inside it (Pyrex 15¼ × 9¼-inch and 13 × 9-inch baking dishes work well)
Colored glass pebbles or ordinary pebbles
12-inch clay pot
Hopper feeder
Black oil sunflower seed
Thistle sock or small feeder
Nyjer seed
Suet cake
Wire cage suet feeder with handle
Small magnetic metal hook
Potted 'Wave' petunia, other potted plant, or other seasonally appropriate decorative item (optional)

Step 1. Place the wagon upside down on a level work surface. Use a 20-penny nail and a hammer to punch holes in the floor of the wagon for drainage—three holes at each corner edge.

Step 2. Paint the floor of the wagon with primer, according to the manufacturer's directions. Use spray paint for the lightest, most even coat. Allow the paint to dry for at least 1 day.

Step 3. Cover the bottom of the wagon with a 2-inch layer of hay or dry pine needles.(You'll want to replace this layer occasionally when it becomes too soiled or wet.)

Step 4. Nest the smaller casserole inside the larger one, and set the larger dish on the hay at one end of the wagon.

Step 5. Fill the gap between the dishes with pebbles. (The pebbles add weight to stabilize the water dish. Colored glass pebbles attract airborne birds.)

Step 6. Place the clay pot upside down on the hay at the other end of the wagon.

Step 7. Load the hopper feeder with sunflower seeds and set it on top of the clay pot.

Step 8. Position the wagon handle diagonally over the wagon. Fill the thistle sock with nyjer and hang the sock from the wagon handle so that it dangles over the ground beside the wagon.

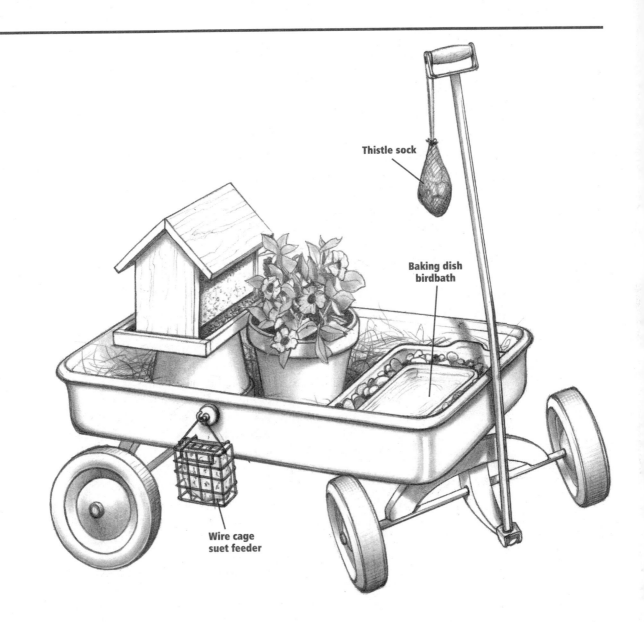

Thistle sock

Baking dish birdbath

Wire cage suet feeder

Step 9. Place the suet cake in the suet feeder. Attach the magnetic hook to the side or back of the wagon and hang the suet feeder on the hook.

Step 10. Fill the smaller baking dish with water. You'll need to change the water every few days, as debris from the feeders will tend to end up in the water.

Step 11. If desired, set a potted 'Wave' petunia, potted mum, or gourds between the hopper feeder and water dish for a decorative touch.

Set the Right Scale

Avid birders will tell you that feeding stations can become an all-consuming passion—the place where you invest most of your spare time and hobby dollars. But when you're just starting a station, design one that you can manage without investing too much time. Keep in mind that just about any feeder will need to be restocked once a week to keep birds returning. Consider both how many feeders you can maintain and whether you're willing to deal with the more time-consuming feeders, such as those you have to hang high or those enclosed within a wire screen. Fresh fruit will need to be replaced frequently, so fruit feeders aren't the best choice for someone who travels a lot for work or pleasure.

And although it's a myth that birds will suffer if you start feeding them and then stop abruptly (they do have other options), each time you take a long break from feeding you'll have to build up your clientele again, which can really compromise your bird-watching enjoyment. It's better to keep up with a few feeding options at a manageable station than to splurge on a magnificent station that's devoid of food most of the time.

Starter Station

A good starter station might include a house-style sunflower seed feeder that has built-in wire cages for suet cakes on the side. Hang a thistle sock from the bottom and set up a birdbath on the side. The sunflower seeds will draw chickadees, nuthatches, kinglets, and cardinals, to name just a few, and the suet will attract woodpeckers, wrens, thrashers, and creepers. The nyjer will appeal to finches, pine siskins, and the like. Best of all, your station should require only 30 minutes to refresh once or twice a week.

Test your feeding station design first using inexpensive feeders like those on pages 112 to 113. You may discover that nuthatches won't visit a feeder close to your house, or that you can't see the tube feeder when it's hung 12 feet below an overhanging tree branch. You'll want to learn these things when you're still dealing with feeders made of plastic soda bottles, not a $50 deluxe model from the farm store.

Consider Your Climate

Be sure to factor in your climate when designing a feeding station. If you live in a region that's warm year-round, for example, you can supply birds' needs more easily with plants, such as nectar-producing flowers and fresh berries. But you might not have much success with suet feeders, since the suet will go rancid in about 3 days if the temperature rises above 70°F.

In rainy areas, you'll be able to provide wonderful water features for your feathered friends and grow lots of moisture-loving berry bushes, but you might want to choose small feeders over large. That way, you can refill them often and not have to throw out large quantities of seeds because they got damp and spoiled. You can also favor large, whole nuts—the kind jays love—that are impervious to water.

In areas that have months of below-freezing temperatures, suet feeders are key. By contrast, you wouldn't center your feeding station on a watering hole that will be frozen much of the time.

Add Mealworms to Your Station

What's a brooding bluebird's favorite power snack? That would be mealworms, in a tin feeding cup or special mealworm feeder that she can find readily so she doesn't have to leave her eggs for long periods of time. Bluebirds also feed mealworms to their offspring, and it's jolly fun to watch the parents fly the babies down to the feeder to sample a couple. Nesting orioles snap up mealworms in the spring, too, and chickadees and nuthatches think that protein-rich mealworms are a great addition to the buffet table in the winter, when insects are scarce.

Consider putting out a mealworm feeder just for nesting season or for short periods during the winter. You probably won't want to stock them on a regular basis, however, because they can be pricey. To keep costs down, you can raise your own mealworms at home. They're clean and do not carry human diseases. You can buy a starter package at a pet store, then set them up in a shallow plastic container with a layer of cornmeal or oatmeal on the bottom. Cover the container with aluminum foil and poke several airholes in the foil, or use a piece of mesh screening as a lid.

Put a small piece of cloth on the surface of the cornmeal to provide an area where the adult beetles can lay eggs. To keep the meal properly moist, put a damp paper towel on top of the cornmeal, then add a banana peel or a slice of potato or apple. Discard the peel or slice once a week and add a fresh one. Put the container in your basement or garage.

The mealworms will burrow below the surface of the cornmeal and molt several times. This will take a couple of weeks, depending on the temperature. After the last molt, the larvae will come to the surface and metamorphose into naked white pupae. After a resting period, the pupae will metamorphose into adult beetles, which have wings but rarely fly.

The adult beetles will lay their eggs between 1 and 3 weeks after they emerge and then die. The eggs will incubate for 4 to 19 days before becoming mealworms. At any time after this, you can sift the meal with a colander or sifter you reserve just for this purpose and remove as many mealworms as you need.

Match Your Landscape Style

Defining the style of your feeding station may be the most important step in the process. What style will fit in best with your existing, or potential, gardening and landscaping projects? You can design a feeding station to match almost any motif, including a country garden, a natural landscape, or a romantic Victorian garden (see the designs on pages 114 through 117). Even the sophisticated landscaper who favors gazing balls and lawn sculpture can find elegant feeders that will match her garden style and please the local birds.

If you like things to look natural, you can use log feeders and natural wreaths to attract birds such as orioles, woodpeckers, and titmice. To appeal to insect

continued on page 115

This Is Only a Test

When you're trying

to figure out which feeders to use and where to place them to attract the most birds, you'll want to work with something simple, rather than diving into a complicated woodworking project or spending a lot of money on expensive commercial feeders. Test the waters with a feeding station that you can assemble in less than an hour, using recycled materials. This station includes three of the most popular types of feeders: a hopper feeder, a suet feeder, and a tube feeder.

MARGARINE BOX SUET HOLDER

Step 1. Use a craft knife to cut a grid of ¼-inch-square holes in the two wide faces of an empty cardboard margarine box (such as the type Parkay is sold in). Space the holes in the grid about ¼ inch apart, and leave a 1-inch-wide uncut margin all around the grid.

Step 2. Place a suet cake inside the box.

Step 3. With a sharp paring knife or Phillips screwdriver, poke a string-size hole about ½ inch from the top of each narrow side of the box.

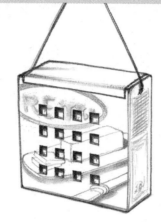

Step 4. Thread an 18-inch piece of string through one hole, inside and across the box, and out the other hole. Adjust the string so that both ends extend equally outside the box.

Step 5. Close the box top and tape it shut with duct tape.

Step 6. Tie the ends of the string together to form a hanger.

SODA BOTTLE TUBE FEEDER

Step 1. Remove the labels from a 20-ounce plastic soda bottle. Wash it with soapy water, rinse it, and allow it to dry thoroughly.

Step 2. Use a nail or a large safety pin to make two small holes in the bottom of the bottle, about 1 inch apart. The holes should be just big enough to thread fishing line or thin florist's wire through.

Step 3. Thread a 2-foot piece of fishing line or wire through one

hole and out the other. Twist or tie the ends together to make a loop for hanging the feeder.

Step 4. Tape the holes shut with a small piece of duct tape to keep the food dry.

Step 5. Use a drill with a ⁵⁄₁₆-inch twist bit to make two sets of holes on opposite sides of the bottle just below the point where the bottle begins to taper toward the neck. Poke an unsharpened pencil through each pair of holes.

Step 6. For a sunflower seed feeder, use a ⁵⁄₁₆-inch bit to drill

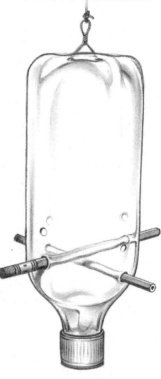

holes about 1 ½ inches above each end of the pencil perch. For nyjer seed, the openings should be ¼ × ⅛-inch slots; use a razor blade to carefully cut the slots.

Step 7. Fill the bottle with seeds and screw the cap on.

Step 8. Turn the feeder over and hang it from the loop.

MILK CARTON HOPPER FEEDER

Step 1. Wash an empty half-gallon milk carton well with soapy water and allow it to dry completely.

Step 2. Close the top of the carton and tape it shut with masking tape or duct tape.

Step 3. Use a sharp pencil to poke a hole through the center of the sealed top edge of the carton.

Step 4. Cut rectangular flaps on opposite sides of the carton, starting 2 inches from the bottom of the carton. The flaps should be about 3 inches wide and 5 inches high.

Step 5. Hold one flap open and poke a small hole about ½ inch from the edge of the flap. Repeat this with the other flap.

Step 6. Thread one end of a 2-foot piece of string through the hole in one flap and knot it in place. Thread the string through the hole in the top edge of the carton, drawing the flap open and up as

you go, until the open flap is at a right angle to the carton.

Step 7. Thread the end of the string through the other flap and tighten it until that flap is also at a right angle to the carton, then tie off the string. (The flaps will act like awnings to keep rain out of the feeder.)

Step 8. Below each flap, centered and flush with the bottom of the carton, poke two facing holes big enough for a pencil.

Step 9. Push an unsharpened pencil through the two holes. This will serve as a perch.

Step 10. Use the sharp pencil to punch several tiny holes in the bottom of the carton for drainage.

Step 11. Pour seeds into the bottom of the feeder, to about ½ inch below the open flaps.

Step 12. Thread a long piece of string through the hole in the top edge of the carton and knot it.

HELPFUL HINTS

If you plan to use the milk carton feeder as a test for a feeder that will rest on a flat surface, omit the perch and the hanging apparatus. Instead, when you set out the feeder, put a few lead sinkers in it along with the birdseed. The heavy weights will prevent the feeder from tipping or blowing away.

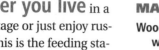
Woodland-Look Feeding Station

Whether you live in a rustic cottage or just enjoy rustic style, this is the feeding station for you. Nature provides many of the basic building materials, including logs, vines, and even a pile of brush. With just a few tools and plenty of food, you can create a primitive feeding station that birds will love.

The brush pile will attract many tiny creatures and feathered friends scouting for bugs and cover. Toss a few sunflower seedheads under the brush, and you'll have fun watching the songbirds and squirrels wrangle over the discovery.

Birds also will visit the dust bath regularly once they realize that it is near food. Quail, pheasants, sparrows, and kinglets might come to bathe.

HELPFUL HINTS

If you don't have a woodstove or wood-burning fireplace, seek out a friend who does and ask if you can have a can of ashes for the dust bath. Or check with a local campground, barbecue restaurant, or pottery supply store.

MATERIALS

Wooden 4 × 4 post, metal post, or wrought-iron shepherd's crook

Pole-mounted hopper feeder

Three 6-penny nails or sturdy twine

Smooth branch with several forks, at least 3 feet long and about 1¼ inches in diameter at the base

Grapevine or other natural-looking feeder (see "Grapevine Wreath Feeder" on page 41)

Cup hook

Wire cage suet feeder

Flat rock

16-inch-diameter clay plant saucer

Brush

Several sunflower heads

Shovel or tiller

Rocks

Sand

Sifted ash

Brush pile

Dust bath

Step 1. Mark off an area that includes a tree or shrub (for shelter and a windbreak) and at least 2 square yards of level, open ground.

Step 2. Set up the post. (For directions for setting posts, see pages 207 through 212.)

Step 3. Mount the hopper feeder on the post.

Step 4. Use the nails or twine to attach the branch to the feeder. This will provide extra perching spots for birds awaiting their turn at the feeders.

Step 5. Hang the grapevine feeder from the branch.

Step 6. Mount a cup hook on the bottom of the hopper feeder and hang the suet feeder from the hook.

Step 7. Out of range of the feeder's spill area but not more than a few feet to the side, set the flat rock on the ground and put the saucer on top.

Step 8. Also beyond the spill area, layer brush lattice style to form a pile about 3 feet tall. Leave enough space so that birds can hop around inside the brush pile, but not enough so that a cat could crawl in. Also discourage feline predators by including some thorny brush, such as holly or wild blackberry. Toss a few sunflower heads under the brush.

Step 9. In a spot beyond the spill area, preferably in full sun, dig a 1-yard-square patch 6 inches deep.

Step 10. Make a rock border around the shallow pit.

Step 11. Mix equal amounts of displaced soil, sand, and sifted ash. Fill the pit to within 1 inch of the top of the rock border with the mixture.

Step 12. Fill the feeders with the appropriate foods. Fill the saucer with water.

continued from page 111

lovers such as robins, leave some lawn unmowed and some fallen leaves unraked.

If you like your lawn well manicured, consider creating a feeding station that serves only hulled seeds, nuts, and nectar and dressing the area below feeders with a thick layer of wood chips. That way, you won't have to fuss with as many hulls and the bird droppings won't be as evident.

Stick to Your Budget

Over time, stocking several feeders can run up a hefty bill for birdseed and treats. Some birds prefer relatively expensive black oil sunflower seed; others, such as goldfinches, which dine almost exclusively on nyjer, have even more expensive tastes. When you're planning your station, you'll need to set a budget and pick feeder types that will help you stick to it.

If you like the songbirds that are drawn to sunflower seeds, for example, choose a hopper feeder or tube feeder enclosed by a wire cage to stop jays, grackles, and pigeons from downing the whole lot in one sitting. And if hulled sunflower seed or nyjer are cost prohibitive, focus on birds that will happily scarf hulled oats or white millet at an ordinary tray feeder, such as cowbirds or song sparrows. The same is true of woodpecker feeders. It's better to create a station that incorporates a simple homemade feeder that you can restock with peanut butter if you can't afford the costly commercial woodpecker mixes that fit into a commercial wire cage suet feeder. If you're on a tight budget—now or permanently—consider the feeders for birds that favor bread crumbs and generic seed mixes, including mockingbirds, starlings, dark-eyed juncos, and grackles.

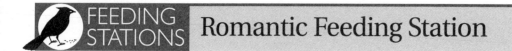

Cascades of pink blooms; soft scents wafting on the summer air. Use your most romantic gardening notions to create an elegant al fresco dining area, with roses and lavender to draw bugs and birds, and vintage touches to make the most down-to-earth bird foods seem gourmet.

Set up this station in an area that you can see from the deck or a convenient window, or that is about 10 feet away from an outdoor seating arrangement (if you plan to stock the station only during warmer months). If possible, place the station along a footpath. The rose-bushes and lattice will provide most of the necessary shelter.

MATERIALS

Two 10-foot-long 4 × 4s, painted white

4 × 8-foot piece of lattice, painted white

2 climbing or shrub roses (Choose a type or cultivar adapted to your growing conditions. Pink or white blossoms are particularly nice for this project.)

2 vintage towel hooks or plant hooks and mounting hardware

Decorative glass hummingbird feeder

White thistle sock

Wide cloth ribbon, preferably pink

Soil-based potting mix

2 or 3 potted lavender plants

Vintage planter, wrought iron or faux marble

Vintage pedestal sink or old-fashioned white birdbath

Small bistro-style or rectangular glass-top patio table

Ceramic glue

2 china teacups and saucers (Shop for these at flea markets.)

Adhesive-backed Velcro strips or dots

Shepherd's crook

Hanging basket planted with strawberries (see "Hanging Strawberry Basket" on page 96)

Step 1. Along one edge of your chosen site, set the 4 × 4s in place and mount the lattice on the posts. Set the posts 2 feet deep. (For directions, see "Wooden Post Mount" on page 209.)

Step 2. Plant the roses in front of the lattice.

Step 3. Install the hooks toward the top third of the lattice, one on each side.

Step 4. Hang the hummingbird feeder from one hook.

Step 5. Tie the thistle sock closed with the ribbon, leaving a loop available for hanging the sock. Hang the sock from the other hook.

Step 6. Use the potting mix to plant the lavender in the planter, spacing the plants at least 18 inches apart. Set the planter to the right of the roses.

Step 7. Set the pedestal sink or birdbath in front of the roses and fill it with water.

Step 8. Position the table near the lattice and birdbath.

Step 9. Use the ceramic glue to attach the teacups to the saucers and allow the glue to dry.

Step 10. Turn the saucers upside down (with the cup attached) and attach several 1-inch pieces of Velcro to the bottom of each saucer. Stick the corresponding Velcro

pieces to the top of the patio table and attach the saucers to the table.

Step 11. Fill the cups with safflower seeds and millet, or with suet and/or your choice of other bird foods.

Step 12. Insert the shepherd's crook into the ground to the right of the roses and hang the strawberry basket from it.

HELPFUL HINTS

Most songbirds don't particularly like lavender, but butterflies, bees, and moths all adore this nectar-rich, fragrant herb. And where insects go, songbirds follow! Lavender likes full, hot sun and demands excellent drainage.

Roses provide hips that emerge in late summer and attract fruit-eating birds, including bluebirds, blue jays, chickadees, catbirds, cedar waxwings, flickers, and robins. Aphids, which birds love, also feast on roses, and the dense, thorny branches of wild roses provide cover and nest sites for thicket birds such as brown thrashers. Roses are sun lovers and will tolerate dry to moist soil. If you already have established shrub or climbing roses in your yard, you have the option of using them as the backdrop for this feeding station rather than planting new ones.

MAINTAINING YOUR FEEDING STATION

Once the birds discover your feeding station, they'll be active there daily. In peak times, you may need to fill feeders nearly every day. Throughout the year, even if traffic is low, check your feeding station at least once a week to see if any feeders need cleaning or refilling. Also check the ground below the feeders to see whether spilled seeds are accumulating.

Keeping It Clean

Some birds prefer to forage on the ground, making it tempting to toss seeds or kitchen leftovers such as stale pancakes on the ground, particularly when it's snowy or icy cold outside. Resist this temptation. Although some seeds and other bird foods will inevitably end up on the ground, you want to minimize the problem, not add to it. Foods that sit on the ground for even a day are susceptible to contamination by dampness, mold, bacteria, and animal droppings.

One way to deal with debris below feeders is to spread a 3-inch layer of wood chips or bark mulch on the ground. The mulch will disguise hulls and bird droppings and also allow ground-feeding birds such as doves and juncos to pick through the mulch for leftover morsels. Turn the top layer of mulch with a garden hoe or rake once a month or so to bury the hulls and spruce up the area.

Cleaning Feeders

Feeders should be cleaned about once a month, or whenever you see moldy, damp, or bad seeds in them.

Feeders made of plastic, ceramic, or glass are easy to clean. Wash them in a bucket of hot soapy water fortified with a capful of chlorine bleach, or run them through the dishwasher (by themselves, not with a load of dishes). Wash wooden feeders by hand, and substitute ¼ cup of vinegar for the bleach so that the wood won't fade. When you wash feeders by hand, be sure to rinse them thoroughly afterward.

If you find dead birds near your feeding station, stop putting out food for a few days and thoroughly clean all your feeders. The birds may be victims of a fungal disease spread through moldy seeds or infected droppings. Rake up the debris under the feeders, bury it, and rinse the rake tines with a solution of one part bleach and nine parts boiling water.

Weathering the Seasons

In a birder's garden, you have unique opportunities both to attract new birds and to assist birds as one season follows another. In a typical four-season region, the most important time to offer supplemental food is in cold weather, when birds' other options—such as live insects, fresh berries, and foraged seeds—are depleted or exhausted.

However, other seasons also present some prime feeding opportunities. In the fall and spring, for example, when certain species migrate, you may be able to attract new varieties to your yard, especially if you tailor your feeder offerings to match the transients' tastes. Birds that ordinarily migrate but decide to stay in your area because it's an unusually mild winter also may require special foods and will flock to your yard if you offer them. Also in the spring, when birds are feeding their young, they have a particular need for high-protein offerings for themselves and their offspring.

Winter Checklist

When winter arrives, keep these items in mind as you maintain your feeding station.

Supply grit. In snowy climates, you may see flocks of birds along the side of the road after the snowplows have passed. They're after the grit. With no teeth, birds require dirt, sand, and pebbles to help grind their food. Adding grit to your feeder is helpful year-round, but particularly in the winter, since natural sources may be covered with snow. (For suggestions on how to supply grit, see page 39.)

Heat the water. If your feeding station includes a water source, don't neglect it during the winter. Although it's not that important for birds to bathe during the cold months, they still need drinking water. See page 182 for ideas on how to keep birdbaths from freezing during the cold months.

Shelter ground feeders. If you have lots of snow in your area, consider moving ground-level feeders, which birds such as juncos and grouse prefer, under some sort of cover, so that the food won't end up covered with snow. A flat rock set under some low-growing evergreen branches is ideal. Or make a lean-to shelter from a piece of plywood propped up with two notched 1-foot pieces of 1-by-2. You won't be able to see birds eating at these feeders unless you have good binoculars, but they'll keep reporting to your station when the snow's off the ground and you can start feeding them in plain view again.

Serve some hulled seeds. Many of the birds that depend on insects as food, including warblers and flycatchers, must migrate south for the winter to find bugs. Now and again, unusually mild winter weather lures such birds, including northern flickers, Carolina wrens, and pine or yellow-rumped warblers, to stay in the North for the winter. When temperatures sink, they need food, but they don't have the right type of beak for cracking seed shells. That's the time to offer a hopper or tray feeder filled with hulled sunflower seeds and mixed nuts.

You can also offset the wintertime absence of insects by offering mealworms. Small overwintering songbirds such as chickadees and nuthatches will appreciate them, too. (If you want to try raising mealworms to serve the birds, see page 111.)

Spring Checklist

Birds' needs change with the arrival of spring. Migratory birds are passing through, and others are choosing nest sites and laying eggs.

Stock more millet. Birds that eat small seeds, such as indigo buntings, finches, and pine siskins, are much more likely to stop at your feeding station in early spring, so be sure to stock plenty of millet for them in a tray or hopper feeder. You can even give your budget a break and put out more millet in place of black oil sunflower seed.

Offer mealworms for bluebirds. If you're trying to encourage bluebirds to visit your feeders, offer mealworms during bluebird nesting and nestling season. You can put out a special mealworm
continued on page 121

Evergreen Christmas Treat Station

If you're lucky enough to have an evergreen shrub or small tree planted where you can see it from a window, turn it into a Christmas tree for the birds. Of course, you can't wait until December and expect the birds to flock to the tree, so make it a year-round site for a tube feeder. That way, chickadees, cardinals, woodpeckers, finches, and nuthatches will already know where it is. As the winter holiday draws near, turn the tree into a full-fledged feeding station for those same birds by adding a medley of treats.

MATERIALS

Strings of fresh cranberries or peanuts in the shell

Pinecone treats, enough to space them about 3 feet apart all around the tree (see "Simple Pinecone Treats" on page 79)

Inexpensive bright metallic Christmas balls, enough to space them about 1 foot apart all around the tree

Unrendered beef suet

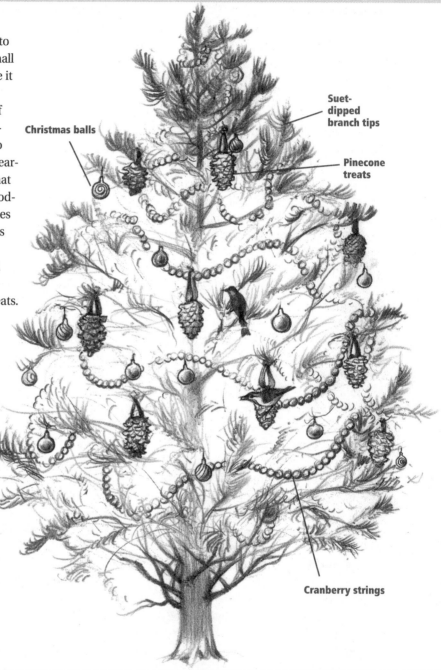

Christmas balls

Suet-dipped branch tips

Pinecone treats

Cranberry strings

Step 1. Drape the treat strings around the tree. Unless you already have lots of established fruit eaters in the area, the cranberries may prove to be strictly decorative, but you can add them to your compost pile come New Year's.

Step 2. Attach the pinecone treats to the tree.

Step 3. Hang the metallic balls, which should reflect the sun and catch birds' attention.

Step 4. Melt the beef suet in a small saucepan on the stove.

Step 5. Wearing oven mitts or heavy gloves, carry the pan outdoors to the tree and carefully dip some of the branch tips into the suet. The suet will harden in the cold, and visiting nuthatches and chickadees will cling to the ends of the flexible branches to eat it.

An Extra Touch

Add even more holiday flair to your Christmas tree by using bright holiday ribbon instead of wire to attach your pinecone treats to the tree. When you prepare the treats, don't wrap the pinecones with wire. Instead, cut a 1-foot length of ribbon for each pinecone. Then mix ¼ cup light corn syrup and 1 cup granulated sugar in a small saucepan and bring it to a boil. Boil the mixture until a candy thermometer registers between 290°F and 310°F, or until ½ teaspoon of the mixture drizzled in very cold water produces a brittle strand.

Put a drop of the syrup in the center of the flat end of each pinecone treat and attach one end of a piece of ribbon to each drop of syrup. The syrup will dry as a bird-friendly glue that will cement the ribbon to the pinecone. To hang the pinecones, simply tie each ribbon to a branch.

continued from page 119
feeder or simply serve mealworms in an empty tuna can nailed to your tray feeder. Migrating tanagers, thrushes, and other insect eaters also may enjoy a mealworm meal.

Provide oranges for orioles. Most species of orioles overwinter far south of the United States, but they travel north for nesting season. If you hope to spot orioles at your feeding station, provide orange halves on platform feeders or on homemade fruit feeders as they arrive. Some orioles seem interested in oranges only at that time and soon switch to insects, but others will go for the oranges throughout the spring breeding season.

Set out shells. Female birds that are preparing to lay their eggs need extra calcium. Finely crushed eggshells or oyster shells (put the shells in a brown paper bag and run over them with the car!) are perfect supplements. Mix the shells with sunflower seeds in a tray or hopper feeder, or hang a shallow tray feeder filled with crushed shells from a hook fastened to the bottom of a popular tube or hopper feeder.

Secure some emergency rations.
Keep an extra stock of sunflower seed,
nyjer, and peanut butter on hand just in
case the weather reverts to a hard freeze
or snowstorm, catching migrating birds
off guard. Purple martins and bluebirds
are particularly hard-hit by cold snaps, so
make sure you have mealworms available for them.

Summer Checklist

Traffic at your feeding station may
slow in the summer as birds turn to the
natural food supplies in your gardens
and around your yard as their major food
source But don't abandon your feeding
station routine. If you keep it stocked,
you may enjoy a view of nestlings just
setting out on their own, as well as the
usual crowd of backyard birds.

Slow down. Load less food into all
your feeders, or switch to smaller or
fewer feeders. That way, seed won't go to
waste—or be eaten by undesirables such
as squirrels and other rodents.

Plant sunflowers. Supplement the
seed supply from your feeders by planting a patch of sunflowers in a sunny spot.
(For growing sunflowers for the birds, see
"Sized-to-Fit Sunflower Plantation" on
page 62.)

Tempt tanagers and company. Although natural food is abundant in the
summer, parent birds still appreciate a
high-protein diet. Fill a log feeder or a
muffin tin with a mixture of one part
peanut butter, one part vegetable shortening, four parts cornmeal, and one part
flour. This sticky mixture will attract lots
of birds that usually focus on insects, including tanagers, thrushes, and warblers.

Switch suet. When temperatures rise,
raw fat can melt and become rancid. It's
safer to use commercially rendered suet
cakes in the summer, because the rendering process kills bacteria. Or switch to
serving suet in jar lids—just a couple of
tablespoons at a time. Nail a lid to a tray
or platform feeder, and the birds will have
it empty before the fat begins to drip.

Add a nectar feeder. Hummingbirds
and several other types of birds will be
regular customers at a nectar feeder. If
you've already put out a hummingbird
feeder in the spring, consider adding a
larger nectar feeder with a perch for orioles and maybe even "sweet-beaked"
woodpeckers.

Clean nectar feeders often. Sugar
water ferments fast in the hot summer
months, so hummingbird feeders need a
weekly cleaning.

Fall Checklist

Provide millet. As you did during the
spring, offer plenty of millet—now for
sparrows, which move through in droves
in the autumn, winging their way to their
southern wintering grounds. Juncos follow close on their tails. Both birds like
white proso millet in open-tray feeders
and will feed on spilled seeds as well.

Keep up with hummers. Hummingbirds need lots of sugary fuel before their
grueling trip south, so keep the nectar
feeders stocked as long as hummers continue to visit.

COPING WITH UNINVITED GUESTS

When you set out tempting foods in your
yard, it's inevitable that some creatures

you didn't intend to feed will show up to share the bounty, whether it's pesky starlings, irrepressible squirrels, or predatory hawks. Although you can do some things to discourage uninvited animal guests, there are no foolproof solutions. It's best to keep a philosophical attitude. After all, these critters are part of Mother Nature's scheme, too. Read on for some tactics to discourage unwanted takers at your feeding stations.

Deterring Pest Birds

Sometimes you just can't welcome birds of every feather at your feeders. Pest birds include grackles, starlings, blackbirds, and pigeons. Not only do they deplete the food at your stations, but they may run off songbirds as well. Plus, when pest birds find a ready food supply, they're more likely to stay in the area to nest. The following strategies may help in discouraging pest birds.

Try safflower seed. Pest birds often won't eat it, but chickadees, titmice, and cardinals will.

Switch to a nyjer feeder. Buy either a tube feeder with adjustable holes and a tray underneath or a finch feeder that offers larger perches for slightly bigger birds. The holes will be too small to give pest birds access (they're not that fond of nyjer anyhow), but finches, chickadees, juncos, and song sparrows will still come around.

Change your seed offerings. Offer black oil sunflower seed only in a tube feeder enclosed in a wire cage. If you can't bear to deprive the big birds entirely, at least put most of your rations in a selective feeder. The cage openings

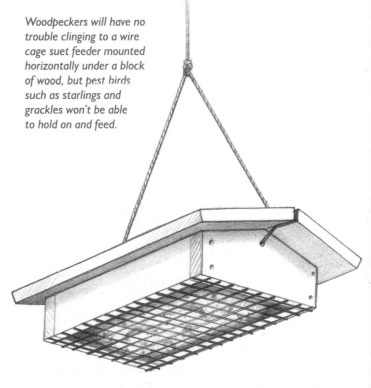

Woodpeckers will have no trouble clinging to a wire cage suet feeder mounted horizontally under a block of wood, but pest birds such as starlings and grackles won't be able to hold on and feed.

should allow chickadees and other small birds to come and go freely, but not the bigger birds. Be sure there's enough space between the cage walls and the feeder tube to keep the seeds out of reach, as grackles and starlings may land on these feeders and poke their heads through the bars of the cage.

Be protective about suet. Set out suet cakes in a wire cage suet feeder enclosed in a larger wire cage with openings too small for grackles. Or consider a suet feeder with a wooden top and wire mesh below. Desirable birds such as chickadees and woodpeckers will either hover beneath it or cling to the underside of the holder—something grackles, starlings, and blackbirds can't do.

Double up on feeders. If you simply can't bear to turn away any bird, stock a feeder just for the pest birds. Fill it with a seed mix they find appealing.

Solving Squabbles with Squirrels

If squirrels live in your neighborhood, you can count on them visiting your feeding station, possibly sticking around until they've eaten all the food in sight—and the feeders to boot. It's too much to expect a squirrel-free zone, but there are ways to minimize their presence. Try these strategies for keeping squirrels away from the goodies meant for songbirds.

Give them a station of their own. Aside from their hearty appetites, squirrels are unpleasant because of their tendency to chase away songbirds. Use this territorial nature to your advantage! Weeks before you set out a feeding station for birds, pick a place a few yards away from your feeding station site and set up a feeding area that will appeal to squirrels. Stock it with corn, acorns, and cracked corn (but don't give them a taste for black oil sunflower seed). As long as you keep it stocked, they're less likely to forage at the bird-feeding station you set up later. (There is a potential downside to this strategy, as we will explain on page 128.)

Be selective about seeds. If you opt to provide millet, safflower, and nyjer exclusively, you won't get much interference from squirrels.

Serve suet unadorned. To keep squirrels out of the suet, choose the plain stuff—no berries or bits of seeds. Or, in place of ordinary suet feeders, place suet cakes in wire peanut feeders (the ones designed for shelled nuts). The holes in these feeders are too small for squirrel "hands" and mouths, but large enough for most beaks.

Mount a feeder on a metal pole. Never underestimate a squirrel's physical capabilities. Squirrels can jump 5 feet in the air from the ground—straight up. Perched on a tree trunk, most squirrels can spring laterally about 10 feet. If they're jumping from a branch above a feeder, make that about 12 feet. If you're setting up a feeder that includes any squirrel-enticing foods, locate the feeder at least 12 feet below the nearest overhanging tree branch and 6 feet off the ground, mounted on a 3-inch-diameter metal pole. And be careful where you place the birdbath! It can be a favorite launching pad for squirrels. (For other squirrel-proof mounting options, see the pole-blocking projects on page 239.)

continued on page 128

✔ *For the Record*

Controversial Cayenne

One popular recommendation for foiling birdseed-eating squirrels is to lace the seed with cayenne pepper. Sources say that it's quite effective and claim that the substance doesn't harm birds or deter them from eating.

However, using cayenne as a squirrel deterrent is now being called into question. Although squirrels are a nuisance, some people say that it's cruel to tempt them with birdseed and then punish them with cayenne. (How would you like an unexpected mouthful of the hot stuff mixed into *your* dinner?) And some ornithologists point out that there's no proof that ingesting cayenne, especially over the long term, has no negative effects on birds.

Homemade Squirrel Baffles

A squirrel baffle is intended to thwart a squirrel from navigating up a feeder pole or down a feeder hanger (chain, fishing line, clothesline, or extra-strength wire) to reach the food. A motto for baffles: Try anything. Most squirrels will figure it out eventually, but it's a lot of fun watching them try to crack the code. The important thing is that the baffle rest between the bird food and anything the squirrel can climb. For extra protection, use two baffle systems, one atop the other.

■ **PVC spinners.** For feeders hung clothesline style, string the clothesline with 3-inch sections of PVC (polyvinyl chloride) pipe. Then hang the feeder from the clothesline using string, a bent wire coat hanger, or some other type of hanger. When the squirrel tries to walk across the clothesline to reach the feeder, the pipe pieces will spin, and the squirrel will roll with them—right to the ground.

■ **Hair curler hang-ups.** Alternatively, you can thread smooth plastic hair curlers along the length of the clothesline instead of PVC pipe.

■ **LP blockades.** To keep a squirrel from shinnying down the twine on which a feeder is suspended, block the way with old vinyl LPs. Space the LPs a few inches apart along the twine, knotting the twine on each side of the hole in the LPs to hold them in place. In most cases, squirrels can't reach around multiple LPs to get to a feeder (although some highly acrobatic squirrels will find a way). This baffle will also protect tray feeders from snow and rain. This won't work with CDs: The squirrel will just hang on to one of the CDs with one "hand" and use the other to swing and grab the feeder.

For more ideas, check out the suggestions for homemade baffles in "Collar Those Criminals" on page 238.

Easy Squirrel Feeders

A feeding station of their own may distract squirrels from raiding your bird feeders—and at the very least provide the squirrels with new playground equipment where their antics will amuse and amaze you. Locate these feeders, in combination or individually, at least 30 feet from the nearest bird-feeding station.

Keep in mind that squirrels are voracious predators of eggs and nestlings. The better fed the squirrels around your yard are, the more young they may produce, thus posing a bigger threat to songbirds. You may want to take it easy on refilling the food supply at your squirrel feeders.

MATERIALS

Wooden half barrel (optional)
Four 12-penny finish nails
Hammer
16-penny nail
Scrap of 1 × 4
3 ears of field corn
Suet-seed cake
Wire cage suet feeder

STUMP THAT SQUIRREL (NOT!) FEEDER

Step 1. Scout out a tree stump in your yard that is visible from your window or deck. If your yard has no suitable stumps, place an upended wooden half barrel in an easily viewed spot instead.

Step 2. Hammer three of the 12-penny nails into the side of the stump or barrel, at least 10 inches above ground level and about 4 inches apart.

Step 3. Hammer the remaining 12-penny nail into the stump 2 inches below the rim and laterally separate from the other three nails by at least 10 inches.

Step 4. Hammer the 16-penny nail through the 1 × 4. Set the 1 × 4 on a flat surface. One by one, push each ear of corn onto the nail, then remove it. This creates a hole in the cob so that you can easily mount the cobs on the nails on the stump.

Step 5. Push an ear of corn onto each of the first three nails that you hammered into the stump.

Step 6. Place the suet-seed cake inside the suet feeder and hang it from the fourth nail.

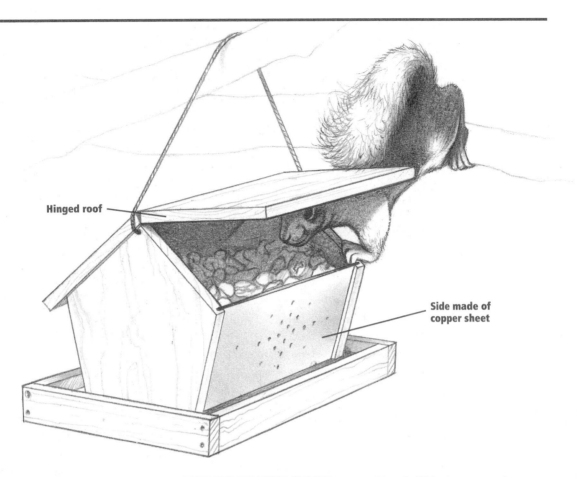

Hinged roof

Side made of copper sheet

MATERIALS

Small, commercially made wooden hopper-type feeder that has a tray, a hinged roof, and clear plastic, removable sides

2 heavyweight 8½ × 11-inch sheets of craft copper, such as Magic Metal

Tin snips

Safety glasses

Unshelled peanuts, acorns, or large-nugget dog food

THROUGH-THE-ROOF NUT FEEDER

Step 1. Remove the plastic sides from the feeder.

Step 2. Using one of the plastic sides as a template, cut new sides for the feeder from the copper sheets, using the tin snips and wearing safety glasses while you work. (Squirrels can't chew through copper.) If you want to get fancy, you can buy inexpensive tools and decorate the copper with holes or lines.

Step 3. Slide the copper sheets into place on the feeder, pushing them flush to the bottom so that no food can escape into the tray.

Step 4. Fill the feeder with the nuts, placing just a few pieces in the tray to attract squirrels. Hang the feeder from a visible tree or post, then watch the fun as the squirrels discover how to open the hinged roof to collect their prizes.

continued from page 124

Hang it with care. If you must hang a feeder from a tree branch or near trees, select a hopper feeder that's designed with a spring-loaded perch that will trip under the weight of a squirrel, closing a door to the seed supply. Or select a tube protected with metal mesh that has holes large enough to let in songbirds but too small for a squirrel to squeeze through. Note that a determined squirrel can eventually chew through any so-called squirrel-proof feeder made of plastic.

Out with Other Pests

Sometimes even rather large wildlife will think that the birdseed you've put out is intended for them, not your beloved songbirds. Follow these tips if the pests consuming your birdseed are in a higher weight class than squirrels.

Deer

In areas with a large deer population, these four-footers may come to feast on the fruit, nuts, or even seeds at your feeding station. To deter them, take a tip from orchard owners: Hang bars of soap—the stronger smelling the better—from branches of the trees and shrubs you are trying to reserve for other members of the wildlife community. With the paper on (to make it last longer in the rain), drill a hole through the bar of soap, insert a piece of twine, and hang it like a Christmas tree ornament.

Cats

Cats aren't after the birdseed, of course, but they are after the birds. Domestic cats are one of songbirds' worst enemies, in part because naive owners believe that well-fed pets won't hunt. That's just not true. Cats are biologically programmed to stalk almost anything that flies or crawls. So aside from keeping your own cats inside, you can hang or mount feeders out of range of soft-textured shrubs or dense flowerbeds, which are places where feline hunters could hide. If you want to plant a groundcover beneath a birdbath or feeder, make it a thorny one, such as barberry or holly, or something very low growing, such as periwinkle.

Hawks

If you've solved the cat problem in your neighborhood but still discover a pile of feathers near your feeder, you'll know there's a hungry hawk or falcon perched nearby. Cooper's hawks, sharp-shinned hawks, merlins, and kestrels are attracted to the heavy concentration of small birds at feeders, particularly in the winter. It's best to resign yourself to this circle of life playing out at your feeders. Just be sure that your feeding station is positioned close enough to some protective cover so that your birds at least have the hope of escape. You can also feed your birds early in the morning, and only as much as they'll eat at that time. Ordinarily, hawks and falcons don't hunt until later in the morning or early in the evening. The other positive news: Hawks and falcons are so territorial that you're unlikely to tangle with more than one monogamous pair.

If you're strongly opposed to letting a hawk hunt around your feeding station, your only option is to stop putting out food. Ordinarily, after a few days to a
continued on page 132

Cat-Proof Feeding Station

Pyracantha is an evergreen shrub with clusters of white blossoms and bountiful red or orange berries that is also known by a more descriptive common name: firethorn. The fierce thorns of this tall, sprawling shrub can cause a painful burning sensation in humans. Fortunately for bird lovers, cats find pyracantha just as unpleasant as we do. They can't climb its branches without getting their tender paw pads poked, and they can't sneak underneath because it sprawls to ground level.

If felines are a constant problem in your yard, a protective hedge of potted pyracanthas is worth a try. If a cat should enter the circle of pyracanthas, it will be in full view of any birds that visit the feeder. Most cats will soon realize that the pickings are no longer easy at this bird hangout, and they'll seek happier hunting grounds elsewhere.

Step 1. Set up a small feeding station, allowing an open area about 5 feet wide all around the station.

Step 2. Measure the circumference of the area around the station.

Step 3. Go to a local garden center or nursery and select enough potted pyracantha plants to encircle the feeding station, leaving one opening wide enough for you to pass through (so you'll be able to visit the feeders to maintain them). Choose plants that are already sprawling over the sides of their containers.

Step 4. Set out the shrubs in a circle around the feeding station. (Wear sturdy leather gloves, long pants, and a long-sleeved shirt whenever you handle the containers.) Be sure that the thorny branches present an impenetrable barrier, with no room for a cat to hide.

Although it takes time, birds will adjust to coming right to a window of your home to feed. Strategically placed, a window feeding station will provide you and your cat with hours of amusement. Just be sure to pick a window that's on the first floor or looks over a deck, that's near a sheltering tree or bush, and that has strong or full sun if possible. Inside, you'll want a wide windowsill or room for a stool or armchair for your cat's comfort.

Don't fret that your cat will scare the birds. It's likely that he'll crouch quietly for hours to watch them and they'll never know he's there. Or he'll try to pounce once, but he'll be foiled by the windowpane and learn that it's futile. The birds will scatter for a few minutes, but they'll return soon to continue enjoying the treats.

Feeders mounted on windows do not encourage birds to fly into the glass. Birds generally do that because they see a reflection in the glass. Window feeders and decals actually help to break up the reflection.

MATERIALS

2 or 3 holly bushes (or creeping grape holly, if you live in the Northwest)

Metal shelf bracket with mounting hardware

Squirrel-proof tube feeder

Lightweight metal chain or flexible wire

Nyjer feeder with top hanging mount

Windowsill feeder (see "Clear-View Windowsill Feeder" on page 50)

Plastic or metal soap dish with suction cup mounts

Pedestal birdbath

Removable decals (optional)

Step 1. Plant the holly bushes beneath the window where you plan to set up this feeding station (unless the area is already planted).

Step 2. Mount the shelf bracket on the exterior of your house beside the window frame, just below the top edge of the frame.

Step 3. Hang the tube feeder from the bracket using the chain.

Step 4. Hang the nyjer feeder from the bracket (it can hold both feeders easily).

Step 5. Attach the windowsill feeder to the windowpane.

Step 6. Attach the soap dish to the windowpane, a few inches to the right or left of the windowsill feeder.

Step 7. Put the birdbath no more than 10 feet away from the window, off to the side and, if possible, within range of a sheltering tree or bush. If the birdbath isn't tall enough that you (or your cat) can see the birds, put the pedestal on top of two cinder blocks to raise it into window view. (Even if the birdbath isn't visible from your window, it does act to draw more birds, which may then come to the window to feed.)

Step 8. If you like, arrange some decals on the window in an eye-pleasing way so that they will break up reflections but not block your view.

Win Them Over to the Window

Follow these tips to increase your odds of attracting birds to your window feeding station.

■ Set up your feeding station only after some birds are already frequenting other feeders in your yard.

■ Don't place the station near bountiful supplies of popular seeds, such as black oil sunflower.

■ Install your station when fresh foods such as insects and berries are in low supply. Like kids, birds are much more likely to try something new when they're hungry.

■ Serve the most desirable treats at your window station.

■ If birds scatter for hours whenever they see movement inside your house, try hanging sheer curtains on the window. Or invest in a commercial windowsill feeder backed by a two-way mirror that prevents the birds from seeing you (or your cat). Usually, though, birds will scatter for only a few minutes and then return when they think it's safe—just as they might if you walked among them outdoors.

■ If fruit eaters such as catbirds or mockingbirds are visiting feeders in your yard, draw them to the window by mixing golden raisins with other soft foods they prefer, such as chopped suet or bread crumbs, set in the soap dish. Jays and Carolina wrens also may come to sample the mixture.

■ If squirrels are a problem around your yard, use only safflower seed (which squirrels don't like) in your window feeders. Only a few types of birds like safflower seed, so there won't be as wide a variety of visitors for you to watch. But if you put out seeds that squirrels like, they will probably monopolize the feeder and keep all birds away.

continued from page 128

week with no feeders—and thus no easy catches—a hawk will lose interest, at least temporarily.

Don't put out poisons or try to trap hawks, since federal law protects all birds of prey, including eagles, owls, and hawks.

Raccoons

Adult raccoons simply adore corn and suet—but will settle for sunflower seeds, fruit, and soft foods. You can go one of two ways with these masked bandits: try to discourage them or give them a food source of their own. One thing in your favor is that although raccoons are great climbers, they're heavy, so you can often lick them by hanging feeders from wire or string too thin for a raccoon to walk across.

For pole-mounted feeders, many of the baffles that work for squirrels will foil raccoons, too, but keep in mind that their reach can be up to 10 inches. That means wire cages must be wider to keep raccoons from sticking an arm in and helping themselves. Raccoons are strong and determined, so don't put plastic feeders where they can reach and destroy them. Instead, use wooden feeders or the wrought-iron feeders sold to deter bears.

If you decide to feed raccoons at a site away from your bird-feeding station, put out the food (such as corn, apples, or bread scraps) in a tray or stump feeder an hour or so before dark.

Bears

There's nothing like a big, hungry bear to leave your feeders in shambles. Preventive medicine works best if you live in bear country. Hang—don't mount—feeders, particularly feeders for nectar, nuts, fruit, or berries. That way, you can take the feeders in at night in the spring, when bear activity (and appetites) peaks. Also consider heavy-duty wrought-iron feeders sold especially to survive bear raids. (For suppliers, see "Resources for Backyard Birders and Gardeners" on page 292.)

CHAPTER 5

Creating Backyard Bird Habitats

Spend an hour or two outdoors watching birds in their natural surroundings, and you'll notice that different birds prefer different settings. Certain birds spend most of their time in shady woodlands, while others are partial to sunny, grassy areas. Some species are drawn to wet places, and others spend most of the daylight hours ranging across the sky. Every kind of habitat appeals to some species, which is encouraging for us gardeners. We envision our yards brimming with bird life—bright orioles flashing to and fro, vivid goldfinches swaying on the grasses, and cardinals raising babies in the rosebushes. In this chapter, you'll find out how to make those visions a reality.

EDUCATED EXPECTATIONS

Creating bird habitats in your yard won't magically lure in new and unusual species of birds. As you learned in chapter 1, some birds are just too wary of people to take up residence in a typical urban or suburban backyard. But many species of beautiful songbirds have adapted well to living near humans, and the more you do to make your yard a welcoming place for these birds, the more willing they'll be to linger longer on your property.

Birds travel through large territories every day—several blocks or even half the town, depending on the species. Even that faithful robin nesting by the front door is fickle: It may leave your yard for part of every day to check out the worms in your neighbor's yard. Other birds, such as indigo buntings and many native sparrows, can't be considered true backyard birds because they usually nest in wild places, visiting backyards only for the tempting array of feeders.

A Measure of Success

Instead of wishing for unlikely rare birds in your yard, consider your habitat projects a way to make the typical backyard species feel more at home around your place. When you make habitat improvements, you can expect that both resident backyard birds and transient visiting birds will spend more time in your yard than they do now. Habitat changes that create a sense of sheltering safety will make these friends more likely to nest in your yard, and they will spend hours there, filling your outdoor space with life and song. And remember, although it's a real thrill to have birds select your yard as a nesting site, you can count your habitat creation efforts a success as soon as you begin seeing more birds in your yard more often—even if none of them chooses to give your efforts the nesting seal of approval.

TAILORING HABITATS TO SUIT YOU AND THE BIRDS

Backyard habitats offer birds a place to eat, find shelter from the weather and predators, sleep safely at night, and raise their families. Plants are the cornerstone of any habitat, and you'll start your backyard bird sanctuary by installing multipurpose plantings for birds. Then you'll bolster the appeal of those plantings with water features and nest boxes. (We'll cover water features and nest boxes in detail in chapters 6 and 7.)

When you install multipurpose plantings for birds, the results will be amazingly swift. For example, plant a thorny rosebush or a hemlock or other evergreen tree, and birds will use it as a retreat where they can feel safe. Almost as soon as you put your shovel away, you'll see birds arriving to investigate the new shrubs, berry bushes, or other plants you've added just for them.

Even young trees, which take a while to grow to a large size, offer bird value. As skinny saplings, they may not look very good to us. But to birds, these young trees supply useful perching places as the birds move about your yard or pause to sing.

A Question of Style

Creating habitats for birds is a matter of dovetailing your taste with theirs. If you like a formal appearance, with all your ornamentals groomed to look their best, you won't be happy with a casual garden corner where lanky wildflowers spill over one another, no matter how many goldfinches it attracts. But you can easily plant a collection of luscious Japanese irises, bold cattails, and other marsh plants into a wet area that will satisfy your sense of style and provide food, shelter, and nesting materials for birds as well. Remember that it's your backyard, too, not just a habitat for birds. Choose projects that appeal to you and match your garden style. You'll find easy projects in this chapter to create many types of garden areas. Try one or two, or combine them all for a backyard habitat that will tempt a wide variety of birds.

Informal Style

Yards that lean toward the casual are an ideal fit for birds. A less manicured look means that your yard will include many welcoming stretches of plants through which birds can travel in safety or rest undisturbed. And the occasional weeds that spring up in informal yards just make the habitat all the more appealing from a bird's perspective, since weed seeds are favorite foods of many species.

Wildflower gardens. Wildflower plantings need little maintenance, so birds are apt to use them as nest sites as well as feeding stations—for both insects and seeds.

Cottage gardens. A jumble of hardy plants, with some that sow themselves, needs little intervention from you, which makes it an appealing site for nesting and food gathering. It's also a safe corri-

Early Birds

Step outside at noon and look for birds in your yard. You're likely to see only a few, regardless of how many plants you've added or how much naturalistic habitat you've created. This is entirely normal: No matter how bird-rich an area is, most birds lie low during the middle of the day.

Birds are much more active, and thus more visible, in the early morning, from the first brightening of predawn to about 3 hours after sunrise. Be an early bird yourself, and you'll gain a more accurate idea of how many birds, and what kinds, are calling your yard home. Plan to spend a few early mornings in each season watching the activity in your yard and listening to the calls or songs. You may be surprised at how many birds you identify.

Beginning about 2 hours before sunset, birds again become active, though not to such an extent as in the early morning. Observe your yard in the early evening to see who's foraging for supper or singing an evening song before bed.

dor for birds to travel through and has winter food value, thanks to abundant seeds.

Meadow gardens. Flowers and grasses feel like home to native sparrows, quail, and other grassland birds. In a meadow garden, ground-dwelling birds will forage, nest, and find cover and shelter from the weather.

Weedy gardens. Weeds are tops with birds. Because they produce so many seeds over such a long period of time, a single plant can be a veritable banquet. Let a few lamb's-quarters and other weeds remain in your informal gardens, and birds are bound to spot them.

Transform an ordinary flowerbed into a bird habitat by adding small trees, vines, and shrubs, that will provide places for birds to forage, seek shelter, and build nests.

Edge gardens. The natural transition from woods to shrubs to meadow is where the biggest variety of birds is found in nature. Imitate this multilevel magic, and you'll be rewarded with possible sightings of an indigo bunting, a common yellowthroat, or other edge seekers.

Formal Style

At first glance, a formal garden seems to hold little appeal to freewheeling birds. But on closer inspection, evergreen hollies, camellias, and conifers—plus many other trees and shrubs commonly planted as specimen plants—are highly useful to birds seeking shelter or food.

Evergreen groupings. A trio of conifers or broad-leaved evergreen trees or shrubs advertises ideal overnight accommodations to birds seeking a safe place to roost.

Specimen trees. Every plant in your yard holds the potential for attracting birds because of the insects it hosts. Specimen trees are living bird feeders, crawling with insects, and may also provide berries, seeds, or nuts. Such trees make great nest sites; evergreens are particularly popular. A single blue spruce that is 20 feet tall, for example, may hold the nests of several grackles, robins, and house finches, as well as provide nighttime roosting space for dozens of birds.

Water gardens. Birds love water, as you'll discover in chapter 6. All species in the area may come to drink, bathe, and forage for insects.

Suits-All-Styles Projects

Some garden projects can be adapted to fit equally well in a formal or informal garden. Whether you like informality or the manicured look, birds will appreciate the addition of a hedge, marsh garden, multilevel garden, or woodland garden in your yard.

Hedges. A row of shrubs makes a safe travel corridor for birds and offers foraging and nest sites. Evergreen hedges have the added bonus of year-round shelter from the elements. Thorny hedges or those with dense branches offer protection to sleeping birds. Plants that are frequently pruned or clipped won't be as attractive for nesting as undisturbed plants, but birds may still take up residence in a formal privet hedge, for example, because there are generally several weeks between shearings.

Marsh gardens. Wet places abound with insects, a big draw for birds. Tall, clump-forming plants provide shelter. Cattail fluff is sought as nesting material; so is mud. Bog plants are often tall plants with dense upright or large leaves—perfect for a formal garden.

Multilevel gardens. Add some small trees and shrubs—such as blooming azaleas and rhododendrons—beneath your tall shade trees to mimic the understory of a natural woodland. Birds specialized to forage and nest at each level, including the forest floor, the brush, and the treetops, will find such a habitat familiar.

Woodland gardens. Shade gardens are pretty much "plant it, mulch it, leave it alone," and that suits birds just fine. Towhees, thrushes, and other woods dwellers will appreciate having a shady spot to forage and find nest sites. Woodpeckers are particularly at home in a woodland garden, where they can seek out insects in bark or in the wood, and where they're likely to find a nest site in a dead branch or stub.

Who's Hiding in the Hedge?

How can you tell whether birds have a nest in your formal hedge before you whip out the hedge cutter? Walk slowly and closely along both sides of the hedge before you begin to trim. If you notice a bird nearby acting excited, or if you hear scolding "chip" notes, you may be near a nest.

Pay attention for such activity after you start to trim, too. If you spot an agitated bird, rather than hunting for the exact location of the nest, the best solution is to back off and delay pruning for 2 to 3 weeks, by which time the babies probably will have fledged. Searching for and pinpointing the nest location can make predators curious about what's hidden in that hedge, too.

Safety First

Make your motto "Safety first" when you think about what to plant and how to plan the arrangement of your bird-welcoming backyard. By making birds feel safe, you'll be creating exactly the kind of habitat that attracts them most—a sanctuary where they can move about and raise their families in a setting that mimics their wild surroundings.

Staying out of sight is the main survival tactic of nearly all backyard birds. Keep these basics of bird behavior in mind as you plan your backyard habitat.

- During the day, birds move around continually as they search for food. Most birds prefer to forage in leafy, brushy areas where they're at least partly hidden from view.

- At night, birds are especially vulnerable to cats, raccoons, and other night prowlers, so they choose well-sheltered spots to perch while they sleep.

- Nearly all backyard birds seek out sheltered nest sites where their nestlings will be safe.

- A crouching cat or other enemy can easily nab a bird while it's bathing. Wet feathers make a fast takeoff more difficult, so birds search for private bathing areas where shrubs or other growth shelters them while they splash and preen.

Bigger Is Better for Birds

When it comes to planting for the birds, the larger the space the better. It's a simple statement, but it makes sense. For example, a natural forest that covers thousands of acres can support hundreds of birds. In comparison, if your backyard includes only a few trees and a handful of shrubs, it may shelter only five or six birds—and they probably won't be the same species that would live in the natural forest.

A larger planting will attract birds' attention better from the air, and it will help make them feel more at ease when feeding, roosting, or choosing a nest site because it's less vulnerable to predators. Should a cat climb that single tree in your yard, for instance, birds are apt to depart for your neighbor's place. But if your yard holds more than one tree, the same birds can simply shift over to another tree that hasn't been infiltrated.

Some birds will be attracted by a planting as small as 3 feet square, especially in the winter, when they're looking for seeds, or during their migration. But a much larger planting will garner more interest and more birds of more kinds. For instance, in late fall or winter, walk a country road. Among big roadside colonies of goldenrod and asters, you may spot dozens of native sparrows feeding on the seeds. Some of these species may never show up in your yard even if you plant an entire bed of goldenrod or line your sidewalk with asters. To entice such birds, you'll need a large habitat—perhaps a quarter of an acre—that resembles their favored wild surroundings.

FORAGING HABITATS

Creating a backyard habitat that's tailored to the foraging needs of birds is the most important step you can take to increase your yard's appeal. Since not all birds dine on the same foods or in the same places, your bird population will be boosted if you make additions that serve a variety of birds, from ground-feeding doves, which will happily dine in a wildflower patch, picking up seeds on the ground beneath the flowers, to tanagers and flycatchers, which prefer to hunt for food high up in the trees.

It's easy to see what kind of habitat a robin needs for foraging—the wide expanse of a lawn where earthworms abound. But that's not the full story. Robins also search for food at the edges of ponds and streams, in the dim shade of forests, and along brushy roadsides. Like most of our backyard species, robins are opportunists. They take advantage of whatever food sources they can find. Robins love berries, fruit, and insects just as much as they do worms.

And if you watch chickadees munching happily on sunflower seeds and suet at your feeding station day after day, you might think those are the only foods these little bundles of energy depend on. Not so. When they leave your feeder, chickadees seek out delectable caterpillars, soft-bodied aphids, and other insects. They even catch small butterflies, remove the wings, and swallow the plump midsections.

Oaks and nut trees are bird magnets, too. Their heavy crops of acorns and nuts supply lots of food for jays, pheasants, woodpeckers, and other birds. Other tree seeds are popular, too, like the winged samaras of maples and the dangling beans of catalpa trees. In early spring, grosbeaks and other birds seek out the plump, tender buds of trees just waking for the season. Sap has its takers, too, and so do the grubs and insects that live within rotting wood.

Even weeds are manna to many birds. The fuzzy puffballs of dandelion seeds are an irresistible draw to white-crowned sparrows, bright blue indigo buntings, and goldfinches, which gather in ex-

The Bushtit Band

From British Columbia south through the American West and Southwest and into Mexico, bands of jaunty, noisy, little gray bushtits roam in just about any kind of habitat—wet or arid; coastal, woodsy, or urban—as long as there are plenty of bushes.

A bit smaller than chickadees and common in backyards across their range, these little guys don't linger in one place for long. You may not even know you have them unless you happen to be outside in the right place at the right time. Traveling in companionable, tightly spaced groups of about 6 to 30 birds, bushtits seem to be in constant sweeping motion, flitting from one tree or shrub to another. Laggards dash to catch up should the flock move along without them. It may take them 5 minutes to cross your yard—or just a few seconds.

Whether it's a mossy, dripping Northwest woodland or a residential street in Los Angeles, bushtits are easy to identify because of this here-and-gone habit. They're looking for bugs in the bushes, although they may drop in for a fleeting visit to a suet feeder. A multilevel planting in your yard will slow them down a little so that you can enjoy their antics as they move from shrub to shrub and then up into nearby trees, then back to the shrubs, investigating the possibilities with a flurry of wings and a chorus of sharp, twittering calls.

panding flocks when they find a good big patch of dandelions gone to seed.

The more thickly planted your yard is, the more birds will be interested. To attract a wide variety of birds, plan for a mix of habitat areas: a grassy stretch, a shady side, a bushy hedge, and perhaps a wet patch filled with marsh plants. One easy project to start with is the "Bargain Bareroot Bird Hedge" on page 140.

continued on page 143

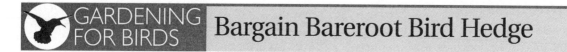

Bargain Bareroot Bird Hedge

Planting a hedge is one of the simplest ways to gain the attention of birds, because hedges offer them so many habitat benefits. Starting a hedge from potted shrubs can get expensive, though, so try this bargain approach instead.

In late winter to early spring, nurseries, garden centers, and catalogs offer bareroot hedge plants at bare-bones prices. You can often find a bundle of three or more bareroot privet, forsythia, weigela, or other deciduous hedge plants for as little as $5. These dormant plants will be spindly sticks that appear to be dead. But if you snap 'em up when you spot 'em, these sickly looking specimens will flourish once they are in the ground. Two years down the road, you won't be able to tell the difference between the bargain plants and the high-priced ones.

Step 1. Shop early for the best selection. The garden centers at discount stores often have the best range of choices (ask the manager when bareroot stock is expected to arrive). Buy four to seven bareroot hedge plants.

Step 2. Open the packages and use a pocketknife to remove any wires, twist ties, or other devices that hold the plants together.

Step 3. Set the roots of the plants in a bucket of water until you're ready to plant them.

Step 4. Dig the hole for the first shrub at the desired location. Fill it with water to "muddy in" the plants. The water also will saturate the surrounding soil so that it won't wick moisture away from the planting hole.

Step 5. Carefully separate the roots of one plant from the others when you remove it from the bucket. Work slowly to avoid breaking off any roots or branches.

Step 6. Make a cone of soil at the center of the planting hole and spread the roots over it. (The hole may still contain some water.) Check that the plant is sitting at the depth it was previously growing.

Step 7. Fill in the hole with the removed soil and press moderately firmly around the base of the plant to firm up the soil.

Step 8. Repeat steps 4 through 7 for each plant, spacing the holes 3 to 5 feet apart.

Step 9. Water the plants liberally when you're finished planting.

Step 10. Spread a 1- to 1 1/2-inch layer of composted manure around each plant.

Step 11. Keep the soil moist but not soaking wet over the coming weeks, as the shrubs leaf out and begin to grow.

Step 12. Nourish the plants with compost tea weekly, pouring about 1/2 gallon around the roots of each plant.

Cone of soil

Roots

Hidden Happenings in a Hedge

A lot of bird life happens out of sight. Birds prefer it that way. Hidden from view, they can move about freely to collect food, make nests, raise their families, or simply find a safe, undisturbed place to sleep.

Birds resent disturbance and will forsake even a favorite place when humans poke around too often. It's best to avoid getting too close to your hedge. Just be satisfied with the knowledge that inside, birds are happily going about their lives.

Set a garden bench at a moderate distance from the hedge, and you may get a glimpse of some of these hedge happenings.

A hearty feast. Hedges provide a banquet of various kinds of food for birds. The foliage holds many delectable insects, and depending on what you've planted, the plants also may offer a bonus of insect-attracting flowers or tempting berries or fruit.

Birds on the move. A hedge is a great travel route for birds because it allows them to stay hidden while on the move. Birds will use your hedge to travel from one part of your yard to another, or from your yard to your neighbor's.

A foul weather hangout. During rain, snow, and hot summer weather, birds will hole up in your hedge. The dense foliage and branches will keep them dry, and the shade will be a welcome respite from the summer sun. In a snowstorm, your evergreen hedge is likely to host a crowd of birds.

Dramatic escapes. Birds will fly fast for the shelter of a hedge when they feel threatened. A prowling cat, a hungry hawk, or even a peace-loving two-legged visitor may raise the alarm. By planting a hedge near your feeder, you will give juncos and other songbirds a better chance of escaping from predators.

Nest construction. Hedges are popular with nesting catbirds, brown thrashers, grackles, cardinals, and mockingbirds, which often use the densely twiggy interior of a hedge plant to hold their deeply cupped nests. Other birds collect thin, dead twigs for nest building from the ground beneath a hedge.

A safe night's sleep. Shh! Birds may spend the night in your hedge, whose twiggy interior will deter cats, snakes, and other nocturnal predators from nighttime raids.

Fledgling exploration. Hedges give a helping hand to young birds just out of the nest. Fledglings can clamber around inside the branches to keep out of harm's way and move about without having to depend on those still-shaky wings.

Plants for Bird Hedges

Look for densely branched plants when selecting shrubs for a bird hedge. You can plant all the same kind or mix things up, with flowering shrubs, berry bushes, and evergreens combined for extra bird benefits.

Hundreds of excellent hedge plants are available for every area of the country. These plants are easy to care for and fast growing, but don't limit yourself to these suggestions. Visit your garden center or nursery and pick the plants you like best. Except where noted, the plants listed here thrive, with minimal care, in average unimproved soil, in Zones 5 through 10.

PLANT NAME	DESCRIPTION AND GROWING TIPS
Barberries (*Berberis* **spp.**)	Spiny branches shelter birds. Many ornamental cultivars available; red-leaved varieties add an extra oomph to landscaping. Thrive everywhere except desert climates.
Lemon bottlebrush (*Callistemon citrinus*)	Eye-catching plumes of red, hummingbird-attracting flowers and glossy foliage. Good choice in arid areas. Hardy only to Zone 9.
Desert willow (*Chilopsis linearis*)	Grows into a small tree. Cut it back once a year to keep it shrublike. Good for adding height to a hedge. Well suited for arid areas; hardy to Zone 9.
Border forsythia (*Forsythia* × *intermedia*)	Gladdens our hearts in spring and makes birds happy for at least three seasons, thanks to its dense branches. Super easy to grow anywhere except deserts.
Rose-of-Sharon (*Hibiscus syriacus*)	Hummingbirds are the bonus for planting this flowering shrub or small tree. Tolerates drought, grows fast, and even self-sows moderately. Not for desert climates.
Privets (*Ligustrum* **spp.**)	Another group of time-honored hedge plants, still among the best if you're looking for easy care. Choose standard dark green foliage plants or newer cultivars with splashy golden variegated leaves. Grow practically anywhere except deserts.
Photinias (*Photinia* **spp. and hybrids**)	Fast-growing evergreens; some cultivars have attractive red leaves on new growth. Look lush but tolerate extended drought once established.
Rhododendrons (*Rhododendron* **spp. and hybrids**)	Thousands of cultivars are available, so pick your favorite color (birds don't care). Need regular watering for at least the first 3 years after planting. When established, look ragged during drought but come back when rain or snow returns.
Rugosa rose (*Rosa rugosa*)	Tough as nails, with wrinkled, glossy foliage and extra-dense thorny branches, plus a bonus of pretty blossoms and colorful rose hips in fall. Thrives in coastal gardens and arid climates.
Bridal-wreath (*Spiraea* × *vanhouttei*)	An old-fashioned favorite that spills a waterfall of white flowers in spring. Often sold in bundled bareroot packages at bargain prices. Easy-care plant: Just plant it and forget it. Thrives practically everywhere except desert climates.

PLANT NAME	DESCRIPTION AND GROWING TIPS
Hemlocks (*Tsuga spp.*)	Graceful, fast-growing, evergreen conifers. Best in Zone 8 and colder. Can withstand some drought once established.
Weigela (*Weigela florida*)	Flowers attract hummingbirds. Grows super fast, filling out from a spindly newcomer to a lush 6-footer in just a couple of years. If older plants become rangy, cut back halfway, after flowering. Not for desert climates.

continued from page 139

ROOSTING HABITATS

Where do birds sleep at night? In many cases, the answer is a mystery. Observations by bird watchers indicate that many birds sleep in dense conifers. Those that nest in cavities or nest boxes often sleep in cavities or boxes, too. Little is known about where birds that favor the treetops, such as tanagers and wood warblers, spend their sleeping hours.

A Sleeping Tree

A good-size evergreen tree is an excellent place for birds to find shelter at night, and almost every yard can accommodate one evergreen. In the East and Midwest, one of the most popular roosting sites in the wild and in backyards is the native eastern red cedar (*Juniperus virginiana*), an upright conifer with foliage that is so prickly it's painful to the touch. A single large red cedar, about 10 feet tall and 3 feet across, may harbor more than a dozen birds every night. This evergreen and other dense conifers, such as arborvitae and spruces, are especially sought after on winter nights, when their foliage helps birds conserve vital body heat. The protective branches also keep birds dry while they sleep. Rain and snow don't usually penetrate the dense interior of an evergreen, and the thick foliage keeps out chilling winds.

Hedges and large, thick shrubs, such as forsythia and rhododendrons, also host overnight guests. House sparrows, white-throated sparrows, juncos, and cardinals are the most common patrons of low-level roosting places such as shrubs.

Roosting Boxes

You can provide roosting habitats for many species of birds by adding more nest boxes, or roosting boxes, which are boxes with perches inside, to your yard.

Titmice, bluebirds, nuthatches, wrens, and chickadees, which spend cold nights in cavities, sometimes show the effects the morning after when they arrive at the feeder. Because such a hole or box may hold as many birds as can pile in, those at the edges often end up with bent tail feathers as a result of being squeezed into the space to make room for all the guests. Using nest boxes for shelter is a good argument for keeping yours up all year. Tree swallows and other swallows, which often arrive in the spring just as the weather takes a sudden turn back toward winter, also may use the boxes.

WEATHER-WISE HABITATS

Feathers are terrific insulation, as those of us with down comforters already know, but their insulating properties don't always keep birds from becoming too hot or too cold. And feathers aren't much use as insulation when they're soaking wet. In times of weather extremes, birds move to more hospitable places, just as we may pull a chaise longue into the shade when the summer sun shifts position.

Beating the Heat

The deep shade beneath the branches of maples, oaks, and other shade trees keeps thrushes, towhees, and flycatchers out of the hot sun in temperate regions. In the desert, quail and other birds search out shady patches beneath sagebrush or under the arms of a saguaro to escape the brutal heat. Large rocks, too, can throw cooling shadows on a sunny day.

Water holes or garden water features are always cool spots on hot days. You'll often see birds bathing or simply enjoying the spray beneath a garden sprinkler on a summer day. For ideas on water features to add to your backyard habitat, turn to chapter 6.

Keeping Away Cold

Cold weather calls for a different strategy. When the thermometer settles into place well below the freezing mark, the evergreen plants in your garden earn their keep. Large-leaved evergreens protect birds from snow and ice, while the thick foliage and branches of large- or small-leaved evergreens and conifers

add insulation to help keep birds from freezing.

Birds also use nest boxes in the off-season to stay warm on cold days or nights. And your feeder offerings of high-fat treats will help birds keep warm in cold weather.

Out of the Rain

Bird "umbrellas" are everywhere in your garden. The big leaves of sunflowers, fig trees, and elephant's ears can become temporary rain gear for hummingbirds, wrens, and other small birds during a sudden deluge, but the birds will quickly forsake them for more protected places to wait out a storm. During the growing season, just about any leafy shrub or tree will do the trick. When deciduous plants are bare of leaves, birds opt for evergreen trees and shrubs to escape the rain. Broad-leaved evergreens, including magnolias and rhododendrons, are ideal places for birds to find shelter from heavy rain.

Showers and light rain rarely deter birds from going about their usual activities. You will see them moving around in your garden, pausing occasionally to ruffle their feathers or give a full-fledged shake like a wet dog.

When a gentle rain falls in the summer, watch the birds in your yard to see whether you can catch any of them in the act of "leaf bathing." Small birds such as chickadees and hummingbirds often make good use of the water that collects in slightly curled leaves, rubbing their bodies in it and throwing it onto their backs with as much abandon as they would at a birdbath.

Shrubs and trees can take months or years to reach a size that will provide decent shelter for birds. But in just a few weeks, fast-growing scarlet runner bean or hyacinth bean vines will race to the top of this tepee, providing a place for birds to sit out summer storms or hide from predators. Set up a tepee in any sunny site in your yard. Use a row of tepees, closely spaced, to mark a boundary line or edge a patio with a temporary hedge. Watch for Carolina wrens, house wrens, and possibly chickadees and titmice investigating the foliage for insects. When the bright orange-red flowers bloom, your tepee will be abuzz with nectar-seeking hummingbirds.

MATERIALS

6 to 8 bamboo or plastic garden stakes, at least 6 feet long

Plastic twine or wire

3 or 4 tent stakes (optional)

1 packet scarlet runner bean or hyacinth bean (*Lablab purpureus*) seeds

Step 1. Choose a site about 4 to 6 feet in diameter in full sun. Remove the surface vegetation and work the soil.

Step 2. Gather the bamboo stakes into a bundle and tie them together at a point about 6 inches from one end of the bundle by wrapping several loops of twine around the stakes.

Step 3. Set the bundle upright at your garden site, with the tied end at the top, and fan out the base of the stakes to form a circle about 3 feet in diameter.

Step 4. The tepee should stand without support, but for extra stability, especially in windy areas, insert a tent stake near every other bamboo stake and tie the base of the tent stake to the bamboo stake.

Step 5. Poke two to four scarlet runner bean or hyacinth bean seeds about 1 inch into the soil at the base of each bamboo stake.

Step 6. Water well and keep the soil moist until the beans are up and growing.

Step 7. When the beans are 1 foot tall, reduce watering to once every few days as needed.

Bamboo or plastic stake

Tent stake

NESTING HABITATS

Ah, nesting—the Holy Grail of backyard bird watching! It's a real treat to discover a nest and observe the family in it. You'll feel almost as proud as the parent birds when those youngsters finally make their big exit—and as worried about their safety, as you recognize the very real threat of every passing cat, crow, or hawk.

Nests and Eggs

Gray Kingbird

One of the most unusual colors of bird eggs is that of the gray kingbird, which lays eggs that are a lovely salmon pink, wreathed at the larger end with brown and lavender. On Sanibel Island and in other coastal areas of Florida, where the gray kingbird is a common sight, a more apt description of the egg color might be seashell pink. In the Florida Keys, another region where the bird nests in abundance, one might dub the color conch pink.

Although the eggs of the gray kingbird are objects of beauty, its nests are nothing to brag about—just frail collections of coarse twigs with a grassy lining. Gray kingbirds can be inexplicably picky about where they nest and live. Many suitable habitats boast no kingbirds or nests, while a short distance away, in identical habitats of cabbage palms, mangroves, casuarinas, and other seaside vegetation, the dapper white-breasted birds are as thick as flies.

If you're lucky enough to be the host of a gray kingbird, you can rest assured that it will be back next year. Nesting birds return to their Florida homesites as reliably as the summer sun and often build their new nests in the same trees as they did the previous year.

Birds' nests are usually difficult to find, for good reason. Way too many critters like to eat birds' eggs and plump little babies, and some will even attempt to swallow the mother bird sitting on the nest. Cats take an enormous toll on nesting birds, and crows, grackles, jays, snakes, and raccoons also take advantage of an easy meal.

Choosing a Nesting Tree

As you plan your habitat, include shrubs and trees that are favored by nest-building birds that frequent backyards. Luckily, that includes a whole slew of plants people like, too. You'll find some top candidates throughout this book, but keep in mind that we've only scratched the surface. Birds have been known to nest in hundreds of species of trees, shrubs, and vines.

Privacy, Please

More important than picking the "right" plant is choosing where to site the trees, shrubs, and other possible nesting locations in your yard. With few exceptions, birds prefer an undisturbed spot, where kids, gardeners, and deliverymen aren't passing by all the time.

Even birds that spend a lot of time out in full view, such as our familiar backyard friend the American robin, retreat to hidden, well-sheltered locations when it comes time to get serious about making a home and rearing a family. Likewise, those loudmouthed jays, who don't seem shy at all about announcing their presence to the whole neighborhood, undergo a transformation at nesting time. Around the twiggy cup that holds their precious eggs, jay parents are the epitome of stealth, remaining absolutely silent and sneaking to and from the nest site. Even experienced birders are often completely unaware of a jay's nest nearby. Such stealth works to keep hawks, crows, cats, and other nest robbers from destroying birds' efforts to raise a family.

Birds that usually nest high in trees, such as orioles, tanagers, grosbeaks, goldfinches, vireos, jays, and flycatchers, may build their homes directly above human activity. It's amazing how many of those nests go unnoticed. Usually the folks down below become curious only when the baby birds cheep loudly at feeding time.

Cavity Nesters

Woodpeckers, chickadees, nuthatches, and titmice all nest in cavities in dead trees or even in dead limbs on living trees. Many trees that look completely healthy and vigorous harbor a discreet dead spot, where a branch broke off long ago or a dead limb or branch stub is still solidly connected to the tree.

Cavity nesters are skilled at finding these places and turning them into custom-made condos. A few hours of diligent pecking, and they can remove enough of the soft deadwood to make room for a family of four (or five, six, or seven, as the case may be). Downy woodpeckers, chickadees, nuthatches, and swallows are small birds that need a hole only a few inches deep and wide to raise a family—exactly the size that can be excavated when a smaller branch dies off.

Post Hole Homes

If you provide the beginnings of a nest hole in a wooden fence post, it may catch the attention of a cavity-nesting bird, who will do the rest of the work. Chickadees nesting in the front yard gatepost? Why not!

Use a drill with a 1½-inch spade bit to drill a hole about 2 inches deep into the side of a post at least 4 inches in diameter that is part of an existing fence, arbor, or other structure. That's all there is to it. Just wait to see if any birds show up to investigate, then watch them finish the excavation and raise a family.

A 1½-inch hole will allow access to chickadees, nuthatches, and titmice. Unfortunately, house sparrows also may investigate the hole. Some may find it too small and give up attempting to squeeze their plump bodies into it, but others may be able to squeeze in and nest there.

If you suspect that your yard is deficient in nest sites for woodpeckers and other cavity nesters, or if you want to add more, you can purposely add potential sites by fastening pieces of tree limb to trellises, posts, or other upright surfaces. One method for doing this is shown in "Deadwood Gulch" on page 149, or you can drill introductory holes in wooden fence posts as described in "Post Hole Homes" above.

Who Nests Where?

Exactly where a bird places its nest on a branch gives experts clues to the species. Eastern wood-pewees, for example, almost always choose a Y-shaped fork along a horizontal branch of a deciduous tree, while olive-sided flycatchers place their nests among the branchlets on a horizontal, thickly needled conifer spray.

It's fun learning such idiosyncrasies of bird species (and finding the nests that don't follow the rules!), but there's no need to become an expert on nest placement in order to choose plants for your garden. The lesson here is that a variety of plant habits will provide good homesites for a variety of birds. This listing is just a partial key to who may nest where.

NEST LOCATION	BIRDS WHO NEST THERE
Young deciduous trees	Goldfinches, hummingbirds, jays, robins, chipping sparrows, vireos
Middle-aged to mature deciduous trees	Blue-gray gnatcatchers, goldfinches, rose-breasted grosbeaks, hummingbirds, jays, orioles, robins, chipping sparrows, tanagers (prefer oak trees), vireos, cedar waxwings
Rosebushes or brambles	Cardinals, catbirds, mockingbirds, brown thrashers
Shrubs	Red-winged blackbirds, indigo buntings, cardinals, catbirds, mockingbirds, orchard orioles, chipping sparrows, song sparrows, brown thrashers
Dense grasses	Red-winged blackbirds, common yellowthroats
Trellised vines	Catbirds, blue jays, house sparrows, brown thrashers, Carolina wrens
Conifers	Cardinals, house finches, common grackles, hummingbirds, jays, kinglets, chipping sparrows
Ground level (hidden in vegetation)	Meadowlarks, ovenbirds, song sparrows, towhees
Bare gravel or bare ground with scattered small stones	Killdeer
Cavities or nest boxes	Bluebirds, chickadees, flickers, kestrels, purple martins, nuthatches, screech owls, tree swallows, violet-green swallows, titmice, woodpeckers

Dead tree limbs that crack off and fall during a storm are just what you need to create potential nest sites for woodpeckers and other cavity-dwelling birds. First you drill a decoy hole in the limb; then you mount it on a porch post, fence post, wooden arbor or gazebo, or existing tree. The decoy hole will get the attention of cavity-nesting birds, which will investigate your offering. If one of them deems it acceptable, the bird will use its beak to enlarge the cavity and entrance hole as needed.

If you don't have any large trees in your yard that are shedding limbs, check with your friends or neighbors. Most likely they'll be delighted to give you what they think of as yard waste.

MATERIALS

Drill

¼-inch twist drill bit

2-inch spade bit

Section of dead tree limb, still solid and uncracked, at least 4 inches in diameter and 10 inches long

Two 12-penny nails

Step 1. Using the ¼-inch bit, drill a starter hole (for nailing the limb to a support) into the tree limb, about 3 inches from one end of the limb. Drill another starter hole at the opposite end of the limb.

Step 2. Using the 2-inch bit, drill into the wood about 2 inches away from one of the starter holes. Continue drilling until this 2-inch-diameter decoy hole is about an inch deep.

Step 3. Choose a site to erect your home for woodpeckers and cavity nesters.

Step 4. Position the tree limb so that the decoy hole is at the top. Nail the limb to the mounting surface, using one nail in each of the pilot holes. Work carefully and handle the limb gently to reduce the chances of breakage.

NESTING MATERIALS

Birds are perfectly capable of collecting their own materials to construct a nest. But just as with feeding stations, it's immensely gratifying to supply desirable materials for birds to use. Putting out nesting materials is also a great way to find out just which birds are building nests in your vicinity and to discover the location of a nest.

Keep watching a bird that selects nesting materials from the pile you've supplied, and you may be able to locate the nest in progress. Do not approach! Your scent won't deter nest-building birds, but your interest can clue in predators to the secret activity taking place, and the birds may abandon the location.

Catalogs and wild bird supply stores now carry specialized nesting material

Nesting Materials Inventory

Think "fibers" when you scour your house looking for possible nesting materials. Birds are weavers, and they use all kinds of soft, pliable material to form their nests. Longer fibers may be woven into the outside of a nest or reserved for the inner lining of a cup of twigs, rootlets, and other coarser materials. Fuzzy, short-fibered materials and feathers are often used to make an extra-soft bed in the center of the nest.

MATERIAL	USED BY
Soft, curled feathers, such as from a feather bed pillow	Chickadees, kinglets, nuthatches, chipping sparrows, house sparrows, barn swallows, tree swallows, titmice, wrens
Short lengths of string, yarn, or twine	Jays, purple martins, orioles, robins, titmice, cedar waxwings
Strands of human hair removed from hairbrush	Chickadees, kinglets, mockingbirds, nuthatches, chipping sparrows, titmice, vireos, wrens
Horse tail or mane hair	Chickadees, kinglets, mockingbirds, nuthatches, chipping sparrows, titmice, vireos, wrens
Dog hair	Chickadees, kinglets, nuthatches, titmice, vireos, wrens
Cattail fluff	Goldfinches, vireos, wrens
Dead blades of ornamental grasses	Cardinals, catbirds, robins, brown thrashers
Moss, such as that sold at craft supply stores	Chickadees, kinglets, mockingbirds, phoebes, thrushes, titmice, wrens
Scraps of loosely woven, coarse fabrics, such as burlap, homespun-type cotton tablecloths, or lap throws	Jays, purple martins, orioles, robins, titmice, cedar waxwings

holders, already stuffed with fibrous offerings that birds find appealing. These holders work very well to attract nest-building birds, but it's also fun to do a treasure hunt through your house and see what other materials you can come up with. As you scout the shelves in the garage and the junk drawer in the kitchen, keep in mind that *fibers* is the keyword: Anything that can be woven into a nest is fair game.

Opportunists at Work

Interestingly, birds adapt to manmade nesting materials and use them just as readily as they do the items that they diligently collect from nature. Historical accounts of nest construction often list horsehair as one of the materials. Nowadays, that's apt to be replaced by fishing line or other synthetic or more readily available fibers.

House sparrows, which seem to have an affinity for tissues, potato chip bags, and other human trash, have even learned to use discarded cigarette butts: They strip off the paper covering and use the soft fiber of the filter in their nests. Crackly strips of plastic wrappers are also a favorite of many birds, including the great crested flycatcher and tufted titmouse, which traditionally use a similar crackly strip of cast-off snake skin in their nests. In the world of nest-building birds, hardly anything goes to waste.

The Simple Approach

Putting out nesting materials can make bird watchers feel the same way we do when we put peanuts in the feeder: It's gratifying to see the birds snatch up our

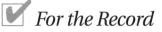 *For the Record*

Snakes in the Nest

Nobody knows why some birds add scraps of snake skin to their nests, and the birds themselves aren't talking. One theory is that the skin frightens away predators. Simply not true, say backyard observers and scientists, who note that marauding snakes and coons pay no attention to the papery reptile skin as they raid nests in search of eggs. Another theory is that birds use snake skin to scare away other birds that might compete for the nest site.

Snakes shed their skins when they molt in the spring, after they emerge from hibernation. A skin may be shed in a single piece, or it may be broken into sections as the snake rubs against rocks or other rough objects to work its way out of its old birthday suit.

Once off the snake, the delicate, translucent skin is a prize to the great crested flycatcher (the bird most often cited as a snake skin fan), tufted titmouse, and blue grosbeak.

offerings with such gusto, but it's disappointing to see how quickly our precious materials disappear.

There's no need to go to a lot of trouble laying out such materials. The simple approach works just fine. Place the materials on the lawn, in a location that you can see from a favorite viewing spot indoors or outdoors. The drawback to this method is that many of the materials will blow away. Although birds will still find your soft feathers and other offerings (they're remarkably adept at ferreting out such items from their natural surroundings), you won't have the pleasure of watching them take advantage of the items you selected just for them.

A Deadly Trap

One absolute must applies when putting out materials for birds to use in their nests: Keep the pieces of fiber short. Birds can get entangled in long lengths of fibers—even human hair!—and die as a result. By far the worst offender is monofilament fishing line.

A fisherman whips his rod backward to make a cast, the line snags in the trees, the fisherman snips the end to free his pole, and the stage is set for a fatal bird encounter. Balled-up line is just as deadly, as birds spot the clump of fibers and attempt to work them free.

To be a friend to birds in the wild, collect any discarded or hung-up fishing line you see whenever you're outdoors. Orioles, which build complicated pendulous nests, and robins are among the documented victims of fishing line, but the list of bird species involved in fatalities due to discarded monofilament is, unfortunately, long.

The Lure of String

An oriole will spend hours stripping fibers from Indian hemp, a plant that grows wild across much of North America. But orioles will just as eagerly use commercially manufactured cotton string. A white string mop is irresistible to northern orioles of the Baltimore race and holds a strong attraction for other orioles, too. The birds will even come onto a porch or deck to retrieve nesting material from this humble source (as long as you stay out of sight inside). You'll enjoy weeks of watching the colorful birds unravel and pull off strings from the mop. You'll marvel at how much force these songbirds exert to yank away at the strings, and how dexterous these birds are—with only their beaks to work with. Other kinds of birds, such as robins and titmice, also may collect strings. One backyard bird watcher was tickled to discover that a mourning dove decided to build its nest—a loose, sketchy collection of sticks—directly on the comfortably cushioned top of the mop head.

Say No to Dryer Lint

Fuzzy clumps of dryer lint, which most of us accumulate in large quantities, are sometimes recommended as nesting material, but lint is not a good choice. Although it's soft and fluffy when it stays dry, it deteriorates too quickly when exposed to the weather. Also, lint in a nest absorbs moisture, and a damp nest can result in hypothermia in the nestlings.

Nests and Eggs

Cardinal

Got roses? If so, you probably have cardinals. Thorny tangles of rosebushes and the canes of climbing roses are favorite places for these birds to build their nests—loose cups of twigs, vines, bark strips, and grasses. You may also detect a cardinal's nest in other brambles or in a vine or shrubby conifer; arborvitae and privet hedges are frequently favored. The weedy proliferation of the notorious multiflora rose offers cardinals lots of ideal nest sites. The eggs—usually laid in a clutch of three or four—are slightly glossy, bluish or greenish white with an overlay of dark blotches and speckles, and heaviest around the bigger end. Cardinals use no leaves in their nests, which is one way to identify their homes in the winter when the birds are long gone.

Mop Strings for the Birds

Children will love this project (and so will you!), because it's super easy and guaranteed to attract any orioles in the neighborhood. Invest just 5 minutes of your time, and you'll be rewarded with 5 weeks of fun. Be sure to describe to the children how the oriole will weave the strings into its pouchlike nest. (See "Nests and Eggs: Baltimore Oriole" on page 155 for a detailed description of the expert nest-builder at work.)

Step 1. Buy a white cotton string mop head, or donate a clean one that you already have on hand to the cause.

Step 2. If necessary, use scissors to clip the ends of the mop loops so that they hang as single strings rather than closed loops.

Step 3. Nail the mop head to a fence post or porch post, letting the strings hang down freely.

Make sure you pick a location where you will have a good view of it.

Step 4. Wait for orioles to arrive.

The String Alternative

Buy one ball of thin and one ball of thick white cotton string. Snip off 10 to 15 six-inch lengths from each ball and lay the pieces on the grass or drape them over a bush. Then sit back and watch as brilliant orange or yellow orioles, familiar robins, shiny purple martins, and other birds arrive to snitch a piece of string for their nests. Replenish the string until the birds have collected all they can use and no longer visit the site.

Nesting Materials Supply Station

Prevent the nesting materials you put out from blowing away by using a wire cage suet feeder or plastic berry box to hold your treasures. Most of these items take up very little room, unless you've managed to collect quite a bundle. It's a good idea to start filling the basket with thin strips of cloth or strings cut from an old mop head.

Using a wire cage allows you to get a good view of birds that come to pick through the pile. Be sure to hang or mount it in a place where you can see it clearly. Enticing orioles with a nesting supply station is an excellent way to get a close look at these vividly colored birds, which spend most of their time in the high treetops.

Step 1. Tear four or more thin strips, ½ to 1 inch wide, from an old cotton or linen shirt. Cut the strips into sections 5 to 6 inches long. Don't remove the frayed threads at the edges of the strips—they're part of the attraction!

Step 2. Assemble your other nesting material offerings: human hair, horse tail or mane hair, dog hair at least 3 inches long, 5- to 6-inch-long pieces of string or dental floss, dried moss, paintbrush bristles, and other likely fibers.

Step 3. Loosely bunch up the cloth strips, then add other materials to the ball, packing them into place as if you were making a snowball. Keep the ball loose, though, so that birds can easily free the fibers and pluck out their favorites.

Step 4. Flatten the ball and stuff it inside the cage. Close and latch the lid.

Step 5. Pull out tendrils of the materials so that they protrude invitingly from the cage. A table fork or a shish kebab skewer makes a good tool to snag fibers through the wire grid.

Step 6. Hang the cage on a post, shepherd's crook, or tree limb. Make sure you have a good view of it from inside the house or a nearby sitting spot, so that you can watch the circus when the orioles, chickadees, and other nest makers arrive to examine the booty.

Nests and Eggs

Song Sparrow

You'll usually find the song sparrow's dense cup of woven grasses by accident. These birds nest very early, so you're likely to stumble upon the nest—we hope not literally—when you're cleaning up the garden in early spring. It's so well hidden, though, that you might not even notice it. Even the three to five small oval eggs are well camouflaged—heavily blotched with browns and purples on a pale green background. The interior of the nest is a neat, cozy cup of fine grasses and hair, small enough to fit in the palm of your hand, but the bird doesn't seem to know when to stop: The outer part of the nest is a large, loose weaving of coarse grasses, leaves, and fibers. Strawberry patches and thickly planted perennial beds are favorite nesting sites. Song sparrows may build and use more than one nest during a season.

Growing Nesting Materials

It's fun to create a small garden of plants that birds can use for nesting materials. Small twigs are always popular, and they're readily available if your yard includes a privet hedge, a maple tree, or any other plant that naturally drops its twigs (which includes just about everything).

Other plants from which birds gather nesting materials aren't as cooperative as those that drop twigs, however. Every bird, from gorgeous orioles to often-despised starlings, spends a lot of time during nest-building season gathering construction materials. A mockingbird may spend an hour or more tediously working to free a strip of grapevine bark, while a goldfinch may repeatedly fly more than 5 miles to collect enough cat-tail fluff to line its nest—one small beakful at a time.

The pleasure of growing plants that supply nesting materials will come when the birds arrive to collect the fruits of your labor. Try planting a garden like the one shown on page 156, and you'll be able to observe familiar birds engaged in activities you've never seen—and working at it with a dedication and single-mindedness that is fascinating.

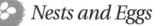 *Nests and Eggs*

Baltimore Oriole

The Baltimore race of the northern oriole is the hands-down winner of the award for most exotic nest in North America (although some of this species' relatives, such as the Bullock's race and the Altamira oriole, are close rivals for the title). Working with its beak alone, the Baltimore oriole threads and knots dozens of strands of fibers into a hanging pouch 5 to 6 inches long.

Work starts at the upper corners of the nest, which the bird fastens to the very tip of a branch of a tall tree. It takes the bird a few days to more than a week of constant weaving to complete the nest. The female does the lion's share of the weaving, but both female and male gather nesting materials, and the male may make a stitch or two to tuck in some strands. The shape of the pouch is roughed in with loosely woven strands; then other threads are added to make a dense, strong weave.

The bird uses its beak like the shuttle of a loom, darting back and forth so rapidly that it is hard to follow as it moves each fiber into place in an ever-growing mass of knotted material. Acrobatics figures into the process, too, as the oriole hangs head down like a parrot to work at the lengthening bottom of the pouch that will hold her babies.

When the nest is finished, it's a comfortable cradle. Fresh air filters through the woven walls, where the eggs and later nestlings stay safe in the bottom, as the nest gently sways in the breeze. Like gold coins in a purse, the mother bird's weight draws the upper edges of the nest together, and the whole family stays cozy and dry.

Look for orioles' nests at the tips of a shade tree's canopy from winter to early spring, when the trees are bare. They are recognizable from quite a distance. Eventually, the fibers of attachment break and the nest, now weathered to a soft gray, falls to the ground.

Nesting Materials Garden

Managing this garden of nesting materials is quite different from taking care of the usual perennial garden. Let the plants grow through the fall; then leave the dead stems standing through the winter and into early summer so that birds can use them. Plan plenty of time to sit in the garden from March through June. Keep a pair of binoculars nearby so that you can see the amazing skill and finesse with which birds remove plant parts.

If you have a natural-looking fence in your yard, it's the perfect backdrop for the grapevine. If not, you can put up a low trellis for the vine to ramble on instead.

Choose a location for this garden where you won't mind its untidiness. As an alternative, cut back the plants in early spring and lay the clippings in a pile. Birds will find it more difficult to separate the fibers from the stems, but they will still make use of them.

PLANT LIST

Potted or bareroot grapevine

Potted weeping willow (*Salix babylonica*)

2 to 6 potted Indian hemp (*Apocynum cannabinum*) plants

3 potted switch grass (*Panicum virgatum*) plants

3 to 8 potted or bareroot daisy fleabane (*Erigeron speciosus*) plants

5 potted or bareroot butterfly weed (*Asclepias tuberosa*) plants

Step 1. Choose a site in full to partial sun. Remove any existing vegetation, especially perennial weeds and grasses. There is no need to spade the soil.

Step 2. If the grapevine is bareroot, set the roots to soak in a bucket of water. Dig a hole near the fence large enough to accommodate the rootball. Fill the hole with water and let it drain.

Step 3. Remove the plant from the pot or bucket and plant it in the hole at the same level it was previously growing.

Step 4. Backfill the hole and apply a 2- to 3-inch layer of wood chips or bark mulch around the plant. You'll follow this same planting technique for the rest of the plants in the garden, except as indicated.

Step 5. Plant the willow, and mulch with 2 inches of wood chips.

Step 6. Plant the Indian hemp in front of the fence, spacing the plants at least 1 foot apart. Choose the number of plants needed to create the size garden you want.

Step 7. Mulch around the plants with 2 inches of bark mulch or wood chips to cover an area 2 to 3 feet wide.

Step 8. Plant the switch grass and apply 2 inches of bark mulch around the plants.

Step 9. Plant the daisy fleabane and butterfly weed. If the plants are bareroot, remove the roots from their wrapping and soak them in a bucket of water for 1 hour before planting.

Step 10. When you set the bareroot plants in place, spread out the thick taproots in a planting hole wide enough and deep enough to comfortably accommodate them without crowding. Space the fleabane plants 6 to 10 inches apart in a staggered arrangement. Set the butterfly weed plants about 12 inches apart in two staggered rows.

Step 11. Apply 2 inches of bark mulch around the plants.

Step 12. Cover any exposed soil with mulch so that it makes a uniform covering that visually ties all the plants together.

Nesting Materials Plants

Refer to this quick guide to learn more about the plants in your nesting materials garden and how birds use them for nesting supplies.

PLANT NAME	PART USED BY BIRDS	COMMENTS
Butterfly weed	Long inner fibers of dead stems; fluff from seedpods	Pods must split open to reveal their fluff before goldfinches, vireos, and other birds can collect it.
Daisy fleabane	Fluff from seedheads	Grows best in cool summer areas. Blooms from early to late summer; let flowers stand through winter. The following spring and summer, birds such as chickadees and hummingbirds will collect the seed fluff.
Grapevines	Bark, twigs, and dead tendrils	Vines will naturally twine around posts and railings. To guide their growth, use ties or garden tape to hold the vines; prune them if they get too rambunctious. Pile the clippings near the fence; they're useful to birds, too.
Indian hemp	Long inner fibers of dead stems	Spreads quickly, creating a moderately dense stand of attractive 3-foot-tall plants with thin, oval leaves and decorative clusters of long, skinny seedpods. Native plant nurseries or prairie plant nurseries are your best bet for finding this plant.
Switch grass	Grass blades at base of clumps	Birds won't select these grass blades until they've turned brown and dry and been weathered by rain and snow.
Weeping willow	Twigs and branchlets	Fast growing and notorious for infiltrating underground water pipes. Plant at least 20 feet away from water or sewage pipes. If you can't, substitute a fall-flowering cherry (*Prunus subhirtella* 'Autumnalis').

HABITAT GARDENING

Now that you've got the big picture of what birds need from a habitat, you're ready to embark on gardening projects that will serve a variety of birds' needs all at once. In fact, you'll discover that most of your gardening efforts can produce multiple benefits, as long as you remember to provide a variety of levels and kinds of plants in your gardens.

Have fun looking over the gardening projects on the pages that follow, but feel free to branch out beyond the plants used in these designs. Without exaggeration, there are thousands of species of plants that have good bird value. Although plants that are native to your region are usually more tempting to birds than nonnative plants, many nonnative species are equally attractive to birds. American dogwoods are well known for their ability to beckon birds to their berries, for instance, but the fruit of the nonnative mulberry tree is even more enticing.

Pick your plants according to what you like, because every plant has some value to birds. All plants host insects (prime bird food!), and all shrubs and trees offer protective shelter. You'll also want to choose plants that will grow well in your area. Local garden centers and nurseries stock plants that are bound to thrive in your climate. All you have to do is check the tag to make sure you're buying shade lovers for your shady side yard or sun lovers for that open area.

Start with Shrubs

Most of us think of flowers first when we're planning a new garden. But a group of shrubs can have much more value when you're creating a bird habitat.

A group of three or more shrubs or a hedge planting of shrubs mimics the preferred natural habitat of many birds, including native sparrows, house sparrows, common yellowthroats, and towhees. Such a planting provides instant appeal for very little effort—and very low cost. Shrubs grow much faster than trees when they are young, filling out to a good size in just a couple of years. By the time they have been in the ground for 5 years, most shrubs will be at their mature height and width.

Shrubs are usually much less expensive than trees and not much more per plant than perennials. Shop around; you can find good shrub plants in gallon containers for less than $10 apiece. After planting your bushes, water well and apply a 2-inch layer of shredded bark, wood chips, or other long-lasting mulch. Allow a bit of space between the mulch and the main stems, and spread the mulch about 1 foot out from the farthest extent of the shrub branches. The mulch backdrop will instantly make even young, puny shrubs look more important.

Thorny Characters

Shrubs that make us say ouch when we brush against them are just the ticket for a bird garden. Birds are adept at perching between the thorns, but three of the most dangerous bird predators—cats, snakes, and raccoons—usually avoid prickly bushes, even if there's a tempting banquet of birdies in the branches.

continued on page 160

A Shrub Stop for Birds

A grouping of shrubs

is a foundation you can build on to expand the variety of birds that visit your yard or to favor the birds that already call your yard home. Try these ideas for incorporating shrubs into your landscape. All these plantings will increase your yard's standing as a bird habitat, because all require little help from the gardener to grow well. And an area that remains largely undisturbed is what birds like best.

■ Plant a group of shrubs beneath taller trees to create a multilevel habitat in which birds can move freely at different heights just as they do in the wild.

■ Plant a patch of meadow flowers in front of your shrubs, or add several clumps of fountain grass (*Pennisetum* spp.) or other low-growing ornamental grasses. This creates an edge effect—a transitional habitat that is notably high in bird appeal. If you garden in an arid area, pair native grasses with ceanothus (*Ceanothus* spp.) and other well-adapted native shrubs.

■ Encourage a "jungle" in subtropical and tropical areas by adding vines such as passionflowers (*Passiflora* spp.) to a shrub planting. The vines will clamber under and over the shrubs, giving birds more hiding places and more insects. Be ruthless with pruners to keep the supporting cast of shrubs from being smothered. Cut back vines about once a month so that they cover no more than one-third of the shrub's exterior.

■ Allow ground-hugging weeds, such as smartweed and chickweed, or attractive tall weeds, such as yellow-flowered mustard, to take over the empty space beneath the shrubs. Finches and other songbirds will seek out the seeds that the weedy plants drop.

■ Plant a group of evergreen shrubs as a living snow fence in northern or mountain regions to collect or redirect snow. Snow will pile up on the windward side of the shrubs just as it would along a fence. Birds will roost at night in the snow-covered shrubs, protected within the insulating blanket of snow that blocks cold winds and helps keep them snug at night.

continued from page 158

Although planting a thick hedge of thorny shrubs is not a surefire solution, it can definitely make a wandering neighborhood cat think twice before trespassing. If cats are the bane of your backyard, consider investing in fast-growing barberry bushes, pyracanthas, or shrub roses. A solid hedge of these thorny plants along the perimeter of your property may be unpleasant enough to give your birds permanent relief from that purring predator. (For a fast solution to a cat problem that you can use while your permanent hedge is growing, see "Cat-Proof Feeding Station" on page 129.)

Retrofit a Flowerbed

Most gardeners love their flowerbeds and borders, but though the colorful displays brighten our hearts, they don't add much value to a bird habitat. Birds will forage for insects, including butterflies, in a flower garden. But birds are unlikely to select it as a nest site or to spend much time in it, because these plantings require regular care, and most birds won't nest in areas where people are frequently active. Some design changes and additions can change that, however, turning your flower garden into a bird destination and perhaps even a residence.

Add low-care shrub roses. Rosebushes, with their thorny stems, offer birds natural nest sites. Snipping and fussing over the bushes cuts down on bird use, so choose roses that can get along just fine without you. Hardy rugosa roses, old-fashioned varieties, and small-flowered floribunda or multiflora roses are your best bets. Birds often sample the fleshy round rose hips that follow the flowers, and in the winter they consume great quantities of the small hips produced by multiflora roses.

Plant a small tree. Plant a flowering cherry or dwarf sour or sweet cherry in the back of the bed. Its open branches and shifting leaves won't put nearby flowers in deep shade, and its flowers or fruit will attract food-seeking birds. Cherry trees also supply excellent nest sites, even when the trees are very young.

Accent with evergreens. You'll thank the birds for inspiring this addition when you see how much difference a few evergreens make to the structure of the garden in winter. The trick is to choose a plant that complements the size and form of the flowering plants in the garden. Generally, broad-leaved evergreens with large leaves are a better match with flowers than are small-leaved evergreens or conifers, which have a finer texture. But as in all matters of home landscape design, the most important rule is to suit yourself. Consider camellias, dwarf cultivars of evergreen azaleas and rhododendrons, or foliage plants such as Japanese pieris and hollies or, in mild climates, citrus. Birds will appreciate the additional shelter that evergreens provide during inclement weather and the protected roosting sites for sleeping.

Grow up with vines. Installing a trellis or tepee of vining plants is a great way for plant fanatics to shoehorn in a little more color. A vine-covered trellis also supplies shelter and potential nest sites for catbirds, cardinals, and other birds. Woody vines, including honeysuckle, trumpet vine, wisteria, and grapes, grow vigorously, boasting the dense, lush growth that nesting birds seek. Make sure the trellis you install is a sturdy one that can remain solidly in place for years.

Add an arbor. If you have about 2 feet of open space at the back of a flowerbed or border, you can erect a romantic arbor with bird appeal. Not only will the arbor provide a backdrop that boosts the effect of the flowers in the foreground, but it also will give birds another coveted high place to perch. Cover the arbor with vines of any persuasion—annual, perennial, or woody—and you'll add more possible nest sites. (One arbor possiblity is the "Patio Pot Grapevine" on page 92.) The sides of an arbor are perfect places for mounting nest boxes, and its location in the flower garden means that you're not likely to overlook the big day when tenants for that birdhouse move in.

Create Layered Plantings

In nature, plants fill every inch of space. Tall trees tower over the smaller trees beneath them; shrubs shoulder up to small trees; and flowering plants, grasses, and ground-hugging plants cover the lowest levels. Our backyards often imitate that multilevel effect unintentionally as we make the most use of our limited space.

If your yard already has plants at various levels, congratulations! You have already succeeded in planting a multistory habitat. More likely, though, your plantings are spread out, with shrubs scattered here and there away from shade trees, and flower and vegetable beds given a place all their own in the sun. In this section, you'll learn how to knit those separate plantings together so that birds have easier, more natural access from one level to the next.

Fill the Space beneath Trees

Many summer residents, such as cedar waxwings, orioles, red-eyed vireos, and flycatchers, spend most of their time in the treetops. Migrating wood warblers, tanagers, and other songsters also find shelter and sustenance in the highest levels of our yards.

The shady space beneath tall trees is usually occupied by lawn grass. This area goes mostly unused by birds, except for robins and the occasional flicker. But the area under shade trees can be a perfect place to add the understory of small trees and shrubs that your habitat-to-be is lacking, as shown in the "Front Yard Makeover" on pages 162 and 163.

Nature's Inspiration

Look at natural woods around you to get ideas for plants that will thrive in these conditions. In the East and Midwest, dogwoods and redbuds are naturally adapted to the conditions below trees. In the conifer-clad West and Northwest, vine maples (*Acer circinatum*), amelanchiers, and western dogwoods are among the adapted candidates. The seedlings of tall trees also contribute to this medium-height layer in wild woods. If you like, you can mimic that by planting young maples, oaks, or other seedlings—or simply allow the tree's own progeny to sprout where seeds happen to fall.

Shrubs take the naturalistic woodland one step lower. Native plants are an ideal choice, or you can include any ornamental shade-loving shrubs that you like. Rhododendrons and azaleas will add a flash of color to your multistory planting.

continued on page 164

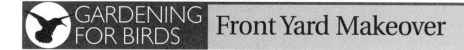
Many homes feature a pair of shade trees in the front yard. Replace the grass that is struggling to grow in the shade of their canopy with this low-care garden that features a multistory design. Borrowing the best from nature, this garden includes attractive plants worthy of a place of honor in the front yard. It's also likely to remain relatively undisturbed, with only occasional walkthroughs, so that birds can settle in and feel safe from intrusion.

The plants in this garden will thrive in Zones 4 through 10, and most are hardy to Zone 3. Bunchberry, spicebush, amelanchier, and Virginia creeper vines will provide hearty crops of tempting berries that are sought by tanagers, robins and other thrushes, cedar waxwings, and bluebirds. Chickadees love the flat, beanlike seedpods of redbuds. The asters and goldenrod bloom in late summer, attracting pollinating insects that also provide food for birds. Potential nest sites are plentiful, too.

Starting from Scratch

If you're not blessed with a pair of shade trees in your front yard, why not plant them now, right where the mature trees are located in this design? Although it takes years for trees to acquire height and fullness, you won't mind the wait because the faster-growing, attractive plants around the trees will take the focus off the spindly saplings. The understory plants in this garden will grow well in sun or shade.

PLANT LIST

Virginia creeper (*Parthenocissus quinquefolia*)

Wreath goldenrod (*Solidago caesia*)

Eastern redbud (*Cercis canadensis*)

Bunchberry (*Cornus canadensis*) or Pacific dogwood (*Cornus nuttallii*)

Amelanchier (*Amelanchier canadensis*)

Rhododendron or evergreen azalea (*Rhododendron* spp. or cvs.)

Spicebush (*Lindera benzoin*)

Christmas fern (*Polystichum acrostichoides*)

Heart-leaved aster (*Aster cordifolius*)

Step 1. Remove the lawn grass in the area you'll be planting. Use a sharp-bladed spade to cut the outline of the planting area.

Step 2. Still using the spade, cut the sod in the planting area into rectangular sections that will be easy to handle.

Step 3. Working with your hands, peel up the edge of a section of sod, roots and all, and slowly roll it up, as if you were rolling up a rug. (Keep a dandelion fork near at hand so that you can remove deep-rooted lawn weeds as you encounter them.)

Step 4. Remove the rolls of sod from the planting area. You can set them near your compost pile to decompose or lay them out in some other area of your yard where you want lawn grass.

Step 5. Plant each plant in the order listed, beginning with those closest to the shade tree and working outward. To plant, dig a hole that will accommodate the plant's rootball, fill it with water, and let the water drain out. Set the plant in the hole, backfill the hole, and tamp down the soil.

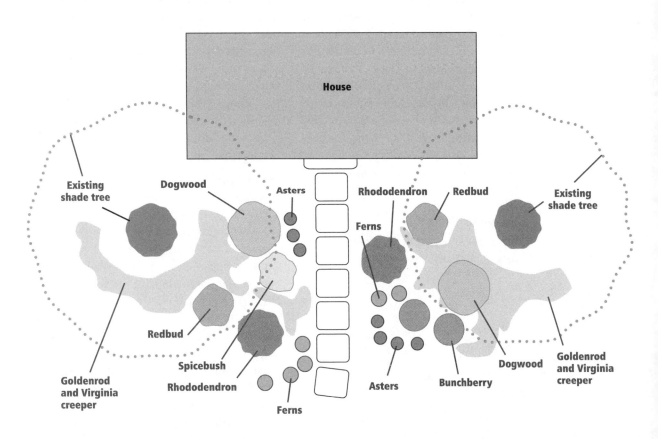

House

Existing shade tree

Dogwood

Asters

Rhododendron

Redbud

Existing shade tree

Ferns

Redbud

Spicebush

Rhododendron

Ferns

Asters

Bunchberry

Dogwood

Goldenrod and Virginia creeper

Goldenrod and Virginia creeper

Step 6. When you have planted all the plants, mulch the entire area with 1 ½ to 3 inches of bark mulch or wood chips. Spread the mulch with a hoe or short-pronged rake. Keep the mulch about 2 inches away from the trunks or crowns of the plants.

Step 7. Water each plant generously once a day for the first week, then once a week for the first 2 months.

HELPFUL HINTS

Continue watering regularly for at least the first year after planting, as woody plants take their time developing roots and becoming established. Expect the asters and goldenrod to spread, by seed and by roots, into ever-larger colonies. That's part of the plan!

Allow fallen leaves to remain in place. They will nourish the soil as they decompose, smother any weeds that try to sprout, retain soil moisture, and provide additional foraging territory for birds.

continued from page 161

Green plants fill the gaps on the woodland floor, whether it's in the wild or in your yard. Look to ferns and groundcovers to make use of that last bit of real estate. You can also leave some areas of ground bare of plants and either cover it with bark mulch or wood chips, or allow fall leaves to cover the soil. Towhees, thrushes, and forest-dwelling sparrows and juncos will find plenty to eat in the decomposing humus of leaf litter.

Up with Vines

Vines get short shrift in most bird gardens, yet many vines provide excellent cover and nest sites. Vines also let you add more bird-friendly habitat in a limited space, as these upwardly mobile plants need as little as 6 inches of ground space. Whenever you congratulate yourself on having a thoroughly planted yard, take another look—chances are there's still room for vines! For one example, check the design of the "Watchable Grape Arbor" on page 166.

Fruit on the Vine

Virginia creeper, every kind of grape, and feathery-seeded clematis vines (such as sweet autumn clematis), along with dozens of other annual and perennial vines, supply delicious fruit, seeds, or berries that birds adore. But beyond the obvious, vines also offer a living cornucopia of tasty insects among their leaves and stems. Caterpillars, beetles, stink bugs, spiders, and lots of other multi-legged creatures await to be uncovered by birds scouring a vine. Vine bark is a popular item for nest construction, and skinny twining twigs, as well as those cute curly tendrils, wind up in nests.

Nests in the Vine

The shady interior of a vigorous vine is valuable real estate to many nesting birds. Carolina wrens sometimes nest in clematis or other vines covering a porch or pole. Catbirds, cardinals, mockingbirds, and thrashers also might choose a vine for a homesite. In winter or at night, those tangled stems of a vine offer shelter from a storm or a safe place for birds to catch forty winks. The dense growth makes it difficult for cats and other climbing predators to reach the sleeping birds or their nestlings.

Grow your vine on a trellis or arbor, and you'll discover another unexpected pleasure: The top rung of such structures is a favorite perching place for backyard birds and hummingbirds.

Wonderful Weeds

As you continue to transform your yard into a bird habitat, take some time to reconsider your attitude toward weeds. No gardener worthy of the name would ever volunteer to let weeds take over a garden bed, but a bird gardener needs to learn how to coexist with weeds. Part of the problem is perception: Many common weeds are actually wonderful plants. But a bigger stumbling block is the psychological one of allowing plants you used to suppress to run wild in otherwise well-tended beds.

You can surmount both of these difficulties by being selective about the weeds you "cultivate"—or, more accurately, tolerate. Judicious weed gardening can lead to a yard that has even more of the plants that birds are naturally drawn to, and one that still looks good, too.

Cultivate Tolerance

It's up to you to decide how many and what kinds of weeds you can tolerate in your yard, but once you see how birds appreciate the seeds of these unloved plants, your tolerance level will likely increase. Of course, you'll want to keep ragweed out of your beds if you suffer from allergies, and thistles are on everybody's pure pest list. But a lawn dappled with buttery dandelions can look mighty pretty, especially when sunny goldfinches, dapper white-crowned sparrows, and brilliant indigo buntings show up as the flowers turn to seed puffs. And since very few of us are perfect weeders, you're likely to be harboring some "intruders" in your beds anyway. Before you yank out that stem of lamb's-quarters, for instance,

you may want to let the seeds ripen to see who comes calling. If you'd like to plan a "weedy" salad garden for yourself and the birds, check out the project on page 168.

Many weeds arrived in North America by intention. Early Europeans brought the seeds of their favorite plants along with them so that they would have the makings for that vital first garden. It didn't take long for these imported plants to escape their cultivated bounds. Two hundred years later, their progeny can be seen blanketing roadsides, vacant lots, and other areas where immigrants made inroads into wild places.

Seasonal Specialties

Weeds to Spare

Many weeds are pretty things, usually sporting tiny flowers and a relaxed habit that can work well as background filler in flowerbeds. Learn to identify these common, widespread weeds so that you can allow them to grow and thus enjoy their benefits to birds, which will visit the plants regularly as soon as they go to seed in late summer or fall. All except pokeweed are unobtrusive in a flower garden. Pokeweed grows so large that it looks almost like a shrub. If you aren't familiar with these weeds, consult a weed identification guide to learn how to identify them at an early stage. (To find a guide, see "Recommended Reading" on page 296.)

- Chickweed
- Purple dead nettle
- Yellow foxtail
- Henbit
- Lamb's-quarters
- Mustard
- Virginia pepperweed
- Pokeweed
- Purslane
- Shepherd's purse
- Smartweed

Watchable Grape Arbor

Grapes are tops with birds, which feast on the multitude of insects on the vines, collect nesting materials from the stems, and depend on the cover of those big leaves during rain or at night. Brown thrashers, mockingbirds, catbirds, and other fruit eaters—many of which also nest in grapevines—adore the abundant fruit.

When you grow these vigorous vines on a full-size arbor, most of the bird activity will be out of sight, as birds will pluck the fruit from the top of the structure. This cut-down arbor gives you a great opportunity to watch birds enjoy the fruits of your labor. You won't be able to walk beneath the arbor, but children will enjoy playing underneath it.

MATERIALS

Four 6-foot-tall wooden fence posts or 4 × 4s

12- to 14-foot-long section of 36-inch-high wire fencing

Twenty 12-penny nails

2 grapevines, any variety suitable for your climate ('Concord' is reliable)

TOOLS

Posthole digger or shovel

Level

Leather work gloves

Step stool (optional)

Staple gun with ½-inch heavy-duty staples

Hammer

Step 1. Choose a sunny location to erect the arbor.

Step 2. Measure and mark the positions for the arbor posts in a rectangular layout. Plan to set the posts about 28 inches apart at the narrow ends of the rectangle. The long dimension of the rectangle

should be equal to the length of your section of wire fencing minus 9 feet (the combined height of two posts when set).

Step 3. Use a posthole digger or shovel to dig a hole about 18 inches deep for each post.

Step 4. Set the posts in place and fill in around them with the removed soil. Use a level to make sure the posts are straight. Tamp the soil around each post firmly with your feet.

Step 5. Wearing gloves, drape one end of the wire fencing over two posts at one end of the rectangle, with the edge of the fencing near

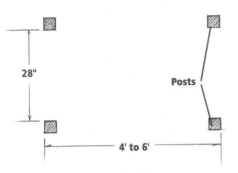

28"

Posts

4' to 6'

the ground. The fencing should extend about equally beyond each post. A helper is handy for this step of the project, as is a step stool.

Step 6. Staple the fencing in place, positioning staples diagonally across joints of the fencing wire in several places up the posts and on top of each post.

Step 7. Unroll the fencing and drape the other end in a similar fashion over the other two posts.

Step 8. Pull on the fencing to remove some slack and staple it as you did in step 6.

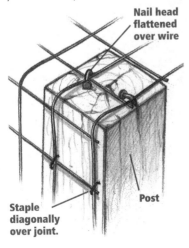

Nail head flattened over wire

Post

Staple diagonally over joint.

Step 9. To secure the fencing permanently, hammer two nails into the top of each post, allowing about 1 inch of each nail head to protrude. Use the hammer to whack the protruding part of the nail over the wire fencing to anchor it.

Step 10. Repeat this anchoring process with more nails down the length of the posts, using three nails for each post.

Step 11. Plant one grapevine at each end of the low arbor, midway between the end posts, on the outside of the fencing.

Step 12. As the grapevine grows, it will cover the fencing to create a lush arbor of short stature, about 4 1/2 feet tall. Bend errant branches into the fencing as needed, and snip off strays with pruners as the vine grows.

Grapevine Happenings

Place a lawn chair or garden bench nearby when the vine shows signs of fruiting (grapes often bear a small crop their first year), so that you can watch the robins, thrashers, and other birds that arrive to feast on the fruit. If you intend the grape arbor to function as a possible nesting location, make your sitting spot indoors instead of near the vine, so that birds have the necessary privacy for a nest site.

Grapes ripen during the summer, when natural food is abundant, so don't be discouraged if birds fail to eat all of the crop. Let the fruit hang on the vine; the birds will finish it off in the fall or winter, even though the grapes may have shriveled into raisins. In the winter, when the branches of the vine are bare, examine the vine to look for the remains of any bird nests. Birds often return to the same location to nest again the following year, so if you're lucky enough to have an old nest in your vine, watch for signs of nesting activity in late spring or early summer. A bird carrying twigs, bark, or other materials in its beak is a sure sign there's construction going on.

Salad Garden for the Birds

For a bird habitat with a different spin—and one that you can enjoy eating, too—plant this garden of salad greens and vegetables. When you've had your fill of greens, or when hot weather causes the plants to bolt and send up flowerstalks, sit back and let the birds eat the rest. Goldfinches, house finches, sparrows, and doves will be among your best customers.

Keep in mind that this patch will attract avian customers only when it goes to seed, and by then the greens look very different from those you snip for your salad bowl. Lettuce, for instance, will shoot up a stem 2 to 3 feet tall, topped by a branching burst of small yellow daisylike flowers. Meanwhile, the leaves may look mighty ragged.

Even so, you'll want to plant this patch front and center of an outdoor viewing area or bird-watching window. With so many birds actively gobbling up the seeds, chances are you won't even notice that the salad plants have lost their looks.

PLANT LIST

1 packet carrot seeds
1 packet chicory seeds
1 packet lamb's-quarters seeds
1 packet lettuce seeds
1 packet mustard seeds
1 packet radish seeds
1 packet turnip seeds

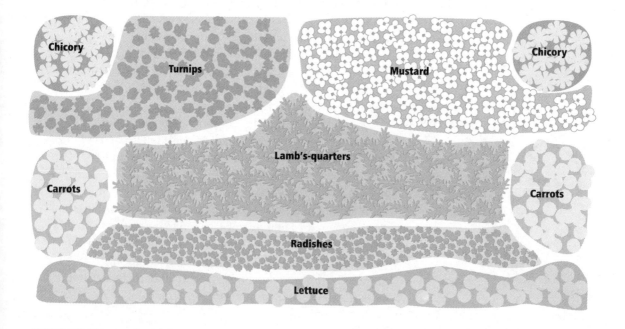

Step 1. Choose a site about 3 × 6 feet in a sunny location with average soil. (You can adjust the size to fit the space you have available.)

Step 2. Prepare the soil in early spring to early summer as you would for any seedbed, by removing existing vegetation and loosening the soil. Rake the soil to a fine texture, then sprinkle the seedbed with a hose, if needed.

Step 3. Plant the seeds in rows, or scatter them in patches. Try to sprinkle out the seeds in each packet to cover the allotted ground area. One packet of each will give you plenty of seedlings in your salad garden.

Step 4. Cover the seeds lightly with a layer of fine soil.

Step 5. Water with a gentle spray.

Step 6. Harvest the greens and vegetables as desired for salads.

Step 7. When the plants send up flower-stalks, let the seedheads stand after they mature. Some seeds that fall to the ground will sprout into new plants, so the garden renews itself without further planting.

Garden Management Tips

Your salad garden for the birds is easy to plant and manage. Here are a few special notes to keep in mind before you begin planting.

■ Lettuce seed packets are sometimes skimpy. You may need two packets, depending on which brand or type of lettuce you buy.

■ For the turnips and chicory, you'll need only about half a typical packet, but it won't hurt your final seed yield to plant them more thickly. Because the size of the roots of the root vegetables (turnips, chicory, radishes, and carrots) is not important to birds, you won't need to thin the stands either.

■ Rather than following the planting plan shown, you can mix all the seeds together and scatter them over the plot. This will produce a weedier appearance than planting varieties in separate areas.

■ Carrot plants are biennial and will bloom the second year. Chicory also may wait until the second season to produce the seed-laden blue flowers that birds find so appealing when the petals fall. All of the others will produce a plentiful crop of seeds the first year.

■ All of the plants are easy to grow from seed, but if you prefer, you can start with potted seedlings for the turnips and chicory.

■ Look for lamb's-quarters seeds in specialty vegetable catalogs or on some seed racks. Lamb's-quarters is gaining popularity as an interesting addition to "wild greens" salads.

■ For a fun alternative, you can transplant the common "weeds" (mustard, chicory, and lamb's-quarters) in this garden using seedlings you find on the roadside or in your flowerbed. Just scoop out seedlings with a trowel and move them to your bird garden, spacing them 4 to 6 inches apart.

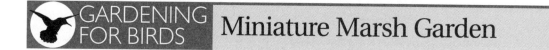

Miniature Marsh Garden

Birds that dwell in a marsh are not likely to show up in your backyard—unless your yard is acres big. But constructing a miniature marsh does have its advantages in a bird habitat. Plants that grow in boggy soil can supply additional food and nesting materials, such as cattail fluff. Even a small marsh—no bigger than a garden pool—may catch the eye of migrating birds in the spring or fall. They won't stick around, but a short visit by a red-winged blackbird, yellow-headed blackbird, or marsh wren is welcome when it happens right at home.

Before you begin your marsh garden, consider that it may turn out to be highly appealing to another marsh dweller: the mosquito. If an increased population of skeeters isn't in your plans, you may want to reconsider adding this type of garden to your yard. However, you may not be troubled at all by mosquitoes, especially if toads and other skeeter eaters move in to munch.

Buckets are the secret for creating this miniature aboveground "marsh." All of the plants grow in water in plastic buckets, thus meeting their requirement for wet feet. You can add a couple of tadpoles, netted at a local pond, to each bucket to help keep the mosquito population in balance. Wait until algae has begun to grow in the water before adding the tadpoles so that they will have an alternative source of food.

MATERIALS

4 to 6 plastic buckets, 2- or 3-gallon size

Plastic drop cloth, about 8 × 10 feet

Black or black-green Krylon spray paint

4 to 6 potted marsh plants (see "Plants for a Marsh Garden" below)

Large handful of duckweed

Ornamental grasses and large rocks (optional)

Step 1. Remove any labels and label residue from the buckets. Wash the buckets with soapy water and allow them to dry thoroughly.

Step 2. Set the buckets on the drop cloth. Spray the inside and outside of each bucket with spray paint. You do not need to paint the outside bottom of the buckets.

Step 3. When the paint is completely dry, arrange the buckets in the site you have selected for your marsh garden. Group them close together, with the rims of the buckets touching.

Step 4. Set each plant, still in its container, inside a bucket. Put the taller plants in the middle of the grouping and the shorter ones on the outside.

Step 5. Add water to each bucket to within 2 inches of the rim.

Plants in the Pool

You can also create a bog garden in a single container: a child's rigid plastic swimming pool. Give the swimming pool the same spray paint treatment so that it blends into the background, allowing the plants to garner the attention of human and avian passersby.

Step 6. Drop a scant handful of duckweed into the water in each bucket. This is the fastest-reproducing plant on earth, and its pretty greenery will soon cover the surface of the water. Not to fret: It won't spread onto the surrounding soil.

Step 7. If you want to screen the containers from view, plant ornamental grasses and place a few large rocks around the grouping of buckets. You may find that you don't mind the look of the discreetly painted buckets, because the unusual shapes and textures of the tall marsh plants draw the eye away from their humble footings.

Step 8. Add more water to the buckets as needed. Expand this small garden whenever you want by adding more plants in painted buckets.

Plants for a Marsh Garden

Common marsh plants that will work well in this garden include yellow flag (*Iris pseudacorus*), common cattail (*Typha latifolia*), dwarf cattail (*T. minima*), pickerel weed (*Pontederia cordata*), and arrowheads (*Sagittaria latifolia* and other species). You'll find these plants at pond supply stores and some garden centers. Buy the smallest container size available, as water plants grow very fast.

If the plants are sold bareroot, transplant each to a 4- to 6-inch plastic pot containing ordinary garden soil topped with a handful of gravel (to prevent the soil from floating out once the plants are submerged).

Duckweed (*Lemna* spp.) is also available at pond supply stores and some garden centers. Or you can net a single scoop of these tiny, bright green, floating plants from the surface of a local pond.

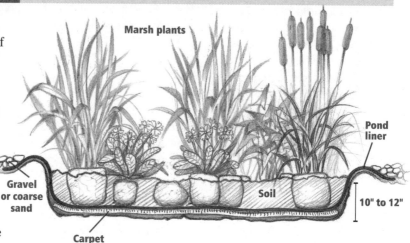

Permanent Marsh Garden

Marsh plants

Pond liner

Gravel or coarse sand

Soil

10" to 12"

Carpet

For those with plenty of space, creating a larger, more permanent marsh garden can be a rewarding endeavor. If your yard does not have a spot where the soil is moist or wet most of the year, you'll need to install a soil barrier—in this case, a flexible pond liner. The barrier will help keep the soil appropriately soggy. You can increase the size of your marsh garden to any dimension you like. As a rule of thumb, you'll want one plant per 4 square feet of garden area.

MATERIALS

Spray chalk, such as that used by engineers and contractors (available at hardware stores)

Piece of old carpet, about 6 × 8 feet

Flexible pond liner, 9 × 11 feet

12 potted marsh plants (see "Plants for a Marsh Garden" on page 171)

Large handful of duckweed

Gravel or coarse sand

Step 1. Use the spray chalk to mark the outline of the marsh area, which should be approximately 6 × 8 feet.

Step 2. Dig out the area 10 to 12 inches deep. Mound the removed soil along the edge of the excavated area. The floor of the garden does not need to be exactly level.

Step 3. To prevent sharp objects from poking holes in the liner, spread the carpet over the excavated area.

Step 4. Unfold the liner over the carpet. The liner should extend all the way up the sides of the excavation and a few inches out over the soil surface. Trim off any excess liner.

Step 5. Remove the plants from their containers and set them on the liner in a pleasing arrangement.

Step 6. Fill in around the plants with some of the removed soil. Tamp the soil moderately firmly into place with your feet.

Step 7. Add the rest of the removed soil, smoothing it to or just below the level of the surrounding soil.

Step 8. Insert the end of a garden hose into the soil in the garden and run the hose until the marsh area is sopping wet.

Step 9. Gently dump the duckweed into the water; it will establish itself from there.

Step 10. Spread an edging of gravel or coarse sand around the marsh area, to cover the edges of the liner and provide a naturalistic approach for birds.

Step 11. Add more water to the marsh garden as needed so that the soil stays constantly wet, or at least very moist. Most marsh plants can sustain occasional periods of drier soil, and some, such as yellow flag, can even adapt to life in a regular flower garden.

CHAPTER 6

Water for Birds

W hether it is dripping, splashing, bubbling, or flowing, water is a welcome addition to a backyard bird habitat. Even standing still, water is a magnet for birds. Most of the time, birds can find water from natural sources, but during a drought or extremely cold weather, supplying water for birds can make a real difference in their health and comfort. In addition, a birdbath is always a source of fun and enjoyment—for the bird watchers as well as the birds! Check out the projects in this chapter to create the drips, plunks, and burbles that will make your yard a year-round spa for birds.

WHY BOTHER WITH WATER?

With your feeding stations in full swing and plans for planting a bird habitat under way, you're ready for new projects that will make your yard even more attractive to birds. Adding a water feature is a great choice. As you learned in chapter 1, birds can usually find enough natural sources of water for drinking and bathing, but you'll be much better able to see and enjoy their bathing antics at a birdbath or other water feature. Most birders report that nearly all feeder birds enjoy the water, and even birds such as cedar waxwings that don't generally come to feeders may visit a water feature. Owls and other night fliers will drink at night, and if you light your water feature, you'll have a wonderful opportunity to observe these little-seen birds.

Experts from the National Audubon Society and other scientists report that most of the time, birds do not have a problem finding drinking water. Whether it's in rural or urban terrain, there are always low-lying areas, puddles, gutters, and ditches that hold water even long after a rain. The only time finding water is difficult for birds and other wildlife is during climatic extremes.

As Dry as the Desert

In dry, arid climates such as a desert, the native species are adapted to tolerate long bouts between drinks of water. However, in the temperate northeastern United States, where summer rainfall is plentiful, birds (and many other animals) depend on a regular routine of drinking and bathing. When there is a serious drought in such areas, some birds and animals can suffer from dehydration. As

with people, the very young and very old, and those already weakened by disease, are the most vulnerable. So even if you don't maintain a water feature in your yard, you may want to add a simple birdbath to your feeding station during an unusually hot, dry summer.

So Cold It Froze Your Toes

As in the case of a drought, freezing temperatures aren't a problem in regions where cold winters are the norm. But when it's unusually cold—such as a dramatic freeze or a blizzard in the Carolinas, or an extended period of below-zero temperatures in Connecticut—birds suffer. Birds have remarkable built-in thermal heaters and a nearly incredible ability to meet their caloric needs, but when they become dehydrated, their systems break down. If it's snowy outside, that's okay, because snow provides water and has a blanket effect—actually providing a buffer from the wind. When there's no snow and it's windy, with severe low temperatures, birds are in danger of hypothermia. The lack of snow for water, when all creeks, streams, lakes, and rivers have frozen, is the problem. A heated water source can be a lifesaver at times like these. (For tips on heating a birdbath, see "Water in Winter" on page 182.)

THE BASIC DRINK AND A BATH

Birds don't know or care whether their midsummer splash or cold-weather sip comes from a triple-tier designer fountain or a dog dish. Thus the type of water feature you make or buy is a matter of what you like, how much money you want to spend, and how much time you want to invest. The minimum goals are to supply some water near ground level and to be sure the feature allows birds to drink and bathe safely.

Vary the Level

In nature, most drinking places are at ground level or lower, and that's where most creatures look for water. For pheasants, turkeys, and other ground-dwelling birds, it's the only place they'll seek water. To ensure that bird visitors can find water in your yard, provide a water feature at ground level, as well as a raised source (waist high or above).

Raise a Saucer

If your birds' bathing and drinking place is on a lawn or in the garden, you may want to raise it above the level of the surrounding grass, groundcovers, or perennials. Ground-dwelling birds such as pheasants will drink from a source that's raised a few inches off the ground, and mourning doves and others prefer

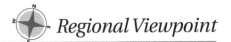 *Regional Viewpoint*

Drought on the Rise

Trying to garden during a drought can be disheartening for home gardeners, but a drought can have even more serious consequences for birds, as food supplies dip and natural water sources dry up. The alarming news is that many parts of the United States have experienced moderate to severe droughts in the past several years, according to the Palmer Drought Index, a measure used by the National Oceanic and Atmospheric Administration's National Environmental Satellite, Data, and Information Service. Here are some of the facts from the summer of 2002—just one of these very dry periods.

■ Drought affected half of the United States between June and August 2002.

■ Global average temperature was the third warmest in recorded history.

■ Twenty-nine states had significantly below-average precipitation.

■ The current drought pattern in the southern and western United States began in 1998.

■ The 12 months from September 2001 through August 2002 were the driest since 1895 in six states (North Carolina, Virginia, Colorado, Utah, Arizona, and Nevada).

■ The same 12 months were the second driest since 1895 in five more states (South Carolina, Georgia, Maryland, Delaware, and Wyoming).

During drought conditions, people suffer on many fronts. Farmers may lose crops, and the tourist industry withers. Wells dry up, and electricity costs increase. In the worst case, people die from extreme heat stress.

For wildlife and plants, the results are equally serious: Old trees become stressed to death, and some animal populations produce fewer young. Entire ecosystems can be damaged. As plants dry up, food as well as water becomes scarce for many birds, amphibians, insects, and other animals, and many deaths occur. Long-term studies on the effects of recent droughts on bird and other animal populations are not yet available, but it doesn't take a scientist to know that drought years are the times when our birdbaths and fountains become more than just pleasant landscape features; they can be lifelines for our birds.

the slight elevation because it offers a better vantage point to watch for predators and other dangers. You can set a large plant saucer on bricks, a fire grate, or any other low, sturdy support you have on hand.

Supply Water Safely

There's no benefit to providing water for birds if you are setting them up for an attack by a predator. Most birds have strong instincts about safety. Some even rely on a scout bird who watches for danger while others bathe. If you don't have any customers at your birdbath, the birds may be sending you a message that your water feature isn't a safe place.

To ensure the safety of bathing birds, place your birdbath at least 6 feet from clumps of flowering plants or ornamental grasses, shrubs, outdoor furniture, or any other potential hiding places for predators. It also helps to provide an elevated perch nearby—such as a tree limb, tall shrub, or trellis—for easy escape upward, as well as a place to duck under cover to escape from a hawk or other raptor. In the case of ground-level birdbaths, a greater distance is needed for safety, since making a getaway is that much harder for a wet bird. Aim for at least a 12-foot space between an inground pond and hiding places for predators.

Remember, too, that some birds, such as bold robins and blue jays, require an open location to feel safe and ensure a getaway. By contrast, a shady, protected spot will be more appealing to warblers and wood thrushes.

Watch Out for Window Hazards

When you're setting up a birdbath or other water feature, analyze the location in relation to the windows of your house,

Overhanging tree limbs or nearby shrubbery (above) can be a point of attack for a neighborhood cat. Place your birdbath in the open (right), but within range of a sheltering tree or shrub to which birds can escape if they're in danger.

especially large windows. You don't want the birdbath to become a takeoff point for fatal crashes into the glass. Place the birdbath (and feeders) such that the natural flight path is well away from all picture windows. Otherwise, birds may become confused upon landing or takeoff and collide with the window. Also, be sure that any large transparent surface is marked with a deterrent, such as decals or hanging balls of feathers, and use blinds and curtains to minimize reflections of the sky.

Just the Right Size

Birds will drink from nearly any container—from a designer birdbath to a plastic bottle cap. Even your roof gutters can serve as a watering trough—preferably with fresh rather than stagnant water.

For a satisfying bath, however, the slope and size of the container matter. Ideally, a birdbath will have a variety of depths, from ½ to 1 inch at the outer edges to 3 inches at the deepest spot, perhaps with occasional stones for perching. Most birds do not submerge themselves while bathing and want a firm footing, so a gradual incline provides security.

Sparrows, chickadees, and goldfinches are among the birds that remain in shallow water; grackles, jays, and robins venture deeper. As for diameter, a 12-inch dish will permit a bath, but a diameter of 24 inches or more is much more attractive to a bird or a whole gang (many birds bathe in groups).

Pedestal Birdbaths

The traditional pedestal birdbath has evolved over the ages, and it meets the need very well. A pedestal birdbath provides shallow water with gradually increasing depth, edges for perching, and a coarse surface so that birds don't slip. It also offers a raised vantage point, where birds can keep an eye out for danger, and easy access for landing and takeoff. (For ideas for adding garden style to a pedestal birdbath, see page 22.)

You can make a pedestal birdbath from materials you have on hand. See the list below and "Keep a Lid on It!" on page 179.

Scavenging for Birdbaths

Although birds don't care what your birdbath looks like, it will probably be a focal point of your yard, so choose something interesting, amusing, attractive, or unique. Attics, yard sales, barns, flea markets, and even the back of a kitchen cupboard are potential sources of homemade birdbath materials. Following are some items that can serve as the base or basin of a birdbath or drinking dish, as is or with a little adaptation.

- Pedestal ashtray
- Pedestal cake stand
- Plant stand with a plant saucer
- Macramé or crocheted plant hanger (for a hanging birdbath)
- Baby bath basin
- Deep-dish pie plate
- Large bowl from a china set
- Casserole
- Chicken feed holder
- Garbage can lid
- Horse feeding bucket
- Lid from a large pot
- Muffin tin
- Soup tureen
- Wok

If you choose to buy a commercial birdbath, you'll have to decide what type of material will work best for you. Lightweight plastic birdbaths are easy to move around and usually hold up through the winter, although some will blow over in a strong wind unless you weight the top with rocks, pour sand into the base (if it's open), or brace it with rocks. Concrete birdbaths offer an appealing rough texture but might be too heavy for you to move around or put away for the winter. Also, concrete baths sometimes crack when the water in them freezes and expands.

Some lovely designer birdbaths made of terra-cotta, ceramic, or even brass pass the style test but may be too smooth for bird comfort, so you will need to add gravel or stones. Likewise, some dark colors may look lovely to us with the water shimmering above them, but to a bird they hint of deep water or danger beneath. Although the outside may be any color, it's best to choose a birdbath with a basin that's light-colored on the inside.

Natural Water Features

A water feature may already be waiting in your yard for you and the birds to take advantage of it. A log or stump has birdbath potential, as shown on page 180. Take a walk around your yard just after a rain and look at the places where water is dripping or accumulating. Can you remove the lower section of the gutter downspout and let the water splash into a dish? Maybe you could place a

continued on page 181

✔ *For the Record*

Help the Bugs Drink, Too

Bees, wasps, and hornets (all important pollinators) will appreciate a drink from your birdbath. In fact, if you have a birdbath, you've probably found dead insects floating in the water. To help insects avoid drowning, supply a "raft" that they can climb on to dry off after a drink, in case their wings are too waterlogged to allow them to fly away. Simply float a twig or wooden block on the water as a matter of course whenever you freshen up the bath.

Other beneficial insects, such as ladybugs, spined soldier bugs, and hoverflies, will benefit from a birdbath, too, but they need a gradual edge from which to approach the water. You can supply this by putting a rock surrounded by pebbles in one part of the bath to provide a little bathing beach for beneficials. And if they fall in while drinking, the pebbles and rock serve as ladders they can climb to escape. Remember that most insects are good for your garden—and a few may even be an attractive bird appetizer.

One of the best sources of an improvised birdbath is a lid (with a handle) from a garbage can or large pot such as a wok or soup pot. The lid rests on a pedestal made from concrete blocks, a piece of tile drainpipe, or a chimney tile. A hidden anchor prevents the lid from tipping or blowing away in a strong wind.

MATERIALS

Rope or clothesline, about 40 inches long

Lid from a garbage can or large pot, preferably 20 inches in diameter or more, with a handle

4 concrete blocks of uniform size; 1 section of 6- to 10-inch-diameter tile drainpipe; or 1 chimney tile, at least 28 inches long

Level

Brick or short piece of heavy pipe

Step 1. Tie one end of the rope securely to the handle of the lid.

Step 2. If you are using concrete blocks, stack the blocks at the desired site, ensuring that the holes in the blocks line up. Use the level to be sure the blocks are set evenly; otherwise, the water in the bath will appear to tilt. If you're using a piece of drainpipe or a

chimney tile, dig a few inches into the ground and set the pipe firmly into the soil. Use the level to be sure the pipe is set evenly.

Step 3. Drop the loose end of the rope into the holes in the concrete blocks or the opening of the pipe. Check that the knot and the handle of the lid fit into the opening as well, so that the lid rests securely on top of the block or pipe. If necessary, pull the rope out and redo the knot so that it will fit.

Step 4. Measure the height of the blocks or pipe. Then measure the rope. The rope should be long enough so that you can tie it around the brick or piece of pipe that you're using as an anchor, such

that the anchor will just touch the ground when the lid is in place on the pedestal. If necessary, cut off some of the rope. (If there is slack in the rope, the lid may tip or blow off.)

Step 5. Tie the loose end of the rope securely around the anchor and drop the anchor through the blocks or pipe. Center the lid.

Step 6. If the lid has a smooth texture, add rocks or gravel to provide a safe footing for birds. Fill the birdbath with water and retreat to your viewing window to watch the show.

Lid

Rope

Drainpipe

Anchor

Basin in a Stump

In a natural-style or
rural garden, fallen logs, large branches, and stumps are often part of the landscape, and they may offer just the right nooks and cavities to become nearly natural water dishes for birds. If your yard is more formal, watch for tree removal projects in your neighborhood or take a walk after a severe storm to find just the right piece of wood to make this birdbath.

Step 1. Collect some bowls, dishes, plant saucers, or other containers that have birdbath potential.

Step 2. Scout your yard for a log or stump with a cavity. If you don't find one, search for one in your neighborhood and bring it home.

Step 3. Measure the diameter of each container and compare that to the cavity in your wood base. You may find one that's a perfect fit.

Step 4. If none of your containers precisely matches the size of the cavity, use a jackknife, utility knife, or other knife to carefully chip away at the wood to create a cavity

that is a little deeper than one of the containers. (Some deadwood is so soft that you can do this easily with a dandelion weeder or screwdriver rather than a knife.)

Step 5. Wedge the container securely into the hollow, adjust it so that it is level, and fill it with water.

Step 6. If you can't see your natural birdbath easily from your house, place a chair within viewing distance and plan to relax or read there occasionally while you enjoy the company of the birds.

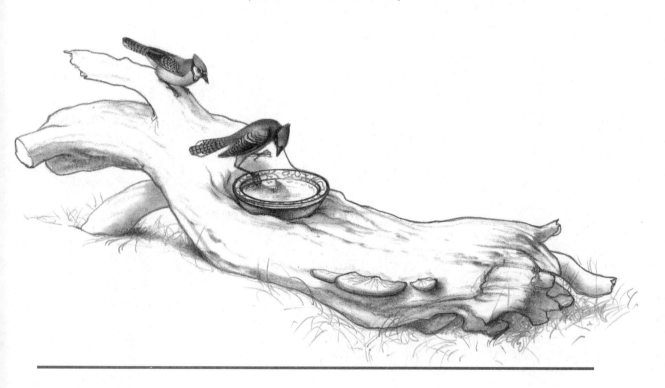

continued from page 178

rock or stump there with a bird-suitable container on top. Is there a dripping eave that would attract birds if you put a large plant saucer under it to make a noisy splash? If your gutter collects water (and grows weeds) and you cannot replace it right away or clean it often enough, you might want to poke a tiny hole in it to create a drain that will drip into a dish below. Natural elements such as logs and stumps also have birdbath potential if you use your imagination.

Keeping It Clean

During a rainy spring, a frequently used birdbath will stay fairly clean, because there is a lot of turnover and because algae don't grow as vigorously as during the hot months. When the scorching sun arrives, however, the green slime proliferates—along with potential bacteria—and it gets worse as the water evaporates. So make it a routine, along with weeding and watering the garden or refilling your feeders, to dump out the old water, remove the algae with a sponge or brush, and refill the birdbath. When a real cleaning is needed, using a light vinegar solution (1 teaspoon per 1 quart of water) is preferable to using a detergent.

Set a Routine

Certain birds, such as chickadees, catch on to people's routines amazingly quickly and adapt to whatever patterns suit their purposes. Other birds take longer to learn the rules in a new setting, but nearly all will figure out what to expect from you. It helps if you establish a routine for refilling, cleaning, and deicing a birdbath. In the frozen North, if you cannot provide a water heater, a daily routine of putting out a dish of tepid water will train some regulars to stop by for a drink and a splash.

Spring. If you put away your birdbaths for the winter, get them back out when spring rains begin. In many parts of the country, rainfall alone will be enough to keep them overflowing. Supplying water at this time of year isn't that important for birds, as they can find it in many places, but it might keep them in the habit of coming to your yard.

Caution: If a freeze is predicted, remember to empty any breakable birdbaths at night so they don't crack.

Summer. As the temperature increases and the rainfall decreases, fungi and bacteria may grow in standing water. This is the time to dump out birdbath water at least once a week and scrub out the bowl. If mosquitoes are a concern, use BTI (*Bacillus thuringiensis* var. *israelensis*), as described on page 182, or add a little pump to keep the water moving.

Fall. Plan to winterize your birdbath with a water-heating device. If the bath is made of a material that will crack when the water freezes, find an alternative made of plastic. Also consider location, as an open summer site might not be suitable when icy winds blow.

Winter. Regular guests or migrating birds may appreciate the water supply most in the winter, when everything else is frozen. Freshen up the birdbath at the same time every day, and check that water-heating systems are working.

Dealing with Mosquitoes

Even nature lovers have never appreciated mosquitoes, and new concerns about West Nile virus, which is carried by some mosquitoes, have made us even more determined to prevent these biting insects from infesting our yards. Bug zappers are not effective mosquito controls, and it takes a lot of citronella or other repellents to keep them away. The most important thing you can do is to remove standing water where mosquitoes breed, such as in abandoned tires, blocked gutters, neglected equipment and buckets, or natural swamps or bogs.

Does a birdbath fit that category? The answer is no—unless you set up the birdbath and never tend to it. You have full control over a birdbath, and all you have to do is dump or change the water every few days during mosquito season. (Mosquito larvae live 4 to 10 days before pupating and becoming adults.) A powerful splash from a hose will displace and remove most of them. In larger pools or bog gardens, you can use BT, a natural larvicide, to kill the larvae.

BTI Products

BT is *Bacillus thuringiensis,* a bacterium that destroys leaf-eating caterpillars and many insect larvae, including mosquito larvae. It does not harm birds or other animals, nor does it have any detrimental effects on plants or water quality. The BT strain known as *israelensis* (BTI) is effective for mosquito management. BTI is available in liquid or powder forms at many garden centers. It also is sold in doughnut-shaped floating pellets that you may find labeled as Mosquito Dunks. BTI has been used to decrease mosquito infestations in large areas and can surely help in your pond. As with any pesticide, even a natural or organic one such as this, always read and follow the label instructions.

WATER IN WINTER

Tending a birdbath in the summer is a fun and easy chore. But when cold wind, sleet, and snow hit, it's not so pleasant to

Water Heating Do's and Don'ts

■ DO read the safety instructions on all heating devices. Some are made for indoor use only. Others can burn out if not submerged.

■ DO use a winter-proof material such as plastic or metal for a birdbath.

■ DO add rocks to your birdbath so that birds can land and drink but can't submerge themselves and bathe. Birds sometimes bathe in heated baths and then freeze to death later when the temperature drops quickly.

■ DO float blocks of wood in the bath, since it helps keep the water open if the heater or timer is off.

■ DON'T use water additives to lower the freezing point of the water, as these may be toxic to birds.

■ DON'T set a heating unit in the birdbath without attaching it to the bath, even if it's too heavy for a bird to lift. A larger, stronger animal may visit your birdbath and bump out the heater as it drinks.

■ DON'T forget that pottery, glass, and ceramic birdbaths and dishes can break, particularly as water freezes and thaws—and thus expands and contracts—when temperatures fall or rise.

Farmers use heat lamps to help keep chickens and other animals warm during the winter, and you can use one to create a sheltered spa for your songbirds. Heat lamps are sold in farm supply stores and cost from $15 to $25. They include a space guard to prevent the hot bulb from touching anything flammable. The fixtures are not intended for outdoor use, and the hot bulbs could easily crack if exposed to precipitation, so use heat lamps only for a birdbath that's protected by a porch roof and completely sheltered from the weather.

Warning: These lamps get very hot and are dangerous if used improperly. Read all the warning labels and instructions.

Step 1. Set up your birdbath on a porch or patio that is covered by a solid roof.

Step 2. Hang the heat lamp from a secure fixture, such as a wall bracket, positioning the lamp about 2 feet above the birdbath. Keep in mind that the distance from which the lamp will be effective is related to how low temperatures drop.

Step 3. Plug the lamp into a GFCI (ground-fault circuit interrupter) outlet. You can turn the lamp on and off manually, attach it to a thermostat (set the thermostat to activate the light when the temperature drops below freezing), or connect it to a timer.

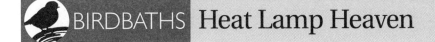

Heat lamp

head outside to dump ice and provide fresh water. Birds don't need warm water, as we humans would prefer, since feathers are much more effective than skin for providing insulation. In the winter, it's important that birds be able to drink, but they don't need to bathe. All you need to do is supply unfrozen water—birds won't mind that it's cold.

One way to do this is to buy a deicer or immersion heater for your birdbath. Many experts say that this is not the place to scrimp, as the cheapest types (sometimes foil or spiderweb-shaped units that lie in the water) aren't always effective and are easily pulled out.

Another option is to fashion a homemade setup for warming a protected birdbath with a heat lamp or lightbulb as shown above and on page 184.

Deicers and Heaters

Small deicing units for birdbaths often have an automatic shutoff feature. Such

An ordinary lightbulb,

such as a 75- or 100-watt bulb, can generate enough heat to prevent a birdbath from freezing over. This simple setup isn't elegant, but it will become an avian hot spot on a cold winter morning. You can find the make-a-lamp kit at hardware stoes and home centers. Also check the holiday decorations section of the store, since many outdoor lighting features will suit this project perfectly.

MATERIALS

Two 6-inch plastic or terra-cotta pots, with drainage hole

Duct tape

Fiberglass insulation (optional)

Plastic grocery bag or other thin plastic (optional)

Make-a-lamp kit

Extension cord rated for outdoor use

75- or 100-watt lightbulb

Birdbath basin (Choose a material not prone to cracking)

Step 1. Place the two pots bottom to bottom, with the drainage holes aligned. Wrap duct tape around the pots at the joint to stabilize item. If you choose not to insulate the pot, go on to Step 3.

Step 2. To increase the effectiveness of this heating device, wrap some insulation around the outside of the top pot. Cover the insulation with plastic and tape the plastic securely in place.

Step 3. Open the make-a-lamp kit. Following the assembly instructions that come with the kit, assemble the parts so that the switch and socket are inside the top pot, pointing up, and the cord dangles down inside the bottom pot.

Step 4. Screw in the lightbulb and turn the switch to the On position.

Step 5. Place the heater base in the desired location. The bottom pot will sit on the cord where it protrudes from the base, but that's okay. If you like, you can make a small chip in the pot to accommodate the cord. Or set the base on a surface with openings—such as a patio table with an opening in the center for an umbrella pole—and feed the cord down through the opening.

Step 6. Set the birdbath on the top pot. Plug the cord into the extension cord. On cold nights, plug the extension cord into a GFCI outlet.

Socket

Cord

features are a good investment to avoid burning out the unit if the bath goes dry. One reliable product is the Ice Eliminator, which lies right in the birdbath and is safe to use with all types of baths.

Birdbaths are available with built-in heating coils, too. If you choose one of these, be sure it is firmly constructed, as some types have been known to warp, so that the dish pops off the heating unit. Wild Birds Unlimited and other specialty bird suppliers offer reliable models that guarantee open water to –20°F. (For information on suppliers, see "Resources for Backyard Birders and Gardeners" on page 292.) Choose a model that can handle the minimum temperature in your region, and compare the wattage used and the type of warranty offered. This is one case where you'll definitely want to buy a durable product.

Timing the Warmup

If the weather in your area has typical periods of freezing nights and warmer days, try plugging the heater into a timer set so that the heater operates only at night. Or take a frugal approach and set the timer so that the water unfreezes only for a short morning or evening period, timed to correspond with the busiest feeding times at your feeders.

When you plug the cord from a heating unit into a timer or extension cord, wrap the connections with electrical tape to prevent snow and rain from penetrating the openings.

THE MAGICAL SOUND OF WATER

Setting up a birdbath or putting out water dishes will meet birds' basic needs to drink and bathe. Adding the sound of dripping water will draw birds more quickly to your backyard oasis. Adding a dripper to a birdbath can be a super-simple project, or you can create an elegant bamboo dripper or even a splashing fountain. You can also buy drippers and misters (sometimes advertised as waterspouts or water drippers) from specialty stores or online suppliers. They cost $25 and up.

If you'd like to see for yourself what a difference adding sound can make, try an experiment. Put two birdbaths in equally bird-suitable locations, one with still water and the other with a dripper or fountain. Observe the baths for a couple of weeks to see which one attracts and keeps more visitors. If you are still skeptical, switch them and observe again.

The birds you attract may vary according to the type of water action you set up. Warblers, for example, can't resist drippers but are intimidated by powerful waterfalls. (In general, gentle fountains and drippers are more attractive to most types of birds.)

The Basic Drip, Drip, Drip

A dripper doesn't have to be artistic to lure in the birds, as long as it makes that dripping noise. The simplest way to add a drip is to hang a 1- or 2-gallon plastic jug from a tree limb, shepherd's crook, eave, or trellis. If you can find a plastic juice jug with a plastic handle around the neck, you'll have a built-in hanging device. Whatever kind of jug you find, poke a hole in the bottom with a pin or tack, starting small. Add some water to the jug and see how frequently the drips emerge. Eight or nine drips per minute will be enough to interest birds.

A jug with a screw-on cap is best for making a dripper, because you can use the cap to help control the rate of the drips. (A tight-fitting snap-on cap creates a vacuum inside the jug, which will prevent water from dripping.) Gradually screw and unscrew the cap to adjust the flow. Enlarge the hole only enough to achieve the right drip rate. At a rate of eight drips per minute, a 1-gallon jug will drip most of the day.

A gutter also works well as a dripping device. Of course, it's usually not a good thing when a gutter leaks—unless it drips where you want it to! But if you have an old gutter, simply poke a hole through it and let the drips fall. A catch basin underneath will increase the sound effect.

Playing with Sound Effects

The sound of your dripper will vary depending on the surface the drips hit. Experiment with the different effects you can achieve. It can be fun for children of all ages to help you with this, as you listen for the pitch, loudness, and tone of those plinks and splashes. Notice how the sound differs when a water drop hits a piece of copper, a pie tin, a bowl of water, a piece of carpet, a stone, or a plastic surface. If you like the effect of the drips hitting a surface other than water, you can add an island to your birdbath and have the dripper drip onto the island. Or set up the dripper as its own water feature, separate from a birdbath. Just the sound of dripping water is a strong attraction for birds, even if no pool is available.

Aiming for Artistic

Hanging a plastic jug of water from a tree to create a dripper will work just fine to attract birds, but the setup won't look very attractive. You can aim for higher style by using a colored glass bottle instead of a plastic jug. You'll need a drill and a diamond-tipped or carbide-tipped drill bit to drill a hole through the glass, or you may find a craft or glass supply store that will drill the hole for you. Another option is to stick with a plastic jug but hide it inside a more decorative container as shown on right.

Japanese garden style offers two beautiful techniques for creating the sound of dripping water: *kusari doi*, rain chains, (shown on page 188) and *tsukubai*, bamboo drippers (shown on page 192).

Double-Duty Dripper

During droughty periods, old, stressed, or recently planted trees may begin to die if they don't receive 8 to 15 gallons of water a week. (And we almost never deliver that much water when we give trees a drink with a hose.) So when a dry spell hits, set up plastic jug drippers not only to attract birds but also to water your landscape trees.

If you want to water a mature tree with strong limbs, hang plastic jugs at varying levels from the lower limbs. (Be sure to pad each limb before you tie the jug to it.) Position the jugs near the ends of the limbs, so that the water will drip where the tree has plenty of active roots to absorb the moisture. You might place pie tins under a few of the drips to hold a little water and let the drips make a pleasing sound.

Depending on where you live, watch for birds such as mourning doves, robins, pheasants, and wild turkeys to stroll by, curious about this new source of refreshment. Your neighbors may be curious, too, and if they ask, you can pass on this low-tech method for watering trees and attracting birds.

A Dripper in Disguise

A clay or ceramic pot

can be just the ticket for disguising that plastic jug dripper. You can select a ceramic pot with an attractive glaze or try hand-painting a clay pot or metal bucket yourself. Tole painting often suits a bird garden style.

Step 1. Wash a 1-gallon plastic jug thoroughly with soap and water.

Step 2. Find or buy a clay pot or other decorative container that is about 2 inches taller than the jug and wide enough to contain the jug. Either buy a pot with a drainage hole in the bottom or make a hole yourself. The hole should be big enough for sturdy twine or clothesline to pass through.

Step 3. Scout out the site where you want to hang the dripper. Any sturdy support—such as a tree limb, the eave of your house, a bracket attached to the wall of a garden shed, or a trellis—will do.

Step 4. Use a tack or small nail to poke one hole in the bottom of the jug.

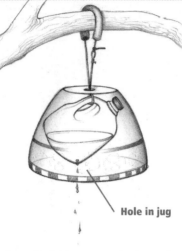

Hole in jug

Step 5. Add water to the jug and see how fast it drips out through the hole. Enlarge the hole, if needed, until the jug drips at a rate of about 10 drips per minute.

Step 6. Tie a length of sturdy twine or clothesline to the neck or handle of the jug. The twine should be long enough to tie to the support and suspend the jug at the desired height. (If the jug is hung in an area where people will be walking, be careful not to hang it at head height.)

Step 7. If you're using a clay pot, you can paint the outside, if you wish. Allow the pot to dry before continuing to step 8.

Step 8. Thread the twine through the hole in the pot or container, from the inside out.

Step 9. Hang the jug and pot from the support. Make a loose knot in the twine around the support at first so that you can experiment with the height of the arrangement. Drips from too high may splash too much and spray too widely, but hanging the dripper too low may scare off birds or look unattractive.

Step 10. Fill the jug with water and let 'er drip!

HELPFUL HINTS

If you're going to hang the jug from a tree limb, pad the twine by laying a piece of plastic tubing or old garden hose over the limb first, and be sure the twine is resting on the tubing or hose. This will prevent the twine from cutting into the tree bark.

Traditional rain

chains, or *kusari doi,* may
be simple or fancy, with
multiple chains, bowls, or
bells. Historically, rain chains
served to move rainwater
from rooftops and gutters to
catch basins, to capture the
water for household or garden
use. For us, rain chains may be
practical, aesthetic, or both.

You can create your own
kusari doi in place of a gutter
downspout, or hang it from a
hook under the eave of your
house. For this project, you can
use any kind of chain, but decorative chains with large links
(such as the kind designed for
hanging lamps or outdoor
lanterns) add the most interest.
You can also experiment with
other types of materials, such as
a mobile or tiered wire egg baskets with dishes placed in the
baskets. Remember, water
droplets will cling to most surfaces until gravity pulls them
downward—creating the steady
drip that attracts birds.

S hook

Basin

MATERIALS

Chain, about 5 feet long
Screw eye (optional)
**S hook, of a size that will fit the
point of attachment and the
links in the chain**
Pliers (optional)
Basin or stone

Step 1. Select a site for the rain
chain where you will hear or see
the pattern of drips or where the
dripping will attract birds after a
rainfall.

Step 2. If you decide to use the
chain as a substitute for one of the
downspouts on your house,
remove the downspout and clean
the opening. (This would be a
good time to clean the gutter, too.)
If you're attaching the chain to the
eave of your house, drill a pilot
hole in the eave and screw in the
screw eye.

Step 3. Hang the S hook from the downspout opening or screw eye. If you are hanging it from a downspout opening, you may have to experiment with the size and angle of the hook, using pliers to bend the upper curve to achieve a firm hold.

Step 4. Hang the chain from the hook.

Step 5. Place the basin under the end of the chain. Then wait for a rain, or use your garden hose to spray water onto your roof to see the effect. You may want to reposition the basin or remove some of the chain links to create a longer distance for drips to fall. Experiment until you're satisfied with the sight and sound of the dripping water. (If you're doing this part by pouring water off the roof, it's very helpful to have an assistant.)

Step 6. Continue watching the rain chain for a month or so to see whether birds are drawn to it and to experience for yourself the relaxation of observing the pattern of the raindrops.

Watering with a Rain Chain

If you have a water-loving or newly planted perennial under the limb of a tree, maximize the watering potential of every rainfall by putting a rain chain over the plant. Just drape the ends of the chain over the tree limb so that the lowest point of the curve in the chain is directly over the plant.

TAKE A JUMP INTO PUMPS

If you move up to a project that uses an electric pump to move water, you'll no longer have to depend on rainfall or remember daily refills to keep a dripper running. You'll also open up lots of delightful possibilities for fountains, cascades, and other effects. Many gardeners worry about the technical details of working with an electric pump, but the calculations for figuring out what size pump you need and the tasks involved in connecting the apparatus aren't difficult. Besides, you'll feel extremely accomplished when you overcome "pump phobia" and can show off your gurgling backyard water feature.

Pumps and Parts Made Easy

Pumps for water features are either *submersible* or *external*, referring to their location in or out of the water. Both kinds of pumps have a motor that runs a set of blades that push the water. Submersible pumps are the easiest and cheapest to use for most water feature projects.

Another choice you'll face when buying a pump is whether to select a *direct-driven* or a *magnetic-driven* pump. In general, magnetic-driven pumps are preferable because they use less energy, but they are usually also more expensive to buy. Check the energy efficiency rating of a pump to gauge which of your choices will require the least electricity to operate.

Determining Pump Size

Pumps are usually sold as miniature (for a dish garden), small (for a little fountain), medium (for an average fountain), and large (for a waterfall or large waterspout). You can determine what size you need based on the volume of water in your project and the distance the water needs to move. Your goal is to choose a pump that can move half the total volume of water in 1 hour. (If you're building a large waterfall or stream, you will need a bigger pump—one that might move the *total* volume of water in 1 hour. However, this type of project is rare for a bird habitat.)

Water garden experts note that beginning water gardeners often buy a pump that is too small. Take the time to calculate the total water volume required for your project, then confirm with a reputable salesperson what size pump you should buy. You'll be disappointed if you assemble your project and discover that the pump won't do the job right.

Start with the Average Depth

In order to calculate the correct pump size for your project, you need to know the average depth of the water in your container or pool. Since many containers have sloping or irregular bottoms and the depth varies, you'll need to do some estimating to come up with the average depth. You don't have to be exact in your measurements, but make sure you estimate the *highest* average depth, so that your pump selection will be based on the largest potential volume of water you want the pump to move.

Create sections. To start with, look at your container or pool and mentally divide it into four to six sections. You will measure the depth in each of these sections. If your container or pool is smaller than 6 square feet or bigger than 100 square feet, measure in fewer or more spots, respectively. The idea is to get a realistic representation of the various depths.

Measure the depths. Use a ruler or yardstick, as appropriate, to measure the depth in each section. (If your container or pool doesn't have water in it yet, measure to the height you expect the water to reach, which is not necessarily the top edge.

Find the average. Add the measurements from each section together, then divide by the number of sections you measured. The result is the average depth.

Figure the Total Volume

Now that you know the average depth of your container or pool, you can move on to calculating the total volume of water. The calculations will vary depending on the shape of your container. When you use the following formulas, express length, width, and other dimensions in feet, not inches.

Rectangles. Measure the length and width of the rectangle.

> Length × Width × Average depth × 7.48
> = Volume (in gallons of water)

Ovals. Measure from the center of the oval to the nearer edge, then measure from the center to the farther edge.

> Distance to nearer edge × Distance to farther edge × 3.14 × Average depth ×
> 7.48 = Volume (in gallons of water)

Circles. Measure the radius (from the center to the edge of the circle).

> Radius × Radius × 3.14 × Average depth ×
> 7.48 = Volume (in gallons of water)

Odd shapes. If you have a kidney-shaped pool or other odd-shaped container, break it into simple units, such as two circles and a rectangle, as best you can. Find the volume for each of those units and add them together to determine the total volume. Or measure the greatest length and the greatest width, then use the formula for rectangles.

Pump Care and Maintenance

When you're working with pumps, remember that the combination of water and electricity can be dangerous when users become careless or overconfident and bypass the rules. This is no place for improvisation. Always read the labels on equipment. Use wiring and cords that are proper for water garden and outdoor use. Place electrical outlets more than 6 feet away from water features to avoid serious accidents. When in doubt, have a professional install your electrical unit or water feature.

Pumps today are sophisticated, usually with oil-cooled motors that prevent them from burning out if the unit runs dry. However, algae and debris will collect at the intake vents on a pump, and the vents will require cleaning occasionally. You can do this with a toothbrush. Some pumps have a filtering screen that you can remove, brush, and wash. If you have questions about your pump's performance and maintenance, check with a reputable supplier, who will be able to assist you with cleaning and replacement parts when needed.

Fountains and Bubblers

Although the variety of fountains and bubblers you can make or buy is amazing, all of these water features share cer-

Doing the Math

Here's a hands-on example of the calculations for figuring the total volume of a container. In this case, we need to find the volume of an oval container that's 1 foot deep.

■ Since the container is basically flat-bottomed, we'll use 1 foot as the average depth.

■ The distance from the center to the nearer edge is 8 inches (0.75 foot); the distance to the farther edge is 1 foot.

■ Distance to nearer edge × Distance to farther edge × 3.14 × Average depth × 7.48 = Volume.

■ That translates to: $0.75 \times 1 \times 3.14 \times 1 \times 7.48 = 17.62$, or about 17½ gallons of water

tain basic elements. Once you understand the component parts, you can make your own fountains or bubblers using your own taste and imagination—in the container or pool of your choice. For one imaginative example, see the "Sparkling Colored-Glass Fountain" on pages 196 through 198.

Start small with your first project, to gain confidence with directing and containing water. Buy a bigger pump than you think you will need, since almost everybody wants a bigger bubbler or a splashier fountain next time.

Container. This could be a preformed water garden, a half barrel, a washtub, a ceramic or clay pot, a hypertufa trough, or a plastic pool. If you use a wooden tub or barrel, you'll need to line it with a plastic pond liner or coat it with asphalt emulsion or epoxy to make it waterproof.

continued on page 195

Tsukubai **is** the Japanese word for a bamboo dripper, a common feature in Japanese gardens. Shinto teachings reveal why the *tsukubai* design causes water to change direction as it flows through the dripper. According to Shinto tradition, evil spirits can travel only in straight lines. If the evil spirit is following the water, it cannot make the turn and falls into the water.

   Once you've assembled this dripper, it's easy to care for. Refill it as needed to keep the water flowing. In the winter, you can take the unit apart and bring it indoors, although it may be a challenge to reassemble. Or you may heat the basin to prevent the water from freezing. In areas with mild winters, floating a ball on the water may be sufficient to maintain a hole in the ice and allow the water to keep flowing.

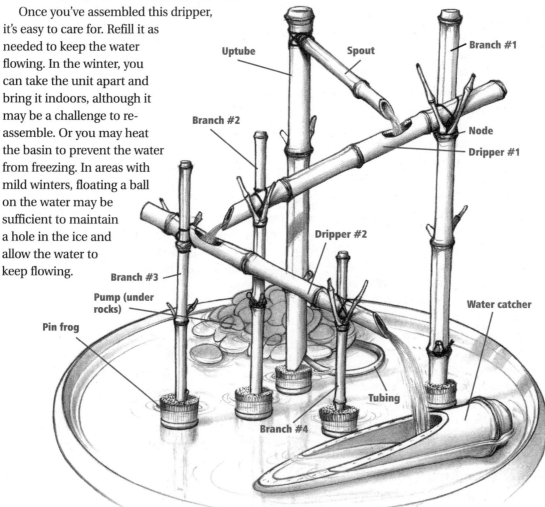

MATERIALS

Three 1½-inch-diameter pieces of bamboo, 15 inches long

¾-inch-diameter piece of bamboo, 8 inches long

24-inch piece of poly tubing to fit the pump output (Select the appropriate diameter to fit inside the ¾-inch-diameter bamboo)

Thin, black poly rope or thin copper wire, about 18 inches long

4 pin frogs (also called needlepoints), or heavy clay or putty

Birdbath or water basin

3-inch-diameter piece of bamboo, 8 inches long

4 bamboo branches with twigs

Mini submersible pump

Black rocks

Wire cutters, scissors

TOOLS

Drill

¾-inch drill bit

Calipers or ruler

Long drill bit or piece of rebar (optional)

Fine-tooth saw

Large, sharp knife or cleaver

MAKING THE UPTUBE

Step 1. Select one piece of 1½-inch-diameter bamboo to be the uptube and decide which end you will designate as the top. Drill a hole in the bamboo about 1½ inches below the top node. The hole should be the same diameter as one end of the ¾-inch diameter piece of bamboo. Use calipers or a ruler to double-check the measurements and ensure a good match.

Step 2. If there are any nodes in the uptube below the point where you drilled the hole, use a long drill bit or a piece of rebar to ream these out. Be careful not to punch out the top node.

Step 3. Use the fine-tooth saw to cut across the bottom of the uptube at approximately a 45-degree angle. This is to accommodate the tubing that will pass through the uptube and connect to the pump.

MAKING AND ATTACHING THE SPOUT

Step 4. To make the spout, cut the ¾-inch-diameter piece of bamboo at a 45-degree angle just above a node.

Step 5. Measure down 6 inches and make a second cut. The cuts should be aligned, but the angle of this cut does not have to be 45 degrees.

Step 6. Insert the poly tubing into the hole in the uptube. Slide the tubing through until about 8 inches protrudes from the bottom.

Step 7. Push the 45-degree-angled end of the spout over the tubing and into the hole near the top of the uptube.

Step 8. Poke the end of the spout into the uptube and secure it in place with a short piece of the rope or wire.

Step 9. Decide where to position the uptube in the birdbath. There will be some minor splashing, so it may be best to place it near the rear of the bath, with the spout facing front.

Step 10. Position one of the pin frogs or a blob of clay or putty at this point, then gently work the bottom of the uptube into the pins or putty. Be careful not to puncture the poly tubing. Point the spout out toward the middle of the birdbath.

MAKING THE DRIPPERS AND WATER CATCHER

Step 11. Take another piece of 1½-inch-diameter bamboo and make a hole in it as you did in step 1. But instead of a circular opening, make an oval one. This piece of bamboo will serve as a dripper.

Step 12. Punch out all the nodes except the top one, as you did in step 2.

Step 13. At the other end of this piece of bamboo, make a wide-angle cut, so that the maximum amount of water will be visible when flowing through the dripper.

continued on next page

Japanese Styling for American Birds *continued*

Step 14. Repeat steps 11 through 13 with the remaining piece of 1½-inch-diameter bamboo to make another dripper.

Step 15. Make an angled cut along the middle of the 3-inch-diameter bamboo piece with the saw. Avoid cutting into the nodes. Use the knife to split the section of bamboo, producing two scoop-shaped pieces. Use one of these pieces as the water catcher; set the other aside.

ASSEMBLING THE TSUKUBAI

Step 16. Visualize how the pieces will fit together. You'll use the bamboo branches to support the drippers. Position the two drippers at the right heights and locations so that water will drip from the spout

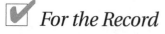

into one of the oval holes, and from there through the dripper and into the oval hole of the second dripper.

Step 17. Cut one of the bamboo branches (Branch #1) to the right height to support Dripper #1. This branch will have to hold Dripper #1 just below the opening in the spout, so that the spout can drip directly into the oval hole of the dripper. You may need to cut the branch a few times to get it precisely right. Insert this branch into a pin frog or piece of clay or putty.

Step 18. Cut a second, shorter branch (Branch #2) to support the lower end of the dripper, and support the branch with a pin frog.

Step 19. Once you're sure the branches are at the right height, tie or wire Dripper #1 onto the twigs.

Step 20. Cut a branch slightly shorter than Branch #2 (Branch #3) to support the upper end of Dripper #2. Cut an even shorter branch (Branch #4) to support the

---

✔️ *For the Record*

Bamboo and Water

Harry L. Abel, owner of Shinkigen in Smyrna, Georgia, teaches about Japanese garden styling and plants—including how to make bamboo water features. He explains that long before American and English gardening began, Asian people were using bamboo for pipes, building, and fencing. (Most bamboos are native to Asia, and there are 120 species of the hollow-stemmed clump-forming and running plants.) Bamboo is light but very strong, endures hard use and weather, and looks natural in the garden—the perfect material to use to deliver water. Harry cautions that bamboo can have sharp splinters. He recommends buying bamboo from a reputable source where it has been stored properly. Also, he says, be sure to use a sharp saw to cut bamboo.

One unusual feature of bamboo is that the nodes (seen as little bumps along the stem, where leaves normally emerge) always have an inner membrane that closes off the stem. This nodal structure makes each segment of bamboo air- and water-tight. When you want to use bamboo as a pipe to deliver water, you have to open up the stem by poking through the membranes. You can do this—carefully—with a long drill bit, a piece of rebar, or a sharp stick.

lower end of Dripper #2. Position Branches #3 and #4 so that Dripper #2 will zigzag, changing the course of the water flow. Support the branches with pin frogs.

Step 21. Tie or wire Dripper #2 to Branch #3 and Branch #4.

Step 22. Position the water catcher under the spout end of Dripper #2. Support the water catcher by wiring it to Branch #4, or secure it in place with a bit of clay or putty.

ATTACHING THE PUMP

Step 23. Find a place among the pin frogs or putty to install the pump. It will draw water in through the underside or low on the pump body.

Step 24. Slip the poly tubing into or over the pump output. Make sure the fit is tight. You may use electrical tape to adjust the sizes of the holes and tape over the connection.

Step 25. Position the black rocks so that they mask the pump.

Step 26. Plug the pump into a GFCI outlet. Be ready to make minor adjustments, as water never does exactly what you think it will. Most pumps have a small valve to control flow, in case there's too much.

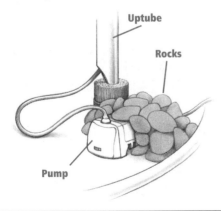

Uptube

Rocks

Pump

continued from page 191

Those products also would work for waterproofing an unglazed clay pot, or you can seal the pot with a polyester resin. Be sure that your container will be deep enough to hide the pump you are using. Also consider whether your project will be outdoors year-round, and select a container that will not crack if you have freezing winter temperatures.

Submersible pump. You'll need a pump that is the right size to move the volume of water in your container, also taking into consideration the height and size of the fountain. (Review "Determining Pump Size" on page 189, if needed.)

Riser pipe or tube. This can be the outlet of the fountain or bubbler itself, or it may be a pipe or tube that feeds into a waterspout or jet of your choice.

Fountainhead. People have made fountainheads out of drip irrigation parts, car grease fittings, lamp parts, and anything with an opening smaller than the riser so that water is forced to spurt out. You may prefer to buy an ornamental fountainhead. The variety available is incredible, ranging from flowers, shells, and animals (spouting water from their mouths) to children holding watering cans or even, ahem, peeing in your pool.

Cover or support for the pump. Some designs feature an inverted pot over the pump, with the riser pipe or tube coming up through the drainage hole in the pot bottom. In other designs, the entire surface of the container is covered with wire or hardware cloth, sometimes decorated with pebbles or marbles. Sometimes garden plants suffice as a cover for a pump that simply sits on rocks or concrete blocks or in a bucket underwater.

Fountains are bird magnets, and this one also offers sparkling colored glass, which may add to the attraction (especially for curious cardinals and blue jays). Some birds may actually splash in the fountain, but its primary purpose is to attract birds to your yard with the sound of water, as well as to provide a pretty focal point for a garden.

Bottle cutters are available at many craft supply stores, or you can ask to have your bottle cut at a store that sells cut glass.

Hunting for Gorgeous Glass

The look of this fountain will depend on your hunting skills. First, search for the prettiest glass bottle you can find—you may be surprised at the choices. For example, there's a type of white wine intended for seafood that comes in a pale green bottle in the shape of a fish. Cobalt blue, amber, and even ruby red glass bottles make beautiful fountains. Translucent or transparent glass of any color will radiate even lovelier shades when sunlit and wet. An alternative would be a cut glass or leaded glass bud vase or narrow vase—perhaps chipped or faulty so that you are willing to sacrifice it for an outdoor fountain. Yard sales, secondhand stores, flea markets, and country auctions may yield the item you want. Keep your eyes open for the unexpected. A lamp parts store, for example, will have lamp bases, which are potentially perfect fountains.

Second, look in a craft supply store or a home decorating store for glass beads or other objects of the same, or a compatible, color as the bottle.

Third, when searching for a container, consider that plain, dark-colored, glazed pottery is elegant combined with sparkling glass.

MATERIALS

Safety glasses or goggles

Sturdy gloves

Bottle cutter or glass cutter

1-liter or larger colored-glass bottle

Small submersible pump, of a size that will move the amount of water in the large container in 1 hour

Large nonporous container, 6 to 12 inches deep and at least 12 inches in diameter, without drainage holes

Pot with drainage hole, 1 to 2 inches shorter than the container but large enough to cover the pump

Tube and fountainhead extension, equal to the length of the height of the pot plus the height of the bottle

Marking chalk

Sturdy ¼-inch wire mesh

Wire cutters

Masking tape (optional)

Glass balls, marbles, pennies, buttons, colored stones, glass chips, or other decorative objects suitable for submerging in water

Extension cord rated for outdoor use

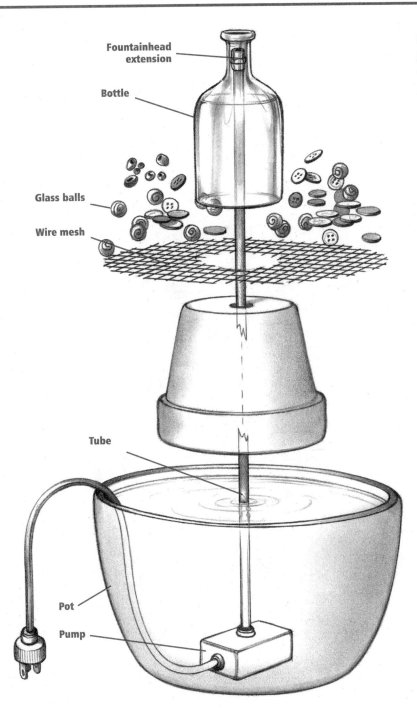

Fountainhead extension

Bottle

Glass balls

Wire mesh

Tube

Pot

Pump

Step 1. Don the safety glasses and gloves, and use the bottle cutter to cut the bottom off the bottle.

Step 2. Set the pump in the center of the container. Be sure the cord of the pump extends up and over the side of the container.

Step 3. Connect the tube to the pump. Thread the tube through the hole in the bottom of the pot from the inside out and upend the pot over the pump.

Step 4. Measure the diameter of the container at a point 1 inch below the rim. Use the marking chalk to mark a circle of slightly smaller diameter on the wire mesh.

Step 5. Use wire cutters to cut a circle of wire mesh along the line marked. Cut a hole in the center of that circle equal in size to the bottom of the bottle.

Step 6. Set the mesh "ring" in place on the inverted pot.

Step 7. Connect the tube to the fountainhead extension.

Step 8. Push the fountainhead extension up through the bottle until the fountainhead is just below the mouth of the bottle. If the extension is wobbly, wrap masking tape around it to thicken it until you have a tight fit in the neck of the bottle.

continued on next page

Sparkling Colored-Glass Fountain *continued*

Step 9. Set the fountain in the desired location.

Step 10. Cover the wire mesh with the glass balls or other decorative objects so that it does not show. Add water to the container. If you are using heavy objects, such as glass balls, marbles, or coins, you can add water all the way to the rim. If, however, you're using lighter objects, such as buttons, add just enough water to cover the mesh and objects.

Step 11. Connect the pump plug to the extension cord and plug the extension cord into a GFCI outlet.

HELPFUL HINTS

Check your fountain frequently during the first few days and after windy periods. You'll need to figure out how quickly water evaporates from the container and spray, and how much water is lost to splashing beyond the bounds of the container. It's critical to keep submersible pumps covered with water, so top off the water as needed.

PONDS AND POOLS

Gardeners generally help wildlife by providing water, but a traditional water garden is often not ideal for birds. Many water gardens have steep sides, are dark and deep, or feature vigorous fountains or waterfalls. Even if you already have a water garden in your yard, you may want to add a shallower inground pool, such as the project shown on pages 200 through 202 that will be attractive to birds.

Alternatively, you can add a natural ramp or ladder to your existing water garden to help birds get down to the water's edge and back out again. For example, you could lay a 3- to 4-inch-diameter log so that it extends from the bank of the pool out into the water, or a pile of rocks at one spot in the water.

About Pond Liners

Some gardeners buy preformed ponds for water gardens or pools, but pond liners provide more flexibility and are much less expensive (as little as one-fourth the cost). Some pond liners are made of fish-grade PVC (polyvinyl chloride), which often is bonded to a backing made of geotextile. The backed PVC liners are more expensive than those without backing, but they are often guaranteed to last a lifetime. If the PVC does not have a backing, you'll have to add a geotextile liner, old carpet, or even ceiling insulation in the floor of the pool before you spread the liner.

Another option is a UV-stabilized rubber liner, which will tolerate very hot sun and last for 25 years or more.

Liner Thickness

The thicker the liner you select, the longer it will last, but also the more it will cost. A 20-mil liner may last only 8 to 10 years, whereas a 32-mil liner may last 20 years or more.

The Realities of Weight

Another factor to think about is the weight of a flexible liner and the number of helpers you will have when you install it. (If your project is a solo performance, you may be able to handle only a small preformed pond.) A 10- by 10-foot PVC liner weighs 15 to 25 pounds, and the same size rubber liner could weigh 30 pounds or more.

Caring for a Pond or Pool

Keep an eye out for mosquito problems. When you see or smell stagnant water or you observe mosquito larvae wriggling in the water, it is time to dump and refill the pond, add a filter, or add fish or BTI. (For details about BTI, see page 181.) Usually just stirring up the water or hosing it regularly is enough to upset the development of mosquito larvae. In a small pond, algae growth and stagnation will not be difficult to manage and will occur only during prolonged warm, rain-free periods.

If you feel that your pond needs some water movement to avoid stagnation and mosquitoes, or if you crave a fountain, bubbler, or little cascade, you can always add a pump. In nature, a healthy pond (usually with some critters that live there) does not need a filter, as the plant and animal recycling of nitrogen, oxygen, and other elements creates a balance. But if you'd like the water in your pond to be clearer than in a natural pond, you may wish to purchase a water filter. Ask a water gardening expert what size will work for the volume of water you have.

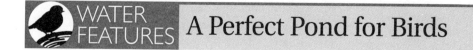

WATER FEATURES A Perfect Pond for Birds

If you don't have a natural pond in your yard, you can create one if you are willing to do some digging and invest in a pond liner and a few water-loving plants. You may even extend the pond to include a bog area, which will increase the number of pond residents, such as frogs and dragonflies. This project is for a pond that measures 5 feet by 9 feet and is 18 to 24 inches deep, but you can vary this size as you wish. (This shallow ornamental pool will not be deep enough for overwintering koi in Zone 6 or colder.)

In this project, planning ahead is important so that you end up with a pond of the depth and shape you want, with a liner that is cut and placed to hold the water where you want it. Measure twice and cut once!

MATERIALS

750 pounds of coarse sand

Flexible pond liner with geotextile backing, 10 × 20 feet

1 pallet cut limestone or sandstone, also sold as flagstones, 150 to 250 pieces (If you are purchasing split stone, 1 square yard, or 1 pallet, will be ample. If you collect them individually, 150 to 250 flagstone-type rocks will be enough, depending on size.)

Turfgrass or low-growing ornamental grasses or perennials

15 to 20 rocks, 6 to 20 inches in diameter

Bucketful of smaller rocks of various sizes

Potted aquatic plants (optional)

TOOLS

Spray chalk, such as that used by engineers and contractors (available at hardware stores), or a length of garden hose

Shovel

Rake

Level

PREPARING THE POND BED

Step 1. Decide on the size and shape of your pond and mark it out with spray chalk or a hose.

Step 2. Dig the pond, leaving an outer ledge ranging from 8 to 12 inches deep and 12 inches wide. Make this ledge level in places if

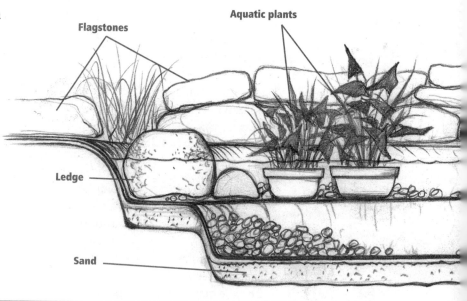

Flagstones

Aquatic plants

Ledge

Sand

you wish to use potted plants. The shallower parts of the ledge are for large rocks or piles of smaller rocks to provide animals easy access to the pond.

Step 3. Remove any protruding rocks and rake the entire pond bed. Loosen the soil at least 6 inches deep to remove all remaining sharp objects. Rake the pond bed smooth, using the level to check and even out the bed and the ledge. If your level is not long enough to span the pond, simply place it on a board that spans the pond to check the level. Keep making adjustments until the entire bed is level.

Step 4. Smooth the area around the lip of the pond, again using the level to check that the entire surface of the outside edge is level. This step will help you achieve a professional-looking result, with no liner showing and an even water level once you've filled the pond.

Step 5. Spread sand carefully and evenly on the pond bed and ledge. Aim for a layer at least 3 inches deep. If you have naturally rocky or gravelly soil, make the sand even thicker. (Under the weight of water, soil compacts and rocks tend to emerge, which may tear the pond liner.)

SPREADING THE LINER

Step 6. Leaving a generous margin on all sides, unroll the pond liner, tucking it into the pond cavity. Make small folds to fit the liner into the sides of the pond, smoothing it as you unroll it. Arrange the liner so that the overlap on all sides of the pond is approximately the same and the folds are evenly distributed.

Step 7. Add a little water to the pond, then recheck the liner placement as the water reveals the folds and the tight areas.

Step 8. Place flagstones around the edge of the pond, with about one-third of each slab extending over the edge.

Step 9. Fill the pond about one-third full, noticing where the liner is pulling under the flagstones. Ease these points of tension by sliding the liner toward the pond.

continued on next page

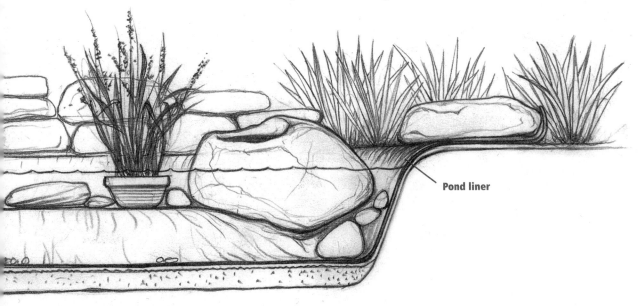

Pond liner

A Perfect Pond for Birds *continued*

FINISHING TOUCHES

Step 10. Add another layer or two of flagstones. The goal is to cover the liner, with only a few inches of the liner extending beyond the outside boundary of the flagstones. An uneven or irregular arrangement of flagstones will look more natural than a symmetrical plan.

Step 11. Fold up the outside edge of the liner to partially enclose the flagstones.

Step 12. Plant turfgrass or low-growing ornamental grasses or perennials around the outside edge of the flagstones to disguise the liner and create a natural look. Don't plant any tall plants that might offer hiding places for predators near the edge of the pond.

Step 13. Place some large rocks, or groups of smaller ones, on the ledge. Vary the groupings from a single large rock to a cluster of smaller rocks 12 inches wide or more. When the pond is full of water, these rocks will provide hiding places for frogs, as well as places for birds and other animals to stand while taking a drink. Place any rock that has a concave side with the indentation facing up, so that it forms a little pool where smaller birds can drink.

Step 14. Fill the pond with water. If desired, place potted aquatic plants on the ledge.

CHAPTER 7

All about Birdhouses

The final touch in a backyard bird habitat is to put up a few cozy nest boxes. Providing birdhouses will allow you to enjoy the brilliance of bluebirds and the glorious song of wrens on a regular basis. It also may make your habitat close to ideal for robins, tree swallows, and perhaps even owls and woodpeckers. Rather than just passing through your yard, these birds may end up raising their families alongside you and your family. Once you know what birds require in their housing—placement, size of house and entrance hole, protection from predators—make a few of the projects in this chapter and see who turns up to feather their nests.

CATERING TO CAVITY NESTERS

A cavity nester is simply a bird that in the natural course of things would choose a cavity or enclosed area in a tree to nest and raise its young. Any bird that is a cavity nester may be tempted to use a constructed birdhouse as long as the size, design, and placement suit its needs.

In the distant past, woodpeckers were the main providers of nest sites for cavity nesters, as they bored holes into trees in search of tasty grubs and other insects. As humans have encroached on natural woodlands, however, there are fewer and fewer stands of undisturbed trees where woodpeckers can find spots to excavate. Think of your own yard: Does it provide any natural cavities where a bird could build a nest? If not, you need to become a birdhouse builder. You can provide a variety of acceptable housing for many species of birds. It's important to understand, though, that each species of cavity nester has its own preferences in size, style, and placement of a home.

Country Bird, City Bird

Cavity nesters can be found in rural, suburban, and urban areas. You won't be able to attract all species to your yard, so set your sights on those that may come your way.

Rural Birds

If you reside in the country, you may be able to play host to any of the following species, as long as your region is in their nesting range.

- Bluebird
- Chickadee
- Wood duck
- Northern flicker
- American kestrel
- Purple martin
- Screech owl
- House sparrow
- Starling
- Barn swallow
- Tree swallow
- Violet-green swallow
- Tufted titmouse
- Bewick's wren
- Carolina wren
- House wren

Suburban Birds

You'll be surprised at the variety of cavity nesters that will take up residence in a suburban backyard. They include the following:

- Bluebird
- Chickadee
- Northern flicker
- American kestrel
- Purple martin
- Screen owl
- House sparrow
- Starling
- Tree swallow
- Violet-green swallow
- Tufted titmouse
- Bewick's wren
- House wren

Urban Birds

If you live in the city, you won't see as many cavity nesters. Choose houses suitable for house wrens, chickadees, house sparrows, or starlings, as these are the birds most likely to raise a family in city surroundings.

Birdhouses All Around

If your property doesn't have wooded groves, open fields, or shrubby areas that birds seek out for nesting, don't despair. Look beyond your yard and ask around the neighborhood to see if you can install birdhouses for everyone to enjoy. Stress that there is no maintenance involved for the property owner. Potential sites for birdhouses that you may want to investigate include farmers' fields, businesses with landscaped surroundings, local parks, churches, nursing homes, hospitals, and schools.

Though considered pests in most places, house sparrows and starlings do have their own niches in cities, tidying up garbage around trash cans. If you can't attract any other birds, it can be fascinating to watch house sparrows raise their young.

BIRDHOUSE MATERIALS

Wood, PVC (polyvinyl chloride) pipe, and gourds are suitable raw materials for making birdhouses. When choosing a material, you'll want to consider how well the material insulates, how it will hold up in all kinds of weather, whether it is safe for birds, and how easy it is to work with.

The Wonders of Wood

Wood is a great material for birdhouses, and it's certainly the most commonly used. That's because wood is a good insulator, easy to work with, and durable. One decision you'll need to make is which type of wood to use. *Never* use pressure-treated wood for building a birdhouse. The chemicals in the wood can be harmful to birds.

Pine boards. Easy to find at do-it-yourself or lumber stores, pine boards come in a variety of sizes, and they're inexpensive. Even a birdhouse made of untreated pine will last 5 to 10 years with proper maintenance. You can finish untreated pine with waterproof primer and paint or stain to help protect and decorate it.

Note: Never paint the inside of a birdhouse. Birds may absorb the paint or stain through their skin, which could be harmful to them.

Cedar or redwood boards. Lovely to look at and longer lasting than pine, cedar and redwood are also more expensive and can be more difficult to find. Redwood, in particular, may not be available from local stores, depending on where you live.

Exterior plywood. In the past, the glues used in making exterior plywood contained formaldehyde, which is toxic, but the glues used today are safe for songbirds. Just be sure to buy exterior plywood, such as T-11 plywood. Avoid interior plywood, is made with waterproof glues.

Natural wood. Slabs of wood with the bark still attached are a charming material for birdhouses. Natural wood houses are especially appealing to chickadees, titmice, woodpeckers, and nuthatches. Your local sawmill may provide you with offcuts—the outermost pieces trimmed from logs before the logs are milled. If you use offcuts, leave the bark in place, and the birds will love it.

Hardware

Most of the projects in this chapter use screws to fasten the pieces of the birdhouse together. The best screws for birdhouse building are rust-resistant screws that will withstand the weather. Choices include brass, stainless steel, or coated screws. The coated screws may be sold as deck screws. Whatever screws you use, predrill holes using a $\frac{1}{8}$-inch twist drill bit to make inserting and tightening the screws easier.

Working with Wood

If you enjoy home repair projects or making wooden crafts or furniture, you may have lots of experience with woodworking tools and techniques. If not, don't worry. Making wooden birdhouses can be very simple, requiring only the use of a power saw, a hammer, an electric drill, and a screwdriver. If you're a novice when it comes to woodworking, though, you may appreciate some general advice and tips for making wooden birdhouses.

Cutting the Pieces

Whenever you're working with wood, the well-know adage "Measure twice, cut once" is always good advice. Here are some other points to keep in mind while you mark and cut out the pieces of a birdhouse.

■ Be sure you've determined which side of your wood is the "weather" (exterior) side.

■ Lay out pieces so that the grain of the wood will run vertically on the front, back, and sides.

■ Keep in mind that the dimensions of dimensional lumber are not exact. For example, a "1 × 6" board is actually ¾ inch thick and 5½ inches wide.

■ If you're using T 1-11 plywood, when you lay out the parts, keep the vertical grooves in the wood away from the edges. Otherwise, you'll have trouble nailing the pieces together.

■ To keep track of the pieces, label each one on the interior surface as you cut it out.

■ If any of the pieces you cut have rough edges and you're concerned about splinters, use sandpaper to smooth them out.

Cutting a Bevel

A bevel is an angled cut on the end or edge of a board. For example, you might need to bevel the back of a birdhouse where it meets the roof, or vice versa. You can cut a bevel with either a handheld circular saw or a jigsaw. The process is essentially the same with either tool.

■ Start by tilting the base on the saw to the angle you need. If you want to perfect your angle, you can use a protractor and a T bevel. (You can find these gadgets at your local hardware store.)

■ Draw a line across the piece of wood at the top point of the angle.

■ Cut along this line with the saw, making sure the blade is tilted in the direction you need.

■ If you find it difficult to saw straight, hold a speed square against the edge of your piece of wood so that you can rest the edge of the saw's base against it for guidance.

Drilling an Entrance Hole

It's very simple to drill a small hole through a piece of wood for a nail or screw. But when you're drilling a larger hole, such as the entrance hole in a birdhouse, you need to take special care to make a clean cut and not to damage the wood you're drilling through. Ensuring that the hole is the proper size also is important, because the size of the entrance hole has a direct bearing on what type of bird will use the house for nesting.

The least expensive way to drill large-diameter holes is to use a spade bit and an electric drill. Spade bits are available in ¹⁄₁₆-inch increments from ¼ inch to 2 inches.

Center the spade bit on the mark you've made to denote the center of the hole, then begin drilling the hole. Drill partway through the wood until the tip of the bit breaks through the opposite side.

Turn the wood over and drill through the other side to finish the hole.

Keeping Things Square

When you're fastening one piece of wood to another, it can be tricky to keep everything lined up precisely and to maintain square corners.

For example, when you make a birdhouse, you may have to hammer a nail through the front face of the house into the edge of a side piece. One good way do this is to place the first piece of wood flat on a workbench or other solid surface. Position the nail and drive it into the wood just until the tip barely peeks out the other side. Only then should you line up the two pieces of wood and finishing driving the nail.

One of the simplest ways to keep pieces aligned as you nail or screw them together is to clamp the pieces in position first. Investing in a clamp or two will make your woodworking life easier. For extra stability, clamp the pieces to your workbench as well.

MOUNTING BIRDHOUSES

Once you've built a birdhouse, the next step is to mount it outdoors. Installing a mounting post securely is as important as building the birdhouse itself. Although western bluebirds and house wrens are happy to move into houses hung from branches and swinging in the wind, many species of birds prefer to have their houses firmly rooted in the ground.

Types of Posts

Wooden posts are a popular choice for mounting birdhouses, but they're not the only option. The top four types of posts

Seasonal Specialties

Put Up Birdhouses in the Fall

Take some time on a pleasant fall day to mount your birdhouses. This allows the houses to weather, which makes them more appealing to birds. Plus, you won't miss the early-spring arrivals. Your yard will be welcoming to the first house hunters on the scene.

for mounting birdhouses are wooden posts (4-by-4s), PVC pipes, metal fence posts, and metal poles. You'll find instructions for installing these four types of posts on pages 209 through 212. All four types have their pros and cons.

Wooden Posts

■ Installing the birdhouse is easy; all you do is screw it to the post.

■ Wooden posts are readily available in up to 8-foot lengths.

■ Wooden posts may rot at soil level.

■ Wooden posts can look chunky.

■ Installing wooden posts requires some heavy work to dig and pack soil and gravel.

PVC Pipes

■ PVC is lightweight but strong.

■ Rain and snow won't damage the pipes.

■ It's difficult for squirrels, cats, and raccoons to climb the smooth surface.

■ You can use PVC flanges or bolts to mount birdhouses.

■ Installing PVC pipes requires heavy work to dig and pack soil and gravel.

Metal Fence Posts

■ Metal posts are lightweight but strong.

- It's easy to secure metal posts in the ground.
- Installing birdhouses on a metal post is simple.
- Metal posts are available only in lengths up to 6 feet, so they don't work for birdhouses that need to be mounted more than 5 feet above the ground.
- Metal posts may rust after a few years of exposure.

Metal Poles

- Metal poles are strong and will last for many years.
- It's easy to secure them in the ground.
- Installing baffles on the narrow poles is simple.
- Telescoping models are available at many bird supply stores.
- It's important to be very careful when using telescoping poles near electric wires. Metal poles don't mix well with electricity!
- The poles may rust after a few years of exposure.

Doing the Job

Installing a post can be a big job or a small one, depending on which type of post you use and what type of soil you have. A shovel is the best tool to use for digging the hole in which you'll secure a wooden post or PVC pipe.

When it comes to mounting the birdhouse, enlist a helper to hold the box in place while you predrill holes and screw the box to the post or pipe.

Safety First

To keep your tenants safe, follow some basic rules when mounting birdhouses

Always provide predator barriers. Eggs and baby birds are vulnerable to predation by snakes, raccoons, cats, and other animals. The best way to keep them safe is to block predators from climbing the post or reaching inside the birdhouse. (For instructions for creating predator barriers, see "Dealing with Predators and Pests" on page 236.)

Avoid chilling winds. Be sure the entrance hole of a birdhouse faces away from the prevailing wind so that baby birds won't catch a chill.

Keep it quiet. Choose a spot that is away from road and people traffic. Most birds won't nest in an area where there's a lot of activity and noise. They look for a nesting site that is in a quiet location where they can come and go without worrying about drawing attention to their brood.

✔️ *For the Record*

Good Neighbors

Swallows are more aggressive than bluebirds, and they will often chase bluebirds away and take over a birdhouse. If there are swallows in your neighborhood and you want bluebirds to move in, mount two bluebird houses rather close together.

This trick works because tree swallows and violet-green swallows will protect their territory fiercely against other swallows. If you place two houses just 15 to 25 feet apart, swallows will probably move into one of the houses well ahead of the more timid bluebirds. The territorial swallows won't allow another swallow couple to nest within their territory, so they'll chase other swallows away from the nearby nest box. They won't mind, however, if bluebirds move in next door.

Wooden Post Mount

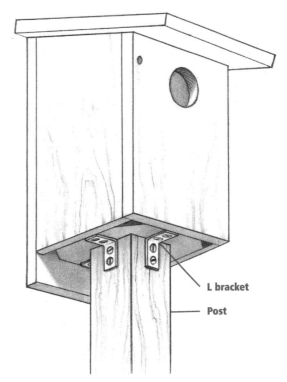

Gravel is the material of choice for mounting a wooden post. You can surround the post with plain soil instead, but gravel will improve drainage and provide a more stable footing for the post. If you have heavy soil, it can become soggy during heavy rains, and the post may tilt.

Using an 8-foot post will allow you to mount the birdhouse about 6 feet above ground level, which is a suitable height for many types of birds that nest in boxes.

L bracket

Post

MATERIALS

Two 50-pound bags of gravel

Scrap of 2 × 4

4 × 4 wooden post, 2 feet longer than the height you want to mount your birdhouse

Four 1½-inch L brackets

Drill

⅛-inch twist drill bit

Sixteen 1½-inch rust-resistant screws

Screwdriver

Step 1. Dig a hole 2 feet deep and about 1 foot wide at the site where you want to mount your birdhouse.

Step 2. Pour a few inches of gravel into the hole and tamp the gravel with the 2 × 4.

Step 3. Place the post in the hole and pour gravel around it until the hole is full. Tamp the gravel until the post is very firmly in place.

Step 4. Center the birdhouse on top of the post.

Step 5. Hold one L bracket in place, centering it against the side of the post and the bottom of the house. Mark and predrill holes for the bracket screws, then drive the screws through the screw holes in the bracket.

Step 6. Repeat step 5 to add a bracket to each side of the post.

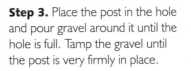

HELPFUL HINTS

When installing a birdhouse that has wooden backboard extensions above and below the body of the house, there's no need for brackets. Instead, simply hold the birdhouse against the post, predrill holes through the top and bottom extensions, and screw the house in place on the post.

A PVC pipe is lighter to handle than a wooden post, and it will last virtually forever. Installing a PVC pipe in the ground is similar to installing a wooden post, but you use different hardware to mount the house on the pipe.

MATERIALS

Three 50-pound bags of gravel, or 2 bags of gravel and one 50-pound bag of sand

Scrap of 2 × 4

3-inch-diameter PVC pipe, 2 feet longer than the height you want to mount your birdhouse

PVC pipe flange

Drill

⅛-inch twist drill bit

Four #10 × ¾-inch rust-resistant screws

Screwdriver

⅜-inch spade bit

⅜-16 × 4½-inch carriage bolt

Step 1. Dig a hole 2 feet deep and about 1 foot wide at the site where you want to mount your birdhouse.

Step 2. Pour a few inches of gravel into the hole and tamp the gravel with the 2 × 4.

Step 3. Place the PVC pipe in the hole and pour gravel around it until the hole is full. Tamp the gravel until the pipe is very firmly seated.

Step 4. Fill the PVC pipe with gravel or sand.

Step 5. Center the PVC pipe flange on the bottom of your birdhouse. Predrill holes in the bottom of the house and drive screws to attach the flange.

Step 6. Mount the house on the pipe by fitting the flange over the top of the pipe.

Step 7. Drill a ⅜-inch hole all the way through the flange and the pipe with the spade bit.

Step 8. Insert the carriage bolt through the holes and secure.

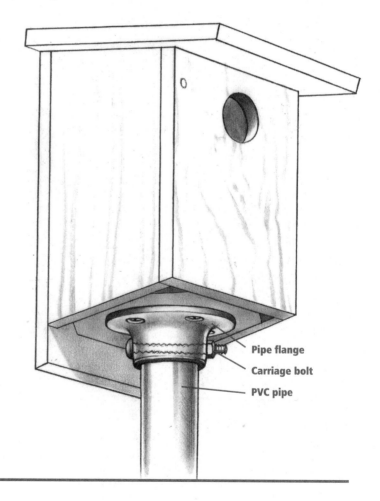

Pipe flange

Carriage bolt

PVC pipe

Metal Fence Post Mount

This style of post is perhaps the fastest to install, and mounting the birdhouse is a cinch, because the post already has holes in it. This type of post won't match a formal landscape, but it's a great choice for mounting a birdhouse in a natural area or at the edge of a field.

MATERIALS

Sledgehammer or other large hammer
6-foot metal fence post
Drill
⅛-inch twist drill bit
Two 1½-inch rust-resistant screws
Screwdriver

Step 1. Hammer the fence post into the ground about 1 foot deep.

Step 2. Hold the birdhouse against the top of the post.

Step 3. Predrill holes through the birdhouse—one near the top, one near the bottom—aligned with two of the holes in the post. Drive screws through the holes in the post and into the birdhouse.

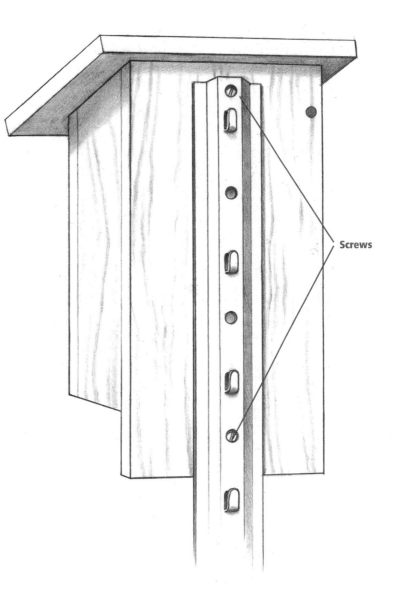

Screws

Metal Pole Mount

Telescoping metal poles are good for mounting any type of birdhouse, but especially for mounting a large house (such as a purple martin house) high above the ground. If you are mounting a martin house, dig a hole for the pole and support it in packed gravel as you would for a wooden post (see page 209). This will allow the pole to stand firmly against the wind.

MATERIALS

Sledgehammer or other large hammer

¾-inch (outside diameter) pipe, 2 feet long

¾-inch (inside diameter) galvanized pipe with threaded end, 1 to 1½ feet longer than the height you want to mount your birdhouse

Pipe flange to fit the galvanized pipe

Drill

⅛-inch twist drill bit

Four 1½-inch rust-resistant screws

Screwdriver

Step 1. Hammer the 2-foot piece of pipe 15 to 18 inches into the ground at the site you've chosen for your birdhouse.

Step 2. Pull the piece of pipe out of the soil. If the pipe resists, rotate it first one way, then the other to loosen it.

Step 3. Insert the long pipe into the hole threaded end up and push it firmly to set it in place.

Step 4. Center the pipe flange on the bottom of your birdhouse. Predrill holes in the bottom of the house and drive screws to attach the flange.

Step 5. Set the birdhouse on top of the pipe and screw the flange onto the pipe to attach the house firmly.

BLUEBIRDS

Almost without fail when discussing birdhouses, the first type that comes to mind is the bluebird house. Bluebird fans and protectors have encouraged anyone who will listen to add bluebird houses to their lawn and garden designs. Bluebirds are affected by a decline in natural nesting cavities—caused partially by humans removing dead and dying trees, which woodpeckers favor for drilling nest holes, and competition from house sparrows, wrens, starlings, swallows, and other assertive cavity nesters.

These beautiful birds have faced perils over the years—primarily lack of housing and food—but they have enjoyed a comeback over the past few decades. This rebirth has resulted from their willingness to move into houses provided by their human friends when natural cavities are lacking. It can be a challenge to encourage a bluebird to nest in a birdhouse in a suburban setting, but you may want to give it a try, especially if there are farm fields nearby.

Bluebird House Design

The bluebird house is simple in essence: It's a box with an entrance hole for the birds, mounted on a pole. The specifics are a bit more exacting: The box floor must be 4 by 4 inches or 5 by 5 inches. The entrance hole should be 1½ inches in diameter (larger for mountain bluebirds) placed 6 inches above the floor. You'll find detailed instructions for constructing a classic bluebird house on pages 214 through 216.

Ideally, the bluebird house should be mounted on a pole about 5 feet from the ground at the edge of an open field, and houses should be situated at least 300 feet apart. It's best if the house is constructed to open from the side or front for monitoring and cleaning. Also be sure that the floor of the house has small holes for ventilation and drainage.

MORE CAVITY NESTERS

Wrens, titmice, nuthatches, downy woodpeckers, swallows, and chickadees all like to nest in bluebird houses. These are appealing birds that you'll enjoy having around your yard, but their presence can prevent bluebirds from nesting. You can actually remove the nests and eggs of some birds, such as those of house sparrows and starlings, from a birdhouse to give bluebirds the nesting advantage, but most songbirds are protected by law (see "'Plant' a Residence for Birds" on page 24 for more information). So if songbirds other than bluebirds move into your bluebird house, settle in and enjoy them. The wren's perky profile and delightful song can be enchanting, and the graceful arc of a tree swallow swooping through the air is quite a show on a warm summer evening.

Ideally, if you have room, it's great fun to provide several houses and watch them fill up with a variety of species. All you have to do is change the dimensions

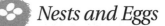

Bluebirds

In all likelihood, if you discover a bluebird nest, it will be in a bluebird house. Although bluebirds will use natural cavities, as they have throughout time, they now depend a great deal on the kindness of human landlords. Male bluebirds arrive in late winter or early spring to look for nest sites, and most return year after year to the same locations, sometimes even the same nest boxes. When the females arrive, the males sing to entice them to the locations they've selected. For the most part, once a female selects her site and her mate (sometimes in that order, finding the site she likes best and accepting the mate who has claimed it), she handles the rest of it—constructing the nest, then laying and incubating the eggs. The cuplike nest, loosely woven of grasses, pine needles, and other plant materials, is often lined with fine grasses and usually houses four to six pale blue eggs. Mountain bluebirds tend to have the palest eggs and the most eggs per clutch (a group of eggs laid and incubated at one time). Often as soon as the nestlings fledge (approximately 20 days), the female will lay another clutch of eggs, and the male takes over the care of the fledglings.

of the classic birdhouse to make it appeal to a wide variety of birds. (For a listing of dimensions, see "Sizing Them Up" on page 222.)

If you like, you can adapt the classic bluebird house design slightly to create a finished product that may be more appealing to swallows, as shown on page 218. You can also build a traditional hanging house that will be perfect for wrens, as shown on page 224, or a simple house out of PVC pipe that will appeal to several kinds of cavity nesters, as shown on page 230.

If you have a spot for mounting a birdhouse near an open field or lawn, this bluebird house will fill the bill. It has a slanted roof and a 1½-inch-diameter entrance hole. It features a hinged side piece that you can open to inspect the nest and to clean out the birdhouse at the end of the season. Simple openings at the corners of the floor allow drainage and air circulation.

MATERIALS

5-foot-long 1 × 10, or ⅝-inch-thick T 1-11 plywood, 14 × 31 inches

4-penny galvanized box nails

Right-angle screw hook, about 1½ inches long

Caulk

TOOLS

Jigsaw or circular saw

Drill

1½-inch spade bit

Assorted small drill bits

⅛-inch twist drill bit

Hammer

Square

2 C-clamps (optional)

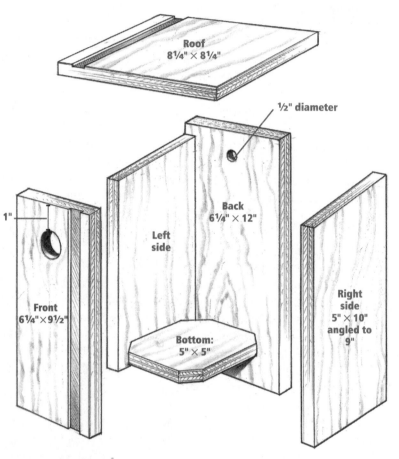

Roof
8¼" × 8¼"

½" diameter

1"

Front
6¼" × 9½"

Left side

Back
6¼" × 12"

Right side
5" × 10"
angled to 9"

Bottom:
5" × 5"

CUTTING AND PREPARING THE PIECES

Step 1. Mark and cut the 1 × 10 or plywood according to the dimensions listed in the illustration above to create the six pieces of the birdhouse.

Step 2. After cutting the side pieces to length, cut the top edge of each side piece so that it angles from 10 inches high at the back to 9 inches high at the front.

Step 3. Bevel the top edges of the front and back pieces by ⅛ inch to allow for the slant of the roof.

Step 4. On the front piece, mark the center of the entrance hole 1¾ inches down from the top and centered from side to side. Drill the entrance hole with the 1½-inch spade bit.

Step 5. On the bottom piece, measure ⅜ inch on each side of each corner and mark. Place a ruler diagonally across each corner and connect the two marks. Using the lines as a guide, saw off the four corners of the bottom. (The resulting blunted corners will create openings in the floor when the house is fully assembled.)

Step 6. On the exterior of the back piece, center a vertical line running 2 inches down from the top. At the bottom of the line, drill a ½-inch-diameter hole for mounting.

Step 7. Measure and mark the following guide marks: On the exterior of the front and side pieces, mark a horizontal line 1 inch from the bottom. On the exterior of the back piece, mark a horizontal line 2½ inches from the bottom.

ASSEMBLING THE BIRDHOUSE

Step 8. Use two nails to attach the right side of the house to the bottom piece, aligning the guide mark on the side with the interior surface of the bottom.

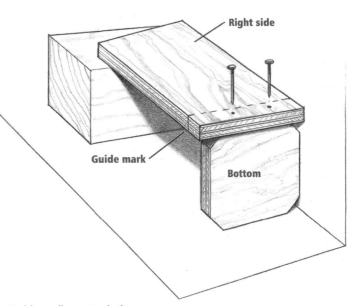

Right side

Guide mark

Bottom

Step 9. Use nails to attach the back piece to the side and bottom pieces, aligning the guide marks on the side and back. Use clamps if desired to keep pieces aligned.

Step 10. Turn the unit to rest on its back. Attach the front piece, aligning the guide marks with the interior surface of the bottom.

Step 11. Fit the left side piece into position. If it is tight, sand it vigorously to make the fit looser. This piece needs to be able to open easily even when the wood swells in wet weather.

Step 12. Drive one nail partway into the bottom and one partway into the front, halfway up the house. Drive the nails just far enough to hold the left side piece in place temporarily. (You will remove these nails later.)

Step 13. On the left edge of the front piece, make a mark 1 inch from the top. Using the square, draw a horizontal line across the left side piece at the mark.

Step 14. At one end of this line, drill a pilot hole using a ³⁄₃₂-inch bit through the front piece and into the edge of the left side piece, then drive a nail into the hole. At the other end of the line, drill a pilot hole through the back piece and into the edge of the side piece. Drive another nail into this hole. These nails will act as hinges to allow the side piece to be lifted open.

continued on next page

The Classic *continued*

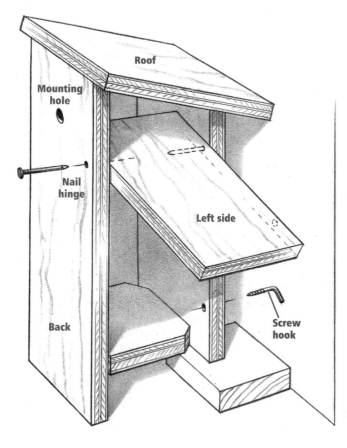

Mounting hole

Roof

Nail hinge

Left side

Back

Screw hook

ATTACHING THE ROOF

Step 17. Run a bead of caulk along the top edge of the back piece.

Step 18. Set the roof piece in place: It should be centered side to side and flush with the back of the house. Be sure the grain runs down the slant of the roof, not across it.

Step 19. Drill two pilot holes at the back of the roof piece using a $1/8$-inch twist drill bit. Drive two nails through the pilot holes and into the back piece.

Step 20. Drill two more pilot holes into the roof where it meets the front piece. Drive two nails through the pilot holes and into the front.

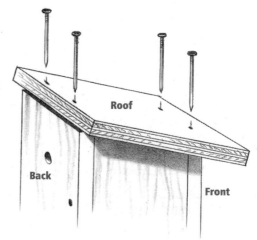

Roof

Back

Front

Step 15. Mark a spot on the front piece 2 inches up from the bottom and aligned with the center of the edge of the left side piece. Drill a small hole about 2 inches deep at this mark. The hole will pass through the front and extend into the left side.

Step 16. Insert the right-angle screw hook into this hole and twist it tight as a locking mechanism. Remove the temporary nails and test the action of the "door."

Bluebirds from Coast to Coast

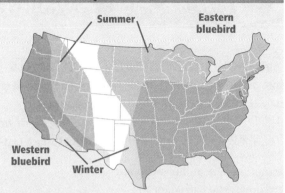

Bird watchers enjoy beautiful bluebirds all across the United States and into Canada and Mexico. Three species—the eastern bluebird, western bluebird, and mountain bluebird—share many similarities in behavior, even though they reside in different regions and wear different plumage.

These bluebirds are cavity nesters that dine primarily on insects, and they need open or semi-open grassland near their nest boxes. Bluebirds like places near their nest sites where they can perch to search for prey or sing to proclaim their territory. Even a good-size suburban lot may attract bluebirds, as long as it provides enough open space. Short grass or bare ground and garden areas where insects are plentiful will fill the bill. If you live in a development near a golf course, cemetery, athletic field, or other large area of open land, it's a good bet that bluebirds will nest in your yard if you provide an appropriate cavity.

Eastern bluebird. The eastern bluebird is perhaps the most widely known bluebird. It has a brilliant blue head and back, a rusty throat and breast, and light underparts. The female is light gray with just a hint of blue when her feathers sparkle in the sun. As its name suggests, this is the bluebird of the eastern United States and Canada. Environmentalists and bird enthusiasts have brought attention to the eastern bluebird's plight of reduced habitat and pesticide contamination of the insects it feeds on.

Western bluebird. The western bluebird complements the eastern bluebird splendidly, covering the western and southwestern United States. The male is a more brilliant blue than its eastern cousin, and it has a blue throat. The western bluebird is one of the few birds that may nest in a house hung from a small branch in a tree. Try this if you are within its range, as such placement helps keep predators at bay.

Mountain bluebird. The brilliant blue mountain bluebird has been known to nest in mountainous areas at an elevation above 12,000 feet, but its range isn't restricted to mountainous terrain. It also thrives near piñon pines, junipers, aspens, and cottonwoods, as well as in grasslands and amid sagebrush. The mountain bluebird covers most of western North America but is present in Canada only during the spring and summer. This bluebird benefits greatly from nest boxes.

 | Swallow Specialties

Swallows may move

into a classic bluebird house just like the one shown on page 214. (Swallows really do help in mosquito control!) If you want to make a house even more tempting to beautiful swooping swallows, you can adapt the classic design there to add a wire ladder inside the house to help fledglings leave the nest. You also can extend the roof overhang and add a wooden block at the entrance hole to help protect against raccoons, prime predators of swallows. To build a swallow house, you'll need all the materials and tools listed for the classic house, plus the ones listed here. If you're cutting pieces from a 1-by-10 board, you'll need a board that's 5 feet 5 inches long.

Place your swallow house in an open area, because swallows prefer clear access to the entrance hole. If you place the house in a quiet area where people aren't active often, it will be less appealing to aggressive house sparrows, which prefer to nest near hustle and bustle.

MATERIALS

2 × 6-inch piece of hardware cloth
Staple gun
¾ × 4 × 4-inch wood block
Two 1½-inch rust-resistant screws

Step 1. Mark and cut the pieces of the birdhouse as on page 214, increasing the size of the roof piece to 8¼ × 13¼ inches (the grain of the wood should run parallel to the long dimension of the roof).

Step 2. Follow steps 2 through 4 on pages 214 to 215.

Step 3. On the inside of the front piece, align the hardware cloth vertically under the entrance hole and staple it in place.

Step 4. Using the hammer, tap the sharp edges of the hardware cloth against the wood to keep them from sticking out and harming birds.

1½"

6"

Staples

2"

Step 5. Drill a 1 1/2-inch hole through the center of the wood block.

Step 6. Place the block on the exterior of the front piece, aligning the holes.

Step 7. Predrill a 1/8-inch hole through the block on each side of the entrance hole. Drive the 1 1/2-inch screws through the holes to attach the block to the front piece.

Step 8. Follow steps 5 through 20 on pages 215 to 216. When you attach the roof piece, note that the added length of the roof provides a protective overhang.

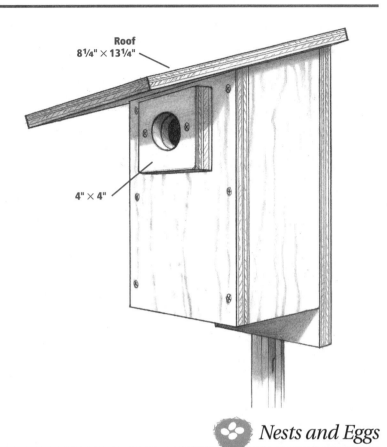

Roof
8¼" × 13¼"

4" × 4"

Nests and Eggs

Tree Swallow

Tree swallows readily move into birdhouses in the spring, with the males arriving first, followed by the females. Swallows don't weave cuplike nests, but their nests are marvelously cozy nonetheless. The female collects dry grasses and straw and fills the bottom of the house or cavity with several inches of this insulation. She then pushes with her breast to make a round, hollow spot for her young. As she lays her eggs, the male brings her feathers, which she arranges to provide comfort and retain warmth in the nest. She positions the feathers shaft down so that the soft part of the feathers covers the eggs and helps keep them insulated. She then presses the soft feathers into the nest during incubation so that the newly hatched baby birds have a comfy bed. These efforts to create a warm, dry nest are essential to the survival of the young in cold, wet weather, which can be deadly. Like the eggs of most cavity nesters, those of the tree swallow are not heavily marked for camouflage, as the cavity provides protection. The female usually lays four to six white eggs per clutch.

Wrens

Wrens will nest in anything. Leave an old flowerpot or your gardening boots or hat on the back porch or shed for a day or two, and you may find a nest when you return. Although these energetic birds are extremely adaptable, you can provide high-class housing for them by building a classic bluebird house (see page 214) with one of two adaptations.

Downsize the Entrance

When you drill the entrance hole, use a 1¼-inch spade bit rather than a 1½-inch bit. This will allow house and Bewick's wrens to enter comfortably, but it will exclude house sparrows, swallows, and bluebirds. It also may exclude Carolina wrens, the largest American wrens.

Change the Entrance Style

Creating a slotlike entrance hole instead of a circular one will make it easier for wrens to bring in the sticks they use to build their nests.

Which Wren Where?

Around the United States, three wren species readily use nest boxes. Their nesting ranges vary, so use geography to help you determine who is most likely to move into your neighborhood.

TYPE OF WREN	NESTING RANGE
Bewick's wren	Mostly in the southern United States and along the West Coast
Carolina wren	Eastern United States, except northern New England, and west to parts of Iowa, Nebraska, Oklahoma, and most of Texas
House wren	Throughout the United States

To do this, use a ruler or straight edge to mark a rectangle on the front piece 4 to 6 inches up from the bottom. The rectangle should be 1 to 1¼ inches high and 3 inches wide. Near the center of the box, drill a ½-inch hole. Then, using a jigsaw and starting in the drilled hole, carefully cut along the marked lines to make the slot. Use a little sand paper to smooth the edges.

To please wrens, locate the birdhouse near shrubs or trees in a semi-open space. You can hang it in a large tree or under the eaves of a building.

Downy Woodpeckers

Downy woodpeckers may investigate your bluebird houses, but the woodpeckers may not nest there unless you fill the bottom few inches of the box with sawdust and wood shavings to encourage them to excavate it.

Chickadees

Chickadees will nest in the same houses that house wrens use. Adding a layer of wood chips about 1 inch thick in the bottom of the house will encourage chickadees to take up residence. The best way to make a house appealing to chickadees is to place the box away from shrubbery, along the edge of a wooded area, and near an open space.

Titmice and Nuthatches

Titmice and nuthatches prefer houses with smaller entrance holes, as described for wrens at left. A smaller hole helps prevent competition from aggressive house sparrows. To encourage titmice, set out pieces of hair, fur, feathers, and thread—all 3 inches or less in length—for them to use in making their nests. (See pages 26 and 154.)

Flickers and Red-Bellied Woodpeckers

Flickers love the mowed lawns that allow them to find ants easily, and red-bellied woodpeckers are often seen at feeders in areas where they nest.

If you build a birdhouse to fit these woodpeckers, pack it full of wood shavings so that they can excavate it. Mount the box on a dead tree or other post in a sunny, semi-open area.

Owls and Kestrels

The same size house can host screech owls, northern saw-whet owls, and American kestrels. Where you place the house will determine who takes up residence. These larger birds need a lot of room (kestrel pairs need an acre) and a flyway to allow for an easy approach. Mount the box 15 to 30 feet above the ground. (If you don't want to climb a tall ladder to hang the house on a long pole, you can mount it on an adjustable pole.) Open woods and abandoned fields are ideal areas for these bigger birds. Beware, though: Kestrels and owls may munch on bluebirds and other similar-size birds, and kestrels may feed over an acre or so of land, so they aren't ideal houseguests in a small garden. You'll want to post the box at least 300 feet from other birdhouses and face it away from smaller houses.

Owls

Although owls are creatures of the night, you have a better chance of catching sight of these mysterious creatures if you provide housing for them. Put 2 to 3

Red-Breasted Nuthatch

The diminutive red-breasted nuthatch, which takes readily to nest boxes when it isn't making its home in a hole of a dead branch or stub, has an odd technique for protecting its clutch of five or six small, freckled eggs. Apparently in an effort to deter predators, this little bird painstakingly carries sticky sap, or pitch, from conifers to the nest hole and smears it all around the entrance. You can imagine that a curious raccoon or snake would probably retreat in a hurry if it encountered the gluey stuff.

inches of wood shavings or dried grass in the bottom of the box for nesting. To attract screech owls, mount the box 15 to 20 feet up on a large, straight tree trunk near an open woodland, perhaps in the shade of a park or orchard. Saw-whet owls prefer forests (mixed, deciduous, or evergreen), woodlots, or swamps.

Kestrels

Just a couple of inches of wood shavings in the bottom of the box will give kestrels, our small common falcons, a perfect spot to build a nest. Ideally, you should have a pole, a tree with a dead branch, or a snag 40 to 90 feet from the birdhouse where the male can perch to pull apart his prey so that he can feed the female while she sits on the nest.

Purple Martins

Purple martins are favorites of many folks who attract birds to their yards. These birds are graceful in flight and catch and eat a multitude of insects. Purple martins nest in colonies. One of the magnificent sights in the fall is seeing many colonies gathered together in huge flocks before they migrate. These groups can contain up to 100,000 birds, and when they move, they do so as one undulating unit.

Because purple martins live in colonies, they will nest only in birdhouses with several rooms or in a cluster of houses hung close together. In the eastern United States, martins are almost entirely dependent on human-supplied housing. See the instructions for "Hanging Assembly for a Martin Colony" on pages 228 to 229. They are attracted to white houses and prefer areas near water.

Sizing Them Up

This table lays out the nest box measurements for many species of cavity nester. Don't be too compulsive about measurements, however. You want to be sure the entrance hole is the minimum size but not larger than needed, because any hole with a diameter larger than 1½ inches may allow starlings to get in.

In the wild, birds nest in oddly shaped cavities, many excavated by woodpeckers—which don't work to each bird's preferred specifications. You've probably never seen a bluebird fly around with a tape measure in its beak! So if your flicker house turns out to be a couple of inches too big or if your nuthatch house is rectangular rather than square, don't worry.

BIRD NAME	Floor Size (inches)	Height (inches)	Diameter of Entrance Hole (inches)	Placement of Hole above Floor (inches)	Height above Ground (feet)	SUGGESTED HABITAT
Bluebird	5 × 5 (or 4 × 4 for eastern bluebird)	12	1½ (1⁹⁄₁₆ for mountain bluebird)	6–7¾	5–10	Open land with some trees for eastern and western bluebirds; open meadows above 5,000 feet for mountain bluebird
Chickadees	4 × 4	9–12	1⅛–1½	6–8	4½–15	Edges of forests, open woodland
Wood duck	12 × 12	24	3 × 4 horizontal oval	12–16	5–20	Wetland with flooded shrubs and trees and some open water
Northern flicker	7 × 7	16–24	2½	14–16	10–20	Farmland, open country
Flycatchers	6 × 6	12	1¾–2	8	6–20	Open, semiarid country for ash-throated flycatcher; open woodland, edges of forests for great crested flycatcher

BIRD NAME	Floor Size (inches)	Height (inches)	Diameter of Entrance Hole (inches)	Placement of Hole above Floor (inches)	Height above Ground (feet)	SUGGESTED HABITAT
American kestrel	9 × 9	15–18	3	9–12	10–30	Farmland, open fields (will nest in suburbs, too)
Purple martin	6 × 6	6	2⅛	2	15–25	Open areas, near water; preferably 40 feet from limbs or buildings
Hooded merganser	12 × 12	24	3 × 4 horizontal oval	16½	At least 5	Very near water: woodland ponds, sheltered backwater, marshes
White-breasted nuthatch	4 × 4	8–12	1½	6–8	5–12	Mature woodland near clearing; edges of forests
Common barn owl	12 × 36	15–18	6	4	12–18	Open farmland or marshland
Northern saw-whet owl	7 × 7	10–12	2½	8–10	8–20	Near dense forests, wooded swamps, bogs; near perches
Screech owl	8 × 8	18	3	9–12	8–30	Farmland, orchards, woodland clearings
Swallows	5 × 5	10–12	1½	6–7	5–10	Open land near water for tree swallows; pastures, fields, parks for violet-green swallows
Titmice	4 × 4	12	1½	6-8	5–12	Mixed woodland, edges of forests
Lucy's and prothonotary warblers	4 × 4	12	1¼	4	5–12	Wooded swamps, above open water
Downy woodpecker	4 × 4	8–12	1½	1¼	5–20	Woodland clearings, edges of forests
Hairy woodpecker	6 × 6	12–15	1½	9–12	12–20	Open woodland, forests
Red-bellied woodpecker	6 × 6	14	2	15	8–20	Open woodland, suburban backyards, orchards, swampland, river woodland
Wrens	4 × 4	9–12	1⅛–1½ for Carolina wren; 1 for house and Bewick's wrens	4–6 (6 for house wren)	5–10	Shrubs, thickets, old fields

Traditional Birdhouse

A traditional birdhouse with a gabled roof will appeal to smaller birds, such as wrens, chickadees, and titmice. One side of the house is designed to pivot on nails so that you can monitor the nest and clean out the box as necessary. The only tricky part is making the angle for the peaked roof. To make this step easier, use a speed square or combination square. You can pick one up at your local hardware or do-it-yourself store—maybe even in the bargain bin.

MATERIALS

4-foot-long pine 1 × 6

Fifteen 1½-inch rust-resistant screws

Two 6-penny galvanized common nails

Hook and eye

TOOLS

Saw

Speed square or combination square (optional)

Drill

1-inch spade bit

⅛-inch and ¼-inch twist drill bits

Screwdriver

Hammer

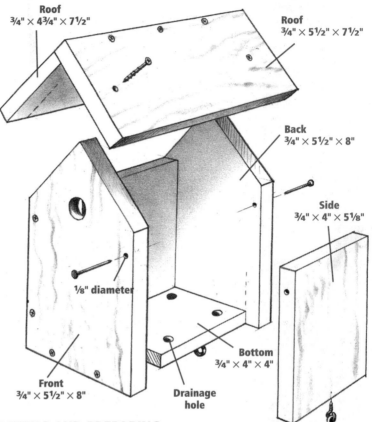

Roof
¾" × 4¾" × 7½"

Roof
¾" × 5½" × 7½"

Back
¾" × 5½" × 8"

Side
¾" × 4" × 5⅛"

⅛" diameter

Bottom
¾" × 4" × 4"

Front
¾" × 5½" × 8"

Drainage hole

CUTTING AND PREPARING THE PIECES

Step 1. Using the 1 × 6, cut the pieces to the lengths shown in the illustration above. (Keep in mind that a 1 × 6 is actually 5½ inches wide and ¾ inches thick.)

Step 2. Cut the side and bottom pieces 4 inches wide. Cut one of the roof pieces 4¾ inches wide. The front, back, and second roof pieces are the correct widths.

Step 3. On the front and back pieces, mark the angled cuts that will form the gable. These are 45-degree angles that meet at the peak. (Your speed square or combination square will come in handy here.) Cut along these lines.

Step 4. Mark a spot on the front piece 2½ inches down from the peak and centered from side to side. Drill the entrance hole at this spot, using the 1-inch spade bit.

ASSEMBLING THE HOUSE

Step 5. Predrill holes in the front and back pieces using the 1/8-inch bit. Screw the front and back pieces to one of the side pieces. The pieces should be flush along the bottom. (The side may appear to be too short. This is intentional to allow for ventilation.)

Step 6. Drill four 1/4-inch holes in the bottom piece for drainage.

Step 7. Slip the bottom into place and use the 1/8-inch bit to predrill holes through the front and back pieces. Drive screws through to anchor the bottom piece in place.

Step 8. Slide the second side piece into place. Drill two 1/8-inch pivot holes, one from the front and into the side and one from the back and into the side. These holes should be 3/8 inch in from the edge and 7/8 inch down from the top of the side. Drive a nail into each hole with the hammer.

Step 9. Predrill a hole for the hook in the center of the bottom edge of the side piece. Screw in the hook.

Step 10. Mark the spot on the bottom of the birdhouse where the eye should be installed. Predrill a hole and then screw in the eye.

Step 11. Secure the side with the hook and eye.

ATTACHING THE ROOF

Step 12. Predrill holes in the roof pieces and screw the two pieces together. Be sure that the wider piece overlaps the narrower piece.

Step 13. Set the roof in place so that the back is flush with the back of the house. Predrill four holes through the roof and then drive screws through the roof and into the front and back pieces.

Which Wire to Use

When you hang a birdhouse for your neighborhood wrens, the wire needs to be flexible enough to work with, but strong enough to support the weight of the house and its occupants. Vinyl-covered clothesline is great because it is strong and flexible, and the vinyl coating prevents the wire from cutting into the tree branch from which you hang the house. Or you can pick up another type of wire from your local hardware or do-it-yourself store. Whatever type of wire you use, be sure to attach it securely to the tree branch. Otherwise, a raccoon may knock the birdhouse, wire and all, to the ground.

Nail head

Hook

Eye

Making birdhouses

out of gourds is a practice that comes to us from Native Americans. Wrens, swallows, chickadees, and purple martins may nest in gourds. You may leave a gourd birdhouse with its own natural look or paint the outside of the gourd white to keep it cooler inside for your guests. Painting is recommended because gourds don't provide as much insulation against heat as wooden birdhouses do.

MATERIALS

Dried gourd, 8 to 10 inches in diameter

Drill

1- to 2-inch spade bit

1/8-inch twist drill bit

Long-handled fork, wooden spoon, or long, narrow metal spatula

Exterior primer

Exterior white paint

2-foot piece of vinyl-covered clothesline or other strong but bendable wire, or a wire coat hanger

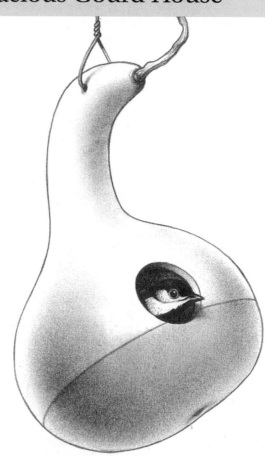

Step 1. Shake the gourd to loosen the seeds and other material inside.

Step 2. Using the spade bit, drill the entrance hole in the center of the fat part of one side of the gourd. Select a 2-inch bit to make a house for purple martins, a 1 1/4-inch bit for wrens or chickadees, and a 1 1/2-inch bit for swallows.

Step 3. Shake out the seeds and other material through the hole.

Use the fork, spoon handle, or spatula to loosen this material so that you remove everything from inside the gourd.

Step 4. Lightly sand the gourd.

Step 5. Brush on primer and let it dry.

Step 6. Brush on two coats of paint, allowing the paint to dry completely between coats.

Step 7. Drill a ⅛-inch hole on each side of the gourd's neck, about 1½ inches from the top.

Step 8. Thread the clothesline through the holes and twist it together over the top of the gourd.

Step 9. Hang the house in a tree if it is for wrens or chickadees (chickadees prefer a location at the edge of a woodland). Or hang several houses in a group in an open area 15 to 20 feet above the ground for purple martins. Swallows also like a house in an open area and don't require houses hung in groups. If you don't want to climb a ladder to mount the martin houses, invest in a telescoping metal pole from your local bird supply or hardware store.

Chickadees

Soft as a cloud, a chickadee nest cuddles its occupants in a cozy bed of soft moss, fur, feathers, thistledown, and even silk (from moth cocoons). You'll probably never get to appreciate a chickadee nest firsthand, however, unless you put up a birdhouse. Chickadees are cavity nesters, and that fluffy mass normally lines a hollowed-out section of a dead tree stub. They raise quite a clutch—usually six to eight tiny white eggs freckled with reddish brown. If chickadees stay in your area during breeding season, they'll readily adopt a birdhouse. Even if you never get the thrill of seeing the nest, you can enjoy the sight of the fuzzy-headed fledglings brought to your suet or soft-food feeder by Mom and Dad.

Grow Your Own Gourds

Bottle gourds (*Lagenaria siceraria*) grow on large, green-leaved vines with soft white flowers that look like crepe paper. The flowers mature into gourds that are suitable for making birdhouses. These vines require a long growing season, but if you live in Zone 7 or warmer, you can grow your birdhouses from seed!

Plant bottle gourds in well-drained soil and full sun. (You can also plant them in a wooden half barrel.)

It's best to support the vine on a trellis or bamboo tepee to keep the gourds off the ground and encourage them to grow with straight necks. As the gourds start to appear, pinch off extra blooms to encourage big, healthy gourds.

After the first frost, cut the gourds off the vines. Wipe the gourds with a mixture of ½ cup bleach and 2 quarts water to combat mold. Dry them thoroughly by placing them in a warm, dry spot near a furnace or on a sun porch, turning them often to allow them to dry evenly. The gourds are dry enough when you shake them and hear the seeds rattling around inside.

Hanging Assembly for a Martin Colony

Many people supply

a hotel-like birdhouse for purple martins, but you can create your own martin colony by hanging many individual houses together in a cluster. Individual martin houses need to be hung high and close together. (A dead tree with many high branches is ideal.) Use a telescoping pole so that you can easily hang the houses in the spring and lower them in the fall for cleaning. This hanging assembly has plenty of room for 12 houses.

MATERIALS

Three 3-foot-long 2 × 4s painted white

Four 8-penny galvanized common nails

2-inch-long eyebolts, one for each house you plan to hang

Nuts to fit the eyebolts

Washers to fit the eyebolts

Two ¼-20 × 2-inch galvanized machine bolts with nuts (These will be inserted through your telescoping pole, so adjust the length accordingly.)

Telescoping pole that extends to at least 15 feet

Individual martin houses

Vinyl-covered clothesline or other strong but bendable wire

TOOLS

Drill

Spade bit slightly larger than the diameter of the telescoping pole

¼-inch twist drill bit

Hammer

PREPARING THE ASSEMBLY

Step 1. In the center of each board, drill a hole using the spade bit.

Step 2. Align the holes and spread the boards out like the spokes of a wheel.

Step 3. Nail the top board to the middle board on each side of the hole.

Step 4. Flip the assembly over and nail the bottom board to the middle board on each side of the hole.

Step 5. Use the twist drill bit to drill holes in the boards wherever you'd like to hang the birdhouses.

Step 6. Thread a nut and then a washer on the shaft of an eyebolt.

Fighting the Competition

House sparrows and starlings are prime competitors for nesting cavities and can take over your martin housing complex if you're not careful. To give martins the edge on claiming space, many martin landlords don't put up their houses until the first martins return in the spring.

If you are serious about attracting purple martins, clean out nests made by starlings or sparrows as soon as you discover them in your martin houses. Laying out crushed, dried eggshells may attract martins. Playing a tape of martin songs also may appeal to the birds. You can find such tapes at many bird supply stores or through the Purple Martin Conservation Association. (See "Resources for Backyard Birders and Gardeners" on page 292). Once a colony of martins begins nesting in your yard, you should register it with this organization.

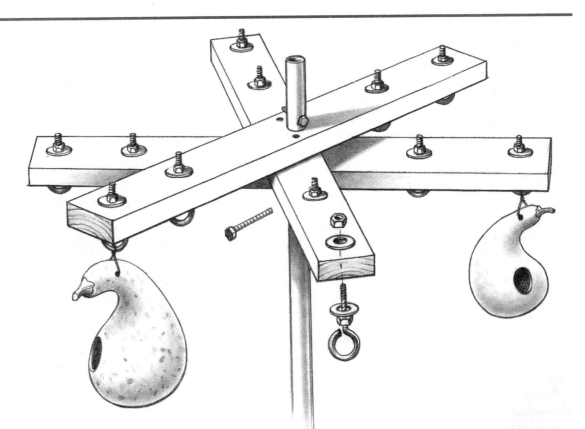

Insert the shaft into one of the holes. Drop another washer over the shaft and secure it with another nut. Do the same for each of the holes you drilled in step 5.

MOUNTING THE ASSEMBLY

Step 7. Use the twist drill bit to drill a ¼-inch hole through the pole approximately 6 inches from the upper end.

Step 8. Insert a machine bolt through the hole and secure it with a nut.

Step 9. Slip the wooden assembly over the pole.

Step 10. Drill a second ¼-inch hole through the pole as close to the wood as you can get it.

Step 11. Insert the remaining machine bolt through the hole and secure it with the nut.

Step 12. Hang the martin houses from the eyebolts with wire.

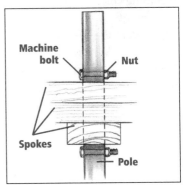

PVC Wren House

For a clean, contemporary look, build a birdhouse out of PVC pipe. You can buy the pipe and fittings from your local home improvement or plumbing supply store. By installing a clean-out cap and plug (which screws in and out), you can open the top to monitor the use of the house and clean it out at the end of the season. PVC is easily cut with a hacksaw, or you can ask your local plumber for a scrap. Also, it's easy to drill through PVC pipe, so you can add some small holes for drainage and ventilation.

To make this wren house more suitable for other birds, including chickadees, nuthatches, bluebirds, and titmice, you'll adapt the design and mount the PVC house on a PVC mounting post. If you need to clean out the house at the end of the season, you can simply unscrew the house from the post.

MATERIALS

4-inch-diameter schedule 40 PVC pipe, 8 to 12 inches long

Marker or grease pencil

Drill

1¼-inch spade bit

¼-inch twist drill bit

4-inch-diameter PVC clean-out cap

Small jar of PVC solvent

¾-inch-long eyebolt with two nuts and washers to fit

4-inch-diameter PVC cap

Strong but bendable wire

Eyebolt
Nut
Washer

Clean-out plug

Clean-out cap

PVC pipe 4" diameter × 8"

Entrance hole 1¼" diameter

PVC cap

THE WREN HOUSE

Step 1. Measure 6¾ inches from one end of the PVC pipe and make a mark.

Step 2. With the spade bit, drill an entrance hole in the pipe, using the mark as the center point.

Step 3. In a well-ventilated area, swab the outside top inch of the PVC pipe and the inside rim of the PVC clean-out cap with PVC solvent. (The solvent comes with its own applicator.)

Step 4. Put the two pieces together and hold for a few minutes to set the seal.

Step 5. Use the twist drill bit to predrill a hole in the top of the clean-out plug. Place a washer and nut over the hole and screw in the eyebolt.

Step 6. On the other side of the plug, place the other washer on the end of the eyebolt and then screw on the nut. Screw the plug into the clean-out cap.

Step 7. Use the twist drill bit to drill three holes in the plain PVC cap for drainage.

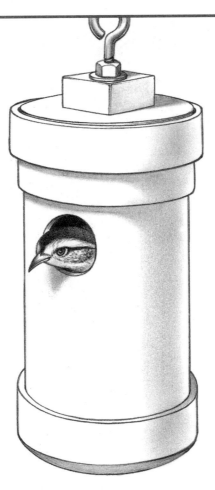

Step 8. Swab the outside bottom inch of the pipe and the inside rim of the plain cap with PVC solvent. Put the two pieces together and hold for a few minutes to set the seal.

Step 9. Thread wire through the eyebolt to hang the house.

THE POLE MOUNT ADAPTATION

Step 1. Follow steps 1 through 4 at left. Skip steps 5 through 7, because there is no need to install the eyebolt to hang the house.

Step 2. Buy a 4-inch-to-3-inch reducer fitting for the PVC pipe. Attach the reducer to the bottom of the wren house (instead of using a plain PVC cap) using PVC solvent.

Step 3. Install a piece of PVC pipe in your garden as described in "PVC Pipe Mount" on page 210. Use a pipe that is 5 to 10 feet long, and be sure to fill the mounting post completely with sand or gravel. This will serve as the floor of the house.

Step 4. Set the house on the pipe and predrill two equidistant holes on each side of the post and reducer.

Step 5. Use 1½-inch screws to fasten the reducer to the pipe.

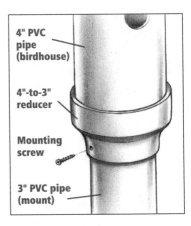

4" PVC pipe (birdhouse)

4"-to-3" reducer

Mounting screw

3" PVC pipe (mount)

Robins and other

phoebes sometimes attempt to nest on very small ledges. For example, they may nest on the piece of 2-by-4 jutting out from your shed, on top of a porch light, or on a 2-inch ledge projecting from a stone barn foundation or wall. Simple nesting platforms offer neighborhood robins good places to raise their families, with a roof to keep off the worst of the weather and a sturdy platform to hold the nest.

MATERIALS

6-foot-long pine 1 × 10

Saw

Protractor (optional)

Drill

⅛-inch twist drill bit

Twelve 1½-inch rust-resistant screws

Screwdriver

Clamp (optional)

CUTTING THE PIECES

Step 1. Mark and cut the pieces as shown in the cutting plan at right. When you mark, be sure to allow ⅛ inch between the pieces to allow for the saw cut. *Note:* The roof and the two side pieces are longer than they need to be. You'll cut them to exact size later.

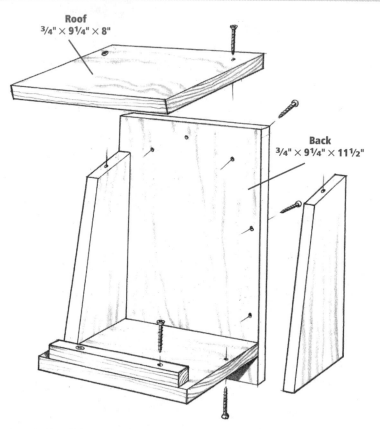

Roof
¾" × 9¼" × 8"

Back
¾" × 9¼" × 11½"

Step 2. Bevel the back edge of the roof piece 15 degrees to allow for the roof's pitch. Lay out this cut so that the final roof length is 8 inches.

Step 3. Cut the side pieces to shape. First, lay out the angled cut

running from the bottom to the top. The pieces should be 5 inches wide at the bottom and taper to 3 inches wide at the top. Make these cuts. Next, mark the top edge of each side to match the pitch of the

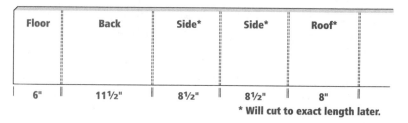

Floor	Back	Side*	Side*	Roof*
6"	11½"	8½"	8½"	8"

* Will cut to exact length later.

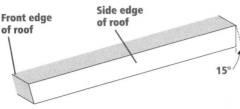

Front edge of roof

Side edge of roof

15°

roof. This angle should be 75 degrees (which complements the 15-degree bevel you cut). A protractor can help with this measurement. Make the cuts.

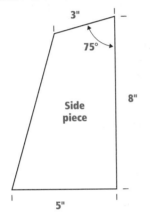

3"

75°

Side piece

8"

5"

Step 4. Cut the front ledge from one of the pieces you cut off of a side piece. It should be ¾ inch x ¾ inch x 8 inches.

ASSEMBLING THE SHELF

Step 5. Predrill two holes and screw the floor to the back piece. The back should extend past the floor by about 1 inch.

Step 6. Add the two side pieces. Predrill the holes; one up through the floor on each side and two through the back will be sufficient. Screw the sides into place.

Step 7. Attach the roof piece to the side and back pieces, beginning by predrilling one hole for each side and two through the back. As you predrill through the back into the roof, angle your drill to match the roof's pitch.

Step 8. Screw the ledge across the front edge of the floor. You may find it easier to keep the pieces aligned if you clamp them together before predrilling.

Step 9. To hang this nesting shelf on a post, drill a hole in the 1-inch overhang at the top of the house and another hole in the overhang at the bottom. Screw the shelf into a post in a protected area of your yard or against a shed or porch.

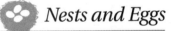

Nests and Eggs

Robins

Robins need a horizontal support, such as a nesting shelf, or a forked branch to hold their mud-heavy nests. Look up to find a robin's nest: Robins build on ledges of houses, in shade trees (maples are a favorite), and in shrubs, but not usually on the ground. Grasses, stems, string, and other fibers are poked and woven through the sturdy, thick cup of wet mud. Robins usually lay four eggs of that famed robin's-egg blue in the soft inner cup of fine grasses. They nest at least twice a season. Robins' nests are prone to disaster in heavy rainstorms, often falling out of trees and landing in collapsed heaps.

To get a firsthand view of nesting birds, mount a birdhouse with a Plexiglas back on a window of your house. Not all birds will be willing to nest so close to human inhabitants, but social birds such as house wrens may. This simple birdhouse has suction cups for easy mounting. Make it easy on yourself and have the Plexiglas cut to the size you need at your local hardware store. Opaque white Plexiglas is available at some hardware stores, or try your local glass supplier. If you can't find it, use clear Plexiglas roughed up with sandpaper to make it translucent. You will need to unscrew a side piece to clean out the house.

MATERIALS

18-inch-long pine 1 × 6

Six 1½-inch rust-resistant screws

Two 2⅜-inch plastic suction cups

5½ × 8¼-inch piece of ⅛-inch thick clear Plexiglas

Twelve ¾-inch #6 round-head brass screws

Two 5 × 8¼-inch pieces of ⅛-inch thick opaque white Plexiglas

TOOLS

Saw

Drill

1-inch spade bit

3/32-inch twist drill bit

½-inch spade bit

Screwdriver

Step 1. Using the 1 × 6, cut the top and bottom pieces to 5 inches long and the front piece to 6¾ inches long.

Step 2. On the front piece, measure and mark a spot that is centered from side to side and 4½ inches up from the bottom. Drill the entrance hole at this spot using the 1-inch spade bit.

Step 3. Line up the top and bottom pieces with the front piece. Using the twist bit, predrill three holes per joint. Attach the top and bottom to the front piece with 1½-inch rust-resistant screws.

HELPFUL HINTS

Drilling Plexiglas is trickier than drilling wood. To avoid cracking the Plexiglas, drill partway through, flip over the Plexiglas, and complete the hole from the other side.

Step 4. Mark two holes for the suction cups on the clear Plexiglas. The centers of these holes should be ¾ inch in from the side edges and 5¾ inches up from the bottom edge. Use the ½-inch spade bit to drill the holes.

Step 5. Place the house on its side, with one of the side panels in place. Using the twist bits, predrill holes for two screws at each end through the Plexiglas and into the wood. Screw the side piece in place with round-head brass screws.

Step 6. Repeat step 5 for the other side piece. You may want to protect your work surface with a rag when you turn the house over, because the screw heads may scratch the surface.

Step 7. Install the back piece in the same manner as the sides, using the remaining brass screws.

Step 8. Push the suction cups through the holes in the back.

Step 9. Hang the birdhouse on the outside of a clean window at eye level, preferably in an area where there's little outside traffic.

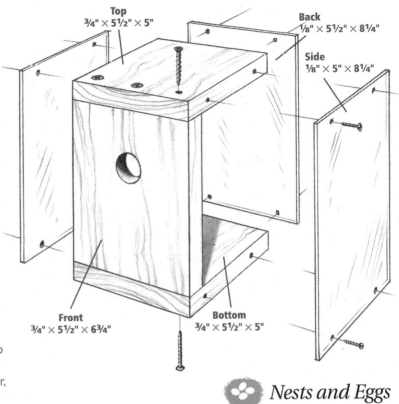

Top
¾" × 5½" × 5"

Back
⅛" × 5½" × 8¼"

Side
⅛" × 5" × 8¼"

Front
¾" × 5½" × 6¾"

Bottom
¾" × 5½" × 5"

Nests and Eggs

House Wren

House wrens are broad-minded nest builders. They'll nest in almost any natural or human-made cavity they come across. The male arrives in late winter or early spring and stakes out his territory by singing and claiming several nest sites. He fills any potential sites with sticks and twigs, which keeps other birds from using the sites and gives the female more to choose from when she arrives. When the female arrives, she chooses her preferred site and builds her nest behind the collection of sticks the male has provided. The nest is a tightly woven small cup of twigs, bark strips, leaves, grass, moss, hair, and string and is lined with grasses and feathers. When the nest is ready, the female lays six to eight white eggs speckled with brown.

KEEPING AN EYE ON THINGS

Monitoring your nest boxes is fun and educational, and if you do it properly, it can benefit the occupants. By taking a few precautions, you can monitor without disrupting the nesting process at all. You'll be able to spot pest and predator problems and take action if necessary.

There are critical times when you should curtail monitoring. These times include the following:

■ During egg laying and incubation, when the female is not active and the male is bringing her food in the nest box

■ During the morning hours, as egg laying often occurs early in the morning

■ On rainy, cold days, when the most important thing is that the nestlings stay dry and warm

■ During fledging (usually about 12 days after the eggs hatch), because if you startle a young fledgling, you may cause it to leave the nest early

Visiting Nest Boxes

Pick a time in the late morning or early afternoon to visit your birdhouse. Approach slowly and open the box slowly: You don't want to be surprised by a snake or a furry creature or frighten the birds. Limit your visit to less than 30 seconds, simply observing how many eggs or nestlings remain, whether the nest is in good shape, and whether the nestlings look healthy. Close the nest box securely when you leave.

If you plan to visit your nest boxes while they're in use, be sure you've protected them from predators by using baffles and other protective devices. Your visit may attract the attention of preda-

tors, and they may follow your human scent or worn trail to investigate.

DEALING WITH PREDATORS AND PESTS

Cats, raccoons, squirrels, insects, snakes, and other birds often plague birdhouses. Raccoons and cats can clean out a birdhouse, and a squirrel's busy teeth can enlarge the hole of your lovely wooden birdhouse so that it can take up residence. In some areas of the country, snakes dine on nesting birds regularly.

You can take several steps to protect young bird families and discourage predators and aggressive species from taking over your houses. Some of these techniques are simple, while others require more diligence.

House Sparrows

House sparrows are a nuisance when you are trying to lure timid bluebirds, tree swallows, or purple martins to your houses. The house sparrow is an introduced species that has taken over much of the bluebird's niche, because this sparrow thrives in the same environment and is persistent and aggressive. House sparrows may take over your bluebird houses if you don't intervene. Even if a pair of bluebirds has built a nest in a house, they may succumb to pressure from a bullying house sparrow and move out.

You will need to decide how tough you want to be on house sparrows in order to keep your houses free for the tenants you desire. If house sparrows start to build a nest, here are some things you can do.

Clean them out. Consistently clean out sparrows' nesting materials to discourage them and force them to move on. House sparrows are very persistent, however, and they may stick it out longer than you, or they may sneak that nest in while you head to the beach for the weekend.

Break some eggs. Destroy the house sparrows' eggs to discourage them even further. They may get tired of trying and move on.

Take down the box. If you can't keep sparrows from nesting in your boxes, you may want to remove the boxes temporarily, or even permanently, rather than allow these pests to reproduce.

Put up more boxes. If you allow sparrows to remain, add more houses to make room for them. House sparrows often nest in houses close to human activity and feeding stations. So be sure to supply housing in areas that get less human traffic for other, more desirable species.

Starlings—Bold and Bigger!

Starlings may be as bothersome as house sparrows to some birdhouse landlords. However, if your houses' entrance holes are of the recommended size for bluebirds, wrens, chickadees, and swallows, you can keep the pesky intruders out. Starlings can become a real hardship for purple martins and larger birds, such as kestrels, flickers, and screech owls, that need larger entrance holes. As with house sparrows, you can consistently remove the starlings' nests to try to discourage them. If you're not successful, you may want to remove the houses rather than allow the starlings to nest successfully.

Insect Intruders

Mites, blowflies, ants, and yellow jackets can greatly impede the growth of your nesting buddies. You can prevent some insect infestations and remove others.

Mites and Blowflies

Mites may infest a nest and feed on the blood, feathers, and skin of the nestlings. Blowflies lay their eggs in damp nests, and the young maggotlike larvae will suck the blood of young birds at night. If you notice the larvae in the nest, you may want to replace it.

Shape a compact, circular nest from dry grass. Put on gloves and a mask to cover your mouth and nose. Carefully move the young birds to a small box or bucket to keep them safe. Remove the infested nest and put it in a trash bag to carry away from the area.

Use a small wire brush or your gloved hands to sweep the box clean. Put the nest you've fashioned inside the birdhouse. Gently place the nestlings on the new nest. Handling the young birds,

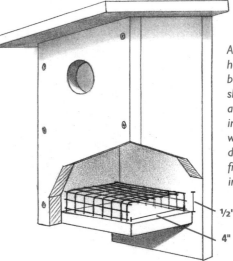

A piece of hardware cloth bent into a U shape will create a raised platform in a nest box that will keep the nest drier and safer from blowfly infestation.

½"

4"

even with ungloved hands, will not cause their parents to abandon the nest.

Ants

These industrious creatures can make their homes in the nest boxes you carefully create. To keep them out, apply a greasy substance—petroleum jelly, vegetable shortening, or axle grease—all around the post the house is mounted on, just underneath the house. Don't put the grease on any surface where the birds could get into it.

Yellow Jackets

Yellow jackets love nest boxes. To prevent yellow jackets from building a nest inside your birdhouse, rub soap or petroleum jelly on the ceiling of the house. This makes it difficult for yellow jackets to attach their nests.

If you have persistent yellow jackets, you'll need to take action. Don't spray chemicals, because the chemicals may harm the nesting birds as well. Instead, use a long stick to force the pests to move on.

continued on page 242

PROTECTIVE MEASURES Collar Those Criminals

Wooden posts are easy for squirrels and cats to climb. To keep these marauders away from birdhouses mounted on wooden posts, add a collar made of a material that's more difficult for them to sink their claws into—a PVC pipe or metal stovepipe collar.

PVC is a great material for predator baffles because it's easy to work with, fairly inexpensive, and too slippery for squirrels and cats to climb easily. You may need to visit your local plumbing supply store to find the wider-diameter pipe needed to fit over 4-by-4 posts, or your plumber may be able to give you a 2- to 3-foot scrap.

Stovepipe comes in 2-foot sections and has an open seam along its length. Instead of using this seam to form a cylinder, simply slip one edge inside the other to fit around your post.

PVC COLLAR

Step 1. Start with a piece of PVC pipe that is 5 to 6 inches in diameter and 2 to 3 feet long. Drill four holes in the pipe equidistant from one another and 1 inch in from one end of the pipe.

Step 2. Slip this collar over your post with the holes at the top.

Step 3. Raise the collar to within an inch or two of the top of the post. (Be sure you leave enough room to mount your birdhouse.)

Step 4. Nail the collar in place through the predrilled holes, using 8-penny nails.

Step 5. Mount the birdhouse.

STOVEPIPE COLLAR

Step 1. Slip one section of 5- to 6-inch-diameter stovepipe over your post.

Step 2. Raise the stovepipe to within an inch or two of the top of the post. (Be sure you leave enough room to mount your birdhouse.)

Step 3. Squeeze the stovepipe to overlap the edges and fit around the post.

Step 4. Use roofing nails to nail the collar in place along the seam.

Step 5. Mount the birdhouse.

Baffles for Metal Poles

You can turn odds and ends of discarded materials into protection for birds. Try these two simple predator baffles for birdhouses that are mounted on metal poles. Be forewarned, though: Determined squirrels will sometimes commit drastic acts—such as chewing right through a plastic bottle—to reach a desirable goal.

Doubling up on baffles may increase their effectiveness.

PLASTIC BOTTLE BAFFLE

Step 1. Use a sharp knife or shears to cut a hole in the bottom of three plastic milk jugs or 2-liter soda bottles and enlarge the opening in the top of each jug or bottle. Make the holes about 1/2 inch larger than the diameter of your pole.

Step 2. Place a hose clamp around the pole about 18 inches above the ground.

Step 3. Slip the jugs end to end onto the pole. The first one will rest on the hose clamp, the following ones on top of the previous one.

Step 4. Mount the birdhouse.

Hose clamp

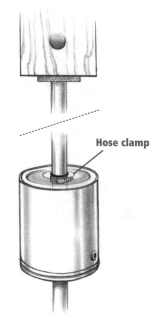

FROM BUCKET TO BAFFLE

Step 1. Drill a hole in the center of the bottom of a 5-gallon plastic bucket. Use a spade bit that is just slightly bigger than the diameter of your pole.

Hose clamp

Step 2. Attach a hose clamp to the pole at least 3 feet above the ground.

Step 3. Turn the bucket upside down and slip it onto the pole, allowing it to rest on the hose clamp.

Step 4. Mount the birdhouse.

To keep nesting birds

out of the reach of raccoons and cats, use a hole guard made out of wood or hardware cloth. The wooden guard shown here is suitable for large birdhouses such as those for flickers and most species of woodpeckers.

If you decide to make the screen guard, wear leather gloves while you work, because the sharp edges of hardware cloth can poke and scratch.

MATERIALS

Four 4 × 5-inch pieces of pine or cedar

Twelve 1½-inch rust-resistant screws (or 16 screws and 4 small metal brackets)

Drill

⅛-inch twist drill bit

Clamp (optional)

Screwdriver

LONG-NECKED HOLE

Step 1. Stand the four pieces of wood on end and shape them into a rectangle, fitting one pair of parallel sides inside the other pair as shown in the illustration below.

Step 2. Predrill two holes into each overlapping joint. If the pieces won't remain steady while you're predrilling, you can clamp them together or have a friend give you a hand.

Step 3. Insert screws into the holes and tighten to form a wooden box.

Step 4. If you're working with a front-opening birdhouse, center the box on the entrance hole and measure the distances from the edges of the box to the edges of the front of the birdhouse. If you're working with a birdhouse where you can't easily access the inside front, skip to step 7.

Step 5. Open the front of the birdhouse and transfer the measurements to the inside of the front piece. Predrill holes through the front and into the box.

Step 6. Still working from the inside of the front, insert screws through the front of the house and into the box sides and tighten.

Step 7. As an alternative to drilling through the front of the house, you can align the box around the entrance hole and place a metal bracket on each side of the box. Predrill holes and screw the brackets in place to secure the box to the birdhouse.

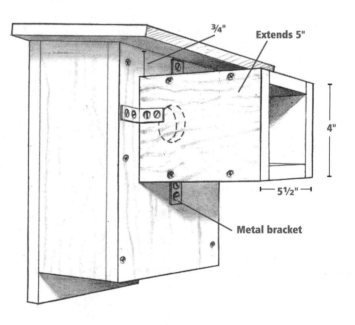

3/4"

Extends 5"

4"

5½"

Metal bracket

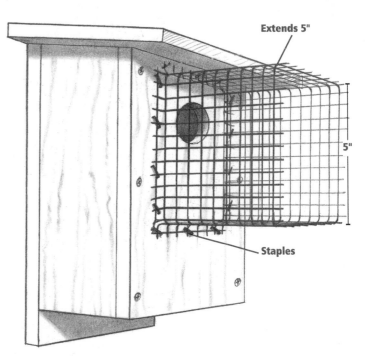

Extends 5"

5"

Staples

MATERIALS

5½ × 16-inch piece of ½-inch galvanized hardware cloth

Tin snips or heavy-duty shears

4 twist ties or four 4-inch pieces of flexible wire (optional)

Staple gun

SCREEN GUARD

Step 1. Measuring from one end of the hardware cloth, use the tin snips or shears to clip in ½-inch (about one square) at 1½, 6½, 9½, and 14½ inches.

Step 2. Form the hardware cloth into an open-ended rectangular tube, bending it at the points you clipped. If the tube doesn't seem to hold its shape, use the twist ties or wire to fasten the edges together.

Step 3. Bend the ½-inch clipped edge perpendicular to and toward the outside of the tube.

Step 4. Place the tube around the birdhouse entrance hole, with the clipped edge flat against the face of the birdhouse. Staple the clipped edge in place, using several staples on each side of the rectangle.

Step 5. On the outer edge of the guard, leave the hardware cloth points sticking out to make it all the more difficult for a predator to reach inside the birdhouse.

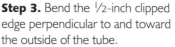

Chew-Proof Entrance

Squirrels can easily chew away at the entrance hole of a birdhouse and make it far too big to deter predators. Downy woodpeckers also may drill away at an entrance hole to make a roost or nest box for themselves. To prevent this, place a metal barrier around the hole. You'll need a metal washer with an interior diameter that is the same size as the entrance.

Drill two holes through the washer, one on each side of the hole in the washer, using a ⅛-inch twist drill bit. Place the washer over the entrance hole, lining up the openings, and drill two holes in the birdhouse, using the holes in the washer as a guide. Screw the washer to the birdhouse using ¾-inch rust-resistant screws.

continued from page 238

Keep an eye on the box, and as soon as you see yellow jacket activity, investigate during the day, when yellow jackets are busy outside their nest. Wear gloves and carry a long stick. Open the box slowly so swarming insects don't surprise you. Using the stick, reach in and knock out the nest. Be prepared to move away quickly if you make the residents a tad angry.

Caution: If you have an allergy to insect stings, don't even try to evict the pests. Have someone else do it while you're away, or wait for winter and clean out the nests yourself.

CLEANING AND MAINTENANCE

The jury is still out on whether cleaning out birdhouses is helpful or necessary. You can find experts on both sides of the argument. There's some evidence that the presence of an old nest may encourage new nest building by some species of birds. However, many old nests are infested with pests that can harm a new family.

A Basic Cleaning Drill

A yearly basic inspection program can be beneficial: It gives you the opportunity to get rid of old, rotting material and check each box to see whether any parts need to be tightened or replaced. You can also decide whether the box needs cleaning. If the nesting material in the box seems damp, or if the material has built up to the point where eggs or young are easily accessible to the probing paw of a predator, it's best to clear out the debris. Take along your screwdriver and hammer and a few extra screws and nails to make any quick repairs, too.

■ Put on gloves and a mask to cover your mouth and nose.

■ Use a stick to clean out nesting material. Look carefully for eggs that didn't hatch. They are great show-and-tell material for grade-schoolers.

■ Use a stiff brush to wipe down the walls and floor. Or take down the house and soak it in a solution of 10 parts water and 1 part bleach. Rinse it with water and let it dry completely.

■ Soap the ceilings to discourage yellow jackets.

■ Tighten any screws or replace any nails that have loosened.

■ If the roof has cracked, replace it or the entire house.

You may find a family of mice inhabiting a house. To keep your houses attractive to birds, you'll need to remove visiting mammals such as these. Just sweep the intruders to the ground. (Don't clear them out with your bare hands, and be sure you are wearing a mask when you do this. Mice can spread diseases, particularly the hantavirus, which is airborne.)

Quick Fix for Entrance Holes

If squirrels or overenthusiastic woodpeckers have enlarged the entrance hole of a birdhouse, you can apply a quick fix rather than replace the house.

Cut a block of wood about 1 inch larger all around than the correct diameter of the hole. Drill a hole of the proper size in the center of the block. Align the hole in the block with the entrance hole and screw it to the birdhouse. To help prevent this from happening again, consider applying a metal washer around the hole, as described on page 241.

CHAPTER 8

Hummingbird and Butterfly Projects

Tempting hummingbirds and butterflies to visit your yard requires a different approach than the projects that attract songbirds. Instead of concentrating on providing leafy, protective cover, hummingbird and butterfly home improvement projects will focus on sunny open spaces and bright flashes of nectar-rich flowers. The other elements of a yard that's friendly to hummers and butterflies are host plants (food for caterpillars), perching places for hummingbirds, and a water source. This chapter also includes habitat ideas to make your yard a possible nesting site for hummers and a wind-sheltered sanctuary for butterflies.

THE HOME TERRITORY

Hummingbirds and butterflies live life in the fast lane: Hummingbirds zoom around in high gear from sunrise to sunset. Butterflies don't move as fast, but they live only a season or two.

Your yard is just one small part of a hummingbird's or butterfly's home territory. The amount of time these beautiful creatures spend on your home grounds is directly related to the amount of creature comforts they find there. For both, food is their most important motivation. As hummingbirds and butterflies cruise around your neighborhood, they'll stop at your place to grab a fast bite to eat or linger for a longer meal if your yard includes plenty of temptations.

Hummer Habits

Hummingbirds have an unconventional lifestyle. In most species, the female alone builds the nest and raises the young. Male hummingbirds mate with any female that will have them, and they leave the nesting and parental duties entirely to the female.

Hummingbirds depend on nectar to fuel their buzzing little bodies. Many species supplement the sugary liquid with bits of protein in the form of insects and spiders, but flowers are an important food source for these brilliant little birds. In your backyard, you can also supply nectar in a feeder filled with sugar-sweetened water. It will be just as popular with hummingbirds as are bona fide blossoms.

Fighting for Food

Both males and females of some hummingbird species are likely to claim a feeder, a nectar-rich garden, or even a particular plant as theirs alone. These tiny feathered terrors will viciously pursue any hummingbird intruder that comes near, as well as dive-bombing trespassing butterflies or songbirds.

Ruby-throated hummingbirds are notorious for monopolizing a nectar feeder for their own personal use. The fiery orange-throated rufous hummingbird of the West is just as possessive, but it often guards a shrub or perennial, such as a fuchsia or a patch of flaming red crocosmia. You may want to provide several garden spots and nectar feeders around your yard to invite hummers to feed without conflict.

A Laissez-Faire Lifestyle

Butterflies don't have "homes" as we're accustomed to thinking of them. Instead, they range widely and erratically as they search for nectar flowers. Monarch, swallowtail, and blue butterflies—as well as many other familiar backyard species—rely on flowers for their daily ration of nectar. If your garden has plentiful nectar flowers, butterflies will spend more time in your yard than in your neighbor's, but eventually they will sail over the fence and away, to return another time.

Some butterflies favor certain species of flowers over others. If you have favorite species of butterflies, research their favorite flowers (see "Recommended Reading" on page 296). When those flowers are at their peak in your yard and local wild areas, you'll see peak populations of your winged favorites flitting around.

Plenty for Everyone

Unlike birds, butterflies aren't territorial—they couldn't care less about other butterflies. They may make a momentary dash at another fluttering visitor that gets too close, but dozens of tiger swallowtails will calmly share a backyard, or even a single patch of blooming oregano. It seems as if they know there is plenty for everyone.

Butterflies don't need to squabble over boundary lines, because they don't form lasting pair bonds as birds do, and they don't need to worry about taking care of their offspring. A female butterfly does make sure that she lays her eggs on or near a host plant on which her caterpillars can feed after they hatch, but that's the extent of it. The kids are on their own.

FLOWERS ARE THE FOCUS

By now, you've figured out that flower gardening projects are key to attracting butterflies and hummingbirds, which isn't the case for songbirds—they have little interest in flowers except for the seeds they may produce or the bugs among their stems and leaves. If you're a flower lover, you can delight in developing flower gardens that will appeal to beautiful hummers and butterflies.

A Great Relationship

Flowers and nectar seekers have evolved together in a mutually beneficial relationship. Flowers can't move around from place to place to distribute their pollen and ensure seed set, but hummingbirds, butterflies, and other creatures can. As the nectar seeker reaches deep into the flower, its body is brushed with sticky pollen that hangs on tight until the pollinator visits the next blossom. In return, the butterfly or other pollinator receives a sweet reward: a sip of nectar.

Feeding Equipment

Hummingbirds remain airborne to feed. Their remarkable wings give them tremendous ability to hover or to fly in any direction—even backward! A hummer positions itself in front of a blossom and extends its extra-long tongue into the blossom to reach the nectary, where its sweet reward awaits.

By contrast, a butterfly lands on a flower before feeding. The butterfly's built-in eating equipment is a thin tube called a proboscis, which coils up neatly when not in use. After landing, the butterfly folds its wings and uncurls its delicate proboscis to dip deep within a blossom and withdraw the liquid. On big butterflies, such as black swallowtails, the proboscis resembles a short length of black thread. On small butterflies, such as dainty hairstreaks, it looks more like a single hair.

Color Is Key

You're practically guaranteed success in attracting hummingbirds and butterflies when you fill flowerbeds and containers with red and purple flowers. That's because plants have evolved to signal their pollinator suitors via their flower color. For example, every plant native to North America that has red or red-orange flowers is pollinated by hummingbirds. Butterflies are less selective, but in general a purple flower is the first cue that draws them to a garden.

If red and purple isn't your color scheme of choice for a garden, not to worry: There are flowers in every color of the rainbow that will suit hummers and butterflies. As you plan your garden, experiment with a range of plants, rather than limiting yourself only to proven butterfly and hummingbird favorites.

Flowers in colors other than red or purple may take longer to catch the attention of hummingbirds or butterflies. So for the fastest payoff in your planting, dot your garden with some red and purple flowers. You'll also want to use these colors if your garden is more difficult for hummers and butterflies to get to: on a raised deck or second-story balcony, for example, or tucked between houses that hide it from full view.

Flower Form Matters

Plant form is also important to nectar feeders. Pollinating birds and insects seek out flowers that accommodate their size, shape, and beaks or mouthparts. Hummingbirds and many butterflies seek flowers with long tubes leading to the nectar. Because hummingbirds hover as they feed, the flowers they favor are usually borne on a spike that extends well above the foliage, such as delphiniums, penstemons, and columbines.

Monarchs and other large butterflies need a secure perch, so they favor blossoms that provide a sizable target to cling to, such as garden phlox and zinnias. Small butterflies can maneuver more easily, so they feed at smaller, lower-growing flowers, such as lavender, verbena, and rock cress.

Delight with Daisies

One great example of a flower with a form that's perfect for butterflies is the simple daisy. That's because a single flower—which may be an aster, a sunflower, or any other flower with a central disk ringed by petals—is a butterfly-size banquet. The central disk, or eye, of the flower is a collection of dozens to hundreds of tiny petal-less flowers.

Because each blossom has so many little flowers to check for nectar, a butterfly often lingers for several minutes at a daisy plant. That gives us plenty of time to enjoy the butterfly, and even to take photos of an especially beautiful or unusual species.

Designing a Garden

Now that you've learned the hows and whys of choosing flowers to attract hummingbirds and butterflies, you're ready to start planting. You can add plants to existing gardens or start a garden from scratch. In the pages that follow, you'll find listings of flowering plants with demonstrated appeal, as well as some complete garden projects.

Full Spectrum Nectar

Designing a garden to attract hummingbirds and butterflies needn't cramp your style. Remember, you're not limited to red and purple flowers. Any flower that has a blossom with a long tube extending from its petals may well attract hummingbirds. Blossoms that grow in a cluster or spike of many small flowers appeal to butterflies.

If you're not sure where to start when designing a garden, try some of the plants listed here. To create a garden that pleases you as well as hummers and butterflies, be sure to include some plants that will bloom in your favorite colors!

Red Flowers

- Crimson columbine (*Aquilegia formosa*): hummingbirds
- Asiatic hybrid lilies (*Lilium* 'Enchantment' and others): hummingbirds
- Zonal geranium (*Pelargonium* x *hortorum*): hummingbirds
- Firecracker penstemon (*Penstemon eatonii*): hummingbirds
- 'Empress of India' nasturtium (*Tropaeolum majus* 'Empress of India'): hummingbirds
- Garden verbena (*Verbena* × *hybrida*): hummingbirds, butterflies

Orange Flowers

- Sunset hyssop (*Agastache rupestris*): hummingbirds
- Cigar plant (*Cuphea* spp.): hummingbirds
- Hybrid torch lilies (*Kniphofia* hybrids): hummingbirds
- Tiger lilies (*Lilium lancifolium*): hummingbirds
- Mexican sunflower (*Tithonia rotundifolia*): hummingbirds, butterflies
- Zinnias (*Zinnia* spp. and cvs.): hummingbirds, butterflies

Yellow Flowers

- Yarrow (*Achillea* 'Gold Plate', 'Moonshine', and other cultivars): butterflies
- Golden goddess (*Bidens* spp.): butterflies
- 'Zagreb' threadleaf coreopsis(*Coreopsis verticillata* 'Zagreb'): butterflies
- Sunflowers (*Helianthus* spp.): butterflies, hummingbirds
- Goldenrod (*Solidago* spp. and hybrids): butterflies
- 'Lemon Gem' marigold (*Tagetes* 'Lemon Gem'): butterflies

Green Flowers

- Flowering tobacco (*Nicotiana langsdorffii*): hummingbirds
- 'Envy' zinnia (*Zinnia* 'Envy'): butterflies

Blue Flowers

- Common ageratum (*Ageratum houstonianum*): butterflies
- Honeywort (*Cerinthe major*): hummingbirds
- Joe-Pye weed (*Eupatorium* spp.): butterflies
- Sages (*Salvia* spp. and cvs.): hummingbirds

Purple Flowers

- Butterfly bush (*Buddleia davidii*): butterflies, hummingbirds
- Common foxglove (*Digitalis purpurea*): hummingbirds
- Common lantana (*Lantana camara*): butterflies, hummingbirds
- Lavenders (*Lavandula* spp.): small butterflies (especially blues)
- Gayfeathers (*Liatris* spp.): butterflies (especially swallowtails and monarchs)
- Brazilian vervain (*Verbena bonariensis*): butterflies

A Sampling of Daisies

The world of daisies (the plant family called Compositae) is a wide one. It includes flowers that any child would recognize as a classic daisy, as well as marigolds, coreopsis, mums, dandelions, and more. Daisies are among the easiest plants to grow from seed. They're also widely available at garden centers, already in bud and bloom. Perennial daisies, such as coreopsis, often produce a few flowers the first year from seeds planted in the spring. All of the following daisies will grow well in all hardiness zones if you buy them already in bud. Those listed as perennials will thrive in Zones 3 or 4 through 10.

DAISIES TO GROW AS ANNUALS

COMMON NAME	BOTANICAL NAME	COMMENTS
Swan River daisy	(*Brachyscome iberidifolia* and hybrids)	Native to Australia, with mounds of airy foliage topped by hundreds of violet, pink, or white flowers
Painted daisy	(*Chrysanthemum carinatum*)	An old-fashioned favorite that's fun to rediscover; flowers often sport pinwheels of contrasting colors
Marguerite	(*Chrysanthemum frutescens*, also called *Argyranthemum frutescens*)	Tidy yellow or pure white classic daisies against neat dark green foliage; nonstop bloom all season
Gazanias	(*Gazania* hybrids)	Abundant dark-eyed blossoms; great for hot, dry areas in full sun; thrive even in sand
Common sunflower	(*Helianthus annuus* cvs.)	Dozens of colors, heights, and flower types, from shaggy dwarfs to giant single blooms
Black-eyed Susan	(*Rudbeckia hirta*)	Also called gloriosa daisy; big, bold flowers in shades of gold and russet
Marigolds	(*Tagetes* spp. and cvs.)	Cheerful orange, yellow, or bicolor flowers on short mounded or tall bushy plants
Mexican sunflower	(*Tithonia rotundifolia*)	Usually a very large plant with bright orange flowers, but dwarf cultivars are available; thrives in poor soil
Zinnias	(*Zinnia* spp. and cvs.)	Long bloom in a variety of colors and sizes; need good air circulation to minimize mildew on foliage

PERENNIAL DAISIES

Golden marguerite	(*Anthemis tinctoria*)	Billows of bright yellow or golden daisies on a sprawling bush of a plant; cut back hard after the first flush of bloom to stimulate another round of flowers

COMMON NAME	BOTANICAL NAME	COMMENTS
Asters	(*Aster* spp. and hybrids)	Purple and pink shades brighten summer-through-fall gardens and beckon to butterflies
Boltonia	(*Boltonia asteroides*)	Airy plants with a relaxed, bushy form dotted with small asterlike flowers in white or pale pink; late bloomer
Chrysanthemums	(*Chrysanthemum* spp. and hybrids)	Pick your favorite color and pop it into the garden in early fall to aid the last of the season's butterflies
Lanceleaf coreopsis	(*Coreopsis lanceolata*)	Sunny gold and easy growing; self-sows to increase your stock
Purple coneflower	(*Echinacea purpurea*)	Easy to grow and so rewarding, with its bouquet of rosy purple, big blossoms that are visited almost constantly by butterflies
Blanket flowers	(*Gaillardia* spp. and hybrids)	A good choice for dry areas; the flowers put on a bright show; although the plants aren't long-lived, they reseed generously (but keep in mind that hybrids won't produce seedlings that are true to type)
Perennial sunflowers	(*Helianthus maximilianii* and other spp.)	Nearly all species spread fast by roots and/or seeds and are difficult to control; best in meadow gardens or informal beds where they can wander
Shasta daisy	(*Leucanthemum* × *superbum*, also called *Chrysanthemum* × *superbum*)	Simple to grow from seeds sprinkled on the soil surface; sow seeds in empty spots in your garden beds in fall and enjoy a bumper crop of white daisies next summer
Rudbeckias	(*Rudbeckia* spp.)	Also called coneflowers and black-eyed Susans; everybody's favorite daisy and a tough, hardy plant to boot

"WEEDY" DAISIES

Hawkweeds	(*Hieracium* spp.)	Flowers look like dandelion blossoms on tall, bare stems; colonies of orange hawkweed (*H. aurantiacum*) are striking, but this is considered a noxious weed in Idaho and some other areas
Oxeye daisy	(*Leucanthemum vulgare*, also called *Chrysanthemum leucanthemum*)	A generous self-sower that is perfect for cottage gardens and meadows; can spread rapidly
Dandelion	(*Taraxacum officinale*)	Eat the leaves in a spring salad; look close to see small butterflies drinking at the blossoms

Rainbow of Nectar Garden

Kids love rainbows, so here's a project just for them—or for rainbow aficionados of any age. Plant this garden in a sunny site where you'll be able to see the living rainbow bloom from an upstairs window. Passersby also will enjoy a leisurely look at the many butterflies that are bound to visit.

Most of the flowers are annuals, and some are super easy to grow from seed. For instant effect, buy six-packs of plants that are already in bud or bloom. All these flowers will bloom from midsummer through early fall.

This plan creates a rainbow that's about 12 feet from end to end. Plant the rainbow's stripes as curving rows, one of each type of plant. Each stripe will fill out to about 9 inches wide. For wider stripes, increase the number of plants.

✔ *For the Record*

Close-Up Focus

For an eye-opening view of butterfly beauty, try a pair of close-focus binoculars. You'll be amazed at the fabulous details of color and pattern that appear when you train these lenses on a feeding or resting butterfly.

Binoculars vary widely in price and quality. The most important factor for butterfly lovers is the minimum viewing distance at which you can still focus crisply. Many pairs focus well at 6½ feet; more expensive models allow you to zoom in when the object of your attention is as close as 6 feet.

Try training your regular binoculars on butterflies before you invest in a pair of butterfly specs. Even if you can't get closer than 20 feet before the lenses lose focus, using binoculars will add an extra dimension to butterfly viewing.

PLANT LIST

- 2 packets bright red-flowered tall zinnia seeds or 24 started plants
- 2 packets 'Profusion Orange' zinnia seeds or 18 started plants
- 2 packets yellow-flowered marigold or golden goddess (*Bidens ferulifolia*) seeds or 24 started plants
- 2 packets 'Envy' zinnia seeds or 16 started plants
- 12 started plants of blue-flowered dwarf-type ageratum
- 8 started plants of Brazilian vervain (*Verbena bonariensis*)
- 1 potted butterfly bush (*Buddleia davidii* blue-violet cultivar)
- 3 started plants of 'Marine' heliotrope

Step 1. Prepare the soil as you would for any annual bed: Remove the existing vegetation, dig to loosen the soil, and rake smooth.

Step 2. Use a garden hose to mark the half-moon outline of the rainbow's outer curve.

Step 3. Beginning at the outside of the rainbow (the red stripe), plant the red-flowered tall zinnias about 6 inches apart.

Step 4. Plant each succeeding stripe, spacing the plants or sowing the seeds according to the package

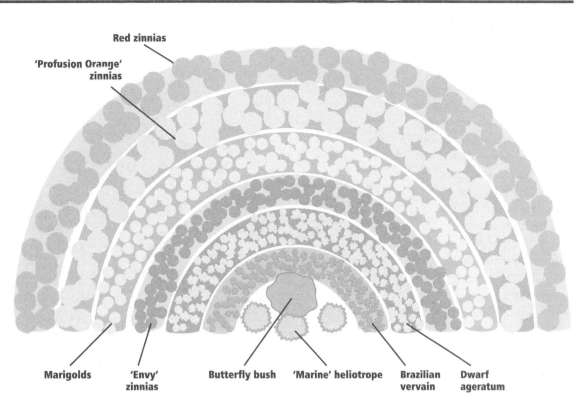

Red zinnias

'Profusion Orange' zinnias

Marigolds

'Envy' zinnias

Butterfly bush

'Marine' heliotrope

Brazilian vervain

Dwarf ageratum

directions. If you're planting seeds, lightly scratch up any trod-upon places in the bed with a hoe before you sprinkle the seeds. If you're using plants, don't bother recultivating; just scoop out a hole for each plant as you work.

Step 5. Dig a hole big enough for the rootball of the butterfly bush. Remove the plant from the container, set the rootball in the hole, and refill with the removed soil.

Step 6. Plant the heliotrope plants in a row in front of the bush.

Step 7. When you're finished planting, water the bed well with a gentle spray from the hose.

Step 8. Mulch around the plants with 2 inches of fine to medium mulch, such as grass clippings, to stifle weeds. If you planted any

seeds, just scatter a light layer of grass clippings over the seedbed. Mulch fully after the seedlings have established themselves.

HELPFUL HINTS

This rainbow is a single-season splendor. Most of the plants are annuals that will fade when frost comes. If you want to renew the garden next year, replant it in the spring. Be prepared for some blurring of the rainbow, though, because some of the plants are likely to self-sow (even during the first season) in random spots. You can weed out the volunteer seedlings or enjoy these variations that result from nature's own garden plan.

Some flowering plants attract both hummingbirds and butterflies, which will usually share garden space amicably. This small garden of dual-appeal plants surrounds a cozy sitting spot for two—two hummingbird or butterfly watchers, that is. The garden's dramatic dark red and soft blue color scheme proves that a planting for hummingbirds and butterflies can be as alluring to us as to our wild friends, although for different reasons!

You'll start this garden with potted plants, except for the sunflowers, which grow from seed. The hardy fuchsia is hardy only to about Zone 6. If you live in a colder zone, you can try planting it and see if it comes back after the winter, or just leave it out of the garden altogether. Replant the sunflowers each spring.

PLANT LIST

4 potted catmint (*Nepeta* 'Walker's Low') plants

2 potted chaste trees (*Vitex agnus-castus*)

1 potted hardy fuchsia (*Fuchsia magellanica*)

2 potted Russian sage (*Perovskia atriplicifolia*) plants

2 potted weigelas (*Weigela florida*); choose a cultivar with dark red leaves

1 packet 'Velvet Queen' sunflower seeds

Step 1. Remove the existing vegetation from the site or plan to mulch extra thickly after planting.

Step 2. Set out the potted plants on the soil surface according to the garden plan shown at right.

Step 3. Dig a planting hole of the correct size to accommodate the rootball of each plant.

Step 4. Fill each hole with water and let it drain. This saturates the surrounding soil so that water won't be wicked away from the roots of the new plants.

Step 5. Remove each plant from its pot and settle the plant in the hole at the depth it was growing in the container. Fill in with soil and tamp moderately firmly around the base of the plant.

Step 6. Prepare the areas for planting the sunflower seeds by turning the soil with a spade or garden fork and breaking up clods. Plant the seeds according to the package directions.

Step 7. Water the entire garden thoroughly.

Step 8. Apply mulch throughout the planting except over the seeded areas. If the soil is bare, spread a 2-inch-deep layer of mulch. If you did not remove the vegetation before planting, spread overlapping sections of newspaper to cover all unwanted vegetation and then apply a layer of mulch 5 inches thick.

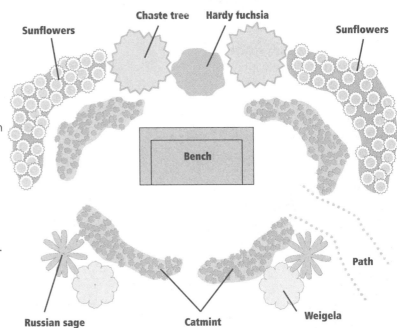

HELPFUL HINTS

Water the garden regularly if rain is scarce, so that the plants get about an inch of water a week. Keep the seeded areas moist until sunflower seedlings emerge, then water them as you do the rest of the garden. Remove weeds as they appear.

Weigelas and chaste trees are woody shrubs. If you wish, prune the weigelas to shape after flowering, and cut old shoots to the ground in the spring as needed to rejuvenate the plants. Chaste trees retain shrub height if left unpruned. If you cut all the stems to the ground each spring before new growth starts, the plant will actually grow taller, to tree height.

Here's a quick, space-saving combo that will appeal to both hummingbirds and songbirds. Try planting this duo along a fence or at the back of a bed. The corn plants serve as trellises for the runner beans.

From mid- to late summer, hummingbirds will seek the orange-red bean flowers for nectar. The corn plants also serve as a windbreak, sheltering any flowers planted in the foreground (which is helpful to visiting butterflies).

In the fall and winter, cardinals, jays, woodpeckers, titmice, and other corn eaters will visit the planting to pluck dried kernels from the ears.

Step 1. Prepare an area in full sun as you would for a bed of annuals or vegetables: Remove any existing vegetation, dig to loosen the soil, and rake smooth.

Step 2. Water the seedbed well a day or two before planting. The moisture in the soil will speed germination.

Step 3. Plant sweet corn or Indian corn seeds 6 to 8 inches apart in a double row, spacing the rows 8 to 10 inches apart. Stagger the placement of seeds from one row to another.

6"   6"   8"–10"   6"   6"

Corn seed   Bean seed

Step 4. Mulch the newly planted seedbed with a thin layer of grass clippings to inhibit weed growth.

Step 5. Water with a gentle spray from the garden hose.

Step 6. Corn seeds sprout within a few days. Keep the soil moist as the corn grows.

Step 7. When the corn reaches 2 to 2 1/2 feet tall, it's time to plant the scarlet runner bean seeds. Poke the beans about 1 inch into the soil along the front, back, and sides of the corn planting, spacing the seeds 6 to 8 inches apart and about 6 inches away from the outside of the double row of corn.

Step 8. Keep the soil moist but not wet to hasten germination of the bean seeds, which should sprout within a few days.

HELPFUL HINTS

If you space the corn and bean seeds 6 inches apart, you'll need about 40 corn seeds and 48 bean seeds to plant an area about 3 feet wide by 10 feet long.

As the bean plants form pods, pick them off. This will direct the vines' energy into producing more flowers for your hummingbirds. After the corn plants mature in the fall, pull the husks away from the ears so that birds can spot the seeds more easily. (Leave the husks attached at the stem end.)

PLANTINGS FOR SMALL SPACES

Nectar seekers are adept at following through on their job description. Migrating hummingbirds will make a detour to home in on a single plant they adore. And butterflies turn up in the most unlikely places as they follow the trail of flowers—windswept buttes in the desert, high mountain meadows, and vacant lots in gritty cities, as well as spacious flower gardens in the suburbs or countryside.

That's good news for gardeners who have very little space—or none at all. Flowers planted in pots and planters can be highly attractive to hummingbirds and butterflies. As mentioned earlier, it is a good idea to include some tried-and-true favorites when your garden size is limited.

Container gardens are the only option for people with limited gardening space, but they're also the way to go if you don't have the time or physical capability to tend a large garden. You'll spend more time watering—usually a daily chore at the peak of the summer—but you'll spend no time weeding.

Check out these container garden designs: "Hummingbird Window Box Garden" on page 256 and "Container Garden for Butterflies" on page 258.

Pots within a Pot

Because the display won't be permanent, as in a garden, try a secret trick to make replacing faded plants quick and easy: "Plant" them in their pots. Then, when a perennial is past its peak or you're ready for something new, you can just pull up the pot and pop another one in. With garden centers brimming with ready-to-go flowers of all descriptions, making a container garden is easier than ever at any time in the growing season.

The potted plants within the container will thrive even though their roots are confined, as long as they get the weekly doses of fertilizer and daily watering that container gardens need to look their best. Compost tea, fish emulsion, and other organic preparations sprayed on the foliage and watered into the soil will keep your "pots within a pot" looking good.

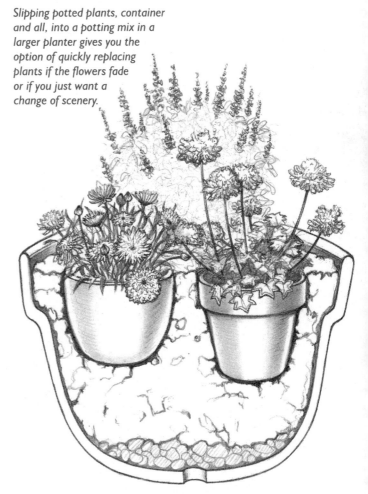

Slipping potted plants, container and all, into a potting mix in a larger planter gives you the option of quickly replacing plants if the flowers fade or if you just want a change of scenery.

Hummingbird Window Box Garden

Here's a window box with a secret only you and the hummingbirds will know. Tucked behind the flowers is a small nectar feeder, which is bound to lure hummers right up to your window.

Window boxes look best when they pack a big punch from a distance. This one can't miss: It holds a simple planting of scarlet sage, which sports fire engine–red flowers. Hummingbirds find it irresistible. Delicate feathery vines of cypress vine, a tiny red-flowered morning glory relative, dangle over the edge. Don't worry if the vines begin climbing the salvia stems; the vines are so thin they won't harm the salvias.

MATERIALS

Lightweight metal hook or mini wrought-iron hook, 6 to 10 inches long

Plastic, metal, or wooden window box, of a size that fits the window where you plan to mount it

Drill

Small nuts and bolts

Soil-based potting mix

Potted scarlet sage (*Salvia splendens*) plants

1 packet cypress vine (*Ipomoea quamoclit*) seeds

Small nectar feeder

Nectar solution

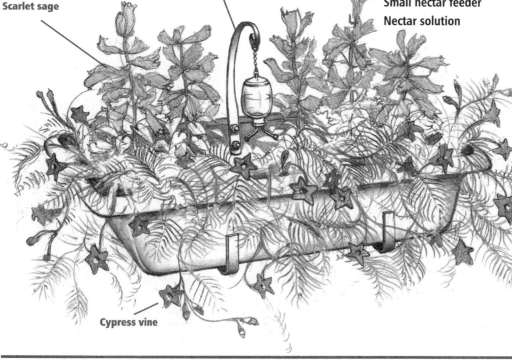

Scarlet sage

Nectar feeder

Cypress vine

Step 1. Hold the hook in position against the box where you plan to mount it. Use a pencil to mark the mounting holes.

Step 2. Set the hook aside and predrill the holes using a twist bit of appropriate size.

Step 3. Use nuts and bolts to secure the hook, inserting the bolts from the outside of the box and attaching the nuts to the bolts from the inside.

Step 4. Put about 2 inches of potting mix in the window box.

Step 5. Remove the scarlet sage plants from their containers. Set the plants, with rootballs touching, in a single row, so that the rootballs are $1/2$ inch away from the front of the box.

Step 6. If your box is wide enough, add a second row of sage behind the first, staggering the positions of the plants from those in the first row. As with the first row, place these plants with their rootballs touching.

Step 7. Fill in around the plants with potting mix. Make sure the mix fills the crevices all around the plants and reaches to within 2 inches of the box rim.

Step 8. Scatter the cypress vine seeds along the front edge and sides of the box, spacing the seeds about $1/2$ inch apart. (You'll see them sprouting in as little as 3 days.)

Step 9. Add more potting mix to within $1/2$ inch of the rim.

Step 10. Water thoroughly with a gentle spray from the hose.

HELPFUL HINTS

Keep your window box looking its best by watering the plants and refilling the nectar feeder regularly. Snip off faded scarlet sage flowers as needed. Don't worry about deadheading faded cypress vine flowers. They will continue to bloom abundantly with no maintenance.

Step 11. Fill the nectar feeder with nectar solution and hang it on the hook.

A Sticky Variation

Avoid the fuss of drilling into the window box to mount bolts for the hook by substituting a plastic hook with a sticky backing on the base instead. Choose a hook with an extra curve at the tip (you may have to search a bit to find one). Check the directions on the package and attach the hook to the back wall of the window box so that the hook is upside down. It's okay for part of the base to extend above the top of the box as long as at least 2 inches of the base is firmly stuck to the box surface.

Press sticky surface to box.

Container Garden for Butterflies

There's a special flair to this container planting that will please both you and a bounty of butterflies. The grouping has a yellow and blue-lilac color theme and includes drought-tolerant, long-blooming flowers of different heights and forms. Plant one, two, or all three of the pots; their contents are coordinated but also look good by themselves. Choose plastic containers to reduce evaporation and thus watering. Be sure all the containers have drainage holes. These flowers do best in full sun. Although they can tolerate dry soil in a garden bed, they will need regular watering in containers.

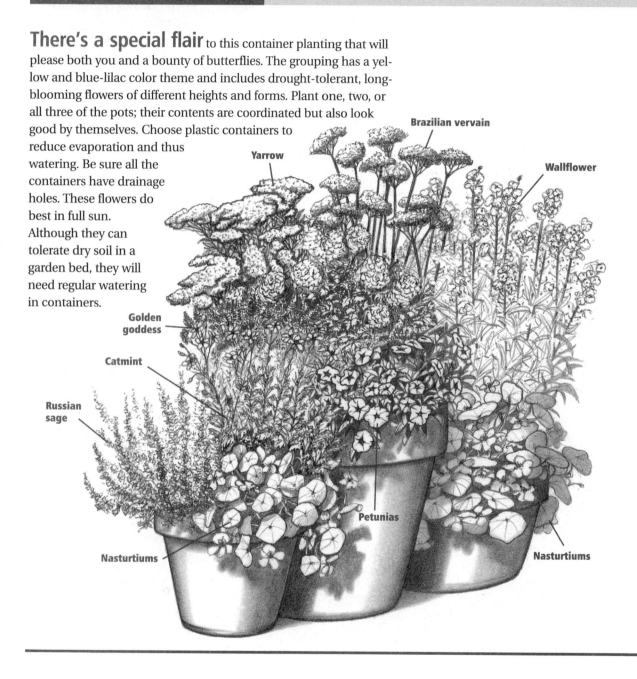

Yarrow

Brazilian vervain

Wallflower

Golden goddess

Catmint

Russian sage

Nasturtiums

Petunias

Nasturtiums

MATERIALS

3 plastic pots of the same or
  similar design:
    1 large (14- to 20-inch-
    diameter),
    1 medium (10- to 12-inch-
    diameter),
    1 low and wide (16- to
    20-inch-diameter)

Soil-based potting mix

PLANT LIST: POT 1

1 potted 'Moonshine' yarrow
  (*Achillea* 'Moonshine') plant

3 started plants of Brazilian
  vervain (*Verbena bonariensis*)

6 started plants of 'Purple Carpet'
  or other lavender-flowered
  sweet alyssum (*Lobularia
  maritima*)

3 started plants of a trailing
  cultivar of golden goddess
  (*Bidens ferulifolia*)

3 started plants of purple-
  flowered milliflora petunias or
  million-bells (*Calibrachoa
  hybrids*)

PLANT LIST: POT 2

1 potted 'Bowles Mauve'
  wallflower (*Erysimum* 'Bowles
  Mauve')

1 packet 'Moonlight' nasturtium
  seeds

PLANT LIST: POT 3

1 potted 'Little Spire' Russian sage
  (*Perovskia atriplicifolia* 'Little
  Spire')

1 potted 'Walker's Low' catmint
  (*Nepeta* 'Walker's Low')

1 packet 'Moonlight' nasturtium
  seeds

Step 1. Fill all pots with moist potting mix to within 4 inches of the rim.

Step 2. Remove the yarrow from its container and plant it near the center of Pot 1.

Step 3. Plant the Brazilian vervain on each side of the yarrow and behind it.

Step 4. Around the edges of the pot, intersperse the sweet alyssum, golden goddess, and petunias, squeezing the plants together for a lush look. Top off with potting mix to about 1/2 inch below the rim. (It will settle when watered.)

Step 5. Remove the wallflower from its container and plant it in the center of Pot 2.

Step 6. Push nasturtium seeds about 1/2 inch deep into the soil around the entire rim, planting the seeds about 2 inches in from the rim and 1 inch apart. Top off with potting mix to about 1/2 inch below the rim.

Step 7. Remove the Russian sage from its container and plant it in the right half of Pot 3.

Step 8. Unpot and plant the catmint in the left half of Pot 3.

Step 9. Poke nasturtium seeds about 1/2 inch deep into the soil around the rim of the right half of the pot. Place the seeds about 2 inches in from the rim and 1 inch apart. Top off with potting mix to about 1/2 inch below the rim.

Step 10. Water all the pots thoroughly with a gentle spray from the garden hose.

HELPFUL HINTS

The nasturtium seeds will sprout in less than a week. Don't try to thin them—you may dislodge neighboring seedlings. Nasturtiums grow well even when crowded.

Water the containers whenever the soil feels dry to a depth of 2 inches. (Check by pushing your finger into the soil.) Fertilize weekly with fish emulsion or compost tea, and snip off fading flowers and stems as needed. The plants will continue forming new buds and flowers into the fall.

Six for Each Season

Once you've succeeded in luring hummingbirds and butterflies to your garden, you may want to move to the next level of sophistication. Your goals will be to draw hummers and butterflies as early in the growing season as possible, and to provide overlapping nectar sources throughout the summer and into the fall. To help you in this endeavor, here's a listing of tubular, nectar-rich flowers for spring, summer, and fall—six for hummingbirds and six for butterflies for each season. These annuals, perennials, vines, and shrubs will help make your yard a hummingbird and butterfly hot spot.

SPRING BLOOMERS FOR HUMMINGBIRDS

PLANT NAME	DESCRIPTION	GROWING TIPS
Wild columbine (*Aquilegia canadensis*)	Perennial with unusual red-and-yellow, long-spurred flowers	Grows well in sun or shade; bloom is perfectly timed to the northward migration of ruby-throated hummingbird; red flowers supply nectar for hungry travelers
Columbines (*Aquilegia alpina, A. caerulea, A. chrysantha, A. vulgaris*)	Perennial with unusual spurred flowers	Bloom slightly later in spring than wild columbine; avoid fussy cultivars such as 'Nora Barlow', which no longer have the simple flower form most frequented by hummers; grow in sun or partial shade
Wintergreen (*Gaultheria procumbens*)	Low-growing groundcover or shade garden plant with white or pale pink summer flowers and fragrant foliage	A shade lover that offers glossy textural contrast at the feet of hemlocks and other conifers
Salal (*Gaultheria shallon*)	Evergreen, shrubby, knee-high groundcover; whitish, waxy, small flowers dangle beneath the leaves	Best in shade and in the Pacific Northwest; spreads moderately quickly
Flame azalea (*Rhododendron calendulaceum*)	Deciduous shrub or small tree with brilliant flowers	Lights up a shady garden; plant Spanish bluebells (*Hyacinthoides hispanica*) beneath it for a great color combo
Flowering currant (*Ribes sanguineum*)	Deciduous shrub with dangling clusters of rosy red, small flowers	A western native that deserves wider appreciation; try it as far north as Zone 4

SUMMER BLOOMERS FOR HUMMINGBIRDS

PLANT NAME	DESCRIPTION	GROWING TIPS
Crocosmias (*Crocosmia* hybrids, especially 'Lucifer')	Bulbs with swordlike foliage and vivid orange or red flowers that arch up over the leaves	Long bloom and bright color add up to more hummingbird fun; bulbs multiply quickly; divide clumps in early spring to increase your plantings
Delphiniums (*Delphinium* spp. and hybrids)	Perennial with tall spikes of flowers in blue, purple, pink, and white	Snip off faded flowerstalks to gain a fresh round of blooms a few weeks later
Cypress vine (*Ipomoea quamoclit*)	Annual vine with a multitude of red mini–morning glory trumpets	Will overwinter in Zone 8 and warmer; self-sows
Rose campion (*Lychnis coronaria*)	Perennial with clusters of fiery red-orange, small flowers	Cut back after flowering to keep the show going until frost; a boon for fall-migrant hummers
Penstemons (*Penstemon* spp. and cvs.)	Perennials with spikes of bright, tubular flowers	One of the favorite flowers of western hummingbirds; look for red species and cultivars to quickly increase the number of hummer visits to your garden
Scarlet sage (*Salvia splendens*)	Annual with spikes of bright red flowers held above the foliage	Simple and gratifying to grow from seed; blooms within weeks; deadhead to prolong bloom; will overwinter in Zone 8 and warmer

FALL BLOOMERS FOR HUMMINGBIRDS

PLANT NAME	DESCRIPTION	GROWING TIPS
Anise hyssop (*Agastache foeniculum*)	Perennial with aromatic licorice-scented foliage and multitudes of blue-lavender, erect, fuzzy spikes of tiny flowers	Bees adore the flowers, too, so plant well back from walkways; self-sows but is never a pest
Cardinal flower (*Lobelia cardinalis*)	Perennial with glossy leaves and majestic spikes of deep red, oddly shaped, tubular blossoms	Grows just as well in sunny garden soil as in its native haunts along shaded creeks; snip off faded flowers to encourage rebloom
Pineapple sage (*Salvia elegans*)	Shrubby tender perennial with aromatic foliage and fire engine–red flowers	Survives and blooms all winter in Zone 8 and warmer
Autumn sage (*Salvia greggii*)	Shrubby tender perennial; tall (5 feet or more) to short (1 1/2 feet) cultivars available; red, pink, white, and pale yellow flowers	Grow as an annual in cold climates; dig up before a killing frost and pot up to spend the winter as a houseplant in a sunny window

continued on next page

FALL BLOOMERS FOR HUMMINGBIRDS *continued*

PLANT NAME	DESCRIPTION	GROWING TIPS
Blue anise sage (*Salvia guaranitica*)	Branching tender perennial with lovely, intense blue flowers	Take cuttings before frost, stick them in a jar of water on a windowsill, and plant the young plants in the garden after spring frosts are over
Mexican bush sage (*Salvia leucantha*)	Tall, shrubby tender perennial with silvery foliage and unusual purple-blue flower spikes	Buy well-started plants because of the late bloom; overwinters in mild-winter areas

SPRING BLOOMERS FOR BUTTERFLIES

Black mustard (*Brassica nigra*)	Annual with myriad bright yellow, small flowers	Often springs up as a weed; look for seeds in the seasonings and spices section of grocery stores
Bachelor's buttons (*Centaurea cyanus*)	Annual with abundant shaggy blossoms in cornflower blue, as well as pink, red, maroon, and white	Scatter seeds on the soil surface in late summer for bloom the following year; a guaranteed success for even nongardeners
Wallflowers (*Erysimum* spp. and hybrids)	Perennials and biennials with sweet-smelling flowers in orange, yellow, white, purplish, and red	Niche plants whose roots can grow into crevices among rocks or in walls; drought-tolerant; may self-sow
Catmint (*Nepeta* cvs., including 'Six Hills Giant' and 'Walker's Low')	Billowy perennials with small gray leaves and masses of blue, extra-long-blooming flowers	A lot of bang for the buck; bloom all season; an occasional shearing keeps growth compact
Moss phlox (*Phlox subulata*)	Ground-hugging mat of foliage smothered with pastel or magenta flowers	Grows on banks, atop walls, and among rocks; fast spreader; slice off divisions to extend the planting
Pussy willows (*Salix discolor, S. caprea,* and other spp.)	Deciduous shrub or small tree with silvery catkins	Surprisingly drought-tolerant plants; watch for butterflies when the silver catkins mature to yellowish puffs

SUMMER BLOOMERS FOR BUTTERFLIES

Lavender (*Lavandula* spp.)	Perennials with gray, scented foliage and skinny spikes of blue to purple flowers	Beloved by nectaring butterflies; shear back by one-third in fall to keep plants bushy and compact
Sweet alyssum (*Lobularia maritima*)	Annual (some plants may overwinter) with mounds of white or purple, tiny blossoms	Self-sows freely, often into cracks in pavement or among gravel; a trouble-free, long-blooming plant

PLANT NAME	DESCRIPTION	GROWING TIPS
Garden phlox (*Phlox paniculata*)	Perennial with trusses of sweetly fragrant flowers in pink, rose, salmon, white, and purple	Snip off faded flower heads to keep bloom going for months
Violet sage (*Salvia nemorosa* 'Mainacht' or 'May Night')	Perennial with dramatic deep blue-purple flower spikes arising from a rosette of foliage	Cut off finished flowers to keep this easy-to-grow plant blooming until frost
Pincushion flowers (*Scabiosa* spp.)	Perennials with fuzzy flowers in blue, pink, and white	Snip off faded flowers for continual bloom; shear back hard if plant becomes mildewy; it will quickly regrow
Stoke's aster (*Stokesia laevis*)	Perennial with large, feathery daisy flowers in shades of blue or white	Flowers held aloft on long, bare stems; plant it at the front of a garden bed to get a better view of nectaring butterflies; may be short-lived

FALL BLOOMERS FOR BUTTERFLIES

'Mönch' Frikart's aster (*Aster × frikartii* 'Mönch')	Perennial with pale blue-purple flowers	Blooms for at least 2 months; no need to deadhead, as the plant continues to produce new sideshoots
New England aster (*Aster novae-angliae*)	Tall perennial crowned by abundant clusters of rich purple, pink, or white blossoms	Lower stems look shabby; hide them with other flowers or ornamental grasses
'Purple Dome' aster (*Aster* 'Purple Dome')	Perennial; tidy mound with deep purple flowers	Break off flexible stems in summer and stick into moist soil; they'll root easily
Heleniums (*Helenium* hybrids)	Tall perennials with masses of flowers in fall colors; also called sneezeweed	Deadhead to prolong bloom; may self-sow
Sunflowers (*Helianthus annuus* and other species)	Annual or perennial depending on species; large, bold daisy flowers and coarse foliage	Perennial types spread rampantly and can take over a garden bed; they're very difficult to control and are best planted in meadows
Chaste tree (*Vitex agnus-castus*)	Deciduous shrub or small tree with grayish leaves and blue-lavender flower spikes	Cut back to ground level in early spring to create a taller plant or if topgrowth is killed during winter; remove bottom branches to train to tree form

NECTAR FEEDERS

While you're developing hummingbird gardens—and even after your gardens are established—you can also attract hummingbirds by hanging nectar feeders around your yard. Serving up nectar in an easy-access feeder is just the ticket for these little gluttons. They will adopt a reservoir of nectar solution and visit it daily, as long as you refill it reliably.

Wherever hummingbirds are found, hummingbird feeders are a hit. And in regions where hummingbirds are sparse, such as the far northern states, nectar feeders may be the extra attraction you need to garner the attention of those that do pass through.

Hummers won't forsake your flowers if you put up nectar feeders. Both sources of nectar will get their patronage. That's why it makes sense to include both when you want to maximize the hummingbird potential of your yard.

When and Why

The big advantage to hummingbird feeders is that they provide practically instant gratification for both you and the birds:

Just assemble the feeder, fill it, and hang it outside. Here are several examples of when and why to use nectar feeders to maximize your yard's hummingbird appeal.

In a new garden. Putting up a feeder lets you take your time planting flowers.

Between peaks of bloom. Perennial gardens often have lulls in the bloom cycle. Feeders fill the gap.

As a relocation aid. Lure hummingbird traffic to another side of your house or to your favorite sitting spot by planting a feeder there.

In early spring. Nectar feeders nourish the early birds before flowers kick into gear.

In the fall. Autumn migrants can get a fast fix and a respite from traveling without expending valuable energy going from flower to flower or yard to yard.

In late fall through winter. For some reason, hummingbird migration patterns have changed in recent years. Some species are lingering longer or straying into unusual areas during what used to be the off-season. Keep your feeder hanging into the winter to nourish these oddball birds. In warm-winter regions, you can keep the feeder up all year. In colder areas, remove it when the temperatures settle below freezing to avoid damaging the feeder.

Choosing a Feeder

A confusing array of designs and styles of feeders are available in stores, from mail-order catalogs, and from online dealers. Hummingbird feeders vary from simple clear glass bottles to artistic globes and tubes. Some have perches; some don't.

Beware of Butterfly Feeders

Maintaining a nectar feeder for butterflies isn't necessary. Nectar-eating butterflies are easy to tempt to your yard with flowers alone, which provide an abundance of the nectar they consume in small sips. Butterfly nectar feeders often suffer from poor design. Butterflies may become trapped in the crevices, which can cause fatal wing damage. For butterflies, stick with flowers as feeders.

The perches themselves vary in placement and size from one style to the next. Drinking holes also vary in size and angle, as does the device that signals their location (such as a molded plastic flower).

The best feeder is one that is easy for both hummingbirds and you to use.

Feeder Features

When you're shopping for a feeder, the best way to evaluate its ease of use is to take the feeder out of its box or remove it from its display stand. Examine it carefully to see how well it fits these guidelines.

Ease of filling. Check the size and location of the opening to the nectar reservoir. Does the design allow you to hold the feeder in one hand or set it on a flat surface while you pour the nectar solution into it with the other hand?

Ease of emptying. It's easier to pour unwanted solution out of a feeder when it has more than one opening. Some artistically designed models, though beautiful, are frustrating to empty and refill because they have only a single narrow opening.

Position of feeding stations. Look for a feeder in which the feeding holes and their connected tubes are located above the bottom of the feeder and point upward. Otherwise, the feeding ports are apt to leak when the feeder is hanging or when you try to refill it. (An exception is the style of nectar feeder modeled after the small water bottles sold for pet rodents. These feeders are designed to have a vacuum seal that retains the liquid in the reservoir. The seal is broken only when a hummingbird dips into the tube to feed.)

Ease of cleaning. Choose a feeder that you can disassemble easily so that you can wash the reservoir and feeding ports. Some are dishwasher friendly, which makes cleaning them much easier. Be sure the feeder and ports are designed so that you can use a narrow bristle brush to remove accumulated mold or other scum. Be wary of designs with inaccessible corners.

Ease of assembly. Is the feeder simple to reassemble after cleaning? Try it out before you buy.

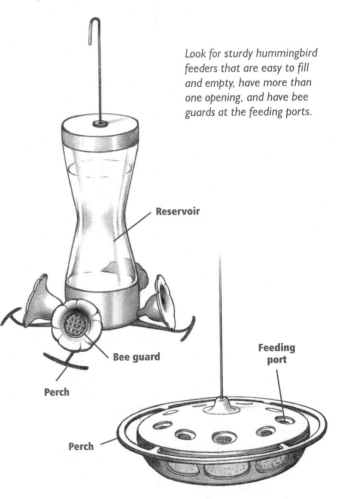

Look for sturdy hummingbird feeders that are easy to fill and empty, have more than one opening, and have bee guards at the feeding ports.

Reservoir

Bee guard

Perch

Perch

Feeding port

Inclusion of bee guards. Wasps, bees, and hornets love sugar water as much as hummingbirds do. Look for a feeder that includes small grids to slip over the feeding holes to discourage insects. You can also buy add-on bee guards. Add-on or not, be sure the guards are glued in place, not just snapped on. Snap-on guards have been known to come off on hummers' beaks, leading to starvation and death.

Quality of manufacture. Choose a feeder made of sturdy materials (including the hanging device). Plastic feeders are fine, but make sure they're strong enough to hold up to repeated disassembly and reassembly. Also, accidents do happen. Clumsy handling, a rowdy dog or child, or a strong gust of wind can dislodge a feeder. Plastic and glass parts should be relatively thick to resist breakage.

Use of an ultraviolet inhibitor. It's important to check whether the colored plastic parts of a feeder contain an ultraviolet (UV) inhibitor. The bright red color often used on feeders is part of their attraction to hummingbirds. Good-quality feeders—which aren't necessarily the most expensive ones—are made of plastic that keeps its color in direct sunlight. Untreated plastic will fade in as little as a week of exposure to UV rays. Hummingbirds may overlook a faded feeder, and a faded feeder also makes your yard look junky. The two types of plastics are indistinguishable to the eye. Feeders made with a UV inhibitor often say so on the packaging. If you can't tell, ask the seller or contact the manufacturer directly to inquire.

Appropriate size. A feeder that's too big can be as impractical as one that's too small. An extra-large feeder may be tempting, because you think you will have to refill it less often. But if you don't host enough hummingbirds to empty the feeder solution within a few days, the solution will spoil, and you'll end up having to empty the feeder and refill it anyway. (If you have a large feeder, keep in mind that you don't have to fill it to the top with solution.) Alternatively, although very small feeders can be fun to use, they require more frequent cleaning and filling. Except in areas of the country where hummingbird populations are highest (the desert Southwest and Texas), the best choice is usually a 1-cup or 2-cup feeder. With moderate traffic (one to four hummingbirds a day), 1 cup of nectar solution will last about 3 days, depending on what other nectar sources are in the neighborhood.

What's Best for Birds

It's easy to evaluate whether a feeder suits your needs, but it's more difficult to figure out whether your hummingbirds will like the feeder you select. If yours is the only nectar feeder for miles around, it's bound to attract hummers. But if you live in a neighborhood where many feeders are available, hummingbirds may scorn your feeder if it's not tailored to their needs.

Hummingbirds may avoid a feeder if the dimensions don't match up well with the size and shape of the birds. Bill length and perching position vary among hummingbirds. A large, long-billed Anna's hummingbird, for example, will have to contort itself to withdraw its bill after each sip from a feeder if the feeder holes and perches are tailored to the dimensions of the smaller, shorter-billed rufous hummingbird. Sometimes the only way you know you've picked a dud feeder is that you get no takers.

Can hummingbirds possibly be so fussy? It seems unlikely, since the flowers they visit vary so much in size, shape, and arrangement. Yet seasoned feeder watchers know that exchanging a barely used feeder for one of a different style is likely to cause a sudden increase in feeder use—or at least feeder investigation.

continued on page 269

What Happened to All My Hummingbirds?

In the spring, when hummingbirds are migrating, they're focused on food whenever they make a rest stop. Thus there's plenty of action at hummingbird feeders during the spring. Hummers migrating through your area will stop at a yard with a source of sugar water for days or even a week or longer. As with most migrating birds, the vivid males arrive first, in many places about mid-April. One to 3 weeks later, females and last year's young fly in.

Along with the hummers that are just passing through, those that will reside in your area also arrive. When they find a hospitable feeding area, they stick around. Add those residents to the transient birds, and you have a big batch of busily feeding hummers.

As spring changes to early summer, the buzzing hummer traffic at feeders and flowerbeds suddenly dwindles to nothing. Hummingbird hosts are often befuddled by the change. Is it a sudden die-off? they wonder, imagining some disastrous scenario. The truth is nothing so dire. The simple answer is that in early summer, hummingbirds are still around. They're just busy with family life and don't have time to hang out at the local sweet shop—your nectar feeder. Also, they're switching their diet to include more insects, especially spiders, for a protein fix.

Changing Priorities

Once the spring migration is over, hummingbirds have other priorities: courting, mating, and nesting. Males are courting females, performing their spectacular aerial swoops and dives as they wait for the females to signal their readiness. Soon after that display, the females take to nest building and egg laying, and then a few weeks of nurturing the nestlings.

Nesting hummers seek food close to their nest sites. If you're lucky enough to have a hummingbird nesting near your yard, you'll still see the female at your feeder and flowers. But if she's made herself at home down the block, she may never show up in your garden.

Lure Them with Flowers

Flowering patterns also affect how many hummingbirds you see at your feeder and how often they come. As peak bloom arrives in the summer, hummingbirds may desert a garden that holds few high-nectar blossoms. Even if such a garden includes a sugar water feeder, the hummers may seek natural nectar elsewhere, in a garden that's filled with their favorites. To increase your chances of seeing hummingbirds even during the slow summer season, stock your garden with a generous selection of hummingbird favorites with overlapping bloom times.

Homemade Nectar Solution for Feeders

The sweetness of natural flower nectar varies depending on the time of day, the ambient temperature, and the age of the blossom. Plant species also vary in the sweetness of their nectar. Honeysuckle, for example, has some of the sweetest nectar around, but most flower nectar is so subtly sweet that we can barely discern the sweetness. When it comes to nectar solution for hummingbird feeders, the magic formula is four parts water to one part sugar.

INGREDIENTS

Water

Granulated or superfine sugar

2 measuring cups, of the appropriate size

Funnel

Clean plastic milk jug, 1-liter soda bottle, or glass jar, with cap or cover

Check how much liquid your feeder holds by filling it with water and emptying the water into a large (4-cup or larger) measuring cup. Round off the amount to a full-cup measure. For example, if your feeder holds 1¾ cups water, round up to 2 cups. This will simplify the calculations for making the nectar solution. To determine the amount of sugar you'll need, divide the number of cups of water by 4. For instance, if your feeder holds 1 cup of water, add ¼ cup sugar to 1 cup water. (Write down the quantities on a scrap of paper and stick it on your refrigerator so you don't have to refigure them every time.)

Measure out the water and sugar in separate measuring cups. You'll need very hot water to melt regular granulated sugar; you can boil it or heat it in your microwave. Superfine sugar dissolves easily in warm tap water.

Pour the sugar into the water and stir to combine. The solution will taste mildly sweet. Let the solution cool to room temperature, then fill the feeder. Use a funnel to avoid spills. Pour any extra solution into the milk jug or other container. Cap the container tightly and store it in the refrigerator. Use the extra solution to refill the feeder as necessary within the next few days. Use a funnel to add the solution to the partially filled feeder through one of the ports.

HELPFUL HINTS

If you're trying to attract hummingbirds to your yard for the very first time, you may have more luck if you put out an extra-sweet solution. Try a ratio of three parts water to one part sugar. Once you've hooked some hummers on your feeder, drop back to the normal 4-to-1 solution.

Never use honey or artificial sweeteners to make the nectar solution, as these can be harmful to hummers.

There's no need to add red food coloring to the nectar solution, although doing so won't harm birds. The red coloring on the feeder itself will be enough to draw the hummers' attention.

continued from page 267

One Recommendation

Each hummingbird fancier has her favorite kind of feeder. But many swear by the same inexpensive option: the four-perch, 1-cup Perky Pet brand vertical glass bottle model. It costs less than $10, and all hummingbird species will quickly accept it. From the host's perspective, this feeder is easy to clean and sturdily made, and the red plastic top and bottom resist fading even in strong sunlight. If you're new to nectar feeding, or if you don't have as many hummingbirds clamoring at your feeder as you think you should, give it a try.

Homemade Hummingbird Feeders

There's a special thrill when you see hummingbirds visit a feeder you made yourself. Don't depend on such feeders as your sole means of feeding hummers, though; commercial models are much easier to maintain. Try asking your child, grandchild, or a neighbor's child to help you make a hummingbird feeder so that she can share the excitement of spotting your first customer.

The glass test tubes used in the feeder projects below and on pages 270 and 271 are easy to work with. Look for tubes made of Pyrex (borosilicate glass), which resists breakage. Tubes cost from as little as 15 cents apiece to about $1, depending on the size. Use whatever size you find easiest to handle. Small test tubes (from 6 by 75 millimeters to 10 by 75 millimeters) are best for hummingbird bills. Standard laboratory test tubes and those up to 25 by 150 millimeters—which are sometimes sold as spice holders—also will work. There is one drawback to using the larger tubes: Hummingbird bills aren't long enough to reach nectar solution in the bottom half of a tube. (For sources of test tubes, see "Resources for Backyard Birders and Gardeners" on page 292.)

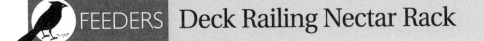

FEEDERS **Deck Railing Nectar Rack**

This project couldn't be simpler. Test tube suppliers also sell inexpensive racks made of plastic or wood to hold the tubes. Order a rack and four to six test tubes sized to fit the rack. Slip the tubes into the rack, add a few red fake flowers, and you have a feeder.

Step 1. Wash the table or deck railing where you want to put the feeder. The railing must be free of dirt and oil so that you can apply an adhesive such as sticky tack.

Step 2. Pull off four pieces of sticky tack and attach one piece to each of the four bottom corners of the test tube rack.

Step 3. Firmly press the rack onto the table or deck railing.

Step 4. Insert the test tubes into the rack in whatever arrangement appeals to you.

Step 5. Insert red flowers into one or more of the unoccupied slots. Clip off the bottom section of each stem, if necessary, so that the flowers protrude 1 to 2 inches above the rack.

Step 6. Fill each tube with nectar solution to just below the rim.

Three-Tube Feeder

A feeder mounted on a patio umbrella is impractical as an everyday nectar source, but it's worth setting up this feeder for the occasional delight of observing the brilliantly colored throat and whirring wings of a hummingbird right at eye level.

MATERIALS

Florist's wire

3 glass test tubes (all one size), with rims

Red silk flower on a stem (for small tubes, use a flower about 1 inch in diameter; for larger tubes, about 2 inches in diameter)

Funnel with a spout small enough to fit inside the test tubes

Nectar solution (4 parts water and 1 part sugar), cooled

Step 1. Cut a piece of florist's wire about 2 feet long.

Step 2. Hold the test tubes in a bunch in one hand. With the other hand, slide the flower stem in the middle of the tubes. Center the flower head over the tubes.

Step 3. Leaving a few inches of wire free at one end, wrap the wire tightly around and around the tubes, just under the rims, for several turns.

Step 4. Twist the short free end of the wire to the long free end to secure it.

Step 5. If the flower stem is flexible, wrap it around the bottom of the tubes until it is secure. If the stem is stiff or won't hold its shape, snip it off and wrap a second piece of wire for several turns around the bottom of the tubes instead. Leave a few inches of wire free on this piece also.

Step 6. Wrap the free ends of the wires around the pole of your patio umbrella.

Step 7. Adjust the flower, if necessary. You may need to pull it a bit higher so that hummingbirds will

be able to see it from a distance. Use scissors to trim off any petals that block the tube openings.

Step 8. Using the funnel, carefully pour the nectar solution into each tube, filling it to within 1/4 inch of the rim, or as full as you can without causing liquid to spill over.

Other Fun Feeder Mounts

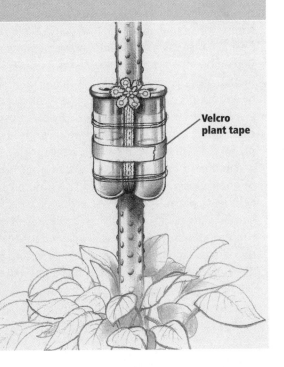

An umbrella pole is just one place to hang a test tube feeder. If you don't have a patio umbrella, you can hang the feeder from a shepherd's crook pole, using the free end of the upper wire to hang the feeder from the crook.

A test tube feeder mounted on a stake can become the centerpiece of a garden bed or container planting located near one of your favorite outdoor sitting areas. Stick a metal plant stake that is coated with textured plastic (this type of stake is available at garden centers and discount stores) firmly into the bed or planter. Snip off the free ends of the wire on the feeder and insert the feeder over the stake. Wrap Velcro plant tape tightly around the tubes to hold the feeder in place. Secure the Velcro snugly by pressing along the entire overlapping section of tape.

Velcro plant tape

SPECIAL FOODS FOR BUTTERFLIES

Butterflies manage to find food in other places besides the flower garden. Juiciness is the main requirement for butterfly food of any kind, because a butterfly must be able to draw the food up through its proboscis.

Fruit trees and bushes, a vegetable garden, and even a barnyard or dog run are sources of butterflies' favorite foods.

✦ Regional Viewpoint

Native Fruits

Butterflies quickly learn to dine on exotic fruits, such as pineapples and bananas, but sometimes it takes a while for them to realize that a particular fruit is edible. By contrast, native fruit choices are usually immediately popular with butterflies. Native fruit plants may be trees, shrubs, vines, or groundcovers, so you're likely to find several native fruits that fit into your gardening plans. Remember that songbirds also are big fans of fruit. Although they may get the bulk of the crop, there should be enough dropped ripe fruit to attract butterflies.

Check out your local woods and fields, or ask at a nearby nature center, to find out what kinds of fruiting plants butterflies in your area have been visiting for generations. In the Northeast, these may include cherries or fox grapes; in the Midwest, persimmons; in the Southeast, papaws; in the West, red or pale blue elderberries. Fruit plants are native to every area of the country, and the plants are well adapted to growing in that climate and usually untroubled by serious pest or disease problems. Keep in mind that "fruit" covers a wide variety of crops, from those we ordinarily put in our own fruit bowls to tiny nuggets of huckleberries or native cranberries or crabapples.

In the pages that follow, you'll find easy projects to attract butterflies such as red admirals, viceroys, red-spotted purples, and hackberries that thrive on a more varied diet.

The Lure of Fruit

Fruit holds temptingly sweet, juicy flesh beneath its outer skin, whether it's a gloriously drippy peach or a crisp red apple. For human fruit eaters, it's a matter of personal preference whether to peel that peach or apple before eating. But for butterflies, tough fruit skin is an insurmountable obstacle. They must wait until the fruit cracks, splits, drops from the tree, or begins to rot before they can feast on the juicy flesh. When birds peck at peaches, apples, or other fruits on a tree, butterflies often follow soon after, collecting around a break in the skin where they can access the juice.

Overripe Is Optimal

For butterflies, overripe or decaying fruit is a prime treat. The bruised, liquefying pulp is so desirable that a crowd of butterflies will gather—a mix of species that is likely to include every fruit-eating type in the area. A single pear past its prime, for example, can easily host two dozen spectacular specimens of red-spotted purples.

When you're assessing your kitchen for butterfly fruit, let your nose be your guide: If it smells bad to you, it likely will be scrumptious to butterflies. This is especially true of melons. When that watermelon or cantaloupe smells "off" and looks soggy, it's reaching prime butterfly ripeness.

You can add fruit to the backyard menu in a feeder, or you can leave the fruit right on the plant (or on the ground below it, when the ripe fruit drops). You can also serve butterfly fruit on a bare patch of ground or lawn. Be sure the fruity offerings are out of the way of foot traffic, though; slipping on a butterfly banana is no joke.

Watching Fruit-Eating Butterflies

It's best to check on your fruit feeder up close now and then, because it's surprisingly easy to miss seeing your visitors. Butterflies usually feed with their wings folded together and upright. The undersides of their wings are generally much less brightly colored than the tops. This is a camouflage device that keeps the butterflies from catching the attention of passing birds, but it also prevents you from spotting them. Dozens of butterflies may be present but, incredibly, also almost invisible to the casual observer.

Try Binoculars

Binoculars are handy for scanning a fruit feeder or beneath a fruit tree from a distance. Train the glasses on one spot for as long as you can to pick up any occasional flutter of wings or other movements that betray the presence of butterflies.

Also walk under your fruit trees now and then when ripe fruit is on the tree and especially when it's on the ground. Two common species of butterflies, the comma and the question mark (named for the tiny white punctuation marks inscribed on their hind wings), are big fruit

Popular Butterfly Fruits

The best fruits to offer butterflies in a feeder tray include the following:

- Apples
- Bananas
- Grapes
- Melons
- Nectarines
- Peaches
- Pears
- Pineapples

If you want to add a fruiting plant that appeals to butterflies to your home landscape, try one of these for starters.

- Crabapple
- Hackberry
- Mulberry
- 'Bradford' callery pear
- Salal
- Sugarberry

eaters and often gather by the score—or even by the hundreds!—at fallen fruit. Even crowds of these butterflies may remain unnoticed, however, because of their tawny camouflage, which looks like nothing more than a bit of dead leaf or natural debris.

The vivid orange-and-black viceroy (similar in coloring to the monarch) is also hard to spot when it sits still with folded wings, as is the lovely painted lady, marked with coral pink on top but a muted potpourri of browns on its underside.

When you stir things up by walking through, the butterflies will take wing, and you're likely to be astounded by how many eager fruit-eating beauties you have in your yard.

This self-serve feeding station takes just minutes to set up. Depending on where you live, you can expect to see viceroy, red-spotted purple, hackberry, question mark, and comma butterflies gathering to feed. If you live near woods, you may host mourning cloak butterflies as well.

It may take several days or longer for butterfly customers to investigate a fruit feeder. Be patient. And remember, the worse the fruit looks to you, the more it will appeal to butterflies.

You may be surprised by some bird visitors to this feeder, including orioles, tanagers, great crested flycatchers, and thrashers. Don't forget to check the feeding station at night, when you may spot interesting moths and beetles. Raccoons and opossums may stop by to feed, too.

Step 1. Choose a flat-topped fence post or flat deck railing where you can mount the feeder. Select a spot away from foot traffic, because the feeder may attract stinging insects. If you prefer, set a single 4 × 4 wooden post in the ground at the location of your choosing. Set the post so that the top is about 4 feet high.

Step 2. Using a few 8- or 10-penny nails, attach a stiff plastic divided dinner plate to the top of the post or railing. Plastic picnic plates available at grocery stores or dollar stores work well for this.

Step 3. Cut some overripe fruit (about 2 cups) into pieces. Cut pears, peaches, and pineapples into chunks or halves. Peel bananas and cut them into chunks. Cut melon into chunks. Slice oranges in half.

Step 4. Arrange the fruit pieces on the plate so that the weight is evenly distributed. Set the heaviest pieces at the center of the plate, directly over the post or railing.

Step 5. Let the fruit remain as long as butterflies continue to visit. It may look awful, but it tastes great to the diners. Replenish the fruit when the number of customers dwindles.

Fruit Smoothie

Lepidopterists (butterfly and moth specialists) call this liquefied fruit concoction butterfly bait. It will lure butterfly guests during the day, but it is also highly attractive to night-flying moths. Butterfly and moth collectors use bait mixtures like this one to attract specimens for netting. There are many personal variations of the recipe. Enthusiasts who collect moths in the tropics often urinate into the mixture to attract butterflies that naturally seek urine.

After you bait your yard with this smoothie, set a comfortable lawn chair strategically nearby so that you can see who shows up to sample it. Scout out nighttime customers with a flashlight.

INGREDIENTS

2 pounds ripe or overripe bananas

3 pounds cheap apples (those with blemishes are fine)

½ cup granulated or brown sugar

½ cup water

Heavy-duty pint- or quart-size resealable plastic bags

Old paintbrush (optional)

Peel the bananas. Place the bananas and apples in a blender or food processor and chop them to a coarse, juicy consistency. Dump the fruit mixture into a large bowl and stir in the sugar and water. Scoop about 2 cups of the fruit smoothie into a plastic bag. Seal the bag tightly, pressing out some but not all of the air. Fill as many bags as needed to use up all of the mixture. Place the bags in the sun. As fermentation occurs, the bags will start to swell with the accumulated gases. When a bag is quite swollen, the bait is ready to use.

Select an open area away from foot traffic to serve the smoothie. Pour or scoop the mixture directly onto a large rock, an open patch of lawn, or bare soil. Or use an old paintbrush to paint the mixture onto the trunk of a tree or a fence post.

Set up as many feeding stations around your property as you wish. Place any extra bags in the refrigerator or in a shady spot outdoors to slow fermentation. The smoothie mixture will keep for about a week.

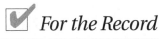 *For the Record*

Nocturnal Fruit Feeders

When you put out a fruit feeder or spread fruit bait, moths and beetles also may come for their share after dark. It's fun to take a flashlight and shine it at your fruit feeder or beneath a fruit tree at night, to see who has come out for a late snack.

Tiny, glowing red eyes are the clue that you have nocturnal customers. If you spot a large triangular moth with nondescript grayish or tan wings patterned with faint lines and squiggles, it may be an underwing moth. The species gets its name from its bright-colored underwings, which flash red, orange, or pink when they fly. If you touch the moth very gently, it may suddenly show its colors for you.

One beetle you might spot is the fantastic eyed elater beetle. This brown beetle is about 1 inch long and has big eyespots on the head end. These eyespots scare away birds looking for a beetle snack.

Crabapple trees were once known for attracting bluebirds, thrushes, and many other songbirds to their plentiful small fruit. But apparently they lost their appeal as breeding programs focused on qualities such as increased bloom, decorative fruit, and disease resistance.

Nowadays, the fruit of many lovely crabapple cultivars remains forlornly on the trees, ignored by foraging birds. But all is not lost: When the fruit finally drops to the ground, it is sure to attract butterflies.

For this simple project, all you need to do is plant a crabapple tree, give it a couple of years to become established, and then set up a viewing spot close by to watch butterflies at the banquet.

Planting a fruit tree to attract butterflies requires a different perspective than planting for birds, which eat fruit from the branches. Here are some things to keep in mind.

■ Choose a crabapple cultivar that drops its fruit in summer or fall, rather than one that retains its fruit all winter. Nurseries and garden centers stock dozens of types of crabapples. Read the labels carefully or ask your local nursery owner for a recommendation. Old-time favorite 'Hopa' and the modern weeping cultivar 'Louisa' reliably drop their fruit in the fall. So do many cultivars that are susceptible to diseases such as scab and rust, which hasten fruit drop.

■ Select a site in an open area in full sun to partial shade, appropriate to the cultivar you have selected.

Make sure the area beneath the tree is clear of other plants. If the fruit drops into flowerbeds or groundcovers, butterflies won't find it. Imagine the tree a few years in the future, with wider branches and more height, and select a location where the fruit will fall onto mulch, gravel, paved areas, or your lawn.

■ Plant the tree according to the label instructions, generally in a hole wide enough to comfortably accommodate the tree's roots and only as deep as it was planted in the nursery pot.

■ For the first 2 years of the tree's growth, supplement rainfall, if necessary, by applying 1 inch of water per week until the tree is well established.

■ Set up an old-fashioned picnic table or a modern bistro set beneath the tree. When fruit falls in the summer or autumn, let it accumulate on the table as well as on the ground. That way, you can sit and enjoy a close-up view of your butterfly friends enjoying the soft crabapples.

■ Most bistro sets are made of painted metal, and some have a tile tabletop. Crabapples are not juicy, but they can mar the finish because of their acidity. You can spray the tabletop with three coats of clear acrylic to help protect it, or have a sheet of Lexan or glass cut to fit as an additional tabletop. If you want to save your expensive outdoor furniture for a more protected place, buy a used bistro set at a yard sale or an inexpensive plastic table at a discount store instead.

Veggies for Butterflies

The vegetable patch holds items of interest to butterflies, too. Here's where you'll find the fluttering wings.

Tomatoes. Blossom-end rot, cracked tomatoes, and other tomato ills are bad news for you but great news for butterflies. Butterflies will eagerly seek out rotting tomatoes to feast on the juice. If you don't mind the stench, let damaged tomatoes hang on the vines or remain where they've fallen.

Cantaloupe and other melons. Butterflies will appreciate it if you split open any extra melons and let them lie. Melon rinds with a bit of flesh still attached also make good butterfly fodder. Add them to the fruit station (see page 274) or put them back in the patch where butterflies can find them.

Watermelon. Sweet, juicy watermelon delights butterflies as well as kids. The vines are usually generous with their fruit, producing enough melons to contribute one or more to the butterfly cause. 'Moon and Stars' and other small varieties are excellent self-contained butterfly feeders. Just split open the melon by dropping it on the ground or giving it a sharp whack with a hoe or shovel. Yellow and seedless varieties will be eaten (we should say sipped) just as eagerly.

Muddy spots. If there's a low spot in your garden that stays muddy, butterflies will visit it for a nutrient boost of minerals. Cabbage white, sulphur, hackberry, and lovely small blue butterflies may be particularly interested if you use composted manure as a fertilizer in your garden.

Manure is the active ingredient in this butterfly attractant. Common white and sulphur butterflies, as well as swallowtails and other species, often gather in flocks around manure to pick up tiny bits of minerals and other essential substances from the moist material. Observe this feeder closely, and you may spot tiny blue butterflies, which are very hard to see unless they are disturbed and flutter about. Composted steer or chicken manure, sold in bags at garden centers, works well for this project, if you don't have another source of manure. You'll need only a small amount; spread the rest around your garden plants as fertilizer.

Step 1. Set a plastic or clay plant saucer in a sunny, open area.

Step 2. Fill the saucer halfway with coarse sand.

Step 3. Pour some bagged composted manure onto a garden bed (in an area where you can spread the leftover manure around your plants). Wearing rubber gloves, sort through the pile and pick out several lumps of unsieved manure. If there are no lumps in the mix, grab a few handfuls of manure instead.

Step 4. Set the manure in the dish. Use a trowel to lightly mix the manure and sand. The materials do not need to be evenly distributed.

Step 5. Spray the mixture lightly with a garden hose to dampen it.

HABITAT FOR HUMMINGBIRDS AND BUTTERFLIES

With nectar gardens and hummingbird feeders in place, the next level in attracting butterflies and hummingbirds to your garden is to introduce habitat improvements that will provide shelter and potential sites for hummingbirds to nest and butterflies to lay eggs. These are the main areas you'll want to consider.

Open space. Sun makes the flowers grow, and sunlight heats up cold-blooded insect bodies, such as those belonging to butterflies. Although some species of butterflies do live in wooded areas, most flock to the sunshine. You'll most likely have planted your butterfly and hummingbird gardens in full sun anyway, so you've probably already created plenty of inviting areas for hummingbirds and butterflies.

Perching places. Hummingbirds like to stop every now and then to rest, so you'll want to make sure your garden has a good selection of places where they can pause. (For simple ideas for adding perches to your yard, see page 280.)

Nesting materials. Try planting some of the raw materials for hummingbird nests, and you may be rewarded with the sight of a female bird gathering bits of fluff. You'll find recommendations for plants that provide hummingbird nesting material on page 157 and in "Nests and Eggs: Hummingbirds" at right.

Spiderwebs. Spiders play a big part in hummingbird life. Hummers eat both the spiders and the small insects the spiders trap in their webs. Female hummingbirds also collect the silken threads of spiderwebs to use in their nests. Keep your yard pesticide-free so that spiders of all sizes flourish.

Shelter. Hummingbirds have very few predators, but one of them may be sitting on your lap right now. Cats are the biggest killers of hummingbirds. Collisions with windows also take a high toll. And the American kestrel, a swift small falcon, can outmaneuver a hummingbird in the air and nab it for dinner.

Butterflies are nothing more than glorified bugs, and birds are among their

continued on page 281

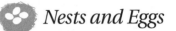

Nests and Eggs

Hummingbirds

Chances are good you'll never be aware of a hummingbird's nest on your property unless you're a sharp-eyed observer or unless you stumble upon the site by happenstance. Hummers build tiny homes for their young, about the size of a golf ball sliced in half. Not only is the nest extremely small, but it's also perfectly camouflaged by the sneaky female hummer, who uses sticky spiderweb material to glue bits of bark, moss, leaves, or other natural disguises to the outside of the little cup.

The outside of a hummingbird's nest may look like scratchy bark, but the inside is as soft and inviting as a bed in a five-star hotel. The female hummer packs it full of tiny bits of fluff that she painstakingly gathers from remarkable sources. The small, puffy seedheads of fleabanes (*Erigeron* spp.), for instance, may yield some of the makings, as can the fuzzy underside of fern fronds or the silky fur of pussy willows. Small, soft feathers are a favorite addition of many species.

That tiny nest holds an even smaller treasure—a couple of itty-bitty white eggs. How small is a hummingbird egg? Next time you're making bean soup from scratch, hold two little navy beans in your hand, and you'll have a rough idea of the incredibly small size of a hummingbird's eggs.

Hummingbirds nest in many types of trees, shrubs, and vines, and most species don't seem to show any distinct preferences for a particular type of plant. Some species, such as the broadbilled hummingbird of the Southwest, show a fondness for oddball supports such as a clothesline or a loop of wire hanging on a wall. Hosting a hummingbird's nest seems to be more a matter of luck than of planting specific trees or shrubs.

If you want to try something new on the market, take a look at the hummingbird nest supports that are showing up in some bird supply stores and catalogs. The metal support mimics a short, naturally forked branch, which can be attractive to a house-hunting hummer. If you're lucky, a hummer will plaster her tiny nest to the "twig," giving you a front-row seat as she raises her family.

Watching hummingbirds in the nest is a real thrill, but supplying nest sites isn't nearly as important as supplying food, in terms of increasing the number of hummingbirds on your property. As soon as the young are out of the nest—wherever it is—the mother bird will show them where the goodies can be found. That's your yard, of course.

Hummingbird Perches

Long ago, so-called authorities on hummingbirds decided that hummers had no feet. It's easy to see why someone could make that mistake, as hummingbirds always seem to be in action and their feet are very difficult to spot while they're whizzing through the air, or even while they're stopped in midair to feed.

If you observe one hummingbird for a while, though, you'll see that it does spend a good bit of time taking temporary rests on convenient perches— and it definitely has feet! The perch must be small enough in diameter for the hummingbird's tiny black feet to get a grip.

Perches that allow an unimpeded view of the surrounding area seem to be what hummers prefer. Also vital is a lack of interfering foliage and twigs, so that the hummingbird can easily maneuver its way to and from the perch. Perches are temporary rest areas; hummers need to be able to zip on and off in a hurry.

Your yard may already hold many suitable perching places for hummingbirds. Try adding other types of perches that hummingbirds are known to visit often.

■ Inexpensive metal arches, which you can find for about $10 in craft supply stores and discount stores, are fast and easy to assemble, and hummingbirds will enjoy perching on the top rung. Plant scarlet runner beans, coral honeysuckle (*Lonicera sempervirens*), or other flowering vines favored by hummingbirds to grow up the arch. That way, you'll provide both nectar and a perfect perching spot.

■ Here's something you undoubtedly have in your yard already: dead twigs. The best perching twigs are those that protrude from the top or side of a garden shrub or small tree. Train yourself to look for that unmistakable small, long-beaked silhouette on the dead twigs in your yard.

■ Young ornamental cherry trees and other young trees that have stretches of bare branches between the leaves offer good perches for hummers. Yoshino cherries (*Prunus* × *yedoensis*) and other flowering cherries have a wide, flaring outward crown of branches, and they don't have thick foliage or dense twigs that would interfere with takeoffs and landings.

■ Young fig trees are sought as perches especially during sudden downpours. The wide, sturdy leaves overhang fairly bare branches, supplying easy entry and exit and a built-in rain hat.

■ Garden ornaments with skinny, protruding parts, such as the tip of the fishing pole of the little boy statue in the fountain, are attractive to hummers. Anything that remains stationary and is small enough to get a grip on appeals to a hummingbird.

■ Tall, twiggy brush that you use to support delphiniums or other top-heavy flowers invites hummers to rest for a moment. Leave these all-natural plant supports in place after you cut back the finished flower heads, and hummers will continue to use them as perches.

■ Ornamental iron trellises are available at discount stores and garden centers, and those made of the thinner metal that best suits hummingbirds (about $1/4$ to $1/3$ inch in diameter) are available for about $20 a section. Push the legs into the soil, plant a vine beside it, and you have a multipurpose addition to the garden. It will supply a desirable perch for hummingbirds (and songbirds), give you more room to grow vining plants, and cast pleasing shade in late afternoon.

continued from page 279

primary predators. A few butterflies, including the monarch and the pipevine swallowtail, are protected from being eaten by their distinctive coloring: Like a flashing warning sign to predators, their coloring signifies that their bodies contain poisonous chemicals. Birds wisely avoid these butterflies and focus on the myriad safe-to-eat species.

It may sound callous, but increasing the population of butterflies in your yard will also increase the number of birds that prey on them. Luckily, a single female may lay dozens of eggs—enough progeny to nourish birds and still carry on the species.

Host plants. Butterflies aren't homebodies as such, but they do search for specific plants on which to lay their eggs. These host plants are easy to work into the garden. Should you spot caterpillars on a plant, you may soon be delighted by the prospect of a hatch, when those larval butterflies complete the transformation and leave their chrysalises on the same day, to fill your flower garden with beautiful wings. We'll cover host plants in detail on page 282.

Basking sites. Butterflies ardently bask in the sun. A butterfly will settle itself on a sunny rock, strip of pavement, or big leaf that faces the sun and open its wings wide to soak up the rays. You may even see a butterfly sunning itself on your deck railing or house siding. Once a butterfly finds a favored basking site, it often returns to the same place day after day.

Water. Hummingbirds are delightful to watch as they bathe in a gentle rain shower or beneath your garden sprinkler.

Sunning Spot for Butterflies

A single large rock or group of rocks is an excellent place for butterflies to absorb heat—directly from the sun and from the solar-warmed rock under their feet. If you have a large rock or rocks in your yard, make them butterfly-friendly by removing any plants nearby that obscure the sun, especially those that block the morning and late-afternoon sun. Or you can position a rock, a concrete paver, or another piece of masonry so that its surface is entirely exposed to the sun. Uniformly flat-topped objects are less appealing to butterflies than natural rocks, however, because the sloping surface of a rock allows a butterfly to reposition itself as needed as the angle of the sun's rays shifts.

Nectar supplies most of a butterfly's liquid needs, but some species eat other food as well, or seem simply to appreciate a drink of plain water. The most basic and quickly adopted water feature for butterflies is wet pavement. For more ideas on supplying water for hummingbirds and butterflies, see page 283.

Butterfly Host Plants

When female butterflies are ready to lay eggs, they seek out specific plants for the caterpillars to eat as soon as they hatch. Caterpillars, or larvae, are notoriously fussy about what they consume. Some eat only a single type of plant, such as the milkweed-munching monarch, while others may be found on several kinds of plants, often of the same family. The plants that sustain this growing generation of would-be butterflies are called host plants.

Plan to include host plants in your backyard plantings so that you can experience the fun of discovering caterpillars, which are often just as strikingly marked as their winged parents. Keep in mind that host plants are made to be eaten and that butterfly larvae have big appetites. These won't be showpiece plants by the time the caterpillars have finished with them! But fresh foliage or flowers should regrow soon—perhaps in time to host another butterfly brood.

Think Native

Native plants are usually a good bet as host plants. Butterflies (and moths) have evolved along with them and are accustomed to using the plants that grow wild in their own backyards, so to speak. But American butterflies have adopted many introduced plants as well. For example, black swallowtail caterpillars will feast on dill, which is native to India and southwest Asia.

You'll know your host plants are a success when you see nibbled leaves and what look like black pepper grains on the foliage or caught in joints along the stem. That "pepper" is really the droppings of caterpillars, which do nothing all day but eat and evacuate.

Find a spot for host plants in your yard, and it will shortly be aflutter with more and better butterflies. More, because the first order of business for new butterflies on the wing is to find food, which they will discover in abundance in your nectar-rich garden. Better because they will be newly hatched, with wings at their peak color. Before long, weather, birds, and other vagaries of life take a toll on butterfly wings, making them look faded or tattered. Butterflies that hatch in your yard are new and perfect for at least the first day or two.

Water

You'll need to create water sources other than a typical birdbath if you want to provide water for hummingbirds and butterflies. The water in a pedestal birdbath or water garden is too deep for these delicate creatures to take advantage of. Try some simple techniques especially for hummingbirds and butterflies instead.

Sprinklers for Hummers

Hummingbirds prefer a shower to a long soak in the tub. They will fly through the water droplets from a sprinkler or the stream of a garden hose, then perch to shake and ruffle, repeating this for minutes at a time. Another bathing technique used by hummers is to perch where the spray of water will land on their backs. Much ruffling and posturing goes on as the tiny birds revel in the spray.

Some sprinklers deliver too forceful a spray, but hummingbirds will figure out a way around this by perching where plant foliage breaks the force of the water. Alternatively, you can switch to a gentler "showerhead," or try a misting head, a device that breaks the water from your garden hose into a superfine spray that hummingbirds can't resist.

A Flying Circus

Hummers look so playful when they zoom back and forth through a fine spray of water that you just know they're having fun. Often two or more birds will join in the activity. Misters are fairly inexpensive, and you can adapt a garden wand mister as a hummingbird shower or buy one especially designed for hummingbirds. For an investment of $10 to $30, you'll enjoy months of hummingbird water play.

Follow the package directions to attach the mister to your hose. Install an on/off toggle switch between the regular hose and the mister hose if it is not part of the device. Or attach a timer to your hose so that the mister automatically runs for a specified period of time every day. Mount the mister so that it sprays upward and outward over an open area of lawn or above a flowerbed.

continued on page 286

Regional Viewpoint

An Exotic Moth

Butterfly watchers in the Pacific Northwest have been baffled by the appearance of a most unusual winged insect in their gardens. About the size of a cabbage white butterfly, this day-flying critter is deep blue-black with geometric red markings and red underwings—a real beauty, but it doesn't show up in any field guide to North American butterflies.

Mystery solved! This insect is actually the cinnabar moth, imported from Europe to help control a noxious European weed, tansy ragwort, that is spreading throughout the Northwest. The caterpillars of this moth feast on the flowers of the weed, preventing it from setting its copious seed.

A Food Garden for Caterpillars

Black swallowtail butterflies lay their eggs on plants that belong to the carrot family, which includes carrots, parsley, dill, and wild carrots (Queen-Anne's-lace). Black swallowtails are so attracted to parsley that their larvae long ago earned the name *parsleyworms*.

This garden of caterpillar food plants also includes broccoli, which is a host plant for cabbage white butterflies. Their larvae are the broccoliworms (officially called imported cabbageworms) that plague your garden crop.

If you plant this garden, will you be causing the pest population to increase? Well, sure, a tiny bit. But you'll never be rid of cabbage whites, so you may as well protect the broccoli plants in your vegetable garden by covering them with row covers, then enjoy watching the butterflies flock to this mini garden planted especially for them. You may spot caterpillars feeding as early as May.

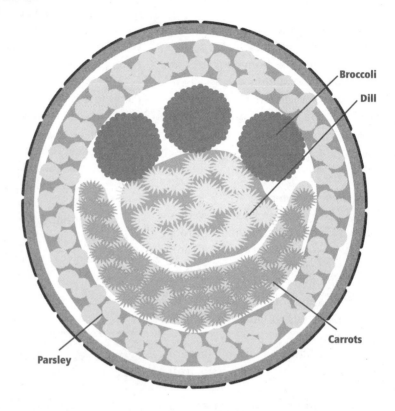

Broccoli

Dill

Carrots

Parsley

MATERIALS

Wooden half barrel

Foam peanuts or clean aluminum beverage cans (optional)

Soil-based potting mix

12 started plants of flat-leaf or curled parsley

3 started plants of broccoli

1 packet carrot seeds

1 packet dill seeds

Step 1. Fill the half barrel about one-third full of foam peanuts or beverage cans, if desired. (This will reduce the amount of potting mix you'll need to use.)

Step 2. Fill the rest of the half barrel to within 3 inches of the rim with potting mix.

Step 3. Plant the parsley plants about 4 to 6 inches apart all the way around the rim.

Step 4. Plant the broccoli plants in an arc as shown in the planting plan at left.

Step 5. Sprinkle the carrot seeds in the area shown in the planting plan. Spread the seeds thinly, but don't worry about overcrowding. The foliage is what attracts egg-laying butterflies, and it can be packed in thickly.

Step 6. Sow the dill seeds in the center of the garden, between the carrots and broccoli.

Step 7. Cover the dill and carrot seeds lightly with potting mix.

Step 8. Water well with a very gentle spray from the hose. Use a watering wand with a seedling noz-zle, if possible, to avoid washing away the carrot and parsley seeds.

Step 9. Maintain the garden by watering regularly with the water-ing wand. Fertilize weekly with an organic nitrogen-rich fertilizer to maximize leafy growth.

Black Swallowtails

The black swallowtail butterfly is so gorgeous that it seems as if it should be a rare tropical species—yet it's one of the most common back-yard butterflies. It has a wingspan of about 4 inches, and the mostly black wings are pat-terned with bits of yellow, orange, and blue. The pièce de résistance of this butterfly's decoration is best seen on newly hatched specimens: Along the bottom edge of the hind wings, on the top side, is the most delicate sprin-kling of pale blue. It looks as though the butterfly was showered with a fine blue powder.

Watch for the pearly eggs of black swallowtails on parsley and other host plants. The butterflies lay eggs individually, and the caterpillars are dark brown when they first hatch. The hatchlings soon shed their skin for a bolder costume: a suit of yellowish-green and black stripes.

When the caterpillars reach about 2 inches long, they disappear. They've found a nearby stem on which to attach their ethereal green chrysalises for the next stage in their transformation. A couple of weeks later, you'll notice velvety black butterflies sailing among your flowers.

continued from page 283

Sipping Spots for Butterflies

Spray your driveway, sidewalk, patio, or brick walkway with a garden hose, and you have an instant butterfly drinking place. You can also fill a saucer or shallow tray with gravel and add water, but in mosquito-plagued areas, this dish can become infested with mosquito larvae.

The jaunty red admiral, a common garden butterfly, is quick to alight on wet pavement to delicately sip the water. Red-spotted purple, hackberry, and painted lady butterflies are among those that will land for a dainty drink. (Generally, your most common visitors for water will be the fruit-eating butterflies.)

Mud adds other possibilities. Butterflies can obtain minerals from soil when the minerals are dissolved in mud, and that makes a mud puddle a popular place. "Puddle" butterflies, including swallowtails, sulphurs, whites, and blues, will gather in groups at an appealing mud puddle, especially if it lingers. Loosen your hose connector at the faucet a tiny bit to create a slow but steady drip, and you'll soon have an inviting spot for butterflies.

Projects at a Glance

W hen project-making day arrives at your house, consult this list of the projects in this book to compare and contrast the choices of feeders, treat recipes, birdhouses, garden projects, and more. There's sure to be a project that fits perfectly with your interests, your budget, and the time you have available.

FEEDERS

Song Sparrow Favorite, 3
Doves at the Dish, 11
A Buffet Tray, 12
Woodpecker Wonder, 14
Sunflower Head Hookup, 33
A Sporty Nyjer Tube Feeder, 34
Flowerpot Seed Bell, 36
Grapevine Wreath Feeder, 41
Gazebo-Style Platform Feeder, 45
Picture-Perfect Tray Feeder, 48
Clear-View Windowsill Feeder, 50
Colorful Coffee Can Feeder, 54
Eating at the Coco Cabana, 57
An Incredible, Edible Garland, 60
Suet Log Feeder, 76
Bagel Feeder, 86
Not for Orioles Only, 100
Margarine Box Suet Holder, 112
Soda Bottle Tube Feeder, 112
Milk Carton Hopper Feeder, 113
Stump That Squirrel (Not!) Feeder, 126

Through-the-Roof Nut Feeder, 127
Deck Railing Nectar Rack, 269
Three-Tube Feeder, 270
Butterfly Fruit Station, 274
Mineral-Rich Manure Feeder, 278

BIRD TREAT RECIPES

Peanut Butter Stretch, 15
Suet–Peanut Butter Filling for
    Pinecones, 80
Suet Muffins, 81
Suet Pie, 82
Dough Ball Treats, 82
Homemade Suet Cakes, 83
Vegetarian "Suet" Treat, 84
Corn Bread Deluxe, 87
Meaty Medley, 99
Homemade Nectar Solution
    for Feeders, 268

BUTTERFLY TREAT RECIPES

Fruit Smoothie, 275

BIRD TREATS

Seed Mosaic for a Snowy Day, 70

Serving the Trimmings, 75

Simple Pinecone Treats, 79

Doughnut Sandwich, 85

Bobbing-Apple Fruit Feeder, 98

A Worm Farm for the Birds, 102

FEEDING STATIONS

Little Red Wagon Portable Station, 108

Woodland-Look Feeding Station, 114

Romantic Feeding Station, 116

Evergreen Christmas Treat Station, 120

Cat's Delight Window Feeding Station, 130

GARDENING FOR BIRDS

Self-Renewing Beginner Bird Garden, 18

Sized-to-Fit Sunflower Plantation, 62

Instantly Accepted Fruit Feeder, 89

Barrel of Fruit, 91

Patio Pot Grapevine, 92

Hanging Strawberry Basket, 96

Bargain Bareroot Bird Hedge, 140

A Tepee for Birds, 145

Nesting Materials Garden, 156

A Shrub Stop for Birds, 159

Front Yard Makeover, 162

Watchable Grape Arbor, 166

Salad Garden for the Birds, 168

Miniature Marsh Garden, 170

Permanent Marsh Garden, 172

Just the Two of Us, 252

Double-Duty Duo, 254

Hummingbird Window Box Garden, 256

Hummingbird Perches, 280

GARDENING FOR BUTTERFLIES

Rainbow of Nectar Garden, 250

Container Garden for Butterflies, 258

Crabapple Picnic Spot, 276

A Food Garden for Caterpillars, 284

BIRDBATHS

Prettified Pedestal Birdbath, 22

Keep a Lid on It!, 179

Basin in a Stump, 180

Heat Lamp Heaven, 183

Light Up Your Birdbath, 184

WATER FEATURES

A Dripper in Disguise, 187

A Homemade Rain Chain, 188

Japanese Styling for American Birds, 192

Sparkling Colored-Glass Fountain, 196

A Perfect Pond for Birds, 200

ENCOURAGING NESTING

A Hanging Basket for Birds, 24

A Bird-Brained Wreath, 25

Furnishing Feathers, 26

Deadwood Gulch, 149

Mop Strings for the Birds, 153

Nesting Materials Supply Station, 154

BIRDHOUSES

The Classic, 214

Swallow Specialties, 218

Traditional Birdhouse, 224

Gracious Gourd House, 226

The Wren House, 231

The Pole Mount Adaptation, 231

Housing the Early Birds, 232
Window on Their World, 234

BIRDHOUSE MOUNTS

Wooden Post Mount, 209
PVC Pipe Mount, 210
Metal Fence Post Mount, 211
Metal Pole Mount, 212
Hanging Assembly for a Martin Colony,
  228

PROTECTIVE MEASURES

Netting a Bush, 95
Homemade Squirrel Baffles, 125
Cat-Proof Feeding Station, 129
PVC Collar, 238
Stovepipe Collar, 238
Plastic Bottle Baffle, 239
From Bucket to Baffle, 239
Long-Necked Hole, 240
Screen Guard, 241

Who Eats What?

Sunflowers, millet, suet: That's all you need to offer to satisfy most backyard birds. But just as your dog will quickly abandon a bowl of kibble to dine on steak, so will birds rush to feeders that are stocked with foods that rank as their favorites. Here are the basic feeder foods readily eaten by various species and good for supplying birds on a day-to-day basis, as well as the special foods they love best.

Note: Treats for the brown-headed cowbird, a common feeder visitor, aren't included in this table because cowbirds parasitize other birds' nests, so songbird lovers don't want to entice them to their yards.

BIRD NAME	BASIC FEEDER FOODS	PREFERRED TREATS
Bluebirds	Suet	Mealworms, peanut butter treats, suet treats
Indigo bunting	Millet	No additional treats needed; millet is the main draw
Bushtits	Suet	Suet treats
Northern cardinal	Sunflower seeds, cracked or whole corn	Sunflower seeds, safflower seeds (once accustomed to eating them), pumpkin seeds, melon seeds
Catbirds	Suet	Suet treats, homemade bird cakes, fruit (especially apples and grapes), homemade bird cakes with fruit, chopped nuts of any kind, baked goods
Chickadees	Sunflower seeds	Peanut kernels, hulled sunflower seeds, chopped nuts of any kind, suet, suet treats, peanut butter, peanut butter treats, doughnuts, homemade bird cakes
Mourning dove	Millet, oil-type sunflower seeds, nyjer	Cracked corn
House finch	Sunflower seeds, millet	Hulled sunflower seeds, canary seeds, flax seeds
Purple finch	Sunflower seeds	Hulled sunflower seeds
American goldfinch	Nyjer, oil-type sunflower seeds	Hulled sunflower seeds, grass seed
Grackles	Cracked corn	Hulled sunflower seeds, pieces, baked goods

BIRD NAME	BASIC FEEDER FOODS	PREFERRED TREATS
Grosbeaks	Sunflower seeds, cracked corn	Hulled sunflower seeds
Jays	Gray-striped and oil-type sunflower seeds, whole corn	Peanuts in shell or shelled, shelled nuts of any kind
Juncos	Millet, cracked corn	Chopped suet, peanut butter treats served in open tray or on ground, canary seeds
Mockingbirds	Suet, cracked corn, sunflower seeds	Suet treats, peanut butter treats, homemade bird cakes, baked goods, fruit (especially grapes)
Nuthatches	Sunflower seeds, suet	Chopped nuts of any kind, suet treats, peanut butter, peanut butter treats, homemade bird cakes
Orioles	Cut oranges	Grape jelly, nectar
American robin	Bread, baked goods	Earthworms, crumbled homemade bird cakes, fruit, raisins, mealworms
House sparrow	Millet	Canary seeds, baked goods
Song sparrow	Millet	Grass seed
White-crowned sparrow and other native sparrows	Millet, oil-type sunflower seed, nyjer	Hulled sunflower seeds, baked goods, crumbled suet treats, chopped peanuts
Thrashers	Suet	Suet treats, peanut butter treats, homemade bird cakes, baked goods, fruit
Titmice	Sunflower seeds	Shelled peanuts, chopped nuts of any kind, suet treats, peanut butter treats
Starlings	Millet, oil-type sunflower seeds, cracked corn	Baked goods, suet treats, peanut butter treats
Woodpeckers	Sunflower seeds, suet, cracked or whole corn	Chopped nuts of any kind, suet treats, peanut butter, peanut butter treats, homemade bird cakes, dried corn on cob
Carolina wren	Suet, millet	Suet treats, peanut butter treats, homemade bird cakes, fruit (especially apples), homemade bird cakes with fruit, chopped nuts of any kind

Resources for Backyard Birders and Gardeners

SUPPLIES FOR FEEDING, NESTING, AND PROJECTS

Arcata Pet
600 F Street
Arcata, CA 95521
Phone: (800) 822-9085
E-mail: sales@arcatapet.com
Web site: www.arcatapet.com
Birdseed, feeders, and nest boxes; suet cakes that contain insects

The Audubon Workshop
5200 Schenley Place
Lawrenceburg, IN 47025
Phone: (812) 537-3583

BestNest.com
1923 Berkshire Road
Cincinnati, OH 45230
Phone: (513) 232-4225
Fax: (513) 232-4118
E-mail: customerservice@bestnest.com
Web site: www.bestnest.com
Wide variety of feeders and birdhouses; suet cakes that contain insects

Bluebird Love
PO Box 872
Cochranton, PA 16314
Phone: (814) 425-2388
Web site: www.bluebird-love.com
Mealworm feeders, nest boxes, and other accessories for bluebirds and other songbirds

Droll Yankees, Inc.
27 Mill Road
Foster, RI 02825
Phone: (800) 352-9164
Fax: (860) 779-8938
E-mail: custserv@drollyankees.com
Web site: www.drollyankees.com

Duncraft, Inc.
102 Fisherville Road
Concord, NH 03303
Phone: (800) 593-5656
Fax: (603) 226-3735
E-mail: info@duncraft.com
Web site: www.duncraft.com
A wide variety of feeders and other bird supplies, including heavy-duty bear-resistant feeders

eBirdseed.com
27823 86th Avenue South
Hawley, MN 56549
Phone: (218) 486-5607
Web site: www.ebirdseed.com

PETGUYS.com
3535 Hollis Street
Building B
Oakland, CA 94608
Phone: (800) 360-4144
E-mail: info@petguys.com
Web site: www.petguys.com
Birdseed, feeders, and nest boxes; turtle and fish food that contains insects only

Pipestem Creek
7060 Highway 9
Carrington, ND 58421
Phone: (800) 446-1986
Web site: www.pipestemcreek.com
Handmade edible feeders and bird-houses; raw materials for nature crafts

Shinkigen
3431 Landrum Drive
Smyrna, GA 30082
Phone: (770) 434-9955
E-mail: shishi@aol.com
Web site: www.shinkigen.com
Traditional bamboo plumbing for water features; bamboo birdhouses; carved lava rock basins

Wild Birds Forever
PO Box 4904
27214 State Highway 189
Blue Jay, CA 92317
Phone: (800) 459-2473
Fax: (909) 336-6683
Web site: www.birdsforever.com

Wild Birds Unlimited
11711 North College Avenue
Suite 146
Carmel, IN 46032
Phone: (800) 326-4928
E-mail: webmaster@wbu.com
Web site: www.wbu.com
Retail bird supply stores in most areas of the United States and a few locations in Canada

Wildlifers
90 Morgan Road
Baie d'Urfe, QC H9X 3A8
Canada
Phone: (514) 457-4144

Wild Wings Organic Wild Bird Foods
220 Congress Park Drive #232
Delray Beach, FL 33445
Phone: (800) 346-0269
Web site: www.wildwingsorganic.com

ORGANIZATIONS AND PROGRAMS

American Bird Conservancy
PO Box 249
The Plains, VA 20198
Phone: (540) 253-5780
Fax: (540) 253-5782
E-mail: abc@abcbirds.org
Web site: www.abcbirds.org
Dedicated to conserving wild birds and their habitats; members receive Bird Conservation *magazine and* Bird Calls *newsletter*

Backyard Wildlife Habitat Program
National Wildlife Federation
11100 Wildlife Center Drive
Reston, VA 20190
Phone: (800) 822-9919
Web site: www.nwf.org
Free information on developing a bird-friendly backyard; provides a certificate if you follow through

The Hummingbird Society
PO Box 394
Newark, DE 19715
Phone: (800) 529-3699 or (302) 369-3699
Fax: (302) 369-1816
Web site: www.hummingbird.org

National Audubon Society
700 Broadway
New York, NY 10003
Phone: (212) 979-3000
Fax: (212) 979-3188

Web site: www.audubon.org
Active worldwide in issues that affect wild birds as well as conservation issues in general; join a local branch to meet other birders, participate in bird counts, and enjoy other bird-related activities

The North American Bluebird Society (NABS)

PO Box 244
Wilmot, OH 44689
Phone: (330) 359-5511
Web site: www.nabluebirdsociety.org
Advice on how to contribute to bluebird recovery

Project FeederWatch

Cornell Laboratory of Ornithology
159 Sapsucker Woods Road
Ithaca, NY 14850
Phone: (800) 843-2473
Web site: www.birds.cornell.edu/pfw
Collects data from individuals who take counts of feeder birds in their yards and analyzes it to determine changes in bird populations and distribution; annual fee covers project newsletter and participation

The Purple Martin Conservation Association

Edinboro University of Pennsylvania
Edinboro, PA 16444
Phone: (814) 734-4420
Fax: (814) 734-5803
E-mail: pmca@edinboro.edu
Web site: www.purplemartin.org
Devoted to the scientific study of purple martins and their habitat requirements; publications available online; quarterly magazine for members

SOURCES OF SEEDS AND PLANTS

Bear Creek Nursery

PO Box 411
Northport, WA 99157
Phone: (360) 733-1171

Canyon Creek Nursery

3527 Dry Creek Road
Oroville, CA 95965
Phone: (530) 533-2166
E-mail: johnccn@sunset.net

Comstock Seed

917 Highway 88
Gardenerville, NJ 89410
Phone: (775) 746-3681
Fax: (775) 746-1701

Edible Landscaping

361 Spirit Ridge Lane
Afton, VA 22920
Phone: (434) 361-9134
Fax: (434) 361-1916
Web site: www.eat-it.com

Forestfarm

9990 Tetherow Road
Williams, OR 97544-9599
Phone: (541) 846-7269
Fax: (541) 846-6963
Web site: www.forestfarm.com

Johnny's Selected Seeds

955 Benton Avenue
Winslow, ME 04901
Phone: (800) 879-2258
Fax: (800) 437-4290
E-mail: homegarden@johnnyseeds.com
Web site: www.johnnyseeds.com

The Native Plant Nursery
PO Box 7841
Ann Arbor, MI 48107
Phone: (734) 677-3620
E-mail: plants@nativeplant.com
Web site: www.nativeplant.com

Niche Gardens
1111 Dawson Road
Chapel Hill, NC 27516
Phone: (919) 967-0078
Fax: (919) 967-4026
Web site: www.nichegdn.com

Plants of the Southwest
3095 Agua Fria Road
Santa Fe, NM 87507
Phone: (800) 788-7333 or (505) 438-8888
Web site:
www.plantsofthesouthwest.com

Prairie Nursery
PO Box 306
Westfield, WI 53964
Phone: (800) 476-9453
Fax: (608) 296-2741
Web site: www.prairienursery.com

Sunlight Gardens, Inc.
174 Golden Lane
Andersonville, TN 37705
Phone: (423) 494-8237
Fax: (423) 494-7086
E-mail: sungardens@aol.com

Thompson & Morgan, Inc.
PO Box 1308
Jackson, NJ 08527
Phone: (800) 274-7333
Fax: (888) 466-4769
Web site: www.thompson-morgan.com

Tripple Brook Farm
37 Middle Road
Southampton, MA 01073
Phone: (413) 527-4626
Fax: (413) 527-9853
Web site: www.tripplebrookfarm.com

WATER GARDEN PLANTS AND SUPPLIES

Lilypons Water Gardens
6800 Lilipons Road
PO Box 10
Buckeystown, MD 21717-0010
Phone: (800) 999-5459
Fax: (800) 879-5459
Web site: www.lilypons.com

Van Ness Water Gardens
2460 North Euclid Avenue
Upland, CA 91784-1199
Phone: (800) 205-2425
Fax: (909) 949-7217
E-mail: vnwg@vnwg.com
Web site: www.vnwg.com

William Tricker, Inc.
7125 Tanglewood Drive
Independence, OH 44131
Phone: (800) 524-3492
Fax: (216) 524-6688
Web site: www.tricker.com

Recommended Reading

BOOKS

Barker, Margaret A., and Jack Griggs. *The FeederWatcher's Guide to Bird Feeding.* New York: HarperCollins, 2000.

Bird, David M. *The Bird Almanac: A Guide to Essential Facts and Figures on the World's Birds.* Toronto: Key Porter Books, 2004.

Cebenko, Jill Jesiolowski, and Deborah L. Martin, eds. *Insect, Disease and Weed I.D. Guide.* Emmaus, PA: Rodale, 2001.

Ehrlich, Paul R., David S. Dobkin, and Darryl Wheye. *The Birder's Handbook: A Field Guide to the Natural History of the North American Birds.* New York: Simon and Schuster, 1988.

Kress, Stephen W. *National Audubon Society: The Bird Garden.* New York: DK Publishing, 1995.

Laubach, René, and Christyna M. Laubach. *The Backyard Birdhouse Book.* Pownal, VT: Storey Books, 1998.

Newfield, Nancy. *Enjoying Butterflies More.* Marietta, OH: Bird Watcher's Digest Press, 2001.

Roth, Sally. *Attracting Butterflies and Hummingbirds to Your Backyard: Watch Your Garden Come Alive with Beauty on the Wing.* Emmaus, PA: Rodale, 2001.

Roth, Sally. *The Backyard Bird Feeder's Bible: The A-to-Z Guide to Feeders, Seed Mixes, Projects, and Treats.* Emmaus, PA: Rodale, 2000.

Sibley, David Allen. *Sibley's Birding Basics.* New York: Alfred A. Knopf, 2002.

Stokes, Donald, and Lillian Stokes. *Stokes Backyard Bird Book: The Complete Guide to Attracting, Identifying, and Understanding the Birds in Your Backyard.* Emmaus, PA: Rodale, 2003.

Tekulsky, Matthew. *The Hummingbird Garden.* Boston: Harvard Common Press, 1999.

Thompson, Bill III. *Bird Watching for Dummies.* Foster City, CA: IDG Books Worldwide, 1997.

Xerces Society and the Smithsonian Institution. *Butterfly Gardening.* San Francisco: Sierra Club Books, 1998.

MAGAZINES

Birder's World
PO Box 1612
Waukesha, WI 53187-1612
Phone: (800) 533-6644
Web site: www.birdersworld.com

Birds and Blooms
5400 South 60th Street
Greendale, WI 53129
Phone: (800) 344-6913
Web site: www.birdsandblooms.com

Bird Watcher's Digest
PO Box 110
Marietta, OH 45750
Phone: (800) 879-2473
Web site: www.birdwatchersdigest.com

Organic Gardening®
33 East Minor Street
Emmaus, PA 18098
Phone: (800) 666-2206 (subscriptions)
Web site: www.organicgardening.com

BIRD FIELD GUIDES

The Audubon Society Field Guide series. New York: Alfred A. Knopf.

Brock, Jim P., and Kenn Kaufman. *Butterflies of North America.* New York: Houghton Mifflin, 2003.

Kaufman, Kenn. *Birds of North America.* New York: Houghton Mifflin, 2001.

Peterson, Roger Tory [birds], and Paul Opler [butterflies]. *The Peterson Field Guide series.* Boston: Houghton Mifflin.

Sibley, David Allen. *The Sibley Guide to Birds.* New York: Alfred A. Knopf, 2000.

Stokes Field Guide to Birds: Eastern Region and *Stokes Field Guide to Birds: Western Region.* Boston: Little, Brown, 1996

Index

A

Agastache foeniculum, <u>261</u>
Anise hyssop, <u>261</u>
Anthemis tinctoria, <u>248</u>
Ants, 238
Apples
  as bird favorite, 95
  fruit feeder of, 98, **98**
  recipes using, 15, 82–83, 275
Aquilegia spp., <u>260</u>
Arbors, 161, 166–67, **166, 167**
Argyranthemum frutescens, <u>248</u>
Asters (*Aster* spp. and hybrids),
  <u>249, 263</u>
Azalea, flame, <u>260</u>

B

Bachelor's buttons, <u>262</u>
Bacillus thuringiensis var.
  israelensis (BTI), 182
Backyard birds, 3–5
  all-season, 4–5, <u>6–7</u>
  attracting, 5
Baffles for Metal Poles, 239, **239**
Bagel Feeder, 86, **86**
Bagels, feeders of, 86, **86**
Bamboo, <u>194</u>
  in water dripper, 192–95, **192,**
    193, 194
Bananas, recipes using, 275
Barberries, <u>142</u>
Bargain Bareroot Bird Hedge,
  140, **140**
Barrel of Fruit, 91, **91**

Basin in a Stump, 180, **180**
Bathing, leaf, 144
Bay leaves, moths and, <u>42</u>
Beaks, 67–69, **69**
Beans, planting, <u>254</u>, **254**
Bears, feeders and, 132
Beetles, feeders and, <u>275</u>
Berberis spp., <u>142</u>
Berries, 17, 87, 88, 94, <u>95</u>
Birdbaths. *See also* Water
    features
  Basin in a Stump, 180, **180**
  deicers and, 183, 185
  depth of, 177
  heating, 119, <u>182,</u> 183, **183,**
    184, **184,** 185
  Heat Lamp Heaven, 183, **183**
  height of, 175–76
  Keep a Lid on It! 179, **179**
  Light Up Your Birdbath, 184,
    184
  maintenance of, 181
  mosquitoes and, 181–82
  pedestal, 22, **22,** 177
  placement of, 176–77, **176**
  Prettified Pedestal Birdbath,
    22, **22**
  from scavenged materials,
    177
  seasonal care routine, 181,
    182–83, <u>182</u>
  selecting, 177–78
  size of, 177
  vine-draped, <u>23,</u> **23**

Bird-Brained Wreath, A, 25, **25**
Bird feeders. *See* Feeder
    projects; Feeders
Birdhouse mounts, 207–8
  Metal Fence Post Mount, 211,
    211
  Metal Pole Mount, 212
  PVC Pipe Mount, 210, **210**
  Wooden Post Mount, 209,
    209
Birdhouse projects. *See also*
    Birdhouses
  Classic, The, 214–16, **214,**
    215, 216
  Gracious Gourd House,
    226–27, **226**
  Hanging Assembly for a
    Martin Colony, 228–29,
    229
  Housing the Early Birds,
    232–33, **232, 233**
  PVC Wren House, 230–31,
    230, 231
  Swallow Specialties, 218–19,
    218, 219
  Traditional Birdhouse,
    224–25, **224, 225**
  Window on Their World,
    234–35, **234, 235**
Birdhouses. *See also* Birdhouse
    projects; Nesting
  birds preferring to nest in,
    <u>148</u>
  building, 205–7

cleaning, 242
deterring nuisance birds at,
236–37
entrance holes
chew-proof, 241
drilling, 206–7
repairing, 241, 242
hanging, 225
hardware for, 205
insects and, 237–38, **237**, 242
maintenance, 242
materials for, 205
measurements of, 222–23
monitoring, 236
mounting (*See* Birdhouse
mounts)
painting, 205
protecting from predators,
208, 236–37, 238–41,
239, 240, 241, **241**
siting, 208
when to erect, 207
Birds
baked treats for, 86–87
beaks of, 67–69, **69**
caloric requirements of, 53
daily feeding schedule, 135
foraging styles of, 10, 43
as pests, 94, 95, 123–24,
236–37
seed-loving, 31
Birdseed
blends, 37–38
buying, 40, 42
canary seed, 39, 39
canola seed (mustard,
rapeseed), 38–39, 39,
61, 64
cost and value of, 39
cracked corn, 36–37, 39
flax seed, 38, 39, 64
grit, 39–40, 119
harvesting, 64
as major food category, 70
millet, 35

milo (sorghum), 38
mixes of, 39
Basic Mix, 38
creating custom blends of,
104
Special Winter Mix, 38
moths and, 42
nyjer (niger, thistle seed), 35,
39
safflower, 36, 39, 64
storing, 42–43, 42
sunflower seed, 32, 39, 62–63,
62–63, 63
Bird treat recipes. *See also* Bird
treats
Corn Bread Deluxe, 87
Dough Ball Treats, 82–83
Homemade Nectar Solution
for Feeders, 268
Homemade Suet Cakes, 83
variations of, 83
Meaty Medley, 99
Peanut Butter Stretch, 15
Suet Muffins, 81, **81**
Suet–Peanut Butter Filling for
Pinecones, 80, **80**
Fruity Pinecones, 80
Nutty Peanut Butter
Pinecones, 80
Seedy Pinecones, 80
Suet Pie, 82, **82**
Vegetarian "Suet" Treat, 84
Bird treats. *See also* Bird treat
recipes
Bobbing-Apple Fruit Feeder,
98, **98**
Doughnut Sandwich, 85, **85**
Seed Mosaic for a Snowy Day,
70–71, **71**
Serving the Trimmings, 75, **75**
Simple Pinecone Treats, 79,
79
Suet Log Feeder, 76–77, **76**
Worm Farm for the Birds, A,
102–3, **102, 103,** 103

Blackbirds
deterring at feeders, 123,
123
food preferences of, 31
nesting preferences of, 148
Black-eyed Susan, 248
Blanket flowers, 249
Blowflies, 237–38
Blueberries, 87, 88, 95
Bluebirds, 212, 217
birdhouses for, 212–13,
214–16, **214, 215, 216,**
230–31, **231**
dimensions of, 222
protecting from swallows,
208
food preferences of, 99, 111,
119, 121, 290
nesting preferences of, 148
nests and eggs of, 213
preferred habitat of, 222
suet cakes for, 83
Bluejays. *See* Jays
Bobbing-Apple Fruit Feeder, 98,
98
Bobwhites, northern, 31
Bog gardens, 171
Boltonia (*Boltonia*), 249
Bones, as bird treats, 78
Bottlebrush, lemon, 142
Bottles, as fountains, 196–98,
197, 198
Brachyscome iberidifolia, 248
Brambles, 148
Brassica spp., 61, 64, 262
Bread crumbs, recipes using, 15,
82–83
Bridal-wreath, 142
Brown creepers, 77, 83
BTI (*Bacillus thuringiensis* var.
israelensis), 182
Bubblers, 191, 195
Buckets, marsh garden in,
170–71, **170**
Buffet Tray, A, 12–13, **12, 13**

Buntings. *See also* Indigo
    buntings
    beaks of, 68
    food preferences of, 31
Bushtits, 139
    beaks of, 68
    food preferences of, 290
Butterflies
    basking, 281, 282
    black swallowtails, 284, 285
    container gardening for, 255,
        255, 258–59, 258
    feeders for, 264, 274, 274, 278
    feeding habits of, 245
    flowers and, 245–46
    fruit and, 272, 272, 273, 273
    garden for adult, 250–51, 251
    garden for larvae of, 284–85,
        284
    habitat for, 278–79, 281–82
    host plants for, 281, 282–83
    lifestyle of, 244–45
    mud and, 277, 286
    plants attractive to, 246, 247,
        248–49, 262–63, 276
    treats for, 275
    vegetables attractive to, 277
    watching, 250, 273
    water and, 282, 286
Butterfly feeders
    Butterfly Fruit Station, 274,
        274
    Mineral-Rich Manure Feeder,
        278
Butterfly Fruit Station, 274, 274
Butterfly treat recipes
    Fruit Smoothie, 275
Butterfly weed, 157

C

Callistemon citrinus, 142
Canary seed, 39, 39
Canola seed (rapeseed, mustard),
        38–39, 39, 61, 64
Cardinal flower, 261

Cardinals, northern, 4
    beaks of, 68
    food preferences of, 31, 290
    identifying, 6
    nests and eggs of, 152
    nesting preferences of, 148,
        150
Carthamus tinctorius, 64
Catbirds
    beaks of, 69
    food preferences of, 290
    nesting preferences of, 148,
        150
    suet cakes for, 83
Catmint, 258, 262
Cat-Proof Feeding Station, 129,
        129
Cats
    coping with, 9
    protecting birdhouses from,
        238–41, 239, 240, 241
    protecting birds at feeders
        from, 128, 129, 129
Cat's Delight Window Feeding
        Station, 130–31, 130
Cattail fluff, 150
Cavity nesters, 148, 204–5
Cayenne, squirrels and, 124
Cedar, eastern red, 143
Cedar shingles and shakes, as
        feeder, 14, 14
Cedar waxwings, 87
    nesting preferences of, 148,
        150
Centaurea cyanus, 262
Chain, for water feature, 188–89,
        188
Chaste tree, 263
Cherries, 89, 160
Chickadees
    beaks of, 68
    birdhouses for, 224–25, 224,
        225, 226–27, 226,
        230–31, 231
    dimensions of, 222

bluebird houses and, 213
food preferences of, 31, 290
foraging habits of, 5, 139
identifying, 6
nesting preferences of, 148,
    150
nests and eggs of, 227
preferred habitat of, 222
sunflower seeds and, 33
wren houses and, 220
Chilopsis linearis, 142
Chrysanthemums
    (*Chrysanthemum* spp.
    and hybrids), 248, 249
Cinnabar moth, 283
Classic, The (birdhouse),
    214–16, 214, 215, 216
Clay saucers, as dove feeder, 11,
    11
Clear-View Windowsill Feeder,
    50–52, 51, 52
Coffee cans, as feeder, 54–55, 54,
    55
Cold, protection from, 144
Collar Those Criminals, 238
Colorful Coffee Can Feeder,
    54–55, 54, 55
Columbines, 260
Coneflower, purple, 249
Container Garden for
    Butterflies, 258–59, 258
Container gardens
    backyard birds and, 28
    for butterflies, 258–59, 258
    planting, 255, 255
    for window sills, 256–57, 256,
        257
Container plants
    dwarf fruit trees as, 90, 91, 91
    grapes as, 92–93, 92
    winter protection of, 93, 93
Coreopsis (*Coreopsis*), 249
Corn
    cracked, 36–37, 39
    planting, 254, 254

Corn Bread Deluxe, 87
Corn bread mix, recipes
 containing, 87
Cornmeal, recipes containing,
 15, 79, **79**, 81, **81**, 82–83,
 84
Cover
 feeders and, 8–9
 necessity of, 20–21
 plants useful for, 27–28
Cowbirds, 31, 290
Crabapple Picnic Spot, 276–77,
 276
Cracked corn, recipes
 containing, 84, 87
Crackers, recipes using, 99
Crocosmias (*Crocosmia*
 hybrids), 261
Crows
 beaks of, 68
 food preferences of, 31
Currants, 87, 260
Cypress vine, 261

D
Daisies, 246, 248–249
Dandelion, 249
Deadwood, as birdbath, 180,
 180
Deadwood Gulch, 149, **149**
Deck Railing Nectar Rack, 269
Deer, feeders and, 128
Delphiniums (*Delphinium* spp.
 and hybrids), 261
Dickcissels, 31
Double-Duty Duo, 254, **254**
Dough Ball Treats, 82–83
Doughnut Sandwich, 85, **85**
Doves
 feeder for, 11, **11**
 food preferences of, 31
 mourning, 5, 6, 290
 rock (pigeons), 123, **123**
Doves at the Dish, 11, **11**
Drainage, and tray feeders, 13

Dripper in Disguise, A, 187, **187**
Drippers, 185–86, 188–89, **188**
 artistic, 186, 187, **187**
 basic, 185–86
 hanging, 186, 189
 tsukubai (bamboo), 192–95,
 192, 193, 194
 watering plants with, 186,
 189
Driveways, birds and, 8
Droughts, 174, 175
Ducks, wood, 222
Dust bath, ashes for, 114, 114

E
Earthworms, 101
Easy Squirrel Feeders, 126–27,
 126, 127
Eating at the Coco Cabana, 57,
 57
Echinacea purpurea, 249
Edge effect, 136, 159
Egg shells, 40, 121
Encouraging nesting. *See also*
 Nest boxes; Nesting
 Bird-Brained Wreath, A, 25,
 25
 Deadwood Gulch, 149, **149**
 Furnishing Feathers, 26, **26**
 Mop Strings for the Birds,
 153, **153**
 Nesting Materials Supply
 Station, 154, **154**
 "Plant" a Residence for Birds,
 24, **24**
Entrance holes for birdhouses
 chew-proof, 241
 drilling, 206–7
 repairing, 241, 242
Erysimum spp. and hybrids, 262
Evergreen Christmas Treat
 Station, 120–21, **120**
Evergreens
 birds preferring to nest in,
 148

 as feeding station, 120–21,
 120
 in formal gardens, 136
 in habitat gardens, 159, 160
 usefulness of to birds, 27, 28,
 143
Eyed elater beetle, 275

F
Fabric scraps, 150
Fats, in birds' diets, 71, 74, 104
"Featherboards," 26
Feathers
 furnishing for nests, 26, 26,
 26
 as nesting material, 150
Feeder foods
 baked goods as, 84, 85, **85**,
 86–87
 basic four, 10, 69
 creating custom blends of,
 194
 fats, 71, 74, 78, 104 (*See
 also* Suet)
 fruit (*See* Fruits)
 nuts, 70–71, 104
 seeds (*See* Birdseed)
 berries, 88
 from cupboards, 84, 86
 eggs (cooked chicken) as, 86
Feeder projects. *See also* Feeders
 Bagel Feeder, 86, **86**
 Buffet Tray, A, 12–13, **12, 13**
 Butterfly Fruit Station, 274,
 274
 Clear-View Windowsill
 Feeder, 50–52, **51, 52**
 Colorful Coffee Can Feeder,
 54–55, **54, 55**
 Deck Railing Nectar Rack,
 269
 Doves at the Dish, 11, **11**
 Eating at the Coco Cabana,
 57, **57**
 Flowerpot Seed Bell, 36, **36**

Feeder projects *continued*
Gazebo-Style Platform
Feeder, 45–47, **45, 46**
Grapevine Wreath Feeder, 41,
41
Incredible, Edible Garland,
An, 60–61, **60**, 60
Mineral-Rich Manure Feeder,
278
Not for Orioles Only,
100–101, **100**
Picture-Perfect Tray Feeder,
48–49, **48, 49**
Song Sparrow Favorite, 3, **3**
Sporty Nyjer Tube Feeder, A,
34–35, **34**
Sunflower Head Hookup, 33,
33
Three-Tube Feeder, **270,**
270–71
Woodpecker Wonder, 14,
14
Feeders. *See also* Feeder
projects; Feeding
stations
attracting reclusive birds to,
66–67
bird foraging behavior and,
10, 43
for butterflies, 264
choosing, 58–59
cleaning, 118
deterring pests birds at,
123–24, **123**
drainage and, 13
food for, 10
garlands, 60–61, **60,** 60
for ground-feeding birds, 3,
3, 11, **11,** 44, 119
hanging, 128
mounting, 124 (*See also*
Birdhouse mounts)
natural feeding habits and,
10, 16–17, 30
nectar (*See* Nectar feeders)

for peanut butter, 11, 14, **14,**
79, **79,** 80, **80**
positioning, 8–9, 11
protecting from animal
pests, 124, 124, 125,
125, 128
protecting from hawks, 128,
132
for seeds, 58–59
hopper (house), 53, 54–55,
54, 55
tray (platform), 11, 12–13,
12, 13, 41, **41,** 43–44,
45–47, **45, 46,** 50–52,
51, 52
tube, 34–35, **34,** 56, 58
suet, 11, 74, 80, **80**
windows and, 177
windowsill, 44
Feeding station projects. *See*
also Feeding stations
Cat's Delight Window Feeding Station, 130–31, **130**
Easy Squirrel Feeders,
126–27, **126, 127**
Stump That Squirrel (Not!)
Feeder, 126, **126**
Through-the-Roof Nut
Feeder, 127, **127**
Evergreen Christmas Treat
Station, 120–21, **120**
Little Red Wagon Portable
Station, 108–9, **109**
Romantic Feeding Station,
116–17, **116**
This Is Only a Test, 112–13,
112, 113
Margarine Box Suet
Holder, 112, **112**
Milk Carton Hopper
Feeder, 113, **113**
Soda Bottle Tube Feeder,
112–13, **112**
Woodland-Look Feeding
Station, **114,** 114–15

Feeding stations. *See also*
Feeders; Feeding
station projects
budgetary considerations
and, 115
cleaning, 118
climate and, 110
getting started, 106–7,
110–11, 115
landscape style and, 111, 115
maintenance of, 107, 110
protecting from animals, 124,
124, 125, **125,** 128, 132
protecting from hawks, 128,
132
protecting from pest birds,
123–24, **123**
scale of, 110
seasonal checklist, 118–19,
121–22
siting, 107
starter stations, 110
temporary, 112–13, **112,**
113
ultimate, 107
Finches
beaks of, 68
food preferences of, 31
house, 4
food preferences of, 290
identifying, 6
nesting preferences of, 148
purple
food preferences of, 290
Flax seed, 38, 39, 64, 87
Fleabane, daisy, 157
Flickers
beaks of, 67
birdhouses and, 221
food preferences of, 31
nest box dimensions for, 222
nesting preferences of, 148
preferred habitat of, 222
Flowerpots, as feeders, 36, **36**
Flowerpot Seed Bell, 36, **36**

Flowers, 8
annual, 17, 20
attractive to butterflies,
245–46, 247, 248–49,
262–63
attractive to hummingbirds,
245–46, 247, 260–62
color of, 246
in container gardens, 258–59,
258
form of, 246
in habitat gardens, 159, **159,**
160
Self-Renewing Beginner Bird
Garden, 18–19, **18, 19**
usefulness of to backyard
birds, 28, 59, 61, 135
Flycatchers
beaks of, 69
great crested
mulberries and, **89**
nesting preferences of, 151
nest box dimensions for, 222
olive-sided
nesting sites of, 148
preferred habitat of, 222
Food. *See* Berries; Feeder foods;
Fruits; Insects; Nuts;
Plants; Suet
Food Garden for Caterpillars, A,
284–85, **284**
Forsythia (*Forsythia*), 142
Foundation plantings, 8
Fountains, 191, 195
Front Yard Makeover, 162–63,
163
Fruits. *See also* Berries;
Container plants;
Grapes
attractive to butterflies, 272,
272, 273
care of, 90
at feeders, 94–95
growing in containers, 90, 91,
91, 92–93, **92, 93**

as major food category, 71
protecting from birds, 94, 95
selecting for birds, 17, 87–88,
90
Fruit Smoothie, 275
Fruit trees, dwarf, 91, **91**
Furnishing Feathers, 26, **26**

G
Gaillardia spp. and hybrids,
249
Game birds, food preferences
of, 31
Garbage can lids, as birdbaths,
179, **179**
Gardening for birds
Bargain Bareroot Bird Hedge,
140, **140**
Barrel of Fruit, 91, **91**
Double-Duty Duo, 254, **254**
Front Yard Makeover, 162–63,
163
Hanging Strawberry Basket,
96–97, **96**
Hummingbird Perches,
280–81, **280**
Hummingbird Window Box
Garden, 256–57, **256,**
257
Instantly Accepted Fruit
Feeder, 89, **89**
Just the Two of Us, 252–53,
252, 253
Miniature Marsh Garden,
170–71, **170**
Nesting Materials Garden,
156–57, **156**
Patio Pot Grapevine, 92–93,
92
Permanent Marsh Garden,
172, **172**
Salad Garden for the Birds,
168–69, **168**
Self-Renewing Beginner Bird
Garden, 18–19, **18, 19**

Shrub Stop for Birds, A, 159,
159
Sized-to-Fit Sunflower
Plantation, 62–63,
62–63
Tepee for Birds, A, 145, **145**
Watchable Grape Arbor,
166–67, **166, 167**
Gardening for butterflies
Container Garden for
Butterflies, 258–59, **258**
Crabapple Picnic Spot,
276–77, **276**
Food Garden for Caterpillars,
A, 284–85, **284**
Rainbow of Nectar Garden,
250–51, **251**
Garlands, as bird feeders, 60–61,
60, 60
Gaultheria spp., 260
Gazanias (*Gazania* hybrids), 248
Gazebo-Style Platform Feeder,
45–47, **45, 46**
Gnatcatchers, blue-gray, 148
Golden goddess, **258**
Goldfinches, American, 4
cattail fluff and, 155
food preferences of, 31, 290
identifying, 6
nesting preferences of, 148,
150
Gourds, growing bottle, 227
Gracious Gourd House, 226–27,
226
Grackles, common
deterring at feeders, 123, **123**
food preferences of, 31, 290
identifying, 6
nesting preferences of, 148
Grape jelly, at feeders, 101
Grapes, 95, 99, 167
arbor for, 166–67, **166, 167**
growing in containers, 92–93,
92
as nest site, 167

Grapevine
  as nesting-material plant,
    157
  wreaths as feeders, 41, **41**
  wreaths as nesting sites, 25,
    25
Grapevine Wreath Feeder, 41, **41**
Grasses
  birds that nest in, 148
  usefulness of to backyard
    birds, 59, 60, 135, 150
Gravel
  birds that nest in, 148
  wooden posts and, 209, **209**
Grit, 39–40, 119
Grosbeaks
  beaks of, 68
  blue
    nesting preferences of, 151
  food preferences of, 31, 291
  rose-breasted
    nesting preferences of, 148
Groundcovers, 88
Grouse, ruffed, 31

H
Habitat gardens
  arbors in, 161
  cherry trees in, 160
  edge effect in, 136, 159
  evergreens in, 136, 159, 160
  flowers in, 159, **159**, 160
  grape arbors in, 166–67, **166,
    167**
  grasses in, 159, **159**
  layering in, 162–63, **163**
  multilayer effect in, 159, **159,**
    161, 164
  for nesting materials, 155,
    156–57, **156,** 157
  plant selection for, 158
  roses in, 160
  salad gardens as, 168–69, **168**
  shrubs in, 158, 159, **159**, 160
  trellises in, 164

vines in, 159, 160–61, 164,
    164
  weeds in, 159, 165, 165
Habitats
  bird safety and, 138
  for butterflies, 278–79,
    281–82
  creating instant, 145, **145**
  for foraging, 138–39
  garden style and, 134–37
    formal, 136–37
    informal, 135–36, **136**
    style-transcending, 137
  hedges, 137, 140, **140,** 141,
    142–143
  for hummingbirds, 278–79,
    281
  marshes, 137, 170–72, **170,**
    171, **172**
  multilevel, 137, 161, 164
  for nesting, 148 (*See also*
    Nesting)
  for roosting, 143, 143
  size of, 138
  trees, 136–37, 139
  weather-wise, 144
  woodland, 137
Hair, as nesting material, 150
Hamburger, recipes using, 99
Hanging Assembly for a Martin
    Colony, 228–29, **229**
Hanging baskets, as nesting
    sites, 24, **24**
Hanging Strawberry Basket,
    96–97, **96**
Hardiness Zone map, **298**
Hardware, for birdhouses, 205
Hawks, protecting birds from,
    128, 132
Hawkweeds, 249
Heat Lamp Heaven, 183, **183**
Heat, protection from, 144
Hedges, 28, 137
  bird life in, 137, 141
  planting, 140, **140**

plants for, 142–143
Heleniums (*Helenium* hybrids),
    263
Helianthus
  annuus, 263
  annuus cvs., 248
  maximilianii, 249
Hemlocks, 143
Hemp, Indian, 157
Hibiscus syriacus, 142
Hieracium spp., 249
Homemade Nectar Solution for
    Feeders, 268
Homemade Squirrel Baffles,
    125, **125**
Homemade Suet Cakes, 83
Hopper (house) feeders, 53, 113,
    113
Housing the Early Birds, 232–33,
    232, 233
Hummingbird feeders
  Deck Railing Nectar Rack,
    269
  Three-Tube Feeder, **270,**
    270–71
Hummingbird Perches, 280–81,
    280
Hummingbirds, 6
  container gardens for, 255,
    255, 256–57, **256, 257**
  feeding habits of, 245
  flowers and, 245–46
  habitat for, 278–79, 281
  lifestyle of, 244
  nectar and, 244
  nectar feeders for (*See* Nectar
    feeders)
  nectar solutions for, 268
  nesting preferences of, 148
  nests and eggs of, 279
  perches for, 280–81, **280**
  plants attractive to, 246, 247,
    260–62
  summer disappearance of,
    267

territoriality of, 244
water and, 281–82, 283
window box for, 256–57, **256, 257,** <u>257</u>
Hummingbird Window Box Garden, 256–57, **256, 257**

I

Ice Eliminator, 185
Incredible, Edible Garland, An, 60–61, **60,** <u>60</u>
Indigo buntings. *See also* Buntings
food preferences of, <u>290</u>
nesting preferences of, <u>148</u>
Insects
ants, 238
as bird food, 8, 16–17
blowflies, 237–38
providing water for, <u>178</u>
yellow jackets, 238, 242
Instantly Accepted Fruit Feeder, 89, **89**
Ipomoea quamoclit, <u>261</u>

J

Japanese Styling for American Birds, 192–95, **192, 193, 194**
Jays, 4–5
beaks of, 68
food preferences of, <u>31,</u> <u>291</u>
identifying, <u>7</u>
nesting preferences of, 146–47, <u>148,</u> <u>150</u>
suet cakes for, <u>83</u>
Juncos
beaks of, 68
food preferences of, <u>31,</u> <u>291</u>
identifying, <u>7</u>
Juniperus virginiana, 143
Just Out of Reach, 240–41, **240, 241**
Just the Two of Us, 252–53, **252, 253**

K

Keep a Lid on It! 179, **179**
Kestrels
American
nest box dimensions for, <u>223</u>
preferred habitat of, <u>223</u>
birdhouses for, 221
nesting preferences of, <u>148</u>
Killdeers, nesting preferences of, <u>148</u>
Kingbirds, gray
nests and eggs of, <u>146</u>
Kinglets, <u>148,</u> <u>150</u>
Kusari doi (rain chains), 188–89, **188**

L

Lagenaria siceraria, <u>227</u>
Landscaping. *See also* Gardening for birds; Gardening for butterflies; Habitat gardens
backyard scorecard for, <u>27</u>–<u>28</u>
Lard, 78, 82
Laurel, California
and moths, <u>42</u>
Lavender (*Lavandula* spp.), <u>117,</u> <u>262</u>
Lawns, birds and, 8
Leaf bathing, 144
Leucanthemum
× *superbum,* <u>249</u>
vulgare, <u>249</u>
Light Up Your Birdbath, 184, **184**
Ligustrum spp., <u>142</u>
Linum usitatissimum, 64
Little Red Wagon Portable Station, 108–9, **109**
Lobelia cardinalis, <u>261</u>
Lobularia maritima, <u>262</u>
Lychnis coronaria, <u>261</u>

M

Magpies, beaks of, 68
Manure, as butterfly attractant, 278
Maps
bluebird ranges, **217**
USDA Plant HardinessZones, **298**
Margarine Box Suet Holder, 112, **112**
Marguerite, golden, <u>248</u>
Marigolds, <u>248</u>
Marsh gardens, 137, 170–71, **170,** 172, **172**
Meadowlarks, 16
nesting preferences of, <u>148</u>
Mealworms, 99, 101, <u>101,</u> <u>111</u>
Meat drippings, 78
recipes containing, 82–83
Meaty Medley, 99
Mergansers, hooded, <u>223</u>
Metal fence posts, for birdhouse mounts, 207–8, 211, **211**
Metal poles, for birdhouse mounts, 209, 212
Migratory Bird Treaty Act of 1918, 24
Milk Carton Hopper Feeder, 113, **113**
Millet, 35, <u>39,</u> 87
Milo (sorghum), 38
Mineral-Rich Manure Feeder, 278
Miniature Marsh Garden, 170–71, **170**
Mites, 237
Mockingbirds
beaks of, 69
food preferences of, <u>291</u>
grapevine bark and, 155
nesting preferences of, <u>148, 150</u>
Mop Strings for the Birds, 153, **153**

Mosquitoes
  birdbaths and, 181–82
  marsh gardens and, 170
  in ponds and pools, 199
Moss, as nesting material, 150
Moths
  birdseed and, 42
  fruit feeders and, 275
Mud, butterflies and, 277, 286
Mulberries, 17, 89, **89**
Mustard, black, 262
Mustard (canola, rapeseed),
  38–39, 39, 61, 64

N
Nasturtiums, 23, **23**, **258**, 259
Nectar feeders, 122, **265**
  bee guards and, 266
  choosing, 264–67, 269
  cleaning, 265
  ease of use, 265, 269
  features of, 265–67
  homemade, 269, 270–71, **270,
    271**
  pole mounted, 270–71, **270,
    271, 271**
  size of, 266
  solutions for, 101
  in window box garden,
    256–57, **256**
Nectar, hummingbirds and,
  244
Nepeta cvs., 262
Nest boxes. *See also* Birdhouses
  for roosting, 143
Nesting. *See also* Birdhouses;
    Encouraging nesting;
    Nesting materials
  calcium requirements
    during, 121
  plants useful for, 27–28
  privacy and, 21, 146–47, 208
  requirements for, 23
  sites for, 148
    cavities as, 147, 147

dead tree limbs as, 149,
  149
Nesting materials
  dangerous
    dryer lint, 152
    monofilament fishing line,
      152
  gardening for, 155, 156–57,
    156, 157
  inventory of, 150
  providing, 150–52, 155
  snake skins as, 151
  string as, 152, 153, **153, 153**
  supply station for, 154, **154**
Nesting Materials Garden,
  156–57, **156**
Nesting Materials Supply
  Station, 154, **154**
Netting a Bush, 95
Not for Orioles Only, 100–101,
  100
Nuthatches
  birdhouses for, 220–21,
    230–31, **231**
  bluebird houses and, 213
  food preferences of, 31, 291
  nesting preferences of, 148,
    150
  red-breasted
    nests and eggs of, 221
  suet cakes for, 83
  suet feeders and, 77
  white-breasted
    identifying, 7
    nest box dimensions for,
      223
    preferred habitat of, 223
Nuts
  custom blends using, 104
  as major food category, 20,
    70–71
  recipes containing, 15,
    82–83
Nyjer (niger, thistle seed), 35, 39
  homemade feeder for, 34, **34**

O
Oranges
  at feeders, 101
  orioles and, 121
Orioles
  Baltimore
    nests and eggs of, 155
  beaks of, 69
  fishing line and, 152
  food preferences of, 291
  nesting preferences of, 148,
    150
  northern
    attracting to feeders, 67
    feeders for, 100–101, **100**
  oranges and, 101, 121
  orchard
    nesting preferences of,
      148
Ovenbirds, 148
Owls
  birdhouses for, 221
    dimensions of, 223
  nesting preferences of, 148
  preferred habitat of, 223

P
Patio Pot Grapevine, 92–93, **92**
Peanut butter
  bird treats containing, 15, 79,
    81, **81**, 82–83, 84
  feeders for, 11, 14, **14**, 15, 80,
    80
Peanut Butter Stretch, 15
Penstemons (*Penstemon* spp.
  and cvs.), 261
Perches
  for hummingbirds, 280–81,
    280
  on strawberry basket, 97
  on suet feeders, 77
Perfect Pond for Birds, A,
  200–202, **200–201, 202**
Perky Pet hummingbird feeder,
  269

Permanent Marsh Garden, 172, **172**
Petunias, **258**
Pheasant, ring-necked, 31
Phlox (*Phlox* spp.), 262, 263
Phoebes
  birdhouse for, 232–33, **232, 233**
  nesting preferences of, 150
Photinias (*Photinia* spp. and hybrids), 142
Picture-Perfect Tray Feeder, 48–49, **48, 49**
Pigeons, 123, **123**
Pincushion flowers, 263
Pinecones, bird treats made from, 79, **79**
Pine siskins, 31
"Plant" a Residence for Birds, 24, **24**
Plants
  backyard scorecard for, 27–28
  as bird food source, 17, 20, 164
  caring for, 253
  for nesting materials, 157
Plastic box, as feeder, 52, **52**
Platform feeders. *See* Tray (platform) feeders
Plexiglas, drilling, 234
Ponds and pools
  building, 200–202, **200–201, 202**
  caring for, 199
  liners for, 199
  mosquitoes and (*See* Mosquitoes)
Posts
  for mounting birdhouses, 207–8, 209–12, **209, 210, 211**
Predator protection
  for birdhouses, 208, 238–39, **239**, 240–41, **240, 241**

for feeders, 124, 124, 125, **125,** 128, 129, **129,** 132
from hawks, 128, 132
Prettified Pedestal Birdbath, 22, **22**
Privets, 142
Projects, complete list of, 287–89
Protective measures
  Baffles for Metal Poles, 239, **239**
    From Bucket to Baffle, 239, **239**
    Plastic Bottle Baffle, 239, **239**
  Cat-Proof Feeding Station, 129, **129**
  Collar Those Criminals, 238
    PVC Collar, 238
    Stovepipe Collar, 238
  Homemade Squirrel Baffles, 125, **125**
  Long-Necked Hole, 240, **240**
  Netting a Bush, 95
  Screen Guard, 241, **241**
Pumps
  care and maintenance of, 191
  for fountains and bubblers, 191, 195
  kinds of, 189
  size of, 189–91, 191
Purple coneflower, 249
Purple martins
  birdhouses for, 226–27, **226,** 228–29, **229**
  dimensions of, 223
  nesting preferences of, 148, 150, 221–22
  preferred habitat of, 223
  protecting from competitors, 228
PVC
  for birdhouse posts, 207, 210, **210**
  working with, 230
PVC Collar, 238

PVC Pipe Mount, 210, **210**
PVC Wren House, 230–31, **230, 231**
Pyracantha, 129, **129**

Q
Quail, Gambel's, 31

R
Raccoons, 132, 240–41
Rain, protection from, 144
Rainbow of Nectar Garden, 250–51, **251**
Rain chain *(kusari doi)*, 188–89, **188**
Raisins, recipes using, 15, 82–83, 87
Rapeseed, 38–39, 39, 61, 64
Raspberries, 95
Recipes. *See* Bird treat recipes; Bird treats
Recycled containers
  as feeders, 112–13, **112, 113**
Rhododendrons (*Rhododendron* spp. and hybrids), 142, 260
Ribes sanguineum, 260
Robins, American, **5**
  birdhouse for, 232–33, **232, 233**
  food preferences of, 101, 291
  foraging habits of, 139
  identifying, 7
  nesting and, 146
  nesting preferences of, 148, 150
  nests and eggs of, 233
Romantic Feeding Station, 116–17, **116**
Roosting habitats
  nest boxes for, 143
  plants useful for, 27–28, 143
Rosa rugosa, 142
Rose campion, 261
Rose-of-Sharon, 142

Roses, 117, 142, 148, 160
Rudbeckia (*Rudbeckia* spp.),
    248, 249

S
Safflower seed, 39, 64
Sages, **258**, 261, 262
Salad Garden for the Birds,
    168–69, **168**
Salal, 260
Salix spp., 262
Salvia spp., 261, 262
Scabiosa spp., 263
Seed Mosaic for a Snowy Day,
    70–71, **71**
Seeds. *See also* Birdseed
    of flowering plants, 59, 61, 63,
        64
    of grasses and grains, 59,
        60–61, **60**, 60
Self-Renewing Beginner Bird
    Garden, 18–19, **18, 19**
Serving the Trimmings, 75, **75**
Shelter. *See also* Cover
    birds and, 144
    butterflies and, 279, 281
    hummingbirds and, 279
    plants useful for, 27–28,
        164
Shoebox, as feeder, 50–52, **51**
Shortening, recipes using, 84
Shrubs
    attractive to butterflies, 262
    attractive to hummingbirds,
        260
    bearing fruit or berries for
        birds, 88
    birds preferring to nest in,
        148
    in formal gardens, 136
    in habitat garden, 158, 159
    as roosting site, 143
    siting for nesting, 146–47
    as snow fence, 159
    thorny, 158, 160

usefulness of to backyard
    birds, 20–21, 28
    watering, 163
Shrub Stop for Birds, A, 159, **159**
Simple Pinecone Treats, 79, **79**
Sized-to-Fit Sunflower
    Plantation, 62–63,
    62–63
Snake skins, as nesting material,
    151
Soda Bottle Tube Feeder,
    112–13, **112**
Song Sparrow Favorite, 3, **3**
Sorghum (milo), 38
Sparkling Colored-Glass
    Fountain, 196–98, **197,
    198**
Sparrows
    beaks of, 68
    chipping
        nesting preferences of,
            148, 150
    food preferences of, 31, 291
    house, 4
        discouraging at
            birdhouses, 228, 236–37
        food preferences of, 291
        identifying, 7
        nesting preferences of,
            148, 150, 151
    native
        food preferences of, 291
    song
        feeders for, 3, **3**
        food preferences of, 291
        identifying, 7
        nests and eggs of, 154
        nesting preferences of, 148
    white-crowned
        food preferences of, 291
Spiraea × *vanhouttei*, 142
Sporty Nyjer Tube Feeder, A,
    34–35, **34**
Squirrels
    cayenne and, 124

deterring at feeders, 124, 124,
    125, **125**, 128
    feeders for, 124, 126–27, **126,
    127**
    homemade baffles, 125,
    125
    protecting birdhouses from,
        238–39, **239**, 241
Starlings, 5
    deterring at birdhouses, 228,
        237
    deterring at feeders, 123,
        123
    food preferences of, 31, 74,
        291
    identifying, 7
Stoke's aster (*Stokesia*), 263
Stovepipe Collar, 238
Strawberries, hanging basket
    for, 96–97, **96**
String, as nesting material, 150,
    152
Stump That Squirrel (Not!)
    Feeder, 126, **126**
Suet
    bird treat recipes containing,
        82–83, 99
    blocks, 73–74
    feeders for, 79, **79**, 80, **80**
    feeder types, 74
    freezing weather and, 73, 73
    Homemade Suet Cakes, 83
    hot weather and, 72, 122
    muffins of, 81, **81**
    protecting from pest birds,
        123, **123**
    protecting from squirrels,
        124
    rendering, 78
    repackaging, 75, **75**
    seasonal feeding of, 72–73
    "smears," 81
    starlings and, 74
    substitutes for, 74, 78
    suet cake variations, 83

Suet feeders, 11, **114**
    logs, 76–77, **76**
    Margarine Box Suet Holder,
        112, **112**
    perches on, 77
    refilling, 74, 77
    repackaging suet for, 75, **75**
Suet Log Feeder, 76–77, **76**
Suet Muffins, 81, **81**
Suet–Peanut Butter Filling for
        Pinecones, 80, **80**
Suet Pie, 82, **82**
Sugar, in nectar solutions, 268
Sunflower Head Hookup, 33, **33**
Sunflowers, 263
    chickadees and, 33
    common, 248
    as hanging feeders, 33, **33**
    hedges of, 62–63, **62–63**, 63
    Mexican, 248
    perennial, 249
Sunflower seeds
    cost and value of, 39
    feeder for, 35
    recipes containing, 82–83, 87,
        99
    from sunflower hedges,
        62–63, **62–63**, 63
    types of, 32, 39
Swallows
    barn
        nesting preferences of,
            150
    birdhouses for, 218–19, **218,
        219**, 226–27, **226**
    bluebird houses and, 208,
        213
    nest box dimensions for, 223
    preferred habitat of, 223
    tree
        nesting preferences of,
            148, 150
        nests and eggs of, 219
    violet-green
        nesting preferences of, 148

Swallow Specialties, 218–19,
        218, 219
Swallowtail, black, 285, **285**
    garden for larvae of, 284–85,
        284
Sweet alyssum, **258**, 262
Switch grass, 157

T

Tagetes spp. and cvs., 248
Tanagers
    beaks of, 69
    nesting preferences of, 148
Taraxacum officinale, 249
Tennis ball tubes, as feeders,
        34–35, **34**
Tepee for Birds, A, 145, **145**
Test tubes, as hummingbird
        feeders, 269, 270–71,
        270
This Is Only a Test, 112–13, **112,
        113**
Thrashers
    beaks of, 69
    brown
        nesting preferences of,
            148, 150
        food preferences of, 291
    suet cakes for, 83
Three-Tube Feeder, **270**, 270–71
Through-the-Roof Nut Feeder,
        127, **127**
Thrushes
    beaks of, 69
    nesting preferences of, 150
    suet cakes for, 83
Tithonia rotundifolia, 248
Titmice
    birdhouses for, 220–21,
        224–25, **224, 225**,
        230–31, **231**
    bluebird houses and, 213
    food preferences of, 31, 291
    identifying, 7
    nest box dimensions for, 223

nesting preferences of, 148,
        150
    preferred habitat of, 223
    tufted
        nesting preferences of, 151
Towhees
    food preferences of, 31
    nesting preferences of, 148
Traditional Birdhouse, 224–25,
        224, 225
Tray (platform) feeders, 11,
        12–13, 43–52
Trees
    bearing fruits and berries for
        birds, 88, 89, **89**
    birds preferring to nest in,
        148
    dead limbs of, 149, **149**
    drippers and, 186, 187
    in formal gardens, 136–37
    growing dwarf fruit in
        containers, 90, 91, **91**
    usefulness of to backyard
        birds, 8, 20, 27, 139,
        146–47
    watering, 163, 186
Trellises, in habitat gardens, 164
Tsuga spp., 143
Tsukubai, 192–95
Tube feeders, 34–35, **34**, 56, 58,
        112–13, **112**
Turkeys, wild, 31
Twine, 150

U

Umbellularia californica, 42
USDA Plant Hardiness Zone
        map, **298**

V

Vegetable gardens
    backyard birds and, 8, 28
    butterflies and, 277
Vegetarian "Suet" Treat, 84
Vervain, Brazilian, **258**

Vines
   attractive to hummingbirds,
      261
   bearing fruits and berries for
      birds, 88
   birdbaths and, 23, **23**
   as bird food source, 17, 20
   growing in pots, 92–93, **92**
   in habitat gardens, 159,
      160–61, 164, **164**
   trellised
      birds preferring to nest in,
         148
   usefulness of to birds, 28
Vireos, 148, 150
Vitex agnus-castus, 263

W
Wagons, as feeding station,
      108–9, **109**
Wallflowers, **258,** 262
Warblers, 68, 223
Watchable Grape Arbor, 166–67,
      166, 167
Water. *See also* Birdbaths; Water
      features
   bamboo and, 194
   butterflies and, 282, 286
   desert climates and, 174
   droughts and, 174, 175
   hummingbirds and, 281–82,
      283
   insects' need for, 178
   natural sources of, 21
   sound effects of, 185, 186
Water features. *See also*
      Birdbaths
   bubblers, 191, 195
   Dripper in Disguise, A, 187,
      187
   fountains, 191, 195, 196–98,
      197, 198
   height of, 175–76

Homemade Rain Chain,
      188–89, **188**
Japanese Styling for
      American Birds,
      192–95, **192, 193, 194**
natural, 178, 180, **180,** 181
Perfect Pond for Birds, A,
      200–202, **200–201, 202**
placement of for safety,
      176–77, **176**
ponds and pools, 199–202,
      200–201, 202
pumps for, 189–91, 195
Sparkling Colored-Glass
      Fountain, 196–98, **197,
      198**
Weeds, 139
   common widespread, 165
   in habitat gardens, 159, 165
   in informal gardens, 135
   usefulness of to birds, 20, 28
Weigela (*Weigela florida*), 143
Whole wheat flour, recipes
      using, 81, **81,** 82–83
Willows
   desert, 142
   pussy, 262
   weeping, 157
Window box gardens, 256–57,
      256, 257, **257**
Window on Their World, 234–35,
      234, 235
Windows
   birdhouse for, 234–35, **234,
      235**
   in birdhouses, 234–35, **234,
      235**
   feeders for, 44, 50–52, **51, 52,**
      130–31, **130,** 131
      nectar, 256–57, **256, 257,**
      257
   water features and, 176–77
Wintergreen, 260

Wire, for hanging birdhouses, 225
Wood
   making birdhouses from,
      205–7
   painting, 205
   posts for birdhouses, 207
      mounting in gravel, 209
   pressure treated, 205
Wooden Post Mount, 209, **209**
Woodland gardens, 137
Woodland-Look Feeding
      Station, **114,** 114–15
Woodpeckers
   beaks of, 67–68
   downy
      bluebird houses and, 213,
         220
      identifying, 7
      nest box dimensions for,
         223
      preferred habitat of, 223
   feeders for, 14, **14**
   food preferences of, 31, 291
   hairy
      nest box dimensions for,
         223
      preferred habitat of, 223
   nesting preferences of, 148
   red-bellied
      birdhouses and, 221
      nest box dimensions for,
         223
      preferred habitat of, 223
   suet cakes for, 83
   suet feeders and, 77
Woodpecker Wonder, 14, **14**
Wood-pewees, eastern, 148
Worm Farm for the Birds, a,
      102–3, **102, 103,** 103
Worms
   earthworms, 101
   producing for birds, 102–3,
      102, 103, 103

mealworms, 99, 101, <u>101,</u> <u>111</u>
Wreaths, grapevine, 25, **25,** 41,
      41
Wrens
    birdhouses for, 220, 224–25,
        224, 225, 226–27, **226**
    bluebird houses and, 213
    Carolina
        food preferences of, <u>291</u>
        nesting preferences of, <u>148</u>
    geographic distribution of,
        <u>220</u>

    house
        nests and eggs of, <u>235</u>
    nest box dimensions for, <u>223</u>
    nesting preferences of, <u>150</u>
    nest sites for, 220
    preferred habitat of, <u>223</u>
    suet cakes for, <u>83</u>

Y
Yarrow, **258**
Yellow jackets, 238, 242
Yellowthroats, common, <u>148</u>

Z
Zinnias (*Zinnia* spp. and cvs.),
    <u>248</u>
Zone map, USDA Plant
    Hardiness, **298**

USDA Plant Hardiness Zone Map

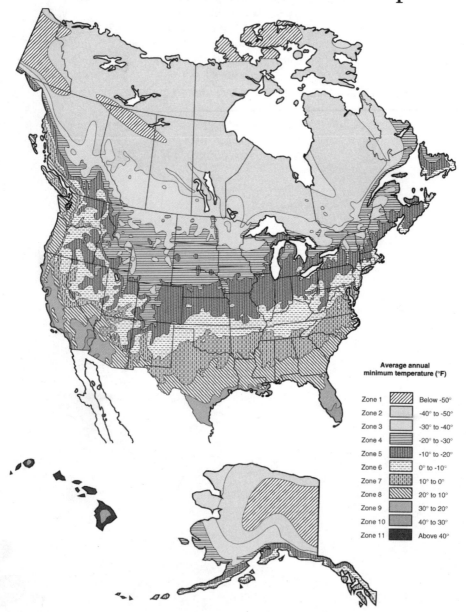

Average annual minimum temperature (°F)

Zone		Temperature
Zone 1		Below -50°
Zone 2		-40° to -50°
Zone 3		-30° to -40°
Zone 4		-20° to -30°
Zone 5		-10° to -20°
Zone 6		0° to -10°
Zone 7		10° to 0°
Zone 8		20° to 10°
Zone 9		30° to 20°
Zone 10		40° to 30°
Zone 11		Above 40°

This map was revised in 1990 and is recognized as the best indicator of minimum temperatures available. Look at the map to find your area, then match its pattern to the key above. When you've found your pattern, the key will tell you what hardiness zone you live in. Remember that the map is a general guide; your particular conditions may vary.